Covert Regime Change

A VOLUME IN THE SERIES

Cornell Studies in Security Affairs

Edited by Robert J. Art, Robert Jervis, and Stephen M. Walt

A list of titles in this series is available at cornellpress.cornell.edu.

Covert Regime Change

America's Secret Cold War

Lindsey A. O'Rourke

Cornell University Press

Ithaca and London

First published 2018 by Cornell University Press

Printed in the United States of America

Library of Congress Cataloging-in-Publication Data

Names: O'Rourke, Lindsey A., author.
Title: Convert regime change : America's secret Cold War /
   Lindsey A. O'Rourke.
Description: Ithaca [New York] : Cornell University Press, 2018. |
   Series : Cornell studies in security affairs | Includes bibliographical
   references and index.
Identifiers: LCCN 2018023380 (print) | LCCN 2018025454 (ebook) |
   ISBN 9781501730689 (pdf) | ISBN 9781501730696 (ret) |
   ISBN 9781501730658 (cloth ; alk. paper)
Subjects: LCSH: Regime change—History—20th century. |
   Regime change—Case studies. | United States—Foreign
   relations—1945–1989. | Cold War.
Classification: LCC JC489 (ebook) | LCC JC489 .O67 2018 (print) |
   DDC 327.1273009/045—dc23
LC record available at https://lccn.loc.gov/2018023380

For Evelyn

Contents

List of Figures and Tables

Acknowledgments

Reflecting back on the many individuals and institutions that have supported this project is heartwarming. Although the long, lonely hours that go into writing a book have, at times, made it feel like a solo endeavor, in reality I owe much to many. I have been able to run my ideas (and drafts) by some of the best scholars in the field while relying heavily upon a wide support network of family, friends, and colleagues the whole time. I am deeply grateful to them all.

This book owes its greatest debt to four scholars at the University of Chicago who generously lent their time and individual talents to this project. First and foremost, John Mearsheimer brought his unrivaled ability to dissect a messy argument down to its core assumptions and then clearly and persuasively articulate those ideas. He is also the model of a courageous scholar, thoughtful mentor, and engaging teacher to which I aspire, and I cannot thank him enough for his spot-on advice and personal support over the years. Charlie Glaser's striking ability to quickly deduce all the logical implications of an argument helped me to refine and improve my theory. Dan Slater brought exceptional intellectual creativity and rigorous comparative methods to the project. Lastly, his reputation having preceded him, I could not wait for Paul Staniland to begin at Chicago. Not wanting to look overly eager, however, I played it cool and waited until his second official day before asking him to join my committee. Thankfully, he accepted, and his high standards and incisive questions were invaluable.

The University of Chicago is an incredibly vibrant intellectual community, and I feel privileged to have called it home. While there, I met an outstanding group of colleagues and friends who provided crucial early feedback on this project and looked out for my well-being in a thousand different ways. My heart will always hold a special place for all of them and Thursday nights at Jimmy's. Thank you to Ahsan Butt, Shawn Cochrane, Keren Fraiman (on loan from MIT), Gene Gerzhoy, Christopher Graziul, Eric Hundman, Morgan Kaplan, Rosemary Kelanic, Joshua Kerr, Monica Lee, Chad Levinson, Adam Levine-Weinberg, Gabriel Mares, Sarah Parkinson, M. J. Reese, and Richard Westerman. I owe a special debt of gratitude to Ahsan. The earliest idea for this project came out of a conversation with him, and thanks to his insights and unwavering good humor, he has become my sounding board for the better part of a decade. Finally, I may not have found myself at UofC in the first place if not for the encouragement of Justin Robbins and my undergraduate mentor, Neil Tennant, and I thank them both for setting me down on this path.

In 2014, I was fortunate to find a new home at Boston College. My colleagues throughout the Political Science Department and its chair, Susan Shell, have been tremendously supportive of this project. Within the IR subfield, I have found scholars whose own research inspires me by asking big questions, and who have been invariably generous with their time and comments. My sincerest thank-you to Tim Crawford, David Deese, Jennifer Erickson, Peter Krause, and Robert Ross. I owe an especially emphatic thanks to Jennifer, who is both brilliant and selfless and has kindly allowed herself to become my go-to source for just about everything. Many others in the department have supported my research, and I thank Jerry Easter and Nasser Behnegar as well as the IR graduate students, Andrew Bowen, Emily Kulenkamp, and Adam Wunische, in particular. I have also relied upon several outstanding undergraduate research fellows, who have spent countless hours tracking down sources, filing FOIA requests, and digging through archival documents on my behalf. A heartfelt thank-you to Joshua Behrens, Maximillien Inhoff, Trevor Jones, Adam Kleinfeld, Theodore Kontopolous, Luna Perez, Caitlin Toto, and Colleen Ward for their meticulous work. Finally, I thank Shirley Gee and Karina Ovalles for making all of my interactions with the university easier.

In October 2015, Tim Crawford chaired a book workshop that brought together a fantastic group of scholars who read my manuscript in its entirety and provided sharp feedback throughout. I thank Ahsan Butt, Dick Betts, Michael Desch, Alexander Downes, Jerry Easter, Jennifer Erickson, Joshua Shifrinson, and Jon Western for their valuable feedback, and BC's Provost Office for funding the workshop. I hope they can see how much I deeply appreciated their constructive suggestions reflected in the final version.

While completing this project, I have twice benefited from yearlong fellowships that facilitated my archival research and introduced me to numerous scholars who supported this project in diverse ways. During my predoctoral fellowship at the Institute for Security and Conflict Studies at George Washington University, I learned much from Stephen Biddle,

Austin Carson, Jeff Colgan, Alexander Downes, Payam Ghalehdar, Charles Glaser, Rose Kelanic, Sameer Lalwani, Harris Mylonas, Elizabeth Saunders, Joshua Shifrinson, and Caitlin Talmadge. During my postdoctoral fellowship at the Dickey Institute for International Understanding at Dartmouth College, I benefited greatly from the insights of faculty members Daniel Benjamin, Stephen Brooks, Jennifer Lind, Daryl Press, Benjamin Valentino, and William Wohlforth, and my peers Jeffrey Friedman, Joshua Kertzer, Victor McFarland, Maria Sperandei, and Laura Thaut Vinson.

Many other scholars have supported this project in various ways. Anatoly Arlashin was indispensable for the statistical analyses in Chapter 4. Jeremy Bigwood helped me to uncover many of the archival documents used in Chapter 6. Alexander Downes, Keren Fraiman, Joshua Rovner, and Joshua Shifrinson have all given valuable comments on multiple occasions. I also thank the audiences for the comments following various presentations at the University of Chicago, George Washington University, Dartmouth College, Boston College, Yale University, Princeton University, and MIT, as well as at the annual conferences of the American Political Science and International Studies associations.

Over the past eight years, I have received additional financial support that made my archival research possible from the Division of Social Sciences at the University of Chicago, the Jewish Family Service Association of Cleveland, and the College of Arts and Sciences at Boston College. I also owe a great debt of gratitude to the many archivists who have assisted my research and patiently answered my questions at the National Archives and Records Administration, the National Security Archive, and the Truman, Eisenhower, Kennedy, Johnson, Nixon, Ford, Carter, and Reagan presidential libraries.

I greatly appreciate the sharp and constructive feedback from my editor at Cornell University Press, Roger Haydon, series editor, Robert Jervis, and production editor, Erin Davis. Though I may not know the identity of my anonymous external reviewer, I have been singing his or her praises for careful and constructive comments.

Arguments derived, in part, from theories developed in chapter 4 have previously appeared in Alexander B. Downes and Lindsey A. O'Rourke, "You Can't Always Get What You Want: Why Foreign-Imposed Regime Change Seldom Improves Interstate Relations," *International Security* 41, no. 2 (Fall 2016): 43–89; and Lindsey A. O'Rourke, "Covert Calamities: American-Backed Covert Regime Changes and Civil War," *Canadian Foreign Policy Journal* 23, no. 3 (2017) 232–45.

I thank my parents, Michael and Saundra O'Rourke, for stressing the importance of education and being a constant source of love and support my entire life. My brothers, Pete, Phil, and Steve O'Rourke; and my in-laws, Jenny and Mariam O'Rourke; and George, Judy, and Brad Boyerinas have provided unflagging encouragement and considerable hospitality as I worked on this project. Finally, like most of the good things in my life, this book was made possible by my husband and best friend, Ben Boyerinas. I owe him countless small thank-yous for helping me find time to write and proofreading on request and one enormous thank-you for making every other aspect of my life better.

It seems fitting to dedicate this book to my daughter, Evelyn Boyerinas, because its end will forever be tied in my memory to her beginning. Thanks to the help of her incredible nanny, Abril Johnson-Nieves, I completed most of its final revisions during her first year. Although Evelyn may be little, her personality is undeniable, and she inspires me every day with her innate tenacity, curiosity, and kindness. Evie: this book is a small token of my love for you. Thank you for everything that you are.

Covert Regime Change

The False Promise of Covert Regime Change

> Many more princes have lost their lives and their states through conspiracies than through open warfare.
>
> —Niccolò Machiavelli, *Discourses on Livy*

Although the policy of regime change is often associated with the US-led invasions of Afghanistan (2001) and Iraq (2003), the practice has a long historical precedent. Foreign-imposed regime changes created the modern world. John Owen, for instance, identified 209 cases of interstate regime change between 1510 and 2010, and Alexander Downes and Jonathan Monten found one hundred cases since 1815 alone.[1] Yet, these works, like most academic studies, focus on overt cases—that is, operations involving the direct and publicly acknowledged use of military power to overthrow another state. States, however, seldom resort to outright war to topple another country's government. Instead, when a state wants to overthrow an adversary, it often attempts a covert regime change—by assassinating a foreign leader, staging a coup d'état, manipulating foreign elections, or secretly aiding dissident groups in their bids to oust a foreign government.

History suggests that covert regime change is a common instrument of statecraft for great powers. One early example, for instance, occurred in 227 B.C.E., when the Crown Prince of the Chinese state of Dan tried to assassinate Qin Shi Huang to prevent the much stronger Qin dynasty from conquering his territory.[2] The Republic of Venice planned or attempted approximately two hundred foreign political assassinations between 1415 and 1525.[3] During the Reformation, both Catholic and Protestant leaders sought to assassinate their foreign rivals, most notably Philip II of Spain's attack on William of Orange, the leader of Holland.[4] During the 1570s and 1580s, foreign leaders tried to assassinate Queen Elizabeth I of England at least twenty times. She employed assassins herself in Ireland.[5] More recently, Woodrow Wilson covertly supported anti-Bolshevik forces during the Russian Civil

War.[6] Indeed, history is so rife with cases of covert regime change that it is difficult to imagine the modern world without it.

Despite the fact that covert regime changes have long played a central role in international politics, comprehensive theories to explain how, when, and why states launch these operations are lacking, possibly because of the special challenges involved in studying covert actions. Nonetheless, American actions during the Cold War offer a unique opportunity to study the covert actions of a great power. The combination of the US government's declassification rules, congressional inquiries, and journalistic coverage has revealed much of what American officials have sought to conceal. Building on archival research of declassified US government documents, this book introduces an original dataset of all US-backed regime changes during the Cold War, containing forty-five more covert regime change attempts than the most expansive existing academic study.[7]

The dataset reveals that the United States pursued a remarkable number of regime changes during the Cold War (1947–89) and that the vast majority of these interventions were conducted covertly—sixty-four covert interventions compared to six overt ones. Twenty-five of America's covert operations saw a US-backed government assume power, whereas the remaining thirty-nine failed to achieve that goal. As table 1.1 indicates, these missions targeted all types of states: adversaries and allies, powerful and weak, democratic and authoritarian, communist and capitalist alike. In many cases, US-backed forces squared off against Soviet-backed adversaries. Sometimes Washington conspired with other countries to topple a foreign government; at other times, the US government intervened alone. Some missions would not have occurred if not for America's covert interference; in other cases, Washington played a secondary role in covert plots hatched by actors abroad. Some of these operations are just now coming to light; others have long been a source of international controversy—such as Washington's efforts to overthrow Iranian prime minister Mohammad Mossadegh (1953), Guatemalan president Jacobo Arbenz (1954), and Cuban leader Fidel Castro (1960–68).

Perhaps given the notoriety of these cases, covert regime changes are sometimes viewed as an artifact of the Cold War. Regime change is not, however, just a Cold War phenomenon. On the contrary, each American administration in the post–Cold War era has embraced regime change, intervening overtly and covertly in places such as Haiti (1994), Afghanistan (2001), Iraq (2003), Libya (2011), and Syria (2012). This preference for regime change seems unlikely to change anytime soon. The United States and other great powers will likely continue to undertake both covert and overt missions regularly. To understand modern world affairs, it is therefore necessary to determine how and why states launch these operations. Toward that end, this project analyzes the causes, conduct, and consequences of foreign-imposed covert regime change.

Table 1.1 US-backed regime change attempts during the Cold War (1947–1989)

Offensive		Preventive		Hegemonic	
Covert	Overt	Covert	Overt	Covert	Overt
Albania (1949–56)	North Korea (1950)	France (1947–52)*	Lebanon (1958)*	Guatemala (1952–54)*	Dominican Republic (1965)*
Belarusian SSR (1949–56)	Libya (1986)	Italy (1947–68)*		Cuba (1960–61)	Grenada (1983)*
Bulgaria (1949–56)		Iran (1952–53)*		Dominican Republic (1960–61)*	Panama (1989)*
China (1949–68)		Japan (1952–68)*		British Guiana/Guyana (1961–71)*	
Czechoslovakia (1949–56)		Indonesia (1954–58)		Dominican Republic (1961–62)*	
East Germany (1949–56)		Syria (1955–57)†		Chile (1962–73)*	
Estonian SSR (1949–56)		Lebanon (1957–58)*		Haiti (1963)	
Hungary (1949–56)		Laos (1959–73)		Bolivia (1963–66)*	
Latvian SSR (1949–56)		Congo (1960)*		Brazil (1964)*	
Lithuanian SSR (1949–56)		South Vietnam (1963)*		Dominican Republic (1965–68)*	
Poland (1949–56)		Angola (1964–72)		Haiti (1965–69)	
Romania (1949–56)		Mozambique (1964–68)		Bolivia (1971)*	
Soviet Union/Russian SSR (1949–59)		Somalia (1964–67)		Grenada (1979)†	
Ukrainian SSR (1949–56)		Thailand (1965–69)		Nicaragua (1979–80)	
North Korea (1950–53)		South Vietnam (1967–71)*		Suriname (1982–85)	
Tibet (1958–68)		Iraq (1972–75)		Chile (1984–89)*	
North Vietnam (1961–64)		Italy (1972–73)*		Haiti (1986–88)	
Cuba (1961–68)		Portugal (1974–75)*		Panama (1987–89)	
Afghanistan (1979–89)*		Angola (1975–76)			
Nicaragua (1980–89)*		South Yemen (1979–80)			
Poland (1981–89)*		Chad (1981–82)*			
Cambodia (1982–89)		Ethiopia (1981–83)			
Libya (1982–89)		Liberia (1983–88)			
		Philippines (1984–86)*			
		Angola (1985–88)			

* Denotes that the US-backed forces assumed power; † denotes that the intervention was aborted before implementation.

Causes: Why Do States Launch Regime Changes?

What logic drives policymakers to launch regime change operations? Stated differently, why would political leaders decide that pursuing a regime change—as opposed to another foreign policy tool—was the best way to secure their interests?

In simplest terms, states launch both covert and overt regime changes to increase their security and the security of their allies. Sometimes this means overthrowing a foreign government that poses a specific military threat; at other times, states pursue regime change to increase their relative military power vis-à-vis rivals. To better understand this behavior, I introduce the following typology to categorize the three main types of security interests that drove the United States to intervene:

Offensive operations aim to overthrow a military rival or break up a rival alliance. During the Cold War, these missions pursued the foreign policy strategy of "rollback," and the United States attempted twenty-three covert and two overt missions of this nature against the Soviet Union and its allies. These missions came in two waves. First was a major effort beginning in the late 1940s to weaken the Soviet Union by supporting numerous secessionist movements within its borders as well as dissident groups in the Eastern European countries that it had come to dominate as a result of World War II. After these interventions failed entirely and Washington recognized the difficulties associated with overthrowing a consolidated Soviet ally, American leaders largely avoided offensive operations until the last decade of the Cold War, when fissures in the Soviet system once again provided an opening for the United States to support anti-Soviet groups, thus enabling covert interventions in Afghanistan, Nicaragua, Poland, and Cambodia.

Preventive operations attempt to maintain the status quo by stopping a state from taking certain actions—like joining a rival alliance or building nuclear weapons—that may pose a larger threat in the future. In Cold War terms, these correspond to Washington's twenty-five covert and one overt "containment" operations targeting states believed to be in danger of joining the Soviet alliance system. Over the course of the Cold War, the United States pursued a variety of covert missions toward this end: Washington first worked to ensure that it would have great power allies in its looming confrontation with the Soviet Union by backing moderate and rightwing pro-American political parties during democratic elections in France, Italy, and Japan. Later, as the superpower conflict expanded to include the Middle East, Southeast Asia, and Africa, US covert interventions followed suit, including notable cases such as the 1953 coup that ousted Iranian prime minister Mohammad Mossadegh, the failed attempt to oust Indonesian leader Sukarno in 1958, the inadvertent assassination of South Vietnamese president Ngo Dinh Diem during a 1963 coup, and covert support for Angolan rebels during the 1970s and 1980s.

Lastly, *hegemonic operations* seek to keep target states politically subordinate. In these cases, the intervener is trying to acquire or maintain hegemony over a certain geographic region to obtain the military, political, and economic benefits associated with being a regional hegemon. Although the United States attempted eighteen covert and three overt operations of this type during the Cold War period, they do not reflect a specific Cold War strategy per se, but rather a strategy of regional hegemony that was first articulated in the Monroe Doctrine of 1823 and has driven US policy in the hemisphere ever since. In these cases, Washington foresaw the rise of a potentially hostile government that would challenge the US-led regional order and potentially encourage other states to defect from it as well. To head off this possibility, the United States sought to install a friendly and reliable pro-American regime in its place. Given the context of the Cold War, some target regimes were viewed as sympathetic to communism, although US officials debated the extent of their direct ties to the Soviet Union, such as Jacobo Arbenz's Guatemala or Salvador Allende's Chile. Still others, however, entered America's crosshairs not because the target government was considered too leftist, but rather because they were governed by unpopular repressive dictators whose continued rule, Washington feared, could lead to instability and popular revolutions, such as Rafael Trujillo's Dominican Republic or Francois "Papa Doc" Duvalier's Haiti.

Why do policymakers try to change who holds the reins of power in a foreign government? The idea that leaders launch regime changes to increase their state's security provides only half an answer. When a country finds itself embroiled in an interstate dispute, it may respond in a number of ways—for example, through negotiation, coercion, sanctions, limited military action, or outright war. Why choose regime change rather than one of these other foreign policy initiatives? The answer is that regime change holds a unique appeal for policymakers. Unlike most foreign policy strategies, regime change offers the possibility of altering the underlying preferences of a foreign government. That is, most efforts to alter another state's behavior rely on negotiation, brute force, or coercion. Although these tactics may persuade a state to change its behavior temporarily, none of these efforts will change that state's underlying interests if its leadership remains unchanged. If one state hopes to maintain ongoing influence in another's affairs, it will therefore require repeated attempts at coercion or subjugation to persuade the foreign government to act against its interests. By its nature, however, regime change promises a deeper solution to intractable conflicts like these. Regime change allows a state to install a foreign government that shares the intervening state's preferences and interests. In theory, such a move is mutually beneficial to both parties and has the potential to fundamentally transform the relationship between the two states. If the operation is successful, the new government will share mutual interests with the intervener, meaning that it will then act in the intervening state's interests without having to be bribed or coerced into doing so.[8] This, in turn, should reduce tensions between the two states. The stage is set for future cooperation as a foe becomes a friend. In the best-case scenario, the new regime will become a reliable client state and pursue the intervener's interests at home and abroad.

Given this remarkable potential to transform adversaries into allies, we might reasonably expect states to pursue regime change more often than they do. Indeed, why would a powerful state choose to live in a world of sovereign rivals when it could potentially live in a world filled with compliant puppet regimes? Most interstate disputes, however, do not lead to a regime change because of two necessary—but not sufficient—preconditions for intervention. These two preconditions reduce the potential pool of cases where a state may theoretically pursue regime change to a smaller subset of disputes in which states are actually likely to intervene.

The first precondition is that the dispute must be based on the perception of a chronic, irreconcilable divergence of national security interests. The hardest disputes to reconcile occur when the target government fears that they will lose power if they comply with the intervening state's demands.[9] The most common catalysts for regime change, therefore, involve disputes where the intervener demands that the target government take an action that could jeopardize its future ability to rule, such as relinquishing its military capabilities, forgoing an alliance with a great power protector, or abandoning a fundamental political position without which it would struggle to maintain power.[10] Disputes of this nature are particularly difficult to resolve via other foreign policy tools, such as negotiation or coercion, because the intervening state's demands place the target government in a catch-22: Acquiescing to the intervener's demands will weaken the target government's grip on power and thus increase the odds that it will be overthrown by domestic or foreign opponents. Failing to comply with the intervener's demands, however, means the intervening state may overthrow it directly. Faced with these unpleasant alternatives, some governments targeted for regime change decide to reject the intervener's demands, leading policymakers in the intervening state to believe that regime change is their only way for the two states to break their political gridlock.[11]

A second precondition is that the intervener must be able to identify a plausible political alternative to the government it is trying to overthrow. The best alternatives have both the capacity to administer the target state and preexisting support from the state's population.[12] Most importantly, from the perspective of the intervening state, the alternative regime must also share similar policy preferences. That is, its members must want to rule their country in a manner consistent with the intervener's interests. If all plausible replacements for the current leadership are likely to behave in the same manner as their predecessors, then there is no benefit to regime change. Although it may seem that finding a foreign leader willing to play ball would be a relatively easy task, US officials often struggled to identify foreign political actors with similar interests and enough political power to be considered viable, and variation in the availability of these leaders over time was one of the key factors determining when Washington intervened.

Interestingly, US policymakers did not seem to believe that any one type of foreign government would be more likely to pursue their interests. Some ideological theories of regime change predict that states will be more likely to install foreign governments with the same type of regime as their own because they believe that similar regimes share similar interests. US interventions during the Cold War, however, confound the expectations of these theories. The United States supported authoritarian forces in forty-four out of sixty-four covert regime changes, including at least six operations that sought to replace liberal democratic governments with illiberal authoritarian regimes. Yet, Washington's proclivity for installing authoritarian regimes was also not absolute. In one-eighth of its covert missions and one-half of its overt interventions, Washington encouraged a democratic transformation in an authoritarian state. This suggests that US leaders were pragmatic in their choice of whom to support. When US policymakers believed that the majority of the target state's population shared their interests, they promoted democratization. When they believed that only a smaller subset of the population shared their preferences, they supported whatever type of government would bring that subset to power—be it a military junta, a single-party authoritarian regime, or a personalist dictator. In most Cold War interventions, US leaders believed that an authoritarian regime would be most likely to pursue their interests. However, that may not always be the case. After communism's popular appeal declined alongside the Soviet Union, democratization has taken on a larger role in US foreign policy in the post–Cold War world. The most famous example is Iraq (2003), when President George W. Bush maintained that given the opportunity to freely select their own government, the Iraqi people would select leaders who shared American values and held a similar vision for the future of their country.[13] Taken together, this suggests that US leaders are open to promoting different types of regimes, and history suggests that when promoting democracy serves US interests, Washington will do so.

Conduct: Why Do States Intervene Covertly versus Overtly?

Leaders decide how to intervene in the same way that they decide most foreign policy decisions: by debating the risks and rewards of the options available to them. In broad terms, these include two kinds of considerations: (1) tactical factors, including the likelihood that an operation will succeed and its potential costs, and (2) strategic factors, reflecting the intrinsic strategic value that the intervener attaches to replacing the target government as well as the intervener's desire to demonstrate either restraint or resolve on the international stage. In most cases, both tactical and strategic considerations favor covert conduct, which explains why Washington chose covert rather than overt action by a ratio of 10 to 1 during the Cold War.

Tactical considerations include the two major operational concerns that policymakers evaluate when deciding how to intervene: the mission's estimated costs and its likelihood of success. Covert action has a significant bearing on both concerns. On the one hand, covert conduct lowers a mission's potential military, economic, and reputational costs because the heart of covert action is "plausible deniability," or the belief that the intervening state can hide its role in the operation by deflecting blame onto others. Covert regime changes are designed so that domestic opposition forces in the target state take on the heavy lifting of toppling the foreign regime, as well as the blame if the operation fails. This allows the intervener to disavow involvement in the plot, which in turn lowers the likelihood that the intervener will experience military retaliation from the target state. It also lowers the potential reputational costs of intervention because covert action enables the intervener to behave hypocritically by secretly acting in ways that contradict its purported values or public positions.

At the same time, however, covert operations fail to replace the government of the target state more often than their overt counterparts. One reason why is that many covert regime changes face a fundamental trade-off between size and secrecy. The type of large operation required to overthrow a powerful state is extremely difficult to organize covertly and carry out while maintaining plausible deniability. Overt missions, by contrast, face no such restrictions. In comparison to their covert counterparts, overt regime changes can typically employ more resources, and are generally better supervised and more thorough in their contingency planning.

Policymakers thus face a tactical dilemma in many cases. If they attempt a covert regime change, its potential costs may be lower, but it is also more likely to fail. If they intervene overtly, the mission's likely costs are higher, but they stand a better chance of success. Faced with these two possibilities, US leaders have overwhelmingly chosen the covert option, recognizing that this increased the odds of mission failure. In most cases, policymakers believe that the low potential costs of covert conduct make this option worth the higher chance of failure—particularly because they expect covert failures to remain hidden. In fact, covert conduct may lower an operation's anticipated costs to such a degree that it shifts the cost-benefit calculation from the point where intervention would not seem desirable to the point where it becomes worthwhile.

These tactical considerations are only half of the equation. Policymakers must also assess the overall strategic value of replacing the target government and whether they want to signal restraint or resolve on the international stage. The greater a state's strategic value, the greater the costs leaders are willing to incur to replace that state's regime. Even in such cases where policymakers are willing to intervene overtly, however, I find that they still generally prefer to intervene covertly to minimize the operation's costs. Nevertheless, covert regime change might not always be an option. Successful covert missions require time. The intervening state needs preexisting intelligence on the target regime and a connection to a feasible domestic opposition group in the target state. Thus, when a government must act quickly in response to developing situations in strategically important states, covert action may not be a practical option, and policymakers may prefer overt intervention. Such a course of action, however, carries its own set of risks. Governments targeted for regime change seldom back down without a fight. With its very survival in the balance, the target regime may want to use all the military resources at its disposal to maintain its hold on power. Knowing this, policymakers intervene overtly only when they believe they can secure a quick and decisive military victory without risking protracted war.

The case studies and chapter 5, which provides an overview of all US Cold War cases, confirm my theoretical predictions. Of the six overt regime changes conducted by the United States during this time, Washington escalated to overt conduct only after first trying and failing to overthrow the target state covertly in four cases (Lebanon, Dominican Republic, Libya, and Panama)—leaving one case where the United States intervened overtly from the beginning (Grenada) and one case where the United States launched concurrent covert and overt efforts to replace the regime (North Korea). In each of these cases, I argue that the United States was willing to overtly intervene because policymakers believed that rapidly developing events on the ground necessitated a quick response and that Washington would achieve a quick and decisive victory, thus sending a strong signal of American resolve.

Consequences: How Effective Are Covert Regime Changes?

Policymakers may have compelling tactical and strategic reasons to prefer covert rather than overt conduct, but the question remains whether covert regime change is a wise choice. That is, do covert regime changes generally secure their desired foreign policy objectives? Chapter 4 analyzes both the short- and long-term consequences of these operations. In both regards, I find that states tend to overestimate their value as a policy tool. Attempted covert regime changes failed to overthrow their target more than 60 percent of the time, and even when they did, most operations failed to remain covert, and many sparked blowback in unanticipated ways.

Chapter 4 first analyzes short-term effectiveness by asking, "Did the covert regime change successfully replace the foreign government?" During the Cold War, US-backed covert regime changes succeeded in replacing their targets 39 percent of the time, compared to a 66 percent success rate for their overt counterparts. However, the covert operations that easily toppled their targets also tended to be the ones that were least needed from a geostrategic perspective in that they involved overthrowing weak states with limited international political or economic influence, such as Guatemala or the Dominican Republic. Washington was far less successful when it targeted powerful military adversaries, such as during its many efforts to install pro-American leaders in Soviet satellite states. To understand why, I ask whether certain characteristics of the target state—such as military capabilities, regime type, alliance membership, or level of domestic political stability—made it a better or worse target for regime change. My statistical analysis then shows that the best candidates for covert regime change are weak states, democracies, and American allies.

Another key factor influencing the success rates of covert missions was the relative domestic power of the groups backed by the United States. When the US-backed forces had already amassed sufficient resources to their side and enjoyed widespread domestic support, Washington had to do comparatively little to tip the scales in their favor—indeed, some likely would have come to power even without US covert support. When the opposition forces were weak relative to the regime, however, Washington struggled to provide enough aid to have a decisive impact without blowing its cover or becoming overtly entangled in the conflict. This dynamic is reflected in the low success rate of covert interventions to support armed dissident groups in their bids to topple a foreign government: because the dissidents backed by the United States were generally quite weak relative to their central governments, only four of thirty-five attempts overthrew their targets. Other covert tactics that typically backed stronger opposition forces had higher rates of success. For instance, nine out of thirteen US-backed military coup attempts successfully ousted their targets. Likewise, I identified sixteen cases where Washington sought to influence the result of a foreign election by covertly funding and spreading propaganda on behalf of its preferred candidates, often doing so beyond a single election cycle. Of these, the US-backed parties won their elections three-quarters of the time. Yet, it is reasonable to assume that many of these parties would have won their elections anyway, given that they were leading in the polls before the US intervention. Taken together, I conclude that America's Cold War covert regime change attempts were most likely to succeed when the domestic conditions favored intervention and Washington's contribution to the effort could be relatively limited.

Successfully changing a regime, however, does not necessarily make a mission a long-term success. In this regard, very few covert regime changes worked out as US planners intended. Policymakers launch regime changes to install foreign leaders with similar policy preferences, with the expectation that when the newly installed leaders then pursue their own interests, their actions will benefit the intervening state as well. Despite the simplicity of this plan, it often proves much more difficult in practice than interveners anticipate.

Operations that succeed in toppling a foreign regime are still besieged by a "principal-agent" problem. The reason why is that for an interstate dispute to have escalated to the point of regime change in the first place, the target government must have had a compelling reason not to acquiesce to the intervener's demands when the dispute first arose. For instance, the intervener's demands may have clashed with the target government's enduring geostrategic interests or brought them into conflict with powerful domestic opposition forces. Unfortunately for the intervener, this means that even if it succeeds in replacing the foreign government, the same political pressures that compelled the first government to act against their interests often continue to hold true for its successor as well. Consequently, I find that the only installed leaders who were willing to act as long-term agents for the United States were those who remained highly dependent on US aid. Such leaders, however, usually faced great difficulties maintaining power domestically. The new leader's opponents often accused the government of being a US puppet and, in some cases, even took up arms against the regime. In fact, approximately half of the governments that came to power via a US-backed covert regime change during the Cold War were later violently removed from power through assassination, war, revolution, or coup. So great was the domestic opposition against them that many leaders installed by the United States acted on behalf of American interests for only a short time, or the United States had to commit an inordinate amount of resources to keep them in power.

Covert operations that fail to replace their targets can also spell trouble for the intervener. Although policymakers launch covert operations with the expectation that the mission's plausible deniability will shield them from the negative repercussions of trying to topple a foreign government, in practice, this often proves more difficult than planners anticipate. In more than 70 percent of America's Cold War interventions, Washington was publicly accused of meddling in the domestic affairs of the target state at the time of the regime change attempt. As a result, when these missions failed to oust their target, US policymakers found themselves in the awkward position of having to do business with foreign leaders who knew that Washington was actively trying to remove them from office. Unsurprisingly, this often had the effect of further souring their country's already negative relationship with the United States. This, in turn, increased the likelihood that the two states would come to blows in the future.

To test these theoretical predictions, chapter 4 asks how America's covert interventions influenced the quality of relations between Washington and the target states. Contrary to the expectations of policymakers, I show that the United States was more likely to experience militarized interstate disputes with the states that they targeted for covert regime change compared to similar countries where they never intervened. Covert interventions also appeared to harm Washington's relationship with the target state at lower levels of cooperation, such as United Nations voting behavior and foreign policy portfolio similarity. Given that Washington already had hostile relationships with these states, however, one potential criticism is that these post-regime change conflicts were the result of a selection effect: namely, that the United States was more likely to target states for covert regime change where the possibility of conflict was already present. To guard against that possibility, chapter 4 introduces several models that use the statistical data preprocessing method of matching to compare the cases where the United States intervened to a set of similar cases where it did not intervene, but which showed a similar propensity for conflict, to confirm that the breakdown in relations was a result of the intervention. The chapter then explores the impact of covert interventions on the targeted states by analyzing the target state's subsequent levels of democratization, civil war, adverse regime changes, and episodes of mass killing compared to similarly matched samples of cases. Here too, the results paint a grim picture: states targeted in a covert regime change operation appear less likely to be democratic afterward and more likely to experience civil war, adverse regime changes, or human rights abuses.

I conclude that states underestimate the negative consequences of covert regime change. The costs in American dollars and lives lost during the Cold War tell only part of the story. Many operations also incurred considerable indirect costs, such as a rise in anti-American sentiment and a loss of international trust. The case studies develop this theme further and illustrate how covert interventions often backfire in unanticipated ways. For instance, chapter 6 shows how early US-backed missions to topple Soviet-backed regimes in Eastern Europe helped to convince Stalin that postwar cooperation with Washington was no longer feasible. Likewise, chapter 7 illustrates how the 1963 plot to oust South Vietnamese premier Ngo Dinh Diem had precisely the opposite effect of its intention; rather than stabilizing the country in order to facilitate an American withdrawal from Vietnam, it upended the South Vietnamese political order and drew the United States deeper into the conflict.

Why Regime Change Matters

Regime changes have broad and long-lasting effects for all states involved. For target states, the consequences are often catastrophic. Covert and overt regime changes have fueled bloody civil wars, brought brutal dictators to power, and increased the odds of government-led episodes of mass killing. For intervening states, the consequences can also be dire. Poorly conceived operations have helped bring about long, costly wars, such as following the 1963 US-backed coup d'état that ousted South Vietnamese president Ngo Dinh Diem or the 2003 overt intervention to remove Saddam Hussein in Iraq. Overt interventions and exposed covert operations can provoke an international backlash, which in turn can weaken a state's diplomatic and political authority. Domestically, covert missions can undermine a state's democratic ideals by creating situations in which political leaders are unaccountable to their citizens. On the other hand, scholars have also identified ways that foreign-imposed regime change operations may have positive effects. For intervening states, successful missions can bolster their security by replacing hostile regimes with friendly ones, by creating buffer zones, or by neutralizing threats abroad before they can spark unrest at home. Successful missions may also provide material benefits for the intervening state by protecting its economic interests or by ensuring access to the target state's markets. In certain situations, these actions may even foster interstate stability and peace. Finally, regime changes appear to have played a key role in stopping several humanitarian disasters: for instance, Vietnam's 1979 invasion of Cambodia overthrew the brutal Khmer Rouge regime and ended a genocide believed to have claimed roughly 2 million lives.[14]

Regime changes occupy a unique position relative to the major international relations theories. On the one hand, the motives cited earlier—overthrowing a military rival, increasing one's relative military power, preventing a new military threat, and establishing regional hegemony—are the same ones that Realist scholars have long provided to explain war.[15] On the other hand, however, the strategy of regime change—replacing the political leadership of another state in order to change that state's behavior—has received surprisingly little attention from Realist scholars. Perhaps the reason for this omission is that some prominent Realist theories view all states as unitary, self-interested actors. Neorealists, in particular, famously "blackbox" the state—meaning that they do not look to a state's domestic politics to explain its international behavior. Instead, they believe that all states, regardless of who is in charge, will behave in predictable patterns based on their geostrategic position and available resources.[16] If states really viewed one another as "black boxes," however, regime change is an odd goal.[17] Why would a state care who is in charge of a foreign government if domestic politics are irrelevant for explaining international relations? Nevertheless, the frequency with which states launch regime changes suggests that leaders do care a great deal about the political leadership of foreign powers and frequently intervene—covertly and overtly—to influence the makeup of that leadership.

To fill that void, this book aims to provide a Realist explanation for covert regime change. I argue that states pursue covert regime change to increase their relative power within the international system—by overthrowing current military adversaries, dividing enemy alliances, and ensuring that their existing allies and states within their sphere of influence are governed by leaders who will remain committed to that alliance. In my telling, systemic factors—such as the distribution of the balance of power—create the broad incentives for states to pursue regime change, while factors internal to the intervening and target states—such as policymakers' perceptions regarding the efficacy of different military strategies and the availability of foreign opposition groups to support—affect the specific foreign policy decisions regarding the timing and conduct of regime changes.[18]

This study also has important implications for the existing literature specifically on regime change. Despite the frequency that states launch covert regime changes, most studies on the causes of regime change have focused only on overt operations, causing scholars to misinterpret the basic causes of covert regime change. Ideological accounts focusing on the regime type of the intervening and target states often break down once covert operations are considered. Contrary to what many of these accounts predict, states are not restrained from covertly overthrowing their ideological equivalents or secretly cooperating with their supposed ideological foes. Alternative explanations focusing on norms are similarly misspecified. Norms do matter, but not as much as some authors believe, nor in the way that they imagine. Contrary to the claims of some existing studies, international norms do not restrain states from attempting regime change. Norms only constrain states from conducting *overt* operations. When policymakers want to conduct an operation that they know violates international norms, they simply conduct it *covertly* to hide their involvement. Finally, studies arguing that military or economic interests motivate regime change fare better, but they are applicable only to a narrow subset of cases as currently formulated, and each fails independently to account for most cases.

Definitions and Data

To ensure that readers understand the specific vocabulary used in this study, it will be helpful to define certain terms. *Regime* is used to mean either a state's leadership or its political processes and institutional arrangements.[19] *Regime change* thus refers to an operation to replace another state's effective political leadership by significantly altering the composition of that state's ruling elite, its administrative apparatus, or its institutional structure. This study focuses only on cases in which an intervening state intends for the target state to retain its juridical sovereignty or, in the case of secessionist movements, to obtain its juridical sovereignty. Consequently, cases of territorial conquest, colonization, or annexation are not included.[20]

Covert regime change denotes an operation to replace the political leadership of another state where the intervening state does not acknowledge its role publicly.[21] These actions include successful and failed attempts to covertly assassinate foreign leaders, sponsor coups d'état, influence foreign democratic elections, incite popular revolutions, and support armed dissident groups in their bids to topple a foreign government. Although many different types of foreign actions can be conducted covertly, the study avoids other secretive actions not designed to replace a foreign state's leadership—espionage, counterintelligence, diplomacy, operational security, and propaganda.[22] This definition aligns with the US government's classification of covert regime change, laid out in National Security Council Directive 10/2 in 1948:

> The National Security Council . . . has determined that, in the interests of world peace and U.S. national security, the overt foreign activities of the U.S. Government must be supplemented by covert operations . . . so planned and executed that any U.S. government responsibility for them is not evident to unauthorized persons and if uncovered the U.S. Government can plausibly disclaim any responsibility for them. Specifically, such actions shall include covert activities related to propaganda; economic warfare; preventative direct actions, including sabotage, anti-sabotage, demolition, and evacuation measures; subversion against hostile states, including assistance to underground resistance movements, guerrillas, and refugee liberation groups, and support of indigenous anti-communist elements in threatened countries of the free world.[23]

Overt regime change includes operations involving the direct and publicly acknowledged use of military force to replace the political leadership of another state. States can go to war for regime change, but the definition also includes smaller military actions designed to replace foreign political leaders, such as air strikes or limited invasions.

A few definitional caveats before I proceed. First, my data exclude efforts to covertly prop up a state's allies through publicly unacknowledged financial or military aid.[24] For instance, the United States reportedly provided covert support to the Saudi royal family during the Cold War to help them maintain their position of power and stability in the region.[25] Although, actions of this nature are similar to covert regime change in that they strive to influence the domestic political system of a foreign power, they differ from regime change in that they seek to maintain the status quo rather than revising it. Consequently, I believe covert actions of this nature are better classified as regime maintenance. There is also the question of how to differentiate covert operations to influence the result of a foreign election from regime maintenance efforts. During the Cold War, for instance, the United States sought to covertly guarantee that their preferred candidate would win a democratic election in over a dozen countries. Many of these cases do not pose a definitional challenge for this project because Washington's covert efforts were designed to upend the status quo: either the United

States was trying to bring a new leader to power via the election, or they were trying to influence the first democratic election in a country after it underwent a power transition from another system of government. However, in five cases—Italy (twice), France, Japan, and Chile—the United States conducted operations to ensure that the ruling party would continue to win elections and thus remain in power. One potential objection is that these cases are better considered examples of regime maintenance and therefore should be excluded from my sample. Nevertheless, I decided to include these cases because I believe it is reasonable to view free and fair competitive democratic elections as, by their nature, prescheduled opportunities for regime change. Furthermore, omitting these cases would paint an inaccurate picture of America's covert behavior during the Cold War because the interventions played a major role in US Cold War strategy. Finally, these cases provide a noteworthy exception to one of the main claims of this study—that covert regime changes are most likely to succeed against weak, geostrategically unimportant states and that many operations spark anti-American blowback and resentment. In four of these five cases—US operations in Italy, France, and Japan—the actions succeeded against powerful, important states with few negative repercussions for Washington. In the spirit of transparency, it is therefore important that I include these cases because failing to do so would bias the data in my favor.

In contrast to some studies, my dataset focuses on target countries rather than individual operations. For example, the United States encouraged three separate coups in short succession during its efforts to overthrow Guatemala in 1954. Although some studies treat these coups as separate events, this study treats them as a single covert campaign. Similar to this is the fact that the United States often pursued more than one covert tactic simultaneously against the same state. For instance, during eight years of covert operations against Cuba in the 1960s, US officials backed multiple assassination plots against Fidel Castro as part of a plan known as Operation Mongoose, as well as the Bay of Pigs paramilitary invasion by Cuban exiles. This study groups them together as one eight-year case rather than multiple independent operations. Similarly, when the United States covertly sought to influence democratic elections across multiple election cycles within the same country, I grouped them together as one campaign. Analyzing covert campaigns rather than independent missions is preferable because states frequently launch more than one operation simultaneously, and treating these actions as independent overlooks the fact that they often have mutually reinforcing effects on one another.

Despite the frequency of covert regime changes, international relations (IR) analysts are often ambiguous in their treatment of them. On the one hand, many critics of US foreign policy frequently allege covert American involvement in controversial political events throughout the world. On the other hand, covert regime change generally does not play a major role in America's foreign policy debates, and IR textbooks seldom address it in depth. This ambiguity about the importance of covert attempts at regime change stems from the fact that America's covert activities are more often treated as the subject of speculation than of systematic analysis. The following anecdote from a conversation between Henry Kissinger and Chinese prime minister Zhou Enlai in 1971 reflects this contradictory treatment. When Zhou questioned Kissinger about the Central Intelligence Agency's (CIA) covert actions, Kissinger replied that Zhou "vastly overestimates the competence of the CIA." Yet Zhou pressed on: "Whenever something happens in the world they are always thought of." Yes, Kissinger retorted, "That is true, and it flatters them, but they don't deserve it."[26]

To help resolve this speculation, this study aims to systematically analyze all US-backed regime changes during the Cold War (1947–89). I have chosen to use this sample for both theoretical and practical reasons. Theoretically, I can hold several important features of the international state system constant by focusing on the Cold War. For one, the modern notion of "regime change" is premised on the idea of Westphalian state sovereignty, or that "states exist in specific territories, within which domestic political authorities are the sole arbiters of legitimate behavior."[27] However, this understanding of sovereignty has not always been the norm. Before the age of decolonization, the international system was based on a much more fluid idea of sovereignty. Although Western powers interacted with each other as sovereign equals, they did not treat their colonies, protectorates, or imperial domains in a similar manner. They considered it their legitimate right to replace the domestic leadership of these territories. Thus, the colonial era concept of "regime change" had neither the same connotations nor the same consequences it does today. Likewise, since 1945, only states have launched regime change missions. This too has not always been the case. For instance, in 1855, an individual—Tennessean William Walker—overthrew the Nicaraguan government and ruled as president for several years with only a small, privately funded army. Similarly, in 1910, a corporation—Cuyamel Fruit Company—hired mercenaries to overthrow the government of Honduras to protect its banana plantations.[28] The motives driving these non-state actors likely differ from those of states, and excluding these cases simplifies the study.

There are also several practical reasons to limit this study to US operations during the Cold War. For one thing, the combination of US government declassification regulations, influential Congressional investigations, and journalistic coverage of these missions have severely undermined Washington's ability to keep its covert actions secret. However, the same cannot be said of operations launched by other states or by the United States during different eras. The primary sources used in this study were obtained through archival research at the National Archives and Records Administration, the National Security Archive, and several presidential libraries.

From this effort, I have obtained thousands of declassified documents—mostly from the CIA and the executive branch—outlining the planning, implementation, and effectiveness of these missions. Because the amount of data available per mission ranges from a few reports to thousands of documents, I have imposed a minimum requirement of three primary source documents to verify each case. These primary sources are listed in several online appendixes: Appendix I lists three primary source documents for each of the sixty-four covert cases indicating that the United States attempted to covertly overthrow the target country. Appendix II does the same for each of America's six overt operations. Appendix III covers cases where the United States has been publicly accused of instigating a covert regime change, but where the existing evidence indicates that Washington was not actively involved in the plot, as well as three primary source documents to support why I made that determination. In several cases that are commonly considered the work of the CIA, such as the 1967 Greek coup or the 1976 Argentine coup, I argue that Washington did not take an active role in planning or implementing the operation, although US officials may have had preexisting ties to the coup plotters or foreknowledge that a coup could occur. The coup plotters may also have been emboldened by the knowledge that Washington would likely back them if they succeeded.

Two potential data concerns are worth addressing in detail. One objection is that my dataset may be skewed toward identifying failed operations while overlooking successful covert cases precisely because they have succeeded in remaining secret. I believe this concern is valid, but likely overstated. For one, at several points in its history, US government agencies have compiled internal histories of the nation's covert operations. If unknown successful cases existed, they most likely would have been included in these reports. For instance, during the Watergate hearings, CIA director James Schlesinger ordered agency officials to collect all potentially incriminating actions for review. The resulting report—declassified in 2007 and commonly referred to as the "Family Jewels"—covers the period from the 1950s through 1970s and does not include any cases that this current study has failed to identify.[29] In addition, several individuals interviewed for this project who were involved in the planning of these missions have indicated that the list is comprehensive. Finally, as with any potential data bias, the question arises of whether the bias supports or opposes the argument. There are a few cases where the secondary literature provides compelling reason to suspect that the United States may have pursued a covert intervention, but for which I have been unable to locate primary source verification one way or the other, such as the allegations that the United States sought to covertly influence elections in the Philippines and Greece during the 1950s or sought to organize a coup in Iraq in the early 1960s. However, these cases are entirely consistent with my argument. To the extent that any covert US regime changes could have completely escaped my attention, I believe they are most likely to be small unsuccessful operations. Because I argue that covert regime changes are largely ineffective, however, failing to identify these cases weakens my argument. Selection bias therefore poses fewer problems for this project than one might originally suspect.

A second potential methodological objection is that I have "selected on the dependent variable." This criticism relates to the research practice of analyzing only those cases where the phenomenon of interest was observed (e.g., US-backed regime change attempts) and not analyzing cases where the phenomenon was not observed (e.g., cases where the United States could have attempted a regime change but did not). According to this line of reasoning, if a scholar samples on the dependent variable, any inferences that they make about the causes of their research subject will be invalid because they may have inadvertently overlooked cases where the causal factors that they consider important were present but did not result in the phenomenon. Applying this criticism to this project, I argue that states launch regime change operations in response to chronic, security-based interstate disputes. One could argue that because I selected on the dependent variable by creating a dataset of regime change attempts, I cannot make any causal inferences about the motives for these interventions.[30] Despite the importance of this concern, I believe that it does not pose an insurmountable problem for four reasons. First, and most importantly, a correlation between security-based disputes and regime changes is not the only piece of evidence that I use to argue that the United States launched regime change operations to pursue security interests. My assertion is also based on extensive qualitative analysis of a plethora of different data sources, such as declassified government documents, meeting transcripts, and recordings. Second, my case studies were selected to show variation in policymakers' willingness to launch regime change operations within and across cases. Third, the two prerequisites for intervention are necessary, but not sufficient, conditions. This means that I readily acknowledge that there may be cases where these two factors are present but do not lead to regime change. Fourth, to avoid sampling on the dependent variable while constructing my dataset, I would have had to identify a corresponding control group of situations where the United States could have launched a regime change but did not. However, from a purely practical perspective, it is difficult to imagine what this control group would look like in a large-N study because the proximate catalysts for US intervention varied widely across cases. The potential control group would therefore have to encompass a huge number of public and private interactions that Washington had with foreign governments, for which it would be virtually impossible to gather data.

Chapters 6–8 include three comparative historical analyses of US-backed covert and overt operations in separate geographic regions. Chapter 6 looks at Albania, the Ukrâinian Soviet Socialist Republic, and the negative case of Yugoslavia during the early Cold War. The rollback missions in this chapter were covert efforts to overthrow pro-Soviet regimes in states where the Soviets had a military presence but still faced domestic opposition to their rule. Chapter 7 analyzes the US experience with covert regime change in North and South Vietnam in the run-up to the Vietnam War. I show how American officials sought to contain the spread of communism in Vietnam by launching one series of preventive covert operations to strengthen the leadership of South Vietnam and another set of offensive missions to weaken the leadership of North Vietnam. Finally, chapter 8 investigates a series of Hegemonic operations against the Dominican Republic during the late 1950s and early 1960s. Eisenhower initiated a coup d'état plot against America's one-time ally General Rafael Trujillo that came to fruition under Kennedy and resulted in Trujillo's 1961 assassination. In 1962, Kennedy launched a second covert operation to manipulate the country's upcoming presidential elections. After these covert efforts failed to produce a stable government, Johnson overtly intervened during a 1965 crisis to prevent leftist forces from assuming power. Afterward, he reverted to covert conduct to manipulate Dominican elections in 1966 and 1968.

Each case study creates a strategic narrative regarding the structural forces and strategic decisions that influenced the origins, design, and effectiveness of these operations. Within each case study, I employ process tracing to test whether the perceptions of US policymakers match my theory's predictions, to verify that the sequencing of historical events matches my causal argument, and to compare my causal logic to the alternative explanations. I also use congruence testing to confirm the internal validity of my theory across different environments and to generate external validity for my theory by comparing it to the alternative explanations across cases.[31]

Four criteria were used for selecting cases. First, the cases that I have selected allow me to best test my arguments compared to rival hypotheses. My theory and the alternative explanations each make specific predictions with observable implications for each case, thereby allowing me to weigh the relative merits of each. I have also attempted to select "hard cases" for my theory—where alternative explanations are at their strongest—so that I may evaluate them on their best merits.[32] Second, these cases are representative of the missions conducted in their type (e.g., offensive, preventive, or hegemonic), time, and geographic region, which helps maximize the external validity of my findings. This means that I have selected cases for what Dan Slater and Daniel Ziblatt term "typological representativeness." The advantage of this technique, they argue, is that "strategically choosing cases in search of representative variation can be one effective way to avoid the trap of selection bias. . . . Based on deep knowledge of cases and the categories scholars have used to array them, one can identify the relevant range of outcomes *ex ante* using well-accepted typologies that by definition specify mutually exclusive outcomes that also are *exhaustive* of all empirical variations."[33] Third, I have selected cases that show variation at each step in my causal logic, thus allowing me to test and verify the logic of my entire argument. Finally, given the controversial nature of my research subject, I must substantiate both US decision-making processes and the details of the covert actions. As such, I selected cases with a wide range of available primary sources.[34]

Causes

Why Do States Launch Regime Changes?

> We should cease talk about vague . . . unreal objectives such as human
> rights, the raising of the living standards, and democratization. The
> day is not far off when we are going to have to deal in straight power
> concepts. The less we are then hampered by idealistic slogans, the
> better.
>
> —George F. Kennan, Memorandum to Secretary
> of State Marshall, 1948

In the wake of the Iraq War, regime change has become a hot topic among
scholars and the public alike. At the forefront of this debate is the question
of what motivates states to launch regime changes. In the case of Iraq, debate continues over the relative influence of numerous different justifications
for war: Was it for access to Iraqi oil? To spread democracy abroad? To liber-
ate the Iraqi people from a brutal dictator? To eliminate Iraq's stockpiles of
chemical and biological weapons? To force Iraq to comply with UN resolutions? One key question raised in this debate was whether the Iraq War was
launched for reasons—as many IR scholars claimed—that radically departed
from the normal principles guiding US foreign policy.[1] To answer that question, numerous academic studies have emerged, analyzing the historical
influence of norms, ideas, and economic interests in motivating states to
launch foreign regime changes.

In contrast to those accounts, this chapter presents a security-based theory of regime change. This enterprise involves four tasks. First, I introduce
the existing literature on the causes of regime change and test hypotheses
generated from those works. In the next section, I present a new theory regarding the security motives driving America's Cold War interventions. In
the third section, I discuss how policymakers expect regime change to work.
Finally, I identify two prerequisites for intervention.

Table 2.1 Case selection and alternative hypotheses on the causes of regime change

Alternative Hypotheses	Eastern Europe	Vietnam	Dominican Republic
Normative Hypothesis 1: US-backed regime changes should not violate norms of justified intervention.	✗	✗	✗
Regime Type: Hypothesis 2a: US-backed regime changes should disproportionately target non-democracies.	✓	✓	✓ *(1959–62)* ✗ *(1962–68)*
Hypothesis 2b: US-backed regime changes should promote liberalism and democracy.	✗	✗	✗ *(1959–62)* ✓ *(1962–68)*
Hypothesis 2c: US-backed regime changes should install authoritarian governments.	✓	✓	✓ *(1959–62)* ✗ *(1962–68)*
Economic: Hypothesis 3a: US-backed regime change should promote the private economic interests of American multinational corporations.	✗	✗	✗
Hypothesis 3b: US-backed regime changes should promote America's position as head of a global capitalist order.	✗	✗	✗
Rogue CIA: Hypothesis 4: The CIA launches covert regime changes without executive branch approval.	✗	✗	✗

✗: signifies that the alternative hypothesis makes competing predictions for this case.
✓: signifies that the alternative hypothesis makes similar predictions for this case.

What Do We Know about the Causes of Regime Change?

America's Cold War covert interventions pose a challenge to the four reigning explanations regarding the causes of regime change. Many existing studies of the causes of regime change focus on overt interventions. The appeal of the covert approach, however, lies in its secrecy, suggesting that the mission's political objectives may influence policymakers' preferred conduct. Thus, some theories that offer credible explanations for overt cases alone are less compelling when compared to a sample of covert and overt regime changes. This section reviews four competing explanations to determine whether hypotheses generated from those works can accurately explain America's Cold War regime changes. Table 2.1 summarizes how these alternative hypotheses will be tested in the case studies contained in chapters 6 through 8.

NORMATIVE EXPLANATIONS

The first set of existing explanations asks how norms legitimatize different forms of regime change by influencing what types of actions political leaders consider appropriate for them to undertake. The effect of norms, according to Nina Tannenwald, is to "shape realms of possibility. They influence (increase or decrease) the probability of occurrence of certain courses of action."[2] One of the most salient norms in the international system is Westphalian sovereignty: the belief that "states exist in specific territories, within which domestic political authorities are the sole arbiters of legitimate behavior."[3] Westphalian sovereignty undergirds the modern state system, modern international law, and many international organizations.[4] In that sense, it is a very powerful norm. At the same time, however, states frequently violate one another's sovereignty. In fact, violations are a routine—and often uncontroversial—facet of interstate relations. To figure out why, many scholars have asked how norms influence what types of foreign interventions policymakers will consider legitimate. Two of these accounts—those focusing on the role of norms of justified intervention and democratic peace theory (DPT)—make predictions about when states will launch regime change operations.

One line of this literature investigates how different norms emerge over time that constrain the types of military interventions that states will consider legitimate. From these works, we can derive several predictions for how the United States and other great powers should have behaved during the Cold War.[5] First, according to these theorists, states should not intervene to prop up leaders who infringe on minority rights or perpetrate crimes against humanity.[6] Likewise, in the post-colonial era, states should not launch regime change to enforce the contractual obligations of private parties or to collect public debts.[7] Scholars have also elaborated on how internationally held norms may constrain the ways that states can use their military, for instance, by prohibiting foreign annexations and conquests, interstate political assassinations, and preventive wars.[8]

Democratic Peace Theory (DPT) suggests another way that norms could regulate state behavior. According to normative variants of DPT, democracies do not go to war with other democracies, because liberal norms shape how democratic policymakers view one another and choose to resolve conflict. In his groundbreaking piece on the topic, Michael Doyle argues that liberalism's respect for individual rights manifests itself internationally as a deep respect for the sovereignty of fellow democracies. As a result, he maintains, "Even though liberal states have become involved in numerous wars with illiberal states, constitutionally secure liberal states have yet to engage in war with one another."[9] A large body of IR literature has subsequently expanded on the various normative reasons why democracies "perceive each other as peaceful because of the democratic norms governing their domestic decision-making processes."[10] These reasons include internalized norms of nonviolent conflict resolution, respect for the rule of law, norms of individual freedom, and shared identities among democracies.[11] Combining these arguments about how norms constrain state behavior, we arrive at hypothesis 1:

> Hypothesis 1 *Operations That Violate Norms of Justified Intervention*: The United States should not attempt regime changes that violate norms of justified intervention.

If hypothesis 1 is correct, then Washington's Cold War behavior should reflect the constraining effect of these norms. Looking at overt interventions alone, although far from perfect, the United States has a relatively strong record: the United States has never gone to war against another democracy. It has not gone to war for the primary purpose of securing private economic interests or public debts in the twentieth century. Its last territorial annexation was the 1917 purchase of the Virgin Islands from Denmark. And as chapter 5 shows, Washington went to great lengths to publicly justify its six overt regime changes during the Cold War as being consistent with these norms.

Once covert operations are also included, however, hypothesis 1 breaks down. America's covert operations habitually violated norms of justified intervention: Washington installed brutal dictators. It broke international law. It collaborated with many unsavory organizations, including violent secessionist movements, authoritarian death squads, religious extremists, Mafioso, drug traffickers, and numerous groups known to have committed mass killings. The United States also pursued numerous regime changes for objectives akin to preventive war and was embroiled in several plots involving the assassination of foreign leaders.[12] Time and again, American leaders had no compunction violating these norms as long as their role could be kept secret. The 1954 Doolittle Report reflects this dynamic: "It is now clear that we are facing an implacable enemy whose avowed objective is world domination by whatever means and at whatever costs. There are no rules in such a game. Hitherto acceptable norms of human conduct do not apply."[13]

America's record of covert regime change also poses a strong challenge to DPT.[14] During the Cold War alone, the United States covertly supported regime change efforts that directly or indirectly replaced democratically elected leaders with authoritarian regimes in six cases and covertly tried to influence the outcome of democratic elections in a dozen additional cases.[15] Contrary to the predictions of normative variants of DPT, US policymakers simply ignored norms of respect for fellow democracies when they believed that it served US national interests.[16] A lack of respect for democratic norms is evident in the way US officials spoke about foreign democracies when they objected to the decisions made by their voters. For instance, fearing that the Indonesian Communist Party might win Indonesia's next election, John Foster Dulles remarked in 1958, "They [the Indonesians] cannot turn over their country to communism without something being done about it by the free world."[17] Likewise, remarking on the chance that Salvador Allende's socialist party might win Chile's 1970 elections, Henry Kissinger declared, "I don't see why we need to stand by and watch a country go communist due to the irresponsibility of its own people. The issues are much too important for the Chilean voters to be left to decide for themselves."[18]

DPT proponents have responded to the challenge posed by covert operations in multiple ways. One argument is that the "political regimes targeted by U.S. covert action, especially forcible action, did not meet the threshold conditions for complete liberalism."[19] In other words, the target states were not fully established liberal democracies, so the United States did not treat them as such. Nevertheless, this argument ignores the fact that though some of the target states had short histories with democracy, others—like France, Guatemala, or Chile—were well-established democracies.[20] A second counterargument put forth by DPT proponents is that some CIA interventions were attempted "on *behalf* of democratic governments on occasion, particularly in the early days of the Cold War, as in Italy and France" by supporting anti-communist political parties in foreign elections.[21] In a related vein, Michael Poznansky argues that US policymakers were not constrained by democratic norms of nonintervention when they believed that their inaction could enable a communist victory in a democratic election.[22]

These arguments are also unsatisfying. There were two types of covert operations targeting democracies during the Cold War: one type tried to covertly influence foreign elections so that America's preferred leader would come to power, and the other aimed to topple democratic governments in favor of pro-American authoritarian regimes. Regardless of how DPT proponents may try to spin it, however, both types of intervention reflect a fundamental disrespect for the core liberal values that they claim undergird the democratic peace—such as the right of self-determination, democratic participation, and respect for international law.[23] The authors are probably correct that some US leaders were able to persuade themselves that they were justified overthrowing or subverting leftist foreign democracies for the sake of democracy. Yet, all this may illustrate is the subjective nature of the democratic peace. Many of the leftist parties had repeatedly committed themselves to working within a democratic framework, and in some cases, US policymakers even acknowledged this fact.[24] Instead, it is possible that US leaders redefined what they considered a democracy based not on the actual political situations within the target states, but rather on their strategic interest in fighting communism.[25] As Tarak Barkawi explains, "U.S. Cold War officials and the democratic-peace research program simply equates 'democracy' with 'liberal capitalist democracy' without acknowledgment of the essentially contested nature of this concept."[26] Sebastian Rosato writes: "Scholars will therefore always be able to find 'evidence' that the other state was not perceived to be sufficiently 'democratic' as leaders go about demonizing the enemy. . . . These perceptions may change independently of the objective nature of the other regime, suggesting that it is entirely possible for liberal states to fight one another."[27]

All of this is not to say that norms are irrelevant for explaining American Cold War behavior. Norms are influential, but not in the way that scholars typically talk about them as motivating or precluding certain interventions. A third possibility also exists: nonnormative concerns may motivate a regime change, but norms of justified intervention could influence *how* policymakers intervene. When leaders believe that international observers will consider a mission legitimate, they can conduct it overtly. When policymakers believe the mission violates norms of justified intervention, however, they are more likely to conduct it covertly. Covert action thus allows states to behave hypocritically. It enables leaders to conform publicly to collective expectations for appropriate behavior while secretly violating those norms.

REGIME-TYPE ARGUMENTS

A second set of arguments analyzes how ideology and regime type influence states' decisions to pursue regime change. Here I have grouped three variants that make predictions regarding which types of states the United States should target for regime change and what form of government Washington should install during these operations.

Targeting Non-Democracies. One set of arguments maintains that the greater the difference in two states' political systems, the more likely they will fear one another and attempt regime change as a result. For instance, Suzanne Werner classified all war belligerents between 1816 and 1980 according to the level of regulation, competitiveness, and openness of executive recruitment of their political system. Werner found that "the cumulative effect of changing the value of the variable measuring the differences between the war participant's and opponent's authority structure from the lowest to highest observed value increases the probability of a foreign imposed regime change by 44 percent."[28] This suggests that the United States should disproportionately target non-democracies for regime change. Along this line of thinking, several authors argue that personalist authoritarian regimes—sometimes called rogue states—are the most likely targets of regime change because their leaders have little credibility when it comes to their likelihood of adhering to interstate agreements, particularly postwar treaties. To test this hypothesis, Alexander Downes looked at 134 wars between 1816 and 2003 and found that states headed by personalist leaders experienced regime change more than chance would dictate.[29] Combining these arguments leads to hypothesis 2a:

Hypothesis 2a *Skeptical Democracy*: The United States should disproportionately target non-democracies for regime change, particularly personalist regimes.

To test this argument, table 2.2 codes the regime type of every state targeted during US-backed covert regime changes during the Cold War, in accordance with Barbara Geddes, Joseph Wright, and Erica Frantz's (2014) dataset. It shows that Washington targeted a variety of states during these missions: 28 percent of covert operations targeted democracies—eighteen in all; and the remaining 72 percent were aimed at authoritarian states—eleven personal, twenty-seven single-party, and eight military.[30] To see whether Washington disproportionately targeted any particular type of state for covert regime change, a difference of proportions test was then used to compare the regime types of target states against the proportion of states in the international system by each regime type during the Cold War (measured in country-years). The test reveals that although the United States targeted democracies less often than what random chance would dictate, this difference was not statistically significant. To the contrary, the only statistically significant finding was that Washington disproportionately under-targeted monarchies. In fact, the United States did not target a single monarchy throughout the Cold War, even though they made up 9 percent of the country-years in the sample. If anything, this observation directly contradicts hypothesis 2a. Monarchies have highly dissimilar political systems and low audience costs, which, according to these theorists, should increase—rather than decrease—the likelihood of regime change. Altogether, this suggests that factors other than regime type need to be considered to explain Washington's regime change decisions.

Promoting Democracy. A second related argument holds that states conduct regime change to spread their preferred system of government throughout the international system. Thus, liberal democratic states like the United States use regime change to promote the spread of liberal values. One reason, according to some proponents of DPT, is that liberal states often turn conflicts with nonliberal states into crusades.[31] Doyle explains, "The very constitutional restraint, shared commercial interests, and international respect for individual rights that promote peace among liberal societies can exacerbate conflicts in relations between liberal and nonliberal societies."[32]

In a comprehensive study covering the period 1510–2010, John Owen argues that states conduct regime change operations in historical waves dur-

Table 2.2 Regime type of target states—Difference of proportions test

	US-Backed Covert Regime Change Attempts		Country-Years by Regime Type	
	Number	Percentage of Total	Number	Percentage of Total
Democracy	18	28.1	1,608	34.1
Monarchy	0	0**	431	9.1**
Personal	11	17.2	648	13.7
Single-Party	27	42.2	1,580	33.5
Military	8	12.5	451	9.6
Total:	64	100	4,718	100

Significance Levels: * –10%, ** –5%, *** –1%.

ing periods when transnational elites are highly polarized between two or more competing ideologies, in an attempt to combat both internal and external security threats from their ideological opponents.[33] During the Cold War, he writes, "Neither the Soviet nor the U.S. government seriously feared a domestic overthrow by the other's ideological movement." Instead, "Promotion was a tool to extend or preserve one's sphere of influence and to arrest the spread of the other's sphere."[34] Other scholars also highlight America's record of promoting liberalism abroad.[35] Susan Epstein, Nina Serafino, and Francis Miko declare, "Democracy promotion has been a long-standing element of U.S. foreign policy."[36] Citing examples such as Italy, France, and Portugal, Joshua Muravchik extends this argument to include America's Cold War covert interventions. He writes, "Covert action has probably more often served to advance democracy than retard it. This judgment cannot be made with great confidence because the bulk of covert actions remain secret. We can judge only from that small fraction about which some information has seeped into the public record. Of these, more positive than negative cases appear."[37] If these authors are correct, the United States should disproportionately target nonliberal states for regime change and attempt to democratize them during these operations.

> Hypothesis 2b *Promoting Democracy*: The United States uses regime change to promote liberalism and democracy abroad.

How does this hypothesis compare to the historical record? Again, not well. Overall, I find little support for the hypothesis at either the overt or covert level. Looking first at the overt cases, Owen identifies eight cases where the United States overtly promoted a regime change during the Cold War (excluding the countries that it occupied after WWII).[38] Although these operations sought to curtail the spread of communism, Owen acknowledges that Washington did not promote liberal institutions in the first six cases as the means to do so.[39] Multiple quantitative studies similarly confirm America's poor record of overt democracy promotion during this period.[40]

Once covert missions are also considered, hypothesis 2b fares even worse. Only eight out of sixty-four covert interventions aimed to promote a democratic revolution within an authoritarian state. In forty-four cases, Washington supported authoritarian leaders. This means that the United States not only failed to promote liberalism during most covert operations, but it actively worked against liberal regimes at times.[41] Influential Cold War diplomat George Kennan set the tone for America's interventions when he explained in 1948, "It is better to have a strong regime in power than a liberal one if it is indulgent and relaxed and penetrated by communists."[42]

Installing Dictators. In contrast to the preceding argument, other scholars have argued that democracies have an incentive to install authoritarian regimes abroad. According to proponents of Selectorate Theory, for instance, when democracies go to war, it is typically to secure public benefits, such as increased security or ideological goals. Securing these public benefits, however, requires postwar cooperation from their defeated opponent. But postwar settlements are unpopular, and leaders in defeated states will likely feel pressured to renege on the agreement. This creates a commitment problem for the intervener. How can the victor know its opponent will not renege on a postwar settlement? The answer, according to Morrow et al., is to install a puppet regime. They argue, "A puppet government solves the commitment problem by eliminating the incentive to pursue revisionist demands by defusing them in the domestic politics of the defeated state."[43] For periods of great-power rivalry, Melissa Willard-Foster makes a related argument. She argues that authoritarian states can impose unpopular policies onto their followers without losing power. As a result, autocracies are more likely to acquiesce to the demands of great powers during disputes. This, in turn, means that the great powers are less likely to try to overthrow them. The opposite holds true for regimes that rely on popular support, such as democracies, which cannot acquiesce to such demands without jeopardizing their rule. Thus, great powers have an incentive to overthrow these democratic leaders in favor of compliant authoritarian ones.[44]

Hypothesis 2c *Promoting Authoritarian Regimes*: The United States should promote authoritarian puppet governments to secure its interests.

Of the three regime-type arguments, hypothesis 2c fits the historical record best. Throughout the Cold War, Washington backed authoritarian leaders in its covert regime changes more than 70 percent of the time. Nevertheless, Washington did not always promote autocrats. In one-eighth of its covert interventions and half of its overt operations, Washington promoted a democratic transformation within an authoritarian country. In fact, many well-known US military interventions since World War II have promoted democracies: Germany, Austria, Japan, Italy, Grenada, Panama, Haiti, Afghanistan, and Iraq. On the other hand, it is no coincidence that these cases are well known. As explained earlier, Washington has good reason to conduct democratizing regime changes overtly and non-democratizing operations covertly. Thus, to say that the United States pursues regime changes primarily to install pro-American dictators oversimplifies US foreign policy. The United States clearly believes that promoting democracy serves its interests in certain cases while promoting dictators works best in others. More contextual information is needed to know which type of regime the United States is most likely to promote in any given case.

ECONOMIC INTERESTS

The third set of arguments asks how economic interests cause regime change. One variant argues that states pursue regime change to protect the narrow economic interests of powerful corporations; another claims that states intervene to spread their preferred economic system.

Multinational Corporations. Numerous studies contend that states have used regime change to protect the interests of powerful multinational corporations.[45] Proponents of this theory most often focus on three cases. The first is the joint Anglo-American operation that toppled Iranian prime minister Mohammad Mossadegh in 1953, allegedly for having nationalized the British-owned Anglo-Iranian Oil Company. After the coup, Iranian oil was managed by an international consortium, which granted five US companies (Esso/Exxon, Gulf, Mobil, Standard Oil of California, and Texaco) 40 percent of Iranian oil royalties.[46] The second case is America's 1954 intervention in Guatemala, allegedly to protect the interests of a powerful American multinational corporation known as the United Fruit Company (UFCO). The third is the 1973 Chilean coup, which proponents claim aimed to protect the interests of an American firm, International Telephone and Telegraph (ITT). According to Stephen Kinzer, these cases show that Washington "acted mainly for economic reasons—specifically to establish, promote, and defend the right of Americans to do business around the world without interference."[47] Scholars have also found some empirical support for this theory. Dube, Kaplan, and Naidu, for instance, show how coups and coup authorizations increased the stock returns of partially nationalized US corporations on five occasions during the Cold War.[48] They conclude "that there were substantial economic incentives for firms to lobby for these operations . . . regime changes led to significant economic gains for corporations that stood to benefit from U.S. interventions in developing countries."[49]

Hypothesis 3a *Multinational Corporations*: The United States pursues regime change to promote the private economic interests of powerful American corporations.

How do these theories compare to the historical record? Overall, there is little support. In the clear majority of Eastern European, African, and Asian cases, Washington intervened even though there were no significant existing American business interests at stake. Even in the Western Hemisphere, it is hard to find economic interests at stake for cases like Guyana, Grenada, Haiti, or Nicaragua, where the United States had virtually no direct foreign trade or investment.[50] Furthermore, in contrast to what these theories would predict, Washington did not try to topple several governments in the Western hemisphere that expropriated the assets of American firms, such as when Mexico nationalized several US oil firms in 1938 or when the Peruvian military regime expropriated multiple US firms in the 1960s.[51]

Even in Iran, Guatemala, and Chile—considered the quintessential examples of American economic imperialism—there is also reason to doubt that economic interests played the decisive role. In the case of Iran, for instance, US policymakers expressed little sympathy toward British concerns about the nationalization of the Anglo-Iranian Oil Company. On the contrary, Frank Gavin argues, "U.S. policy recognized nationalization of the oil concern as an inevitable and, in fact, acceptable outcome, as long as it was the product of a negotiated settlement."[52] In the case of Guatemala, CIA agent Richard Bissell, who planned the operation, admitted that UFCO "had quite a lot to do with causing the State Department and others in Washington to focus on Guatemala as the locus of a major communist threat," but "when it came to decision to plan an operation . . . [there is] absolutely no reason to believe that the desire to pull the fruit company's chestnuts out of the fire played any significant role."[53] Guatemalan communist leader Jose Manuel Fortuny agreed, lamenting that "they would have overthrown us even if we had grown no bananas."[54] The case against American involvement in Chile on behalf of ITT is also clear-cut, especially in light of this exchange between Kissinger and Nixon just days afterward:

> KISSINGER: That's another one of these absurdities. Because whenever the ITT came to us, we turned them off. I mean we never did anything for them.
> NIXON: I didn't even know they came.
> KISSINGER: They came once because Flannigan set it up. You didn't know it. I didn't tell you because it required no action and I listened to them and said "thank you very much" and that was that.[55]

Global Economic Order. Instead of focusing on the narrow interests of specific corporations, other economic accounts maintain that states intervene to protect and/or spread their preferred economic order abroad. The Cold War, according to this view, was fueled by each superpower's desire to expand its global economic reach.[56] On the Soviet side, proponents claim that interventions in Hungary in 1956 and Czechoslovakia in 1968 were motivated by a desire to protect its command-economy allies from capitalist revolutions.[57] American interventions, by contrast, sought to promote Washington's position as head of a global capitalist order.[58] For example, Michael Sullivan argues that "the primary strategic goal of the United States since 1945 has been to supplant the major imperial powers of the pre–World War II era—the United Kingdom, France, Germany, and Japan—as the sole economic hegemon of the global capitalist system."[59] The strongest empirical support for this argument comes from Berger et al., who found that CIA interventions to covertly install or prop up a foreign leader led to an increase in US exports to that country in industries where the United States had a comparative disadvantage.[60]

> Hypothesis 3b *Global Capitalist Order*: The United States pursues regime change to promote its position as the head of a global capitalist order.

The case for hypothesis 3b is more complicated. Since World War II, the United States has sought to lock in its advantageous postwar position by establishing a global capitalist order.[61] Indeed, the United States—like all states—has continually tried to increase its economic strength to raise its population's standard of living and because wealth is a prerequisite for military power.[62] Consequently, it is accurate to say that, to some degree, economic interests always motivate US foreign policy. At the same time, the importance of these economic interests varies by operation. Economic interests were most salient when the United States targeted wealthy, industrialized countries—such as Italy, France, and Japan—or countries with large stores of oil—like Iran and Iraq. But the vast majority of operations did not target economic powerhouses or resource-rich countries like these, and in most cases, economic interests played a secondary role to national security interests. Existing economic accounts, therefore, struggle to explain many Cold War interventions in Eastern Europe, Africa, and Southeast Asia, where the United States did not have significant preexisting economic interests and/ or where the country's small population suggested little potential for market growth.

Even in the Western Hemisphere, there is reason to doubt that US interventions were primarily aimed at protecting its capitalist order. If that had been the case, for instance, one might expect to see an increase in bilateral trade between the countries targeted for regime change and the United States. However, a study by Paul Zachery, Kathleen Delougherty, and Alexander Downes, analyzing US-orchestrated successful regime changes in Latin American since 1816, found precisely the opposite. They determined that "U.S. intervention decreases bilateral trade with targeted countries compared to states that do not experience FIRC. This reduction in trade is 37.5 percent."[63] Focusing specifically on the Cold War, my own analysis, reported in chapter 4, found that Washington's covert interventions did not have a statistically significant effect on their target's total amount of trade with either the United States or the Soviet Union. In summary, the evidence for hypothesis 3b is mixed: America's desire to protect its position as the head of a global capitalist order was an important—but secondary—motive for intervention.

ROGUE ELEPHANT: OVERZEALOUS CIA

A final set of explanations looks specifically at US cases.[64] These works contend that an overzealous Central Intelligence Agency (CIA) conducted covert operations recklessly and often without executive approval. In the famous words of Senator Frank Church (D-ID), chairman of a Senate investigation into US government covert operations that began in 1975, "The CIA was behaving during those years like a rogue elephant rampaging out of control."[65] Supporting this claim, the Church Committee investigation found that only 14 percent of the CIA's covert actions between 1961 and 1975 had been vetted and approved by the National Security Council (NSC).[66] Although Church himself later disowned the "rogue elephant" metaphor, the image has stuck, and popular accounts continue to repeat this theme.[67] For instance, Tim Weiner argues, "The CIA's covert operations were by and large blind stabs in the dark. The agency's only course was to learn by doing—by making mistakes in battle. The CIA concealed its failures abroad by lying."[68] The general picture painted in these accounts is of an incompetent CIA predisposed toward meddling in the domestic politics of foreign powers.

> Hypothesis 4 *Rogue CIA*: The CIA launches covert regime changes without executive approval.

As a theory of covert regime change, this explanation is unsatisfactory. To begin with, it seems highly unlikely that any president would willingly cede such independent authority over its foreign policy to a government agency. Moreover, proponents often blur the boundary between covert action and covert regime change and thus overestimate the latter. They are correct that the CIA did operate independently when conducting small covert actions, particularly in the early years of the Cold War, when elements within the CIA behaved in ways that seem reckless in hindsight. This rash behavior did not, however, extend to independently launching regime changes. In that capacity, the CIA never proceeded without some form of presidential approval. In the early years of the Cold War, CIA authorizations came in the form of general NSC directives, which would call on the CIA to use covert action against the target regime, but would leave the operational details up to the agency.[69] During this period, according to the Church Committee, "loose understandings rather than specific review formed the basis for CIA's accountability for covert operations."[70] Following a series of congressional reforms in the mid-1970s, however, executive and congressional oversight of the CIA's covert actions was greatly strengthened, and executive authorizations to pursue covert regime change afterward were much more specific.[71]

In many ways, the CIA appears to be a victim of the "plausible deniability" inherent in covert actions. As Robert Gates, who served as director of Central Intelligence under George H.W. Bush and secretary of defense under George W. Bush and Barack Obama, explained: "The CIA is a uniquely presidential organization. Virtually every time it has gotten in trouble, it has been for carrying out some action ordered by the President—from Nicaragua to Iran. Yet few presidents have anything good to say about CIA or the intelligence they received."[72] The case studies in this book therefore paint a somewhat more sympathetic picture of the CIA than its popular image would suggest. In many cases, CIA analysts and agents, who were often more familiar with the target country than executive-branch officials, expressed serious reservations about carrying out certain operations and only did so after their objections were overruled.[73]

The Strategic Logic of Regime Change

Regime change is a common and important instrument of statecraft used by states to secure their national security interests in the intense security environment of the international system. Although no study to date has sought to provide a thorough security-based theory of the regime change efforts of a great power, several existing studies have discussed the security motives behind certain operations. In addition, historical accounts of the Cold War frequently describe the national security interests motivating Soviet and American interventions.[74] Historians, however, attempt to provide descriptive narratives of historical events, rather than offering comprehensive theories explaining when and why states launch regime changes. Although political scientists typically pursue this type of research, existing studies within the political science literature have only identified two security-oriented reasons why states may attempt regime change.

The first rationale comes from Clifford Carrubba, Dan Reiter, and Scott Wolford, who find that countries often seek regime change following a war when they fear that their adversary cannot credibly commit that they will adhere to a postwar agreement once they recover from their wartime losses.[75] A second reason comes from Tanisha Fazal, who argues that powerful states often target "buffer states"—that is, weak countries geographically positioned between two great-power rivals—for regime change.[76] The problem with these studies is not that they are incorrect—states do in fact pursue regime change for these reasons; however, by their own design, these accounts do not attempt to explain the motives behind most cases. For instance, the explanation focusing on postwar settlements helps to explain when states will impose a regime change after they are victorious in war. However, it does not try to explain covert regime changes, which were often pursued as an alternative to war, nor explain when states will go to war for the purposes of regime change. Likewise, accounts focusing on buffer states do not aim to explain missions against non-buffer states, which constitute the majority of targets for foreign-imposed regime changes.

Expanding beyond these existing theories, this section aims to provide a security-oriented theory of regime change. I argue that states pursue regime change for motives akin to the ones that Realist scholars have provided to explain war. Interestingly, though, whereas Realists have well-developed theories on the causes of war—and many other uses of force, such as coercion, deterrence, and sanctions—one foreign policy tool seldom discussed by Realists for combating security threats is regime change. As aforementioned, one potential reason for this omission is that one of the central tenets of Neorealism is that the specific composition of a state's domestic leadership is irrelevant for explaining its international behavior because great powers behave in similar predictable patterns given their relative share of material power and geostrategic position.[77] If this is true, then states have little incentive to pursue regime change because the pressures of the external environment are likely to make the newly installed government behave the same way as the one that was overthrown.[78] Nevertheless, the frequency that states launch regime changes suggests that leaders care a great deal about regime change and believe that by changing the leadership of another state, they can change that state's behavior.

The remainder of this section shows how states can pursue regime change to increase their national security. Just as with the causes of war, there is no single security motive driving states to intervene, and operations may have multiple overlapping motives. Nevertheless, the security-oriented motives that drove the United States to intervene can be grouped into three ideal types: *offensive*, *preventive*, and *hegemonic*. Each aimed to increase America's relative power in a different way.[79]

OFFENSIVE REGIME CHANGE

States launch offensive regime changes to replace governments that they consider current military threats with less hostile regimes, with which the intervener hopes to have friendlier relations. Whether conducted covertly or overtly, offensive regime changes are launched for a reason similar to those for which states often go to war: to decrease the threat posed by a current military adversary.[80] States may be considered threatening—and therefore more likely to be targets of offensive regime change—for several reasons: having a high share of relative power and offensively oriented military capabilities, being close geographically, appearing to have aggressive intentions, and/or having already attacked the intervening state.[81] Because Realists view all power as relative, any loss of power for a rival that results from the regime change equates to a gain for themselves. In that regard, offensive operations are a revisionist strategy designed to weaken a current adversary.

History provides numerous examples of overt offensive regime changes. Perhaps the most famous would be the Allies' decision to demand unconditional surrender from Germany, Italy, and Japan during World War II so that they could replace the hostile Axis governments with friendlier regimes afterward.[82] Another famous example is the Sixth Coalition's decision to overthrow Napoleon and restore the Bourbon dynasty in France at the end of the Napoleonic Wars.[83] Although these examples targeted states that posed a major and direct military threat to the interveners, other offensive operations target weaker states within a rival alliance. In these situations, the intervening state attempts to fracture its rival's alliance system and potentially even gain a new ally for itself, thereby increasing its own bloc's relative power. The Korean War is a famous example of this type, as the Soviet Union and China tried to capture South Korea from the US alliance system while the United States and its UN allies sought to remove North Korea from the Sino-Soviet sphere of influence.[84]

As chapters 5 and 6 explain, the United States conducted twenty-three covert and two overt offensive regime changes during the Cold War. These missions were part of a larger US strategy to roll back Soviet influence into neighboring states and decrease the military threat posed by the Soviet bloc. A 1949 NSC memo first explained America's goal: "Our over-all aim with respect to the satellite states should be the gradual reduction and eventual elimination of preponderant power from Eastern Europe without resort to war."[85] A 1951 memo from the Joint Chiefs of Staff to the secretary of defense explains why the United States pursued regime change toward that end: "The objectives would be the establishment of friendly regimes not under Kremlin domination. Such action is essential to engage the Russian attention, keep the Kremlin off balance, and force an increased expenditure of Soviet resources in counteraction."[86] By fracturing the Soviet bloc, the United States would increase its relative military power and gain access to strategic territory in the event of war.[87] At the same time, American officials assiduously sought to avoid direct military conflict while conducting these operations. They understood that war with the Red Army would be extremely costly and potentially suicidal once the Union of Soviet Socialist Republics (USSR) acquired nuclear weapons.

PREVENTIVE REGIME CHANGE

If offensive regime changes seek to revise the status quo, preventive opera-tions seek to maintain it. As the name would suggest, preventive regime changes seek to prevent another state from taking certain actions—like join-ing a rival alliance, building nuclear weapons, or increasing the size of its military—that may threaten the intervener's security in the future. Unlike offensive interventions, preventive operations target states that do not cur-rently pose a major military threat—indeed, they may even be a current ally—but policymakers have reason to believe that they will become more threatening in the future. In that regard, preventive regime changes are pur-sued for goals like those that Realists associate with preventive war. Jack Levy explains, "The preventive motivation for war arises from the percep-tion that one's military power and potential are declining relative to that of a rising adversary. . . . There is an apprehension that this decline will be ac-companied by a weakening of one's bargaining position and a correspond-ing decline in the political, economic, cultural, and other benefits that one receives from the status quo."[88]

Realists have identified two scenarios when states launch preventive wars.[89] The first occurs when a state "wants to knock down a rising poten-tial challenger before it has the confidence and additional power to back up a bolder or more aggressive foreign policy."[90] Probably the most famous ex-ample of this type of preventive war is Japan's surprise attack against the United States at Pearl Harbor in 1941. In that case, Japanese leaders feared that America's crippling oil embargo would erode Japan's relative power and threaten its ability to control its newly conquered empire.[91] The United States' 2003 invasion of Iraq followed a similar logic: US policymakers feared that if Iraq were allowed to develop nuclear weapons, it would be embold-ened to challenge US interests throughout the Middle East.[92] The second sce-nario occurs when a declining great power fears a future war against a ris-ing challenger. If the declining state feels that war is inevitable, its leaders may seek to start a war early in the power transition while the balance of power is still in their favor. Dale Copeland writes, "States in decline fear the future. They worry that if they allow a rising state to grow, it will either attack the latter with superior power or coerce them into concessions that compromise their security."[93] Realists have cited this motive to explain German behavior in WWI and WWII. In both cases, Germany feared that if Russia—a country forty times greater in territory and three times larger in population—could industrialize, it could quickly overwhelm German defenses, and therefore went to war before this transition could occur to lock in its power advantage relative to Russia/the Soviet Union.[94]

Preventive regime changes can be launched in response to both scenar-ios, and a third motive should be added to that list: to prevent foreign coun-tries from joining rival alliances.[95] In these cases, the intervening state is less concerned about a growth in the relative power of the target state. Indeed, the target country may be comparatively weak and nonthreatening on its own. Instead, the potential shift in power is toward a rival military alliance. To maintain the status quo and prevent this from happening, the intervening state attempts to install a foreign leader who will, at the very least, refuse to join their rival's alliance, and in the best-case scenario, become a reliable ally to the intervener, thereby eliminating a future threat and bolstering their own alliance's power. Preventive regime changes frequently occur in competitive bipolar systems because both great powers fear that a small number of defections could upset the tenuous balance of power or cause a cascade of defections favoring their rival.[96] For this reason, the USSR attempted numerous preventive regime changes against states they feared would join the American camp during the Cold War—Angola, Congo, Ethiopia, Mozambique, and Yemen are famous examples.[97]

As chapters 5 and 7 show, Washington also pursued a number of preventive regime changes during the Cold War.[98] These operations were part of the broader US strategy of containment, which emerged shortly after WWII and continued throughout the Cold War.[99] Toward this end, American policymakers conducted twenty-five covert missions and one overt preventive mission to install friendly governments in states believed to be in danger of joining the Soviet camp. As one 1954 NSC report explains, these missions sought to provide "support for indigenous and anti-communist elements in threatened countries of the free world."[100] If the United States failed to do so, another NSC memo warned, "The Soviets will continue to seek to divide and weaken the free world coalition, to absorb or win the allegiance of the presently uncommitted areas of the world, and to isolate the United States, using cold war tactics and the communist apparatus."[101] Over the course of the Cold War, the geographic focus of these operations shifted across regions, depending on where the Soviet Union was believed to be trying to expand. The first interventions aimed to consolidate a pro-American bloc in Western Europe and targeted left-wing parties in French and Italian elections. Afterward, policymakers shifted their attention to the Middle East in the 1950s, Southeast Asia in the 1960s and 1970s, and Africa in the 1980s.

HEGEMONIC REGIME CHANGE

States launch a third type of regime change in pursuit of the goal of regional hegemony—a position that offers many important military, political, and economic benefits. A hegemon is a state "so powerful that it dominates all the other states in the system. No other state has the military wherewithal to put up a serious fight against it."[102] Hegemonic regime changes include missions in pursuit of this goal. They can be either offensive in nature—as an aspiring hegemon works to achieve a dominant position over weaker states within a certain geographic region—or defensive in nature—as an established regional hegemon works to protect its dominion from internal or external threats. Unlike in the preceding two types of regime change, however, the states targeted in hegemonic missions do not need to pose a current or future threat to the intervening state. Instead, the defining feature of a hegemonic regime change is the desire to maintain a hierarchical relationship between the intervener and the target state as part of the former's effort to establish regional hegemony.[103]

Offensive Realism provides one rationale for why states pursue regional hegemony. According to proponents, the anarchic structure of the international system compels states to maximize their relative power whenever possible with the ultimate objective of becoming a global hegemon. As Mearsheimer explains, "The pursuit of power stops only when hegemony is achieved."[104] Nevertheless, as he goes on to argue, it is virtually impossible for any state to achieve global hegemony given the difficulty of projecting power across oceans. As such, states settle for the second-best outcome: "to be a regional hegemon and possibly control another region that is nearby and accessible over land."[105] Once a state reaches this position, it no longer faces any security threats from within its region and therefore "is free to roam around the globe and interfere in other regions of the world."[106]

In addition to these security benefits, regional hegemony offers numerous political and economic benefits as well. According to proponents of Hegemonic Stability Theory, hegemons help to create and establish stable international systems by providing public goods to minor powers, such as military protection and/or international legal and financial orders. In exchange, minor powers acquiesce to the hierarchical system and support the hegemon's core interests.[107] This benefits the hegemon in multiple ways. For one, it allows the hegemon to set the economic policy of weaker states so that it can enjoy the benefits of deeper economic integration.[108] Moreover, it enables them to influence the domestic political behavior of weaker states to their favor.[109] They also gain legitimacy from the support of subordinate states in international institutions for actions against third parties or, as one 1953 NSC directive described it, "hemisphere solidarity in support of our world policies, particularly in the UN and other international organizations."[110] Finally, hegemons can provide a forum for minor powers within the region to settle disputes among themselves, thus preventing those conflicts from escalating to the point of war.[111]

Hegemonic regime changes target neighboring states that the hegemon considers within its sphere of influence or against former colonies or protectorates. Indeed, history provides many examples of great powers using regime change as part of their efforts to achieve regional hegemony. Revolutionary/Napoleonic France overthrew twenty-eight political systems in its bid for hegemony in Europe between 1792 and 1815.[112] Nazi Germany pursued eight regime changes as part of its strategy to conquer Europe in WWII.[113] Following WWII, the Soviet Union pursued nine regime changes to consolidate its control over Eastern Europe. The only great power to have ever successfully achieved lasting regional hegemony, however, is the United States in the Western Hemisphere. Toward this end, Washington conducted a large number of hegemonic regime changes during the early portion of the twentieth century, overthrowing the governments of Nicaragua (1909, 1910, and 1926), Honduras (1911), the Dominican Republic (1912, 1914, and 1916), Mexico (1914), Haiti (1915), and Costa Rica (1919) as part of its efforts to secure regional hegemony.[114]

Chapters 5 and 8 describe how the United States, having achieved this elusive goal, attempted eighteen covert and three overt hegemonic regime changes during the Cold War to defend its position of regional hegemony and the military, economic, and political benefits that go along with it. Washington's objective during these interventions, as one 1953 NSC report explains, was to encourage "an orderly political and economic development in Latin America so that the states in the area will be more effective members of the hemisphere system . . . [and] the safeguarding of the hemisphere."[115] Toward this end, US leaders pursued regime change "in the interests of U.S. national security . . . to replace local leadership with indigenous leaders who are more amenable and sympathetic to the need for eliminating the breeding areas for dissension . . . seeking to insure that modernization of the local society evolves in directions which will afford a congenial world environment for fruitful international cooperation and for our way of life."[116]

Despite occurring during the Cold War, these operations did not reflect a particular Cold War strategy. Rather, they reflected the strategy of first obtaining and then maintaining regional hegemony that has driven US policy in the Western Hemisphere ever since the Monroe Doctrine (1823).[117] In the context of the Cold War, this meant that the United States tried to prevent left-wing regimes from assuming power out of fear that they would spark a series of defections from the American-led regional order. Unlike during many preventive interventions, however, US policymakers were not concerned about sparking a direct confrontation with the Soviet Union during these hegemonic interventions. Indeed, as chapters 5 and 8 show, many of the target governments had no clear ties to Moscow. The Cold War hegemonic regime changes discussed in this book therefore resemble preventive operations in that they are trying to prevent communist or socialist governments from coming to power. Despite the particular anti-communist form that they took during the Cold War, however, these interventions share a common objective of promoting American regional hegemony that both predates and survives the Cold War. Thus, we can see, for instance, continuity between the objectives that drove the United States to pursue covert regime change attempts against Haiti during the Cold War (1963, 1965–69, and 1986–89) with those that motivated Washington to pursue regime change against Haiti before (1915) and after (1994) the Cold War.

How Does Regime Change Work?

Given these strategic objectives for regime change, the question arises as to how policymakers actually expect regime change to work. That is, why does the intervening state expect the new government to behave any differently from the one that it just overthrew?

Policymakers launch regime changes to modify the policy preferences of another state. The logic behind regime change is simple: if the intervening state can install a foreign leader whose policy preferences align with their own, then the new leader's self-interested actions should reflect their interests as well.[118] Once in power, the new government should stop pursuing the unwanted policies and instead pursue the intervener's preferred agenda. Afterward, disputes between the two regimes are less likely to arise because the target state will automatically act in the intervener's interest. Thus, a contentious relationship is transformed into a cooperative one. For example, if a state wanted to prevent another country from adopting a communist platform, the former could use regime change to install a right-wing leader with significant land-ownership or business interests. In order to protect his or her business interests, the new leader will be more likely to pursue the type of capitalist policies on the international stage that the intervener prefers as well. The two states are then free to enjoy all the benefits of a cooperative relationship.

This potential to transform the underlying preferences of foreign governments makes regime change a uniquely appealing strategy to policymakers. Most foreign policy strategies rely on coercion or brute force to resolve disputes on a case-by-case basis. Regime change, by contrast, promises a more permanent solution to interstate disputes by eliminating the underlying source of the disagreement: the conflicting preferences of the two states.[119] If both states want the same thing, the dispute can be settled once and for all, and the intervening state can continue to get its way without having to repeatedly bribe or coerce the target government into compliance. From a policymakers' perspective, the benefits of such an action can hardly be overstated. Both theoretic and experimental studies confirm that the "greater the conflict of interest, the more likely it is that conflictful behavior will follow."[120]

Installing foreign leaders with similar policy preferences also helps states alleviate a second common source of interstate conflict, namely, the fact that states can never be certain of one another's intentions.[121] The myriad of problems caused by states' uncertainty of one another's intentions are well known to international relations scholars. As Brian Rathbun notes, "The force of uncertainty is central to every major research tradition in the study of international relations. . . . It is arguably the most important factor in explaining the often unique dynamics of international as opposed to domestic politics."[122] The root problem caused by the fact that states can never be certain of one another's true intentions is that any time a state enters into an agreement, it cannot be sure that the other side will maintain its side of the bargain. If the other side cheats and their state abides by the agreement, they risk the possibility of suffering the "sucker's payoff."[123] In the economic realm, this poses high—but generally not insurmountable—barriers to cooperation. For instance, states use rules, norms, and institutions to help predict the intentions of one another.[124] Still, these institutions are costly to construct, and states continue to "spend considerable sums of labor and money in the quest for information."[125] In the security realm, however, cooperation is even more difficult. States that fail to discern the military intentions of others can face grave consequences.[126] For this reason, the concept of the uncertainty of intentions lies at the core of Realist theory.[127] Offensive Realists maintain that states can never assume that their rivals do not harbor malign intentions. What's more, even if a state could somehow signal its true benign intentions, those intentions could always change in the future.[128] Defensive Realists, though more sanguine about the potential for cooperation, still note that under certain circumstances, uncertainty of intentions can lead to arms races, instability, and war because "many of the means by which a state tries to increase its security decreases the security of others."[129] Discerning other states' intentions thus remains a top priority for any government.

Regime change can decrease a state's uncertainty regarding its rival's intentions in three ways. First, as mentioned earlier, states install foreign leaders believed to share mutual interests. Because they expect the new leader to protect those interests, they can make their assessments of their rival's future intentions with much greater confidence. Second, leaders may be less fearful of one another if they share similar substantive beliefs about the proper values and order of the international system.[130] One benefit of regime change is that policymakers can install leaders believed to share a similar worldview to their own. Third, some scholars have even contended that the process of regime change can help the new leadership to accept the intervening state's authority. For instance, Alexander Wendt and Daniel Friedheim argue that regime change constructs an "intersubjective structure of authority" wherein the intervening state gains informal authority over the new regime in exchange for having created the opportunity to rule for actors who otherwise would not rule or would have had to make major concessions to domestic rivals.[131] Moreover, once the new regime is in power, John Ikenberry and Charles Kupchan maintain that "a process of socialization in which the norms and value orientations of leaders in secondary states change more closely reflect those of the dominant state," which reinforces the legitimacy of this social order.[132] Building on several case studies, they argue, "The process of socialization can lead to outcomes that are not explicable simply in terms of the exercise of coercion. . . . In particular, socialization leads to the legitimation of hegemonic power in a way that allows international order to be maintained without the constant threat of coercion."[133]

Interestingly, and in contrast to existing regime-based explanations, I find that US leaders did not believe that any one form of government would be most likely to share their policy preferences. Rather than promoting any one type of regime, US policymakers promoted whatever regime type they felt would best serve US interests in that particular state. This suggests that US behavior was guided less by ideology and more by pragmatism. When most of a target state's population shared US interests, policymakers would encourage a democratic transition. When a smaller proportion of the population shared US preferences, they supported whatever type of government would bring that group to power. Sometimes this meant supporting a military junta; at other times, a single-party authoritarian regime or a personalist dictator was thought to be best. In most Cold War cases, US leaders promoted authoritarianism. However, this preference for authoritarianism is not written in stone and may not hold for the post–Cold War era. When US policymakers believe that the majority of a foreign population shares US interests but their authoritarian leaders do not, Washington may promote democracy.

When Will States Launch Regime Changes?

If regime change has the potential to transform a contentious interstate relationship into a cooperative one, why don't states launch these operations more often? One of the shortcomings of earlier studies on regime change is that they tend to predict far more interventions than actually occur. Regardless of the cause under consideration, the potential precipitating events for each theory greatly outnumber the actual occurrences. Yet, it is quite clear that not every interstate dispute sparks a regime change. Instead, interstate disputes vary greatly in their severity, and policymakers calibrate their response in proportion to the dispute's importance. Roughly speaking, foreign policy options available to states range in risk and cost from traditional diplomacy to coercive diplomacy including threats of military force and sanctions, military clashes, regime change, war, and conquest. Because regime change falls on the more aggressive end of the spectrum, policymakers will only attempt it under select circumstances.

This section aims to identify the circumstances under which a state might launch a regime change, by determining the minimum requirements for intervention. I argue that regime change is best suited to address disputes that meet two necessary—but not sufficient—conditions for intervention: (1) the interstate dispute should be based on a chronic divergence of policy preferences between the intervening and target state, and (2) the intervening state must be able to identify a plausible domestic political alternative to the target regime. Variation in the availability of these two conditions over time helps to explain when and where policymakers decide to pursue regime change.

INCOMPATIBLE POLICY PREFERENCES

Regime change is best suited to address chronic interstate conflicts where the intervening and target states have fundamentally incompatible policy preferences over the issue at hand. When a state faces a one-time dispute or even an occasional disagreement, traditional diplomacy or coercion will probably be sufficient to resolve the conflict.[134] Given its potential costs, regime change would be overkill in these situations.[135] Instead, regime change is better geared toward interstate disputes when there is a long history of disagreement between the two states. Given the lack of trust permeating these relationships, even if the two countries could overcome their conflicting preferences to reach an agreement, they may struggle to credibly commit to adhere to its terms.[136] To break this gridlock, policymakers in the intervening state seek the type of transformative solution to their dispute that is promised by regime change.

Most regime changes involve great powers overthrowing minor states.[137] This raises the question of why the weaker state did not simply acquiesce to the stronger state's demands when the dispute first arose, rather than resisting, which risked an even worse outcome—being removed from power by the stronger state via a regime change.[138] Nonetheless, there are at least two scenarios where even very weak states will still have strong incentives not to cooperate with the demands of a great power. These scenarios are difficult to resolve with diplomacy because they place the target government in a catch-22: acquiescing to the stronger state's demands will increase the odds that it will be overthrown by its domestic or foreign opponents; refusing to comply with the stronger state's demands, however, increases the risk that the stronger state will overthrow it directly. Faced with these two unpleasant options, some weak states decide to reject the stronger state's demands. Thus, any attempts by the intervener to coerce their opponent is unlikely to succeed, and the stronger state may consider it more efficient to replace the target government than to try to coerce it on an issue-by-issue basis.

First, states often cannot resolve disputes that require one side to relinquish its military capabilities or jeopardize its future security.[139] Even if two states could reach an agreement where the weaker state cedes some of its capabilities to avoid conflict, the stronger state must still somehow commit not to renege on the deal and exploit its opponent's weakened position after the opponent has disarmed.[140] Further complicating things, the intervening state may not be the only external security threat that the target state fears, suggesting that even if the intervener could credibly commit not to attack the weaker state in the future, the target government may still be unwilling to accept the deal out of fear that it may facilitate predatory attacks from others.[141] Therefore, when a state wants a rival to take an action that weakens that rival's military position—such as surrendering territory, forgoing an important ally, relinquishing its nuclear weapons, or pursuing a less aggressive foreign policy—regime change may be the only option.

A second type of chronic dispute over incompatible policy preferences occurs when a state demands that a rival government abandon a fundamental position of its political platform, without which the rival believes that it could not maintain power domestically.[142] This meshes with Robert Powell's finding that weak states resist more powerful opponents when the stronger state's demands would cause a rapid shift in the domestic balance of power that would expose it to domestic threats.[143] In the Cold War context, American officials repeatedly demanded that rising leftist regimes renounce key portions of their political platform and embrace a free market agenda. However, for many political leaders, the costs of complying with these demands—abandoning strongly held beliefs and alienating their base of support—simply outweighed the potential costs of resistance. In these situations, American attempts to coerce or bribe the target state into submission were likely to fail, leading policymakers to believe that only by installing a new cooperative regime could they satisfy their demands.

PLAUSIBLE POLITICAL ALTERNATIVE(S) AVAILABLE

For a regime change to work, the intervening state must also identify a plausible alternative leader to take over after it has overthrown the target state's current leadership. From the perspective of the intervener, there are two major characteristics of a plausible alternative.

First, the alternative must be strong relative to the target regime. The best alternatives should have the capacity to overthrow the target government, eliminate any lingering threats posed by supporters of the previous regime, and effectively govern afterward.[144] The stronger the domestic alternatives are relative to the target regime, the greater the mission's chances of success.[145] Second, and most importantly from the perspective of the intervening state, the alternative government must share its policy preferences. If all plausible alternative leaders are likely to behave in the same manner as the current government, then regime change is irrelevant, and the intervener would be better off pursuing another foreign policy strategy. Given the importance of this factor, aspiring coup plotters hoping to overthrow their government often seek out foreign backers for their efforts by stressing their shared interests. Indeed, Cold War history is rife with stories of émigré and dissident groups, civil war combatants, and ambitious military officers approaching the superpowers for help with their causes. For instance, Michael Grow's analysis of eight American interventions in Latin America during the Cold War found that "none of the interventions was entirely unilateral in nature. In every case, local political actors influenced the U.S. decision to intervene."[146]

If it cannot find a plausible alternative, the intervening state may try to construct a new regime from scratch. Though possible, the success rate for these operations remains quite low. For instance, after analyzing seven American nation-building exercises since World War II, James Dobbins found only two successful operations—Germany and Japan—while the others fell short of their goals. He concluded that "the most important determinant [of success] seems to be the level of effort—measured in time, manpower and money."[147] Other authors have come to similar conclusions about the prospects for foreign-imposed democratization and occupation.[148] This suggests that states should only pursue regime changes that they anticipate will require significant nation building afterward when the target government has great strategic importance for them.

This chapter analyzed the causes of regime change and has put forth four main arguments. First, I argued that because most existing theories of regime change focus predominantly on overt operations, they overlook many disconfirming covert cases and misinterpret the motives driving states to intervene. Second, I presented my security-oriented theory for why states attempt regime change and introduced a typology of missions: *Offensive* operations seek to overthrow a current military rival or rival alliance. *Preventive* interventions aim to stop their targets from taking certain actions that may threaten the intervener in the future. *Hegemonic* operations protect a state's strategic and economic interests by ensuring a hierarchical relationship between the intervening state and target government. Third, I asked, why do states pursue regime change to secure these interests? That is, how do policymakers expect regime change to work? The answer is that by installing a foreign government with similar policy preferences, the intervening state hopes to transform its relationship with the target state. Finally came the question of when states are likely to attempt regime change. To explain why most interstate disputes do not lead to regime change, I introduced two prerequisites for intervention: the dispute had to be based on a long-term dispute caused by misaligned security preferences, and the intervening state had to be able to identify a plausible alternative government. If the situation met those prerequisites, policymakers may choose to topple the recalcitrant regime rather than trying to coerce it on an issue-by-issue basis.

CHAPTER 3

Conduct

Why Do States Intervene Covertly versus Overtly?

> Political warfare is the logical application of Clausewitz's doctrine in times of peace. In broadest definition, political warfare is the employment of all the means at a nation's command, short of war, to achieve its national objectives. . . . Understanding the concept of political warfare, we should also recognize that there are two major types of political warfare—one overt and the other covert.
> —George Kennan, Policy Planning Staff Memorandum, 1948

The preceding chapter explained why states pursue regime change and how it promises several unique benefits as a foreign policy tool. Now that we can see why leaders would want to intervene, however, the question arises of how best to conduct these operations. This chapter addresses that question by asking, why do states intervene covertly versus overtly during their regime changes?

I argue that policymakers decide how to conduct an operation by weighing two types of considerations: tactical and strategic. Tactical considerations relate to the mission's operational plans, such as the likelihood that the operation will succeed and its potential costs. Interestingly, I show that these two tactical factors are at odds during most regime changes: covert missions typically have lower potential costs than their overt counterparts, but they are also less likely to succeed, thus forcing policymakers into a trade-off between minimizing costs versus maximizing efficacy. Strategic considerations, by contrast, refer to the way that the regime change fits into the intervening state's overall foreign policy agenda, and reflect the broader geostrategic value that policymakers attach to replacing the target government. For the clear majority of cases, I find that both tactical and strategic considerations point to covert conduct as the preferred way to intervene. This explains why the United States attempted nearly eleven times more covert operations during the Cold War (sixty-four covert versus six overt) and why in four out of its six overt regime changes, Washington first intervened covertly before sending in US troops.

This chapter proceeds in five parts. First, I discuss the two major tactical factors weighed by policymakers. Next, I analyze leaders' broader geostrategic considerations. Third, I explain why both tactical and strategic considerations favor covert conduct, and I discuss the conditions under which states will intervene overtly. Fourth, I lay out the five types of covert tactics employed by states during their regime changes. Finally, I argue that the conduct of a regime change is best thought of as falling along a continuum between truly covert and directly overt action, and I investigate the phenomenon of "pseudo-covert operations," that is, regime changes where the intervening state officially denies its role even though all parties involved seem to know of its participation.

Tactical Considerations

Policymakers weigh two major tactical concerns when deciding how to intervene: the mission's predicted costs and its likelihood of success. Whether the operation is conducted covertly or overtly significantly affects both factors.

PREDICTED COSTS

Covert conduct significantly lowers several potential costs associated with overthrowing a foreign government. This occurs because the heart of covert action is the idea of "plausible deniability," or the belief that the intervener can hide its role in an operation by deflecting blame onto others. In theory, plausible deniability enables states to pursue risky or selfish interests yet escape blame for their actions, which in turn decreases the security, material, and reputational costs associated with an intervention.

Trying to topple a foreign government is an inherently risky act. Any state that attempts to do so risks provoking a military response from its target, if not an outright declaration of war. If the intervening state can deflect the blame onto other actors, however, it stands a good chance of avoiding military retaliation. Covert regime changes are designed to achieve precisely that. All the covert operations in this study involved collaboration with domestic actors from the target state, such as dissident movements, rival political parties, or coup plotters. These individuals not only do the heavy lifting of actually overthrowing the regime but are also positioned to take the blame if the mission should fail. Officials in the intervening state hope that even if the target government suspects that they are ultimately behind a mission,

covert conduct will create enough ambiguity about the extent of their involvement to deter a military response.[1]

As the case studies show, US policymakers calibrated the scale and risk
of exposure for their covert interventions to minimize the mission's potential security costs. For instance, one 1949 policy planning staff paper argued,
"Proposed [covert] operations directed at the satellites must consequently
be measured against the kind and degree of retaliation which they are likely
to provoke from the Kremlin."[2] Likewise, NSC-174, a 1953 policy recommendation, declares that the United States should "encourage and assist the
satellite peoples in resistance to their Soviet-dominated regimes, maintaining their hopes of eventual freedom from Soviet domination, while avoiding: a. Incitement to premature revolt; b. Commitments on the nature and
timing of any U.S. action to bring about liberation; c. Incitement to action
when the probable reprisals or other results would yield a net loss in terms
of U.S. objectives."[3] The report goes on to warn, "Continuing and careful attention must be given to the fine line, which is not stationary, between ex-
hortations to keep up morale and to maintain passive resistance, and invita-
tions to suicide. Planning . . . should be determined on the basis of feasibility,
minimum risk, and maximum contribution to the fundamental interest of
the United States."[4]

In addition to minimizing the risk of military retaliation, covert conduct
can also lower a mission's material costs because the resources necessary to
instigate a regime change via covert means—such as assassinations and coup
d'états—are much lower than those typically required for overt missions. This
discrepancy becomes evident when the costs of America's covert and overt
regime changes are compared. (All of the following costs have been converted into 2015 dollars to adjust for inflation.) On the covert side, for example, the United States spent between $900,000 and $178 million to incite the 1953 coup in Iran depending on how costs are calculated;[5] between
$26.6 and $62 million during its 1954 Guatemalan campaign;[6] approximately
$71.9 million during its efforts to oust Chilean president Salvador Allende
in the early 1970s;[7] $2.4 million during the 1971 Bolivian coup;[8] and roughly
$70.8 million supporting Kurdish dissident groups within Iraq between
1972 and 1975.[9] However, even the smallest of America's overt Cold War
regime changes cost multiple times more than these covert interventions.
For instance, the Department of Defense estimates that the United States
spent $321.6 million in 1983 to overtly overthrow Grenada—one of the
weakest states in the world—and $314.4 million during its small-scale mili-
tary intervention to oust Panamanian dictator Manuel Noriega in 1989.[10]

The cost-efficiency of covert conduct holds true for larger regime changes
as well. For example, the unsuccessful covert Bay of Pigs invasion of Cuba
in 1961 is said to have cost the United States approximately $370.4 million.[11]
However, compared to what it would have cost to invade Cuba with American troops, these expenses are minimal. For instance, declassified docu-

ments from the Kennedy administration show that America's overt activities during the Cuban Missile Crisis cost roughly $1.3 billion,[12] and 1962 casualty estimates for a direct US invasion of Cuba project "up to 18,500 casualties in the first ten days of operation" even without the use of nuclear weapons.[13] For another crude comparison, one can consider the costs of America's covert and overt regime changes in Afghanistan. During its covert intervention in the 1980s, the United States spent an estimated $6.6 billion to fund the Afghan resistance's successful campaign against the Soviet Union—making it America's most expensive covert regime change of the era.[14] By contrast, America's 2001 overt intervention to overthrow the Taliban regime—an operation praised for its cost-efficiency—is estimated to have cost $20.8 billion, meaning that the United States spent three times more to overtly overthrow a much weaker opponent.[15]

Beyond the direct operational costs associated with toppling another state, covert conduct can also decrease the material costs associated with rebuilding the target country afterward. Covert action allows states to avoid what Colin Powell famously described in the run-up to the Iraq War as the "Pottery Barn rule": "You break it, you own it." That is, states that launch overt regime change in the modern era are normatively obligated to protect the target country's population and reconstruct its government.[16] Successful covert missions, however, avoid these responsibilities. Having never publicly "broken" a country, the intervening state is not obligated to "own" it. Here the cost efficiency of covert action becomes even more apparent. For example, following the Soviet withdrawal from Afghanistan in 1989, the United States significantly decreased its covert aid to the rebel fighters and later stopped its funding entirely in 1993.[17] In the sixteen years following its 2001 overt operation in Afghanistan, however, the United States has spent more than $763 billion rebuilding the country.[18] Once the costs of long-term medical care for US veterans and their families, as well as the cost of replacing military equipment, are factored in, the price tag of the 2001 Afghan war is estimated to reach into the trillions of dollars.[19]

In a similar vein, covert action can lower the reputational costs associated with a regime change by allowing the intervening state to secretly act in ways that contradict its publicly held values, official policy positions, and preexisting diplomatic commitments. As discussed in the previous chapter, America's covert interventions repeatedly violated norms publicly held by Washington—such as respect for state sovereignty, liberal values and institutions, and international human rights.[20] It is therefore easy to see the appeal of covert conduct. At least in theory, covertly intervening allows states to pursue regime changes that are considered normatively unacceptable, without suffering a backlash from domestic and/or foreign audiences.

Internationally, covert action shielded the United States from charges of violating other states' sovereignty and liberal norms of justified intervention. Although these norms were not powerful enough to prevent the operation

entirely in the cases where the United States intervened, they were powerful enough, in the words of Bruce Russett, "to drive the operations underground amid circumstances when the administration otherwise might well
have undertaken an overt intervention."[21] Case studies of US covert missions
targeting foreign democracies support this theme as well.[22] For instance, although liberal norms may not have restrained the United States from advo-
cating to overthrow Chile's democratic government in 1970, policymakers
certainly did not want to be caught doing so. This exchange between
Nixon's National Security Advisor Henry Kissinger and Secretary of State
William Rogers explains why:

> ROGERS: I talked to the President at length about it. My feeling—and I
> think it coincides with the President's—is that we should . . . do so dis-
> cretely so that it doesn't backfire.
> KISSINGER: The only question is how one defines "backfire."
> ROGERS: Getting caught doing something. After all we've said about elec-
> tions, if the first time a communist wins the US tries to prevent the con-
> stitutional process from coming into play, we will look very bad.
> KISSINGER: The President's view is to do the maximum possible to pre-
> vent an Aliente [sic] takeover, but through Chilean sources and with a
> low posture.[23]

Covert action also allowed US policymakers to avoid revealing unsavory details of their foreign interventions to the American public. Influential diplomat George Kennan set the tone for America's covert Cold War interventions
in a 1947 letter: "I think we have to face the fact that Russian successes have
been gained in many areas by irregular and underground methods. I do not
think the American people would ever approve of policies which rely on similar methods for their effectiveness. I do feel, however, that there are cases
where it might be essential to fight fire with fire."[24] Kennan's observation
meshes with John Mearsheimer's analysis of when state leaders lie. Interestingly, Mearsheimer found that "leaders appear to be more likely to lie to
their own people about foreign policy issues than to other countries."[25] This
effect is particularly pronounced in democracies because "leaders in a democracy must pay more attention to public opinion. . . . They cannot enun-
ciate a policy that they think is wise but sure to be unpopular and then ignore the political fallout. In such cases, leaders have powerful incentive to
adopt the policy, but not announce the decision publicly, and then lie if necessary to cloak what they have done."[26] Case studies of America's Cold War
interventions highlight these domestic incentives for covert action. David
Gibbs's analysis of Eisenhower's 1960 covert regime change in Congo, for instance, found "secrecy successfully concealed government activities (such
as the efforts to assassinate Lumumba) that were potentially very controversial. Other covert operations, such as the coaching of President Kasavubu,
the efforts to undermine Lumumba's position in the military, the support for

Mobutu's coup would all have been very difficult to justify in public."[27] Similarly, covert action enabled Eisenhower's secretary of state John Foster Dulles to inform Congress at the same time as the United States tried to topple Indonesian president Sukarno's regime, "We are pursuing what I trust is a correct course from the point of international law. We are not intervening in the internal affairs of the country."[28]

LIKELIHOOD OF SUCCESS

The flip side of covert conduct is that it also decreases the second major tactical factor weighed by states—the operation's chances of success. Two characteristics unique to covert operations continuously undermine the odds that they will succeed in replacing their targets: (1) a fundamental limit to how large a covert operation can become while maintaining plausible deniability, and (2) recurrent errors made in the planning and implementation of covert interventions.

When policymakers attempt to conduct a covert regime change, they face a crucial trade-off between wielding resources and being able to plausibly deny their role in the operation. Covert regime changes can only become so large before the target government inevitably learns about them. The larger an operation, the more individuals will become privy to its details—individuals who may not share the intervening state's interests or who may be susceptible to espionage or blackmail. As such, the need to maintain plausible deniability impedes states' efforts to translate military power into successful outcomes. Or as Secretary of State John Foster Dulles lamented while trying to overthrow the Indonesian government, "You reach a point where it is extremely difficult to do much more without showing your hand."[29]

Policymakers' frustration with this trade-off is a recurrent theme in many covert cases. For example, the Official CIA Historical Review of the Bay of Pigs Operation concludes, "The myth of 'plausible deniability' was the caveat that determined the CIA would be the principal implementing arm for the anti-Castro effort. From inception to termination, 'deniability' would be the albatross around the necks of Agency planners."[30] CIA Operations Chief Richard Bissell concurred: "If the United States was sure to be held responsible, then it made no sense to pay a price in terms of impaired operational capability for a result that could not be obtained. Yet this is exactly what we did. It was a major error. . . . Everyone in the Cuban operation moved forward without much debate, confident that the fig leaf of plausible deniability was still in place."[31] In this same vein, the Church Committee, a mid-1970s Congressional investigation of America's covert activities, determined:

The original concept of "plausible denial" envisioned implementing covert actions in a manner calculated to conceal American involvement if the actions were exposed. The doctrine was at times a delusion and at times a snare.

> It was naïve for policymakers to assume that sponsorship of actions as big as the Bay of Pigs invasion could be concealed . . . when the United States resorted to cloak-and-dagger tactics, its hand was ultimately exposed.[32]

In additional to this fundamental trade-off between size and secrecy, covert regime changes are also subject to four recurrent errors made during their planning and implementation that further undermine their odds of success. First, the need to maintain plausible deniability introduces logistical and conceptual ambiguity into the planning of covert operations, which undercuts their effectiveness. To preserve plausible deniability, planners often discuss these missions with "euphemisms or circumlocution," which confuses subordinates about what precisely they want accomplished.[33] Often this occurs in two stages: first between the executive branch and the government agency in charge of organizing the mission, and then again between that office and the foreign operatives carrying it out. At both stages, the desire to conceal the president's role means that planners delegate significant discretionary authority to individuals at lower levels. The result resembles the children's game of telephone. As the agency relays the White House's orders to operatives on the ground, intermediaries—sometimes with their own conflicting political interests—reinterpret the orders away from the executive branch's original intent.

Second, the need for secrecy means that covert operations are usually not vetted by a robust "marketplace of ideas."[34] Instead, the policymaking process for covert operations often resembles what Stephen Van Evera describes as "non-evaluation." He writes, "Confining policymaking to team players and limiting internal analysis prevents leaks that could stymie the policy's implementation, but it allows the policy to escape hard questions during its formulation."[35] Because the executive branch does not rigorously vet covert operations, the United States repeatedly pursued missions that were marred by threat inflation, poor contingency planning, naïve assumptions about feasibility, and short time horizons. Indeed, on several occasions during the Cold War, CIA analysts and diplomats stationed in the target country objected to a covert operation, claiming that the executive branch policymakers did not fully understand the ramifications of their actions, only to have their objections dismissed by the central decision-making body. Joshua Rovner refers to this type of intelligence pathology as neglect and, in these cases, explains that "policymakers ignore intelligence that is pathologically discomforting, and they exploit the organizational diversity of modern intelligence communities by searching out analyses that support their predispositions. They are also more likely to bypass intelligence agencies they believe are ideologically biased against them."[36]

Compounding this problem, a logical flaw often taints the policymaking process for covert operations: because officials assume their role will remain concealed, they believe that the mission's margin of error is greater than with overt operations. However, they overlook the fact that because they have not planned the mission as thoroughly, it often fails to remain covert. For instance, the Church Committee investigation of assassinations concluded, "We find that the likelihood of reckless action is substantially increased when policymakers believe that their decision will never be revealed. Whatever can be said in defense of the original purpose of plausible denial—a purpose which intends to conceal United States involvement from the outside world—the extension of the doctrine to the internal decision-making process of the Government is absurd."[37]

A review of the oversight committees for US covert operations during the Cold War shows that these bodies were typically quite small. Following WWII, the National Security Council and Policy Planning Staff oversaw America's initial covert operations somewhat haphazardly, leading the Hoover Commission to recommend in 1949 that the United States create "an evaluation board or section composed of competent and experienced personnel" to manage Washington's covert interventions going forward.[38] Since then, every president has created a committee to oversee the CIA's covert activities.[39] Until the mid-1970s, the number of officials mandated to participate on these councils was typically between six and twelve individuals. Even so, executive policymakers frequently sidestepped them. The Nixon administration exemplified this practice. For instance, Kissinger preferred to speak with members of the 40 Committee, the executive branch group tasked with evaluating covert actions, individually over the telephone rather than hold NSC meetings. Indeed, during 1973 and 1974, the 40 Committee authorized over forty covert actions without ever meeting in person.[40] Since the mid-1970s, the number of participating individuals has increased. Nevertheless, as scandals such as Iran-Contra have shown, these procedures are easily skirted, as many of the officials charged with supervising covert operations have been reluctant to exercise their oversight. Indeed, as one 1992 congressional study on the matter concluded, "Because covert action is secret, deceptive, and intended to be deniable, it carries an inherent risk: an administration could—without the knowledge of citizens or even Congress—bypass procedures of accountability in the conduct of foreign policies and military activities."[41]

Third, the motives underlying covert operations may undermine their success. In the testimony of CIA director Richard Helms, states opt for covert conduct so that the missions do "not explode in the President's face and so that he was not held responsible for them."[42] Because of this potential for scandal, when media outlets reported the US's role, planners often struggled to rectify the situation. On several occasions, policymakers order an immediate cessation of all activities in the target state—thereby isolating current operatives, abandoning existing intelligence networks, and losing their ability to redress developments on the ground. As the CIA's head of the Directorate of Intelligence, Ray Cline, once explained, "The weak point in covert paramilitary action is that a single misfortune that reveals CIA's connection makes it necessary for the United States either to abandon the cause completely or convert to a policy of overt military intervention. Because such paramilitary operations are generally kept secret for political reasons, when CIA's cover is blown the usual U.S. response is to withdraw, leaving behind the friendly elements who had entrusted their lives to the U.S. enterprise."[43]

Finally, states have learned that the United States is both willing and able to covertly overthrow its rivals. Potential target states have therefore taken steps to protect themselves from similar operations in their country.[44] Fortunately for them, even weak states can afford defensive measures, such as filling critical government positions with ardent supporters, creating parallel intelligence and security agencies to monitor potential dissenters, and tightening border security to hinder international transfers of funds and arms.[45] However, the same does not hold for preventing overt regime changes. Even with foreknowledge of an impending attack, weak states may simply lack the military forces necessary to deter or disrupt a direct military assault from a more powerful state. In fact, James Quinlivan finds that the same measures that help states protect against covert regime change— such as having multiple parallel security agencies—undermine its overt military effectiveness during wartime, suggesting that the more a state does to protect itself from a covert assault, the easier it can be overthrow overtly.[46] Likewise, comparing the battlefield effectiveness of different authoritarian states, Caitlin Talmadge argues, "Regimes facing significant coup threats are unlikely to adopt military organization practices optimized for conventional combat, even when doing so might help them prevail in conflicts against other states."[47]

The combined effect of these four factors is that policymakers often pursue covert regime changes that are doomed to failure from the start. Overt operations, by contrast, do not face these same limitations. When launching an overt mission, states can use whatever resources they would have used covertly, and likely can use much more. They may also have more mission flexibility, direct supervision over actors on the ground, and likely better contingency planning. As a result, overt missions succeed more frequently than their covert counterparts. Ironically, given his administration's penchant for covert action, this was the conclusion of a study commissioned by Nixon in 1969: "Covert operations can rarely achieve an important objective alone. At best, a covert operation can win time, forestall a coup or otherwise create favorable conditions which will make it possible to use overt means to finally achieve an important objective."[48]

Anecdotal evidence suggests that US policymakers understood the limitations of covert conduct. For instance, Kermit Roosevelt telegraphed to CIA headquarters during the 1953 operation to overthrow the Iranian prime minister that he wished to proceed despite the "slight remaining chance of success."[49] John Foster Dulles's estimates for success in Guatemala ranged from less than 20 percent to "better than 40 percent but less than even."[50] When his brother, Director of Central Intelligence Allen Dulles, informed Eisenhower of this estimate, the president appreciated his realistic prediction: "Allen, the figure of 20 percent was persuasive. If you had told me the chances would be 90 percent, I would have had a much more difficult decision."[51] Secretary of Defense Robert McNamara recommended that the United States proceed with the Bay of Pigs invasion despite "a marginal probability of success."[52] CIA director Richard Helms's personal notes from a meeting with Richard Nixon about covert operations in Chile states, "One in ten chance perhaps . . . but save Chile. Worth spending . . . not concerned with risks involved."[53] The success rates of America's covert and overt operations during the Cold War also support this hypothesis. Covert operations had an overall success rate of 39 percent, whereas overt operations succeeded 66 percent of the time (four out of six). Although these findings should not be exaggerated given the small sample size, the fact that several overt operations only came after a series of failed covert missions suggests that policymakers reserved overt conduct as a last resort.

Strategic Benefit of Intervention

Tactical considerations, however, are only half of the equation. When determining how to intervene, policymakers must also evaluate how the regime change fits into their overall foreign policy agenda. In that regard, two strategic factors are most important: the overall political benefit of replacing the target government and whether policymakers want to signal restraint or resolve on the international stage.

GEOSTRATEGIC BENEFIT OF REPLACING THE TARGET REGIME

The first factor evaluated by policymakers is the political benefit of replacing the target regime. This consideration reflects the political value that planners foresee for replacing the foreign government, regardless of whether the operation is conducted covertly or overtly. The precise strategic importance of replacing a target regime is determined by a myriad of factors: military strength, geography, population, economic ties, aggressive intentions, and so forth.[54] In broad terms, however, studies of US grand strategy have found that the United States has historically ranked its national interests—from highest to lowest—as defending the homeland, maintaining peace between the Eurasian great powers, protecting its access to oil, fostering economic openness, and supporting democracy and human rights.[55] The greater a threat a foreign government is believed to pose to these central interests, the greater the political benefit that policymakers will attach to replacing their regime. This means, for example, that from the US perspective, having a friendly government in Canada is inherently more valuable than having a friendly regime in Cameroon because Canada is a much more powerful country, a major trading partner, and geographically contiguous. For this study, however, the important point is that policymakers place some value on replacing the target government based on how valuable they consider that state to be to US national interests. The greater the geostrategic political benefit of replacing the target government, the higher the costs policymakers are willing to incur for regime change.

REPUTATION: RESTRAINT VERSUS RESOLVE

The second major strategic factor influencing the strategic value of a regime change is whether the intervening state wants to demonstrate resolve or show restraint on the international stage. Leaders base this preference on their perception of the threat as well as how they believe the operation is likely to be viewed by foreign audiences. The implication of this factor for their behavior is self-evident: when leaders feel the need to send a strong signal of their resolve and believe that they can successfully pull off a decisive display of force that will do so, they intervene overtly. When restraint is more appropriate, they prefer covert conduct.[56]

In most scenarios, states seem to prefer the appearance of restraint. The reason is that most regime changes, whether covert or overt, involve a great power intervening in a comparatively weak state. On the covert side, chapter 5 shows that few of America's Cold War interventions directly targeted a great power. On the overt side, Melissa Willard-Foster's study of fifty-eight regime changes between 1816 and 2003 found that roughly 75 percent involved an intervention by one of nine great powers.[57] The sheer power imbalance inherent in these operations suggests that international audiences are likely to perceive the great power's actions as unnecessarily belligerent and question their legitimacy. From the intervening state's perspective, this is bad news. Policymakers typically try to avoid establishing reputations as aggressors because a hostile reputation undermines the credibility of their alliance commitments and can provoke other states into taking measures to counterbalance their power.[58] The appeal of covert action in these cases is obvious: it allows stronger states to target weaker ones while maintaining a less threatening image on the international stage.

On occasion, however, states may find it in their interests to send a strong signal of resolve to deter other states from trying to take advantage of them.[59] Deterrence theory holds that "a reputation for resolve—the extent to which a state will risk war to achieve its objectives—is critical to credibility."[60] Particularly when facing an aggressive adversary and multiple, interrelated security threats, proponents argue that a state should accept the costs associated with having a more bellicose reputation because they believe that reputation will serve as a deterrent against potential aggressors and ensure future peace. In these situations, deterrence theory holds that an intervention can strengthen the credibility of a state's deterrent threat by showing it is willing and able to fight to protect its interests; this, in turn, deters other countries from challenging the intervener's interests in the first place. The classic articulation of this line of thinking comes from Thomas Schelling, whose work on coercion and deterrence was instrumental in Cold War policymaking. He wrote, "The main reason why we are committed in many of these places is that our threats are interdependent. Essentially we tell the Soviets that we have to react here because, if we did not, they would not believe us when we say that we will react here . . . the loss of face that matters most is the loss of Soviet belief that we will do, elsewhere and subsequently, what we insist we will do here and now. Our deterrence rests on Soviet expectations."[61]

Demonstrating resolve is especially important when the intervening state believes that an entire region would be destabilized if it failed to act.[62] During the Cold War, these fears were often driven by domino theory—the belief that the "loss" of an allied or neutral state to the Soviet sphere would make that state's neighbors more likely to ally with the Soviets as well.[63] Domino theory provides three rationales for why the United States would want to signal its resolve: first, to deter further Soviet expansion; second, to persuade current allies of the superiority of an alliance with the United States compared to one with the Soviet Union; and third, to signal to non-aligned countries that the United States will intervene if they try to ally with the Soviet Union. Given these potential benefits, proponents of deterrence theory encouraged displays of force to signal US resolve and contain Soviet expansion.

American policymakers throughout the Cold War were acutely concerned about having a reputation for resolve given the worldwide scope of the conflict and the difficulties associated with extended deterrence. For instance, President Nixon argued that if the United States withdrew from Vietnam, "the cause of peace might not survive the damage that would be done to other nations' confidence in our reliability."[64] Following North Vietnam's victory, Kissinger declared, "The U.S. must carry out some act somewhere in the world which shows its determination to continue to be a world power."[65] Similarly, President Reagan argued that if the United States did not prevail in Central America, "our credibility would collapse and our alliances would crumble."[66]

When deciding how to intervene, policymakers thus face a choice of how they want the intervention to reflect on them. Covert action allows states to avoid developing a reputation for hostility and thus minimizes the chances that other states will take steps to counterbalance their power. Although overt actions may make the state appear more hostile, they also demonstrate the intervening state's willingness to risk military confrontation to protect their interests. In certain circumstances—particularly when they face a revisionist adversary across multiple fronts—states may be willing to appear hostile in order to secure the deterrent advantages of having a reputation for resolve. Overt regime change was one such way to do so.

Deciding How to Intervene

Combining the arguments from the preceding two sections, it is apparent that leaders weigh three factors when deciding how to conduct a regime change operation: (1) the mission's predicted costs, (2) its likelihood of success, and (3) the strategic benefit of an intervention. The first two factors—the operation's costs and its likelihood of success—relate to the actual tactical considerations of intervention and vary depending on how the regime change is conducted. Specifically, I find that covert conduct lowers an operation's predicted costs but also decreases its likelihood of success. Overt conduct increases the odds of success. Because the intervening state does not conceal its role in the operation, however, the predicted costs are greater. The third factor—the mission's overall strategic importance—reflects both the intrinsic value of the target state in terms of the intervener's national interests and how policymakers want the operation to be viewed on the international stage. Because these three factors are all weighed relative to one another, a state may be willing to intervene in places where the political stakes appear rather small, if policymakers foresee a quick and decisive victory. Conversely, if they believe the mission will be prohibitively costly or is unlikely to succeed, a state may not intervene even when the strategic benefits of intervention are very high. Richard Haass explains, "To draw a direct connection or parallel between the importance of an interest and a willingness to intervene would be wrong. An interest can be widely viewed as extremely important but military force may not be the best or most appropriate tool to promote or protect it; alternatively, an intervention can only be moderately important but intervening military might be judged to be relatively 'cheap and easy' and worth it."[67]

Which option is better? For the vast majority of cases, I find that both tactical and strategic concerns point to covert conduct as the preferred way to intervene. In relation to tactical considerations, covert conduct means lower predicted costs but also less chance of success. However, policymakers seem to believe that although covert conduct influences both factors, it has a bigger overall effect on a mission's costs. In other words, they believe that whereas covert conduct *moderately* decreases the likelihood that an operation will succeed, it *dramatically* decreases its costs, leading policymakers to conclude that they might as well attempt an operation even if it appears unlikely to succeed. Although policymakers preferred covert conduct because of its low costs, different types of costs were salient in each type of operation.

When conducting offensive and preventive operations, for instance, declassified documents show that US planners preferred covert conduct primarily for security reasons, namely, to decrease the odds of Soviet retaliation. During hegemonic operations, by contrast, security and material costs were less of a concern, given the vast power discrepancy between the United States and the target regimes. In these cases, Washington sought to minimize the reputational costs associated with violating norms of justified intervention, such as installing leaders known to have committed human rights abuses or targeting a democracy. Overall, in terms of strategic considerations, I find that US leaders typically opted for covert conduct to maintain a benign image on the international state rather than gaining a reputation for belligerence. The combined effect of these considerations means that all else being equal, when the United States wanted to overthrow a foreign government, it did so covertly.

In fact, US policymakers appear to believe that covert conduct shifts the cost-benefit calculation for a regime change from where they would not consider the intervention worthwhile to where they consider it viable, suggesting that there are many cases when Washington will intervene covertly in pursuit of objectives for which they are unwilling to risk American boots on the ground. Or as President Nixon once said, "Overt economic or military aid is sometimes enough to achieve our goals. Only a direct military intervention can do so in others. But between the two lies a vast area where the United States must be able to undertake covert actions. Without this capability we will be unable to protect important U.S. interests."[68] US behavior during the Cold War clearly reflects this inclination for covert conduct. During that time, Washington launched twenty-three covert offensive operations, twenty-five covert preventive missions, and eighteen covert hegemonic operations. This amounted to 92 percent of its total offensive missions, 96.2 percent of preventive, and 85.7 percent of hegemonic regime changes.

But if policymakers overwhelmingly prefer to conduct their regime changes covertly, why do states ever intervene overtly? The simple answer is that policymakers intervene overtly when prevailing in the target state is seen as important and covert actions are unlikely to succeed. The more complicated way of saying this is that states opt for overt conduct when the operation's predicted costs are extremely low and/or its strategic benefits are extremely high. In these situations, policymakers may prefer to intervene covertly but are willing to intervene overtly if covert action has already proven insufficient or appears unlikely to succeed. This is consistent with the observation that four of the six overt regime changes attempted by the United States during the Cold War came after a failed covert attempt to replace the target regime.

As mentioned earlier, many US policymakers during the Cold War believed that the best way to deter Soviet expansion into the third world was to send a strong signal of American resolve and that overt regime change was one way to do so. Even so, relatively few interstate disputes actually led to an overt regime change because US officials only sent in troops when they believed that they faced a threatening situation where it was preferable to appear resolute, as opposed to restrained, and where they were confident of victory and, thus, that the operation would send the signal that they intended. This section introduces three circumstances when those conditions are most likely to be met: first, when policymakers believe they can secure a quick and decisive victory; second, when public opinion favors intervention; and/or third, when a rapidly unfolding foreign crisis necessitates a fast response.

Governments targeted for regime change seldom back down without a fight. Facing an existential threat to their political survival, the target regime has every incentive to use all military resources at its disposal to prevent this from occurring. Under such circumstances, intervening states have good reason to want to avoid a prolonged military conflict with the target regime. Policymakers therefore only escalate to overt conduct if they believe that they can achieve a decisive military victory.[69] This means that a balance-of-power logic will prevail, and states will seldom overtly attack others with commensurate military power. Not surprisingly, great powers conduct most overt regime changes against weak states and are reluctant to attack foreign countries allied with a powerful rival.[70] For example, the United States overtly intervened in only two out of the twenty-five offensive regime changes against the USSR and its allies during the Cold War. Washington decided not to directly invade in twenty-three cases because policymakers feared that the Soviet Union was willing to defend its allies militarily if necessary. Nevertheless, this type of deterrence can break down if the intervening state suspects that its rival's alliance is tenuous—for example, if the great power protector has taken steps to distance itself from the target regime or finds itself preoccupied with other security concerns at the time. In the two cases where the United States directly targeted a Soviet ally—North Korea and Libya—during the Cold War, for instance, intelligence estimates at the time assured American leaders that their actions were unlikely to lead to war against the Soviet Union.

To achieve a quick and decisive victory, the intervening state must believe it has a clever military strategy that will allow it to overthrow the target government before it can retaliate through prolonged attrition or guerilla warfare. Thus, aggressors seek a strategy for rapid victory, which in the modern era typically involves the concentrated use of overwhelming force to quickly break through their enemy's frontline defenses and disrupt operations in their rear.[71] Historically, states launch wars and regime changes more frequently when they have developed a novel strategy of this nature. For instance, Napoleonic France sought to conquer Europe following its new developments in mass conscription and maneuver warfare.[72] Nazi Germany did the same following its mastery of Blitzkrieg tactics.[73] Likewise, some

American defense analysts worry that the post–Cold War "Revolution in Military Affairs" (RMA) encouraged the 2003 regime change in Iraq by fostering an "overreliance on the military element of national power."[74]

A second scenario, where policymakers may be more willing to escalate to overt conduct, is when public opinion is on their side.[75] Public support negates one of the main rationales for covert conduct—to avoid reputational costs. Indeed, even if the public merely tolerates a mission, its reputational costs will decrease. If the public enthusiastically supports an intervention, the operation's political benefits will increase, and policymakers will want to make their actions known. Although this project does not attempt to theorize all the factors that influence public support, the existing literature does suggest some scenarios where public support levels are likely to be higher: when media elites support intervention, when the operation adheres to norms of justified intervention, or when it is perceived as a defensive response to a clear military threat.[76]

Lastly, policymakers may escalate to overt conduct when they face significant time pressure to act. The reason is that successful covert missions require time: the intervener will need preexisting intelligence on the target regime and a connection to domestic resistance in the target state. Thus, if a state must act quickly and does not have preexisting contacts within the target state, covert conduct may not suffice. (In terms of the cost/benefit/odds-of-success trade-off, these are cases where the probability of success for a covert intervention is so small that policymakers pursue overt conduct despite the increased costs.) For these reasons, states are more likely to intervene overtly in response to rapidly unfolding scenarios, such as after a surprise attack or to reinstall a recently deposed leader amid a political crisis in the target state. If the state waits to develop the resources necessary for a successful covert mission, the operation's costs will continue to rise as the target regime consolidates its political control and the recently deposed regime loses political legitimacy.[77] We can see this reasoning, for example, in Lyndon Johnson's decision to overtly intervene in the Dominican Republic in 1965, days after the country erupted in civil war, out of fear that if the United States failed to act immediately, leftist forces would consolidate power and the US would soon face a "second Cuba" in the country. In a similar vein, Reagan's 1983 overt intervention in Grenada followed a violent political uprising following the execution of Grenadian leader Maurice Bishop during a military coup.

States are particularly likely to send in troops during foreign crises when they believe that they need to send a strong signal of their resolve to defuse a regional crisis. Chapter 5 shows that many of America's overt regime changes occurred in the context of an ongoing regional crisis where US policymakers feared that multiple states were in danger of rapidly falling to communism. Eisenhower's 1958 overt intervention into Lebanon, for instance, was immediately precipitated by a leftist coup in Iraq and was driven, in large part, by fears that if Washington did not act, "the United States would lose influence not only in the Arab States of the Middle East but in the area generally."[78] In these cases, US policymakers overtly intervened not only to prevent the target government from succumbing to communism but also to deter the Soviet Union from further aggression within the region.

Covert Tactics

Now that we can see why states prefer covert conduct, this section introduces the five major covert tactics employed by the United States during the Cold War. The following chapter discusses the relative effectiveness of these tactics.

ASSASSINATIONS

The planned assassination of a foreign leader was the least common covert tactic employed by the United States during the Cold War. A declassified CIA manual on assassination defines that action as "the planned killing of a person who is not under the legal jurisdiction of the killer, who is not physically in the hands of the killer, who has been selected by a resistance organization for death, and whose death provides positive advantages to that organization."[79] It advises, "Assassination is an extreme measure not normally used in clandestine operations. It should be assumed that it will never be ordered or authorized by any U.S. Headquarters, though the latter may in rare instances agree to its execution by members of an associated foreign service."[80] In these cases, "the specific technique employed will depend on a large number of variables, but should be constant in one point: Death must be absolutely certain."[81]

The United States developed plans to assassinate foreign leaders on several occasions during the Cold War. First, as part of an aborted joint US–UK covert operation in Syria in the mid-1950s, plans were developed calling for the assassination of several Syrian politicians.[82] Second, in 1960, the CIA developed a plan to assassinate Congolese leader Patrice Lumumba, and poisons were shipped into the country for this task, although never used.[83] Third, between 1960 and 1965, the CIA pursued multiple assassination plots against Cuban president Fidel Castro.[84] Beyond these clearer-cut cases, there is also some evidence suggesting that the CIA explored the possibility of assassinating Indonesian president Sukarno, Haitian leader "Papa Doc" Duvalier, as well as an unnamed Iraqi politician.[85] None of these assassination plots succeeded. However, two other foreign leaders—South Vietnam's Ngo Dinh Diem and the Dominican Republic's Rafael Trujillo—were killed by foreign forces without explicit preapproval from Washington during US-backed coups. Democratically elected Chilean president Salvador Allende also reportedly committed suicide during a 1973 military coup.[86] Scholars remained divided, however, on the question of whether the United States took an active role in the 1973 Chilean coup or merely had foreknowledge of its plan. The Church Committee's investigation of the matter, for instance, reported "no hard evidence of direct U.S. assistance to the coup."[87] Nevertheless, the CIA had a long history of covert action in Chile, including directly backing a failed coup attempt in 1970, wherein another influential Chilean official, General Rene Schneider, was assassinated. Although the United States likely did not play a direct role in the 1973 coup, Chile was the target of a US-backed covert campaign to destabilize Allende's regime at the time that may have encouraged the coup plotters to strike.[88] Or as Henry Kissinger phrased it in a telephone conversation with President Nixon days afterward, "We didn't do it. I mean we helped them. [Redacted] created the conditions as great as possible."[89]

After America's role in these assassination plots came to light during the Church Committee's congressional investigation of the mid-1970s, President Ford signed Executive Order 11905, formally prohibiting all US government employees from engaging in assassination.[90] In 1978, President Carter signed Executive Order 12063, expanding this ban to include "persons . . . acting on behalf of the United States Government"—a stipulation reaffirmed by President Reagan in December 1981.[91]

SPONSORING FOREIGN COUPS D'ÉTAT

In his influential study on the subject, Edward Luttwak defined a coup as "the infiltration of a small but critical segment of the state apparatus, which is then used to displace the government from its control of the remainder."[92] By this definition, Washington was involved in thirteen foreign coups during the Cold War, nine of which saw US-backed forces assume power. Almost all US-backed coups supported right-wing military officials over foreign leaders that the United States deemed sympathetic to communism. In all the cases included in this study, US officials took an active role in the mission, ranging from providing foreign coup plotters with arms, intelligence, and funding to organizing and fighting on the coup plotters' behalf. However, in contrast to some other studies, this project does not include cases where the available evidence suggests that the United States simply had foreknowledge that a coup might occur and did not alert the target government—for example, Ecuador (1963), Indonesia (1965), Ghana (1966), and Greece (1967).

COVERT SUPPORT FOR FOREIGN DISSIDENTS

Washington's most common covert tactic during the Cold War was to secretly support foreign revolutionary or secessionist movements in their bids to topple or secede from a target state. In these cases, the United States provided covert funding, weapons, logistical aid, intelligence, propaganda, and/or military training to the foreign dissidents to bolster their efforts to topple an anti-American regime. All told, the United States attempted at least thirty-five of these missions between 1947 and 1989, four of which saw the US-backed forces assume power. Many operations occurred in the context of civil wars, wherein the United States and the Soviet Union each supported opposing sides. In nine cases, however, Washington backed foreign secessionist movements in their bids to secede from the Soviet Union, China, or Iraq.

ELECTION INTERFERENCE

Throughout the Cold War, the United States recurrently sought to influence foreign elections by covertly providing funding, advisory assistance, and propaganda to help its preferred candidates win their elections. These operations often carried beyond a single election cycle.[93] Some of the states targeted in these interventions were well-established democracies that held free and competitive elections; others were authoritarian states, which held competitive subnational elections or partially free national elections. In all cases, however, US covert assistance was designed to tip the election in favor of pro-American candidates whom US policymakers believed might be in danger of losing without additional support. All told, US-supported parties won their elections in twelve out of sixteen covert campaigns.

DEMOCRACY PROMOTION

A final regime change tactic, which is perhaps better described as "pseudo-covert," came to the fore during the early Reagan years. In contrast to the aforementioned efforts to influence foreign elections, this tactic aimed to transform authoritarian states into democracies.[94] President Reagan first publicly laid out his rationale for what became known as "Project Democracy" during an influential 1982 address to the British Parliament: "The objective I propose is quite simple to state: to foster the infrastructure of democracy, the system of a free press, unions, political parties, universities, which allows a people to choose their own way to develop their own culture."[95] Toward this end, Reagan signed NSDD 77 in January 1983, which established an "International Political Committee" under the guidance of the National Security Council for the "planning, coordinating and implementing international political activities in support of United States policies and interests relative to national security. Included among such activities are aid, training and organizational support for foreign governments and private groups to encourage the growth of democratic political institutions and practices."[96]

With this objective in mind, the question arose of how the United States should distribute aid to foreign pro-democracy groups. Some in the administration proposed that the United States distribute aid through state-run agencies, whereas others argued that independent nongovernment affiliated groups were preferable.[97] After a contentious legislative battle, Congress opted for the latter route and authorized funds to create the National Endowment for Democracy (NED), whose stated objective was "to encourage the establishment and growth of democratic development in a manner consistent . . . with the broad concerns of United States national interest."[98] According to its Statement of Principles, the NED is a "privately incorporated nonprofit organization with a Board of Directors comprised of leading citizens from the mainstream of American political and civic life."[99] The House legislation authorizing the NED also reinforced this nongovernmental organization (NGO) status. It stated, "Nothing in this title shall be construed to make the Endowment an agency or establishment of the United States Government."[100]

While technically an NGO, the NED's relationship with the US government is extensive: 99 percent of the NED's total revenue comes from US governmental agencies, and the State Department must first approve of all NED grants.[101] Nonetheless, owing to its NGO status, the US government can use the organization to promote its interests abroad while avoiding, in Alexander Haig's words, the "charges of interference" associated with pursuing these activities through official government agencies, like the CIA.[102] As NED president Carl Gershwin explained in 1986, "We should not have to do this type of work covertly. It would be terrible for democratic groups around the world to be seen as subsidized by the CIA. We saw that in the 1960s, and that's why it has been discontinued. We have not had the capability of doing this, and that's why the endowment was created."[103] Likewise, the NED's first director, Allen Weinstein, explained in 1991, "A lot of what we do today was done covertly twenty-five years ago by the CIA."[104] The NED's NGO status therefore serves a useful purpose: it allows the NED to pursue US-government sanctioned objectives while allowing the government to distance itself from those actions and plausibly deny its role in specific NED programs.

During the Reagan years, the NED was instrumental in several US efforts to promote democratic transitions in Chile, Haiti, Liberia, Nicaragua, Panama, the Philippines, Poland, and Suriname.[105] During these missions, the US government first provided funding to the NED, which in turn allocated funds to four "core constituencies": the American Center for International Labor Solidarity (ACILS), the Center for International Private Enterprise (CIPE), the National Democratic Institute (NDI), and the International Republican Institute (IRI).[106] These groups then distributed grants to selected foreign political parties, dissident movements, student groups, labor unions, and civic organizations in the target states. This structure is reminiscent of the CIA's earlier political action and psychological warfare operations, and many of the NED recipients had longstanding ties to the CIA. According to William Robinson, NED funds were ultimately used for five overlapping pseudo-covert activities: leadership training for pro-American elites, promotion of pro-American educational systems and mass media, strengthening the "institutions of democracy" by funding pro-American organizations in the target state, propaganda, and the development of transnational elite networks.[107]

Even so, Reagan did not launch these operations simply to foster democratization per se. Instead, these missions sought to create an opportunity to rule for pro-American parties. Toward this end, the key objective of many of these missions was to prevent communist and socialist parties from winning their state's elections. For instance, Reagan signed NSDD 101 on Liberia "to promote political and economic stability through the development of democratic institutions." To do so, he called for "adequate assistance to the Liberian transitional process through Project Democracy funding" in order to "develop a moderate and viable political coalition" and "prevent the development of Libyan, Soviet or other hostile influence."[108] Thus, the NED backed moderate and right-wing political movements, but not socialist or communist parties, even when those groups advocated for democratic elections. Likewise, in Nicaragua, the NED spent $13 million between 1988 and 1990 to ensure that Sandinista leader Daniel Ortega did not win the 1990 presidential elections.[109] In Poland, the United States spent at least $9 million funding Solidarity and other moderate to right-wing groups, but no democratic-socialist groups.[110] In the Philippines, the NED gave at least $7 million dollars to the Trade Union Congress of the Philippines (TUCP), a conservative organization, but no aid to the Kilusang Mayo Uno (KMU), a large leftist coalition union, despite its fervent opposition to Marcos.[111] Altogether, Robinson concludes, "U.S. policymakers claim that they are interested in *process* (free and fair elections) and not *outcome* (the results of these elections); in reality, the principal concern is outcome."[112]

The Pseudo-Covert Continuum

On multiple occasions during the Cold War, the United States pursued operations that are perhaps best described as "pseudo-covert"—that is, a regime change operation where the United States officially denied its role even though all parties involved seem to know of its participation. For instance, throughout the 1980s, the United States covertly funneled billions of dollars of aid and arms to Afghan Mujahedeen militant groups fighting against their Soviet occupiers. When Carter launched the operation in 1979, he had solid strategic reasons to do so covertly. However, the United States maintained the charade of covertness long after it seemingly lost the ability to plausibly deny its role. For instance, by May 1983, the *New York Times* was reporting specific details of the US-led operation and citing members of both the House and Senate Intelligence Committees, who acknowledged "a consensus favoring aid to Afghan rebels."[113] By 1985, the United States had begun supplying the Mujahedeen with sophisticated Stinger missiles to target Soviet aircraft—weapons that the Soviets would immediately and undeniably recognize as American made. Despite all of this, US leaders went to great lengths to continue to use covert methods and deny their role in the conflict. What explains this behavior?

Policymakers pursue pseudo-covert operations for the same reason that they pursue missions that they intend to remain entirely secret: to minimize the predicted costs of the operation. Rather than being a clear-cut dichotomy between truly covert and overt action, the decision regarding how best to conduct a regime change can be thought of as falling along a continuum that is governed by the same dynamics discussed earlier in the chapter. This means that when a state wants to take a more aggressive pseudo-covert action—such as providing Stinger missiles to the Afghan fighters—it will decrease the state's ability to plausibly deny its role, thus increasing the mission's potential costs but also increasing its odds of success. Policymakers decide how to calibrate this trade-off by looking at the potential strategic benefits of intervention. The greater the potential benefits, the higher costs that planners are willing to incur, and thus the more willing they are to pursue pseudo-covert tactics that undermine their ability to plausibly deny their role.

Once the cover of a covert regime change has been blown, it might be reasonable to suspect that the intervening state will soon face all the costs associated with the mission, and thus there is nothing to be gained from continuing to intervene covertly. However, that is not always the case. Maintaining the charade of pseudo-covert conduct can still minimize the operation's material, reputational, and security costs for several reasons. For one, pseudo-covert conduct minimizes the material costs associated with toppling a foreign government because covert missions require fewer resources, even after an operation's cover has been blown.[114] In addition, pseudo-covert conduct minimizes media scrutiny of the operation.[115] Journalists who cover covert operations do so without the cooperation of the intervening state, regularly scheduled press conferences, or a guarantee of safe passage with friendly military forces. Thus, operational details are likely to be underreported, and a larger portion of the public will remain in the dark about the operation. For instance, even after the Iran-Contra scandal broke in 1986, and its subsequent congressional hearings in 1987, only 54 percent of the US public knew that the US government had been covertly backing the "rebels trying to overthrow the government" in Nicaragua.[116] Indeed, only 32 percent of Americans surveyed correctly identified Nicaragua as being located in Central or Latin America.[117] In a similar vein, Gibbs's case study of Eisenhower's 1960 covert operation to overthrow Congolese prime minister Patrice Lumumba found that US planners knew their actions had been uncovered in Leopoldville and Moscow, but continued the covert operation because its secrecy concealed specifics of the mission that were still "potentially very controversial."[118] In addition to minimizing audience costs, covert conduct also allows US leaders to bypass the War Powers Act, which requires congressional approval for any deployment of US armed forces for more than sixty days.[119] Covert operations are a distinctly presidential power, meaning that the president can exercise close control over their implementation without having to accommodate the wishes of Congress or rival politicians.

States also pursue pseudo-covert tactics to minimize the security costs associated with attacking a foreign government. A state may decide to conduct an operation covertly—even when it knows that its opponent is aware of the mission—because it understands that an overt intervention would constitute a direct challenge to its opponent's reputation. Thus, to minimize the chances that its opponent will feel compelled to respond to this challenge, the state limits its behavior to covert conduct. A former CIA agent explained the "tacit convention" behind this type of behavior:

> In the professional context of the secret war and covert operations . . . avowal of responsibility has a specific meaning. It is interpreted by the enemy as a threat, since it means in the context, that the avower not only ignores established custom, but also the basis of that custom, which is the maintenance of the international power balance. The avower therefore puts himself in the position of demonstrating indifference to the international political balance; his avowal may even be taken to imply that he intends to change it by any and all means.[120]

This suggests that when the intervening state faces an opponent whom it believes also wants to avoid a direct military confrontation, pursuing nominally covert tactics can help both sides lessen the pressure to militarily escalate the dispute.[121]

KEEPING SECRETS FOR YOUR ENEMY

Now that we can see why an intervening state would maintain a charade of pseudo-covert conduct, an even more interesting question arises: Why would the states targeted in these pseudo-covert operations sometimes go along with this charade? Repeatedly during the Cold War, each superpower uncovered evidence that its rival was attempting a covert regime against one of its allies or a nonaligned state. In most cases, not surprisingly, Washington and Moscow took advantage of these revelations to publicly accuse and embarrass their rival. Given the ideological character of the Cold War, these blown operations could be a major propaganda victory by discrediting its opponent's credibility and the popular appeal of the rival ideology. On other occasions, however, each superpower ignored an opportunity to scandalize the other and instead kept its knowledge of the rival's covert activities unpublicized. Given the high stakes ideological conflict of the Cold War, why would either superpower forgo an opportunity to expose its opponent's covert operation?

There are four reasons why a state may prefer to keep its rival's secret operations unpublicized. First, the targeted state may try to introduce spies and double agents into its opponent's operation, thereby generating intelligence on the opponent and foiling the operation from within. For instance, chapter 7 discusses how North Vietnamese forces managed to infiltrate a large number of spies and double agents into America's covert operation against Hanoi in the early 1960s. Second, the state may prefer to wait and reveal the operation on its own terms to maximize its leverage over the opposing side. For instance, archival documents reveal that the Soviet Union shot down thirteen American reconnaissance planes between 1950 and 1964.[122] However, the Soviet Union chose only to publicize the 1960 incident when Francis Gary Powers was shot down, in essence keeping America's secret for the other twelve missions. This suggests that the Soviet Union weighed the relative merits of exposing the US operations against the disadvantages of inflaming passion between the superpowers, and only revealed information when it best suited Soviet interests. Third, the target government may prefer not to publicize covert operations against it so that the regime's weakness is not exposed to its domestic adversaries. For instance, Moscow did not acknowledge America's early covert operation in the Ukrainian SSR because the ruling regime felt insecure about its hold on power and preferred not to acknowledge the existence of a domestic resistance movement as large as the Organization of Ukrainian Nationalists. Finally, a target state may choose not to expose its rival's covert operation to avoid military escalation.[123] Leaders in the target state may fear war but feel constrained by a nationalistic population that would demand retaliation in response to an attempt to overthrow their state. Bruce Berkowitz and Allan Goodman note, "In the late 1940s, for example, the Soviet government knew that the CIA was supporting resistance fighters in the Ukraine, since Soviet intelligence had penetrated most of the groups. Similarly, the Soviet leadership knew that the United States was supporting the Afghan Mujahedeen in the 1980s. If US leaders had admitted responsibility, Soviet leaders would have felt it necessary to retaliate."[124] By feigning ignorance of the operation, however, the state does not have respond to the embarrassing challenge to its authority. In scenarios where both sides face similar fears of military escalation, each state may choose to keep its opponent's covert activities secret to minimize the chances of military escalation. This explains why, on several occasions during the Cold War, the United States and Soviet Union were able to fight covert proxy wars in the Third World with little danger that the dispute would escalate to outright war between the superpowers.[125]

This chapter asked why states launch regime changes covertly versus overtly. To answer that question, I first argued that states weigh three factors when deciding to intervene: (1) a mission's political benefits, (2) its likely costs, and (3) its probability of success. Whereas the mission's political benefits are dictated by the strategic value of the target state, the other two factors vary depending on whether the regime change is conducted covertly or overtly. Specifically, I claimed that covert conduct substantially decreases the security, material, and reputational costs associated with toppling a foreign government. At the same time, however, covert operations are less likely to succeed than their overt counterparts. Faced with this trade-off between cost and effectiveness, I argued that, in most cases, policymakers opt for the lower costs associated with covert conduct. This explains why Washington conducted 91 percent of its regime changes covertly during the Cold War. In the remaining 9 percent of cases, however, I explained that the United States was willing to overtly intervene—often after a failed covert mission—if a covert operation was either impossible to carry out within a short time horizon or because policymakers believed they could achieve a decisive victory with public support for their cause. Next, the chapter provided an overview of the five main covert tactics used by states during their regime changes. Finally, I investigated "pseudo-covert" operations and explained why, under certain conditions, both intervening and target states found it in their best interest to maintain the charade of covert conduct even after a mission's cover had been blown.

Consequences

How Effective Are Covert Regime Changes?

> The fact is that many conspiracies are attempted but very few reach
> their desired goal.
>
> —Niccolò Machiavelli, *Discourses on Livy*

Now that it is clear why states have so frequently launched covert regime changes, the question naturally arises of whether these operations generally achieve the goals that policymakers set for them. To tackle that issue, this chapter asks two questions: First, why did some covert missions succeed in their short-term objective of toppling the target regime while others failed? Second, what were the long-term consequences of these operations?

Overall, US-backed covert regime changes succeeded in replacing their target 39 percent of the time, compared to 66 percent for America's overt interventions. Moreover, once one looks at the long-term consequences of the covert operations, it becomes apparent that very few ultimately worked out as Washington intended. Time after time, US leaders pursued covert regime change based on the assumption that the missions would provide a cheap and permanent solution to their problem, but these outcomes were seldom delivered. Instead, covert regime changes tended to succeed where they were needed the least—overthrowing weak governments of little geostrategic value. Missions targeting strong countries usually failed. Moreover, the great majority of attacks targeting weak and strong states alike seldom remained covert. Although feasible in theory, "plausible deniability" was extremely difficult to maintain in practice, and domestic forces in the target state accused the United States of involvement in more than 70 percent of the cases. These findings suggest that covert regime changes are only likely to succeed under limited circumstances. States should therefore be far more cautious when attempting them.

The first half of this chapter analyzes the question of short-term success. Are certain types of covert operations more likely than others to topple their target? In general, I argue that covert operations are most likely to succeed when they are limited in scale and pursue modest objectives. The most successful covert missions are therefore those that are designed to tip the scales in favor of one side in a close political competition. Ambitious large-scale missions, by contrast, usually fail due to the difficulty of maintaining plausible deniability. Overthrowing a powerful state requires a powerful opposition, and it is extremely difficult for any foreign power to sponsor such a large opposition without blowing its cover. I also find that the type of covert tactic used during an operation influenced its odds of success. For instance, not a single US-backed assassination plot succeeded during the Cold War, although US actions did lead to a few inadvertent killings during other covert missions. Likewise, covert actions to support foreign dissidents nearly always failed. Of thirty-five attempts, fewer than 12 percent overthrew their targets. The remaining three covert strategies—sponsoring coups, meddling in foreign elections, and promoting democratic revolutions in authoritarian states—were far more successful. Each succeeded in replacing its target more than half of the time.

To determine whether any characteristics of a state would make it a better or worse target for regime change, I then introduce a statistical model that compares several different aspects of the states targeted, such as their military power, regime type, wealth, and level of political instability. Overall, I find that covert operations are most likely to succeed against democratic governments, weak states, and American allies. Combining these factors helps to explain why operations targeting the Soviet Union's authoritarian allies succeeded only 10.3 percent of the time, compared to 42.9 percent of operations targeting nonaligned states, and 69.6 percent of missions targeting American allies, which were frequently democratic. Democracies appear to be particularly susceptible to regime change for three reasons: First, covert operations against democracies involve tactics that are generally more successful and easier to conceal. Second, all democratic states targeted were also US allies, which gave US agents free access to the country. Third, although authoritarian leaders often "coup-proof" their regimes, democratic leaders frequently do not—leaving them more vulnerable to domestic challengers than their autocratic counterparts.

The second half of this chapter is dedicated to an analysis of the long-term consequences of regime change. Several statistical models are introduced, which compare states that have experienced a covert regime change to a sample of similar states that have not. The first question asked is, how did America's covert interventions influence Washington's relationship with the target state? Was the United States able to turn its opponents into allies by installing friendly leaders? Chapter 2 argued that states launch regime changes to install leaders with foreign policy preferences like their own. This suggests that if these operations work as policymakers intend, America's relationship with the target state should immediately improve. However, the data suggests that this is not the case. Contrary to policymakers' expectations, attempting to overthrow a state covertly actually *increased* the likelihood that the United States would become embroiled in a military dispute with that state down the line while *decreasing* the similarity of that state's foreign policy portfolio and UN voting behavior to those of the United States.

The reason is that changing the preferences of another state requires more than just changing the leadership of that state. Whatever political pressures compelled the previous regime to act against American interests will hold true for their successors as well. Consequently, many newly installed leaders balked at their pre-regime change promises and began to behave like their predecessors who were overthrown. Other leaders followed through on their promises and tried to pursue US interests. Doing so, however, often made them quite unpopular domestically. Their opponents were quick to deride them as American puppets, and more than half of all leaders installed during US covert operations were subsequently overthrown via revolution or coup. Unsurprisingly, the governments that took over afterward were often even more hostile to the United States than the regime that was initially overthrown. Finally, there is the question of how US covert regime changes affected the states targeted. Here, my analysis paints an almost unremittingly negative view of covert action. States targeted for regime change were frequently less democratic afterward and more likely to experience a civil war or episode of mass killing compared to similar countries where the United States had not intervened.

Short-Term Effectiveness

Why do some covert regime changes succeed at replacing their targets while others fail? In relation to the question of short-term effectiveness, an operation can be classified as a "success" if the US-backed forces came to power during the mission. An operation is a "failure" if the individuals supported by the United States did not come to power. Overall, I find that the short-term effectiveness of a covert operation hinges on three things: the magnitude of the covert action attempted, the type of covert tactic used, and the nature of the targeted state. This section briefly discusses each of those factors.

The first important factor in determining whether a covert operation succeeded was the magnitude of the intervention attempted. Because of the trade-off between size and secrecy discussed in the previous chapter, states have a difficult time orchestrating large-scale covert operations without blowing their cover. Thus, the relative balance of forces between the opposition forces and the target regime at the beginning of the intervention was a crucial factor in determining the mission's likely odds of success. When opposition forces were weak compared to the central regime, the intervening state had to covertly deliver a significant amount of resources to them if their operation was to stand a chance of success, but the larger a covert operation, the more possibilities of its discovery or infiltration by enemy forces. This problem was particularly acute during US covert operations targeting strong communist governments during the Cold War. For instance, Herbert Weis-shart, a CIA officer who worked on multiple Cold War covert regime changes against the Soviet Union, China, and North Vietnam, estimated that in an anti-Soviet resistance cell of just ten individuals, the odds that the group had been penetrated by security forces were 50 percent.[1] When US-backed opposition forces were already strong relative to the central government, by contrast, the United States had to do far less to tip the scales in their favor. In some cases, strong opposition movements may have succeeded even without US covert assistance, thus making America's covert involvement superfluous.

A second influential factor determining the odds of short-term success is the type of covert tactic employed during the operation. As the preceding chapter explained, Washington employed five covert tactics during its sixty-four Cold War interventions: assassinations, sponsoring coups d'état, supporting foreign dissidents in their bids to overthrow a state, backing favored candidates in foreign elections, and promoting democratic revolutions in authoritarian states. The common feature making these tactics covert is that they were designed to maintain "plausible deniability" of US involvement by using foreign intermediaries who would appear to have acted independently if the operation were uncovered. Frequently, the United States pursued more than one tactic simultaneously, and though some tactics had higher success rates than others, Washington's choice of tactics was governed largely by opportunity. Because all of its Cold War covert operations involved collaboration with opposition forces in the target state, the covert tactics available to US policymakers were largely dictated by the nature of the opposition and its relationship to the target government.

Figure 4.1 shows that the US-backed opposition forces succeeded in assuming power between 0 and 75 percent of the time, depending on which covert tactics were used. Assassinations had the worst record. Not a single assassination plot succeeded during the Cold War, although two foreign leaders were killed without explicit US approval during US-backed coups. After details of some of these plots became public in the mid-1970s, a US Senate committee headed by Frank Church launched an investigation into America's covert actions. The Church Committee's final report on assassinations was highly critical of the tactic, stating, "Running throughout the cases considered in this report was the expectation of American officials that they could control the actions of dissidents that they were supporting in foreign countries. Events demonstrated that the United States had no such power."[2] The committee concluded, "Assassination has no place in America's arsenal."[3]

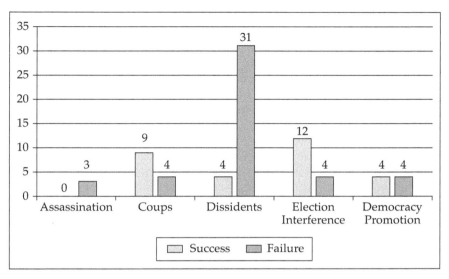

Figure 4.1. Short-term effectiveness by covert tactic.

Covert operations to support foreign dissidents also usually failed because of the magnitude of covert assistance that the United States would have had to deliver to the opposition forces for them to succeed. Of thirty-five attempts, only four overthrew their targets. Furthermore, half of those successes involved additional covert tactics: US missions in Guatemala and Nicaragua also included efforts to promote a coup or influence democratic elections. Only in Afghanistan and Chad did the United States successfully engender a regime change by covertly supporting dissidents alone. However, the operation in Afghanistan is unique in that it was abnormally large and costly, with the United States spending more than $6.6 billion during the 1980s.[4] The mission in Chad was far less costly, but it failed to remain covert, and the United States was criticized for backing Hissene Habre, given his well-established record of human rights abuses.[5] Similarly, and perhaps not surprisingly, all US missions supporting dissidents in their bids for secession failed. Because these groups were trying to gain their independence from states that were much more powerful, the dissidents would have required a far greater amount of military support to overthrow their governments than the United States could have delivered covertly.

On the more successful end of the spectrum, coups overthrew their targets 69 percent of the time. Almost all US-backed coups against democracies succeeded.[6] When faced with rebellious autocrats backed by the United States, democratic leaders had nowhere to turn to defend their government. Coups that targeted authoritarian regimes met with mixed success: three out of six successfully brought down their targets. Interesting, all of the authoritarian governments targeted in US-backed coups were of a personalist or military variety despite the fact that single-party authoritarian regimes were more prevalent during the Cold War. The appeal of targeting personalist dictators for regime change makes sense given the promise that such missions offer for dramatically changing the policy preferences of the target state. As Caitlin Talmadge notes, "Personalism . . . is fragile. Deliberately devoid of institutions separate from the leader, personalist systems require only that a rival arrest or assassinate a single person (and perhaps his immediate circle) to assume the reins of power."[7] By contrast, single-party systems—particularly well-institutionalized ones—make less appealing targets for coups. As Samuel Huntington first argued—and a later wave of scholarship confirmed—well-institutionalized authoritarian regimes tend to be more stable, have better civil-military relations, and are better able to co-opt their potential political opponents.[8]

Covert operations to influence foreign elections also brought America's preferred candidate to power 75 percent of the time. Democracies appear to be particularly vulnerable to regime change for several reasons. To begin with, covert actions against democracies use tactics that are much easier to conceal. For instance, it is relatively easy for a state to covertly transfer money to a foreign political party without revealing these actions to the central state or that party's opponents. Moreover, all democratic target states were US allies or nonaligned during the Cold War, thereby enabling US agents to move within the country and meet with influential politicians without attracting attention from the regime's security forces. However, in many of these cases, it is difficult to determine whether US actions were responsible for their victory. Many of the parties supported by Washington might well have won their elections without US help. For instance, in France, Italy, and Japan, the parties supported by the United States already had a steady advantage over their opponents in the polls, raising the question of whether the covert mission played any role in their victory. Similarly, in Lebanon, US-backed candidates prevailed in the country's parliamentary elections, but the United States had to intervene overtly soon afterward in order to ensure that those candidates could remain in power. The cases in which America's role seems to have been the most decisive required a relatively large commitment. For example, the United States gave at least $20 million to Chilean presidential candidate Eduardo Frei during his 1964 campaign. This amounted to $8 per voter and to over 50 percent of Frei's total campaign costs.[9]

Covert operations to encourage a democratic revolution in an authoritarian state by secretly backing pro-democratic groups were similarly successful. Four of the eight operations (50%) coincided with a democratic regime change in the target state. Again, however, the question of what would have happened without the US intervention remains salient. Good reasons exist to believe that American efforts did not play a decisive role in bringing about these democratic transformations. For one, in many of these cases, Washington began to collaborate with pro-democracy groups after they were already quite powerful. For instance, US covert aid to the Solidarity movement in Poland began after the group had already claimed over 9 million members, suggesting that US support was not instrumental in creating or maintaining the organization.[10] Second, all seven covert operations to promote democratization in authoritarian states coincided with the "third wave of democratization" and gradual collapse of the Soviet Union. As such, they were uniquely positioned to succeed. They came to fruition at a time when a number of global factors were pushing states toward democratization and the Soviet Union was simultaneously retrenching its global influence and decreasing its covert aid to foreign communists.[11] Supporting this argument, several scholars have questioned the effectiveness of the National Endowment for Democracy (NED)—the main instrumented used by Washington during these operations in the 1980s—in promoting democracy.[12] For instance, James Scott and Carie Steele's study of the impact of NED grants on a country's level of democratization between 1990 and 1999 determined that "the democracy promotion hypothesis that suggests that allocation of NED funding results in greater democratization is firmly rejected. . . . NED aid neither produces democracy nor follows democratization."[13]

The third major factor influencing the likelihood that a covert operation will succeed is that nature of the targeted government. To see whether certain characteristics of a target state would make it more or less susceptible to covert regime change, I analyzed the impact of a variety of potential factors on the short-term effectiveness of America's Cold War covert regime changes.[14] In the following analysis, variables with theoretical significance for this project were selected, as well as variables that existing studies have shown to be predictors of victory in interstate or civil war.[15] They include *Regime Type*,[16] *Material Capabilities*,[17] *Instability*,[18] *Economic Development*,[19] *Ongoing Civil War*,[20] *Ethno-Linguistic Fractionalization*,[21] *Alliance*,[22] and *Type of Covert Operation*.[23] Because the dependent variable is dichotomous (i.e., short-term success or failure), multivariate probit analysis was used to compare the effects of the independent variables.[24]

Table 4.1 reports the findings of four probit models. Because of the low number of cases (sixty-four) within the sample, the statistical significance of each individual variable will naturally decrease as additional factors were added (as demonstrated in model 3), so the results were broken into four models. Model 1 analyzes the success rates of the five different covert tactics. Model 2 examines eight major characteristics of a target state. Model 3 encompasses all of the variables in the previous two models. Finally, model 4 calculates each variable independently—without controlling for the others—as a robustness check to capture the direction of each effect.

Four results stand out from the analysis. First, in accordance with the arguments developed earlier in the chapter, model 1 shows that the type of covert tactic used significantly affected the mission's odds of success. Covert

Table 4.1 Probit analysis of short-term effectiveness

Variable	Model 1	Model 2	Model 3	Model 4
Assassination	–0.54		–0.74	0.02
Coup	0.85*		0.70	0.81**
Dissidents	–1.26***		–1.08*	–1.16***
Meddling in Elections	0.78**		0.43	1.26***
Democracy Promotion	0.18		0.002	0.31
Polity Score		0.11***	0.06	0.10***
Material Capabilities		–4.61	–4.52	–9.68*
Instability		–0.34	0.05	–0.30
GDP per capita		–0.17**	–0.10	0.23
Ongoing Civil War		–0.05	0.48	–0.07
Ethno-linguistic fractionalization		0.03	–0.20	–0.13
US Ally		0.93**	0.68	0.97***
Soviet Ally		–0.10	0.09	–0.79**

Significance: * –10%, ** –5%, *** –1%.

operations that involved tactics where the United States typically had to do comparatively little to bolster the power of the opposition forces relative to the central government—coups and covertly meddling in foreign elections—had a positive and significant effect on short-term success. By contrast, the covert tactic that generally required the largest commitment of resources to strengthen the opposition forces relative to the regime—supporting armed dissidents—had a negative and significant impact on the mission's odds of success.

Second, a state's level of democracy had a positive and statistically significant impact on the likelihood of a successful regime change. Specifically, the higher the target state's polity score (i.e., the more democratic the state), the easier it was for the United States to replace the target government. This supports the argument, developed in the previous section, that democracies are susceptible to regime change because of a combination of factors: (1) covert tactics used against democracies are easier to conceal and often more successful; (2) democratic leaders are often ill prepared to defend themselves against military coups; (3) in the cases where the United States tried to covertly influence the outcome of a foreign democratic election, some of the parties may have won their election even without US support, thus artificially inflating the success rate for these operations.

Third, the probit models suggest that a state's Cold War allegiance had an impact on the short-term effectiveness of America's interventions. Although being a US ally had a positive and statistically significant effect in models 2 and 4, being a Soviet ally was only statistically significant in model 4. Given the centrality of the superpower alliance system to the Cold War, this lack of significance for Soviet allies in model 2 is somewhat surprising. One plausible reason is that alliance membership was heavily correlated with other important variables in the model—regime type and

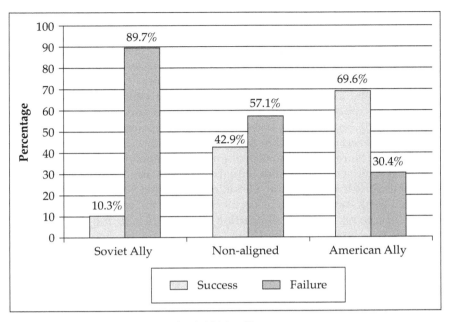

Figure 4.2. Short-term effectiveness by Cold War alliance.

material capabilities—which may have led to its significance being under-estimated by the model.

To see whether Soviet allies were harder to overthrow, figure 4.2 compares the short-term effectiveness of America's covert interventions by the Cold War allegiance of the target state.[25] A Pearson-s chi-squared test on a cross tabulation of the data in figure 4.2 yields a χ^2 of 19.3 and a p-value of 0.000064. This means that the null hypothesis that the target state's Cold War allegiance did not influence its likelihood of success can be rejected with over 99 percent confidence.[26] The historical record also supports this assessment: US-backed covert operations against Soviet allies succeeded in replacing the target government only 10.3 percent of the time because they pitted American-backed forces directly against Soviet military and security forces, thereby limiting the assistance that the United States could offer without risking war. This limitation quickly became apparent during the first wave of offensive missions in the late 1940s and early 1950s. As early as 1952, the State Department's Policy Planning Staff reported, "It has become impossible, with only the existing techniques and contacts . . . to operate in the satellite area of Eastern Europe. The perfection of totalitarian police state techniques is approaching '1984' efficiency to a degree where 'resistance' can probably exist only in the minds of the enslaved peoples of the Soviet orbit in Europe."[27]

Conversely, 42.9 percent of missions against nonaligned states succeeded because they pitted US-backed forces against Soviet-backed oppositions—rather than the Soviet forces directly. Given the bipolarity of the Cold War, both superpowers felt that they could not afford to lose a developing country into their opponent's camp. Thus, in almost every case where the United States targeted a nonaligned regime, the Soviet Union was also covertly backing the opposing side. Because Washington and Moscow each intervened covertly, however, they both faced the same constraints on the amount of military and economic aid that they could provide without risking military escalation. The result was that their efforts cancelled one another out, and each superpower had roughly equal success in the third world. Finally, 69.6 percent of missions against US allies succeeded because they generally targeted weak states with no ties to the Soviet Union, where the United States faced little to no domestic opposition. For instance, during operations in the Western Hemisphere, the United States had on average a military 217 times larger than the targeted state's and a military budget 3,413 times larger.[28]

Finally, one surprising finding was that a state's material capabilities did not have a statistically significant finding in model 2 (although it had a negative and statistically significant result in model 4). Given this study's argument that covert missions targeting strong countries usually fail because of a trade-off between size and secrecy, this finding was unexpected. Again, however, the likely reason for this finding is that material capabilities were correlated with several other important variables in this model—level of democracy and alliance—leading its significance to drop in model 2. Furthermore, the success of a few covert operations to influence elections in particularly powerful states (France, Italy, and Japan) may have skewed the results; if these cases were dropped from the analysis, material capabilities would have a significant and negative effect in model 2.

Combining these insights, we see that not all states made equally good targets for covert regime change. The short-term effectiveness of a covert operation varied depending on the target state's regime type, its material capabilities, its superpower alliance, and the type of covert tactic attempted. If the arguments made in this section are combined, it is clear that the ideal covert regime change for the United States during the Cold War would be a coup or election meddling against a weak, democratic ally of the United States—such as in Guatemala (1954), Chile (1962–1973), or the Dominican Republic (1960–68), as is discussed in chapter 8. The worst possible candidate for a covert regime change would be supporting an armed dissident movement against a powerful, authoritarian ally of the Soviet Union—such as the ones targeted in the covert rollback operations in Eastern Europe that are discussed in chapter 6.

In terms of tactics, another potential policy implication based on these findings is that states should limit their covert regime changes to funding elections, coups, and promoting democratic revolutions. Conversely, if a state finds itself in the position where its only covert options have been largely unsuccessful in the past—an assassination or supporting dissidents—it should seriously reconsider whether the intervention is worthwhile. Although this is sensible advice, three things should be kept in mind. For one, the two most successful tactics—funding elections and promoting coups—also happen to be the ones where the importance of US actions is most in doubt, meaning there is reason to suspect that many of the groups supported by the United States would have won their elections or ousted their target anyway. Second, though certain tactics may appear more successful, they will not always be an option: funding elections will only work in democratic states; promoting a democratic revolution in an authoritarian state requires preexisting pro-democratic groups in the target state; and coups require a willing collaborator in the target state. Lastly, the effectiveness of US-backed coups d'état appears to be declining over time. In fact, America's last successful Cold War coup was in 1973. A reasonable hypothesis for this decline is that greater state capacity in the developing world has made it more difficult for the United States to topple potential targets—unlike some of the weak banana republics that it targeted in the 1950s and 1960s. This hypothesis is consistent with Jonathan Powell and Clayton Thyne's study of all international coups between 1950 and 2010, which found that "the mean success rate is 48 percent during the entire time span. This rate saw early peaks around 1970 and 1980, and then a decline until the turn of the century."[29]

Long-Term Effects on Interstate Relations

Meeting the short-term goal of replacing a foreign government does not necessarily mean that the operation will serve the intervening state's interests in the long term. The remainder of this chapter is dedicated to investigating the long-term consequences of America's covert regime changes. I begin by asking how these operations influenced Washington's relationship with the target government. Recall that in chapter two, I argued that states pursue regime change in order to install foreign leaders who share similar foreign policy preferences, with the expectation that when the new leaders act in their own self-interest, they will be acting in the interests of the intervening state as well, thereby setting the stage for future cooperation between the two states. Now that we can see why policymakers launch these operations, however, the question arises of whether the missions actually achieve these goals. Do covert regime changes improve relations between the intervening and target states? Can interveners acquire reliable allies by covertly overthrowing foreign governments?[30]

Overall, I find that the answer is no. Covert regime changes seldom worked out as intended. Contrary to policymakers' expectations, changing the policy preferences of a foreign government requires more than simply changing the political leadership of that state. To understand why this is the case, one must consider the set of interstate disputes that lead to regime change. Most regime changes—whether they are conducted covertly or overtly—involve the intervention of a great power into a comparatively weak state. As discussed earlier, this raises the question of why the weaker state did not simply acquiesce to the stronger state's demands, rather than resisting, which led to the even worse outcome of being overthrown. This suggests that for the dispute to have escalated to the point of regime change in the first place, the target regime must have had a particularly strong incentive not to cooperate. Sometimes this occurred because the intervener demanded that the target government abandon a fundamental position of its political agenda without which it would be unable to remain in power. At other times, the intervener demanded that the target state take an action that it believed would jeopardize its future security, such as relinquishing certain military capabilities or forgoing an important alliance. Either way, the target government had good reason to refuse to submit to these demands.

Unfortunately for the intervener, whatever political pressures compelled the target government to stand up to its interests will hold true for its successor as well. Consequently, many of America's Cold War covert regime changes unfolded in a similar pattern: Washington installed a foreign leader, hoping that leader would pursue America's interests once in office. After assuming power, however, the new leader was confronted with political pressures similar to those that faced the government that was overthrown. Like the previous regime, the new government soon faced an unpleasant choice—pursuing Washington's interests and upsetting domestic audiences, or appeasing domestic audiences and upsetting the United States. Faced with this catch-22, some newly installed leaders defied their US backers, and conflict between the two countries reemerged.

Other new leaders opted to pursue the policies benefiting the United States. However, such actions came at a cost to them domestically as their domestic opponents were quick to deride them with accusations of being a US puppet. As a result, I find that the only new leaders who were willing to take on this role were those who remained highly dependent on aid from the United States to maintain their position in power. Yet, this arrangement fueled domestic opposition to their rule, which in turn increased the odds that they would be overthrown. Indeed, roughly half of all leaders installed via US-backed covert regime changes were violently removed from power via an assassination, revolution, or coup. Unsurprisingly, the governments that took over afterward often held particularly negative views of the United States, thus paving the way for conflict between the two countries to reemerge.

What about covert regime changes that fail to replace their target? How do failed operations impact interstate relations? If covert operations function as policymakers expect them to, then failed missions should have no effect on the intervener's relationship with the target state because the plausible deniability inherent in covert action should shield the intervening state from any negative repercussions. Yet, this seldom works out as interveners intend. Although governed by different dynamics, failed covert regime changes also have a negative impact on interstate relations because most covert regime changes do not remain covert. As a result, failed covert operations represent the worst possible outcome for policymakers: not only have they failed to topple their target, most likely they have also gotten caught in the act, thus further souring an already negative relationship with the foreign government.

MILITARIZED INTERSTATE DISPUTES

If covert regime changes work as policymakers expect them to, successful operations should change the target government's foreign policy preferences in ways that benefit the United States, and conflict between the two states should decrease. Failed covert operations should have no effect on Washington's relationship with the target state because of plausible deniability, and the level of conflict between the two states should remain the same. To see whether covert regime changes worked as policymakers anticipated they would, the following section analyzes how America's Cold War covert interventions influenced the likelihood of military conflict between the United States and the target state in the years following intervention.

My first dependent variable is whether the United States or the target regime initiated a militarized interstate dispute (MID) against the other state within a ten-, fifteen- or twenty-year period following the covert intervention.[31] MIDs are defined as "united historical cases of conflict in which the threat, display or use of military force short of war by one member state is explicitly directed towards the government, official representatives, official forces, property, or territory of another state. Disputes are composed of incidents that range in intensity from threats to use force to actual combat short of war."[32] MIDs are a good proxy for the quality of interstate relations in my analysis, because I argue that states often pursue covert regime changes in pursuit of objectives for which they are not willing to overtly fight. It is therefore important that I identify levels of interstate conflict short of actual war.

Figure 4.3 shows bivariate correlations between US-backed covert regime changes and MIDs involving the United States during the Cold War. The results show that the baseline probability that the United States would be involved in a MID with a foreign country within a given ten-year period during the Cold War was roughly 5.2 percent. However, this number grows to 35.2 percent for countries that had experienced a US-backed covert operation within the preceding ten years. In other words, states targeted for covert regime change were 6.7 times more likely to experience a MID with the

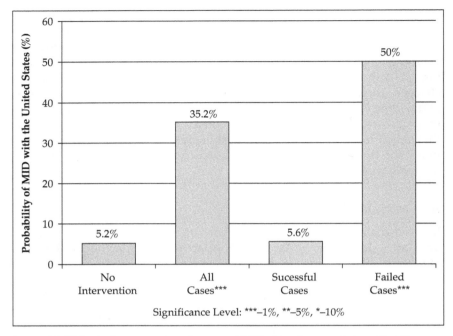

Figure 4.3. US-backed covert regime change and MIDs: bivariate correlations. Significance level: *–10%, **–5%, ***–1%.

United States in the ten years following intervention. Whether that covert operation succeeded or failed in its short-term goal of replacing the target regime, however, had a strong impact on the likelihood of conflict. When the covert operation successfully replaced the target government, there was little difference in the likelihood of a MID with that country compared to America's baseline (5.6% versus 5.2%). When the covert operation failed, however, Washington was ten times more likely to engage in a MID with that state within the next ten years.

Although the bivariate correlations are suggestive, one potential drawback is that they do not control for the possibility of selection bias. The central problem facing this project—or any study that attempts to estimate causal effects—is that this assessment must be made relative to the counterfactual of having not intervened.[33] In this case, one potential objection is that Washington did not randomly select target states for intervention, and the same factors that encouraged the United States to attempt a covert regime change against the target state may also increase the likelihood that the United States would subsequently experience a MID with that regime. If that is the case, then the relationships identified in the bivariate analysis—even though it is statistically significant—may be spurious. Nevertheless, scholars have identified several ways to mitigate the problem of selection bias. One such way is through a method of data preprocessing known as matching.

Matching works by pairing treated cases (i.e., states where the United States did not attempt a covert regime change during a specified period) with control cases (i.e., states where the United States did not attempt a covert regime change during a specified period) that are very similar to those that did. The logic behind matching is that by comparing two sets of cases that are as similar as possible in important regards except for the treatment, any differences that you see between the two groups can then be attributed to treatment effects.[34] Ho et al. explain, "The immediate goal of matching is to improve balance, the degree to which the treatment and control covariate distributions resemble each other . . . without losing too many observations in the process. The result of this process, when done appropriately, is considerably less model dependence; reduced potential for bias; less variance; and, as a result, lower mean squared error."[35]

Although matching may be the best way to deal with the problem of selection bias in this type of quantitative analysis, readers should also be aware of its limitations. In reality, countless factors influence a state's decision to launch a military intervention—many of which are unique and case specific and therefore not easily captured by any large-N analysis. The following probit models should therefore be interpreted as one piece of evidence in support of my arguments, alongside the bivariate correlations, the robustness checks in the online appendix, and the qualitative data presented in the case studies. In the following analysis, the MatchIt statistical program was used to generate a control group with one-to-two exact matching.[36] In other words, for every example of a US covert regime change, two control cases were identified. The variables used for matching were selected because they had been identified by previous studies as affecting the likelihood of interstate conflict.[37] They include *level of democratization, military strength, distance* to the United States, *alliance* with the United States or the USSR, and whether the target state had experienced a *MID with the United States* within the preceding twenty years.

Table 4.2 shows the results of three probit analyses using the same variables that were selecting for matching. Model 1 shows the effect of all covert regime change attempts on MID initiation; model 2 analyzes only successful cases; and model 3 looks at failed covert operations. The pattern revealed by the probit analysis is very similar to the bivariate correlations. The full sample of US-backed covert regime change attempts had a positive and statistically significant effect on the likelihood of a MID. As with the bivariate correlations, whether the covert mission actually replaced the target regime or not had an effect on the likelihood of conflict. Covert operations that succeeded in their short-term objective had a negative but statistically insignificant effect on the likelihood that the two states would experience an interstate dispute. Covert missions that failed had a positive and strongly

Table 4.2 US-backed covert regime change and MIDs: Probit analysis

Variable	Model 1	Model 2	Model 3
Polity score	−0.04	−0.05*	−0.02
Military strength	−8.37	−5.57	−9.89*
Distance to US, log	−0.73**	−0.59	−0.66*
Alliance with US	−0.27	−0.23	−0.08
Alliance with USSR	0.02	−0.08	−0.01
Past MID with US	1.00***	0.95***	1.15***
US Covert, all	0.99***		
US Covert, Successes		−0.39	
US Covert, Failures			1.53***
Constant	5.02	4.31	4.13

Significance: *−10%, **−5%, ***−1%.

statistically significant effect on the likelihood of a MID. These dynamics remained the same in the models looking at the fifteen- and twenty-year periods following intervention.

Measures of Interstate Relations Short of Conflict. To see whether covert interventions had an effect on interstate relations at levels short of a militarized dispute, I replicated each of the previous models, using four alternative dependent variables: (1) whether the target state voted alongside the United States in the United Nations (UN) General Assembly; (2) whether the target state voted with the Soviet Union during UN General Assembly votes; (3) the target state's subsequent foreign policy portfolio similarity (FPPS) with the United States; and (4) the target state's subsequent FPPS with the Soviet Union.[38] The results of these analyses mirrored the MID results. Successful covert operations had no significant effect in most of the models—the one exception being that successful interventions appeared to make target states less likely to vote alongside the United States in the UN General Assembly fifteen and twenty years afterward. This supports the argument that successfully toppling a foreign government did not make that state any more likely to cooperate with Washington. Failing to covertly overthrow a state, however, had a statistically significant effect on each of the alternative dependent variables. That is, states targeted in failed US-backed covert interventions were less likely to vote alongside Washington in the UN and more likely to vote alongside Russia in the ten-, fifteen- or twenty-year period following intervention. Similarly, the FPPS of states targeted in failed covert regime changes with the United States decreased following intervention, whereas their FPPS with Russia increased for all time periods.

A final possibility exists that while Washington's covert interventions did not improve cooperation in terms of the political or military variables discussed above, it did improve the target state's economic cooperation with the United States. To test for that possibility, I ran a series of models analyzing the effects of covert regime changes on target state's subsequent trade with the United States and the Soviet Union. As the online appendix shows, regardless of whether I looked at total trade, imports, or exports, Washington's covert interventions had no significant effect on the target state's subsequent trade with either the United States or the Soviet Union.

Altogether, these findings suggest that, at best, when the covert operation successfully replaced the target regime, the quality of the relationship between the United States and the target government remained roughly the same. Contrary to policymakers' expectations, successful covert regime changes did not improve their relationship with the target government. This trend remained consistent whether I analyzed MIDs, FPPS, UN voting behavior, or trade. These findings mesh with the argument that it is difficult to alter the policy preferences of another state via regime change because the same political pressures that compelled the target government to act against the intervener's interests will hold true for their successor as well. When the covert operation failed, however, it hurt Washington's relationship with the target state. In these cases, the United States was significantly more likely to experience militarized conflict with the state afterward, and the target state was less likely to cooperate with the United States—and more likely to cooperate with the Soviet Union—in terms of its UN voting behavior and FPPS. These findings are consistent with the argument that failed covert operations sour an already negative relationship with the target regime.

Effects of Covert Regime Change on the Target State

The following section explores the impact of America's covert regime changes on several characteristics of the targeted states, including their subsequent level of democratization as well as the likelihood that they will experience a civil war or episode of mass killing in the years following intervention. Although several existing studies have analyzed the effects of overt regime change on all of these factors, there has been little research to date specifically analyzing the effect of covert interventions.

DEMOCRATIZATION

The existing literature is divided on the question of whether states can use regime change to spread democracy abroad. Optimists argue that regime change can increase a state's level of democracy, and point to successful examples, such as West Germany and Japan following WWII, to make their case.[39] Pessimists respond that these successes are outliers and point out that the majority of regime changes do not lead to increased democratization.[40] Virtually all empirical studies measuring the effects of overt regime change side with the pessimists.[41] One assumption implicit in many of these studies is that the United States and other democracies wanted to promote democracy via their regime changes. Considering that these studies only look at overt cases, this assumption may be warranted. When it comes to America's Cold War covert regime changes, however, that assumption does not seem to hold. Although 12 percent of covert cases were designed to bring about a democratic revolution in an authoritarian state, 10.6 percent of cases sought to do precisely the opposite by overthrowing a democratically elected government and replacing them with an autocrat. Most covert regime changes, however, were not designed to change the regime type of the target state one way or the other—that is, either the United States sought to replace one dictator with another, or they sought to help one party win in a democratic election. Given these conflicting objectives, it is unclear if we should expect the interventions to have a consistent effect on their target states' level of democracy if they worked out as policymakers intended. Alternatively, one could imagine that America's covert interventions might unintentionally have a negative impact on the target state's subsequent level of democracy by destabilizing its political system and undermining the state's political institutions. The sole academic study analyzing the effect of covert regime changes found that American covert "interventions"—which includes both regime change and regime maintenance efforts in their sample—decreased the odds that their targets would become a democracy by roughly 30 percent over twenty years.[42] To see whether this trend holds true for my sample of US-backed covert attempts, the following section analyzes the effects of a covert regime change on the target state's level of democracy in the years following intervention.

Figure 4.4 shows a bivariate analysis of US-backed covert regime changes and the average change in a state's polity score during the Cold War. The results show that in a given ten-year period during the Cold War, countries that had not experienced a covert intervention increased their polity score by 0.73 point on average. This baseline is consistent with the gradual worldwide trend toward democratization that occurred during this time. Countries targeted in an unsuccessful regime change, however, had a 1.5-point average increase in their polity score—a finding that is surprising considering that Washington did not actually replace their governments. Countries that the United States successfully overthrew, by contrast, showed a dramatic and statistically significant decrease of 0.79 point in their polity scores in the ten years following the covert intervention, reflecting, in part, the six democratic governments that were ousted during US-backed military coups.

As with the previous analysis of MIDs, the above bivariate analysis is suggestive in its findings but does not control for the possibility of selection bias. In other words, the same factors that led the United States to pursue a regime change against the target government may also have an impact on their level of democracy in the following ten years. I therefore again used

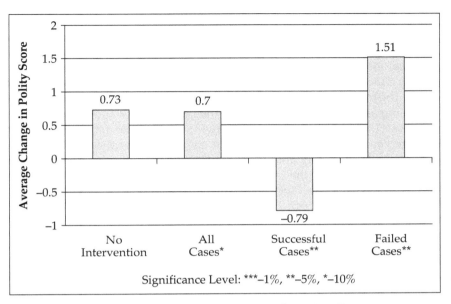

Figure 4.4. US-backed covert regime change and average change in polity score. Significance level: *–10%, **–5%, ***–1%.

matching to control for the possibility of selection bias. The sample of control cases was matched using variables identified by previous studies as influencing a state's level of democratization.[43] These variables include *regime type*, the state's previous *maximum level of democratization, economic development, ethno-linguistic fractionalization, state age, population, civil war, interstate war, geographic region,* and whether the country had been a *British colony.*[44] Once these variables are controlled for and a linear regression is run on the matched sample of cases, Washington's covert interventions did not have a consistent or significant impact on target states' level of democratization in any of the models. This suggests that the bivariate correlations should be taken with a grain of salt. Although some states overthrown by the United States undoubtedly were less democratic afterward, we cannot say that the cumulative effect of all of America's covert Cold War interventions had a significant impact on their targets' subsequent level of democratization once we control for the possibility of selection bias.

CIVIL WAR

What effect do covert operations have on the domestic stability of target states? Are targeted states more likely to enjoy stability afterward, or will they devolve into civil war? Looking only at overt cases, multiple studies have found that regime changes increase the likelihood of civil war. For example, one study by Goran Peic and Dan Reiter argues, "FIRCs make civil wars more likely because they wreck state infrastructural power or change political institutions." However, the authors find that this effect only occurred if the regime change came after an interstate war. In these cases, they find, "The magnitudes of these effects are considerable, as imposing an FIRC following an interstate war increases the risk of civil war onset more than eightfold."[45] A study by Alexander Downes, by contrast, found that regime change can increase the likelihood of civil war regardless of whether it occurred after an interstate war or not.[46] Downes explains, regime change "tends to undermine the imposed leader who—by providing benefits to interveners—sows grievances among his population and raises the risk of rebellion."[47] To see whether the same dynamics occur for covert cases, the following section analyzes the effects of US-backed covert regime changes on a target state's likelihood of experiencing a civil war within ten, fifteen or twenty years of intervention.[48]

Figure 4.5 shows bivariate correlations between US-backed covert regime changes and civil wars during the Cold War. The results show that the baseline probability that a foreign country would experience a civil war within a given ten-year period during the Cold War was roughly 19.9 percent. However, this number grows to 39.7 percent for countries that had experienced a US-backed covert operation within the preceding ten years. This effect was consistent for both successful and failed covert operations. When the covert operation successfully replaced the target government, the prob-

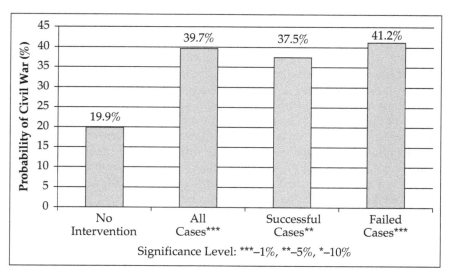

Figure 4.5. US-backed covert regime change and civil war: bivariate correlations. Significance level: *–10%, **–5%, ***–1%.

ability that the state experienced a civil war within the next ten years increased to 37.5 percent. When the covert operation failed, however, the probability of a civil war increased to 41.2 percent—more than twice the rate compared to states that had not experienced an intervention.

Although these bivariate correlations are suggestive, the problem of selection bias remains; namely, the same factors that led to a civil war in the target state may also have encouraged the United States to pursue regime change there. Once again, I used matching to control for this problem. Variables used for matching in this model include *level of democratization, regime age, economic development, population, ethnic-linguistic fractionalization, political instability, percentage mountainous terrain, geographic region*, and whether the state has experienced a *civil war* or *defeat in an interstate war* within the past twenty years.[49]

Table 4.3 reports the results of three probit models. Model 1 shows the effect of all covert attempts on the likelihood of civil war; model 2 analyzes only successful cases; and model 3 looks at failed covert operations. The results are similar to the bivariate correlations. Overall, model 1 shows that the states targeted in a US-backed covert regime change were more likely to experience a civil war within ten years. When the mission succeeded in replacing the target regime, however, the opposite appeared to be true—although this result was not statistically significant. When the operation failed to replace its target, the likelihood of civil war increased and was highly significant. The results remained consistent in the fifteen- and twenty-year models as well.

These findings make sense given what we know about the destabilizing effects that overt regime change have on target states. The same pathways to conflict described in the existing literature for overt regime changes hold true for covert operations as well. In addition, covert regime changes may be particularly predisposed toward civil war because many missions are explicitly

Table 4.3 US-backed covert regime change and civil war: Probit analysis

Variable	Model 1	Model 2	Model 3
Polity score	0.01	0.01	0.02
Wealth	−1.03***	−0.88***	−1.07***
Population	0.18	0.16	0.17
Ethnic fractionalization	0.90*	0.93*	1.04*
Mountainous terrain	0.03**	0.03**	0.03***
Civil war (20 years)	1.57***	1.59***	1.73***
Defeat interstate war (20 years)	0.95*	0.83*	0.96*
New state	0.87	0.78	0.93
Political instability	−1.25***	−1.14***	−1.37***
US Covert, all	0.77**		
US Covert, Successes		−0.21	
US Covert, Failures			1.20***
Constant	3.96*	3.33	4.03

Significance: * −10%, ** −5%, *** −1%.

designed to destabilize the target regime. Moreover, many covert operations directly provide arms to secessionist movements or groups currently engaged in a civil war, which likely extends the length of these conflicts.[50]

MASS KILLINGS

Does covert regime change affect the likelihood that the target government will commit mass atrocities against its population? In a separate study with Alexander Downes, we argue that regime changes often lead to an increase in government-sponsored episodes of mass killing within the target state for two reasons. First, autocratic leaders installed via regime changes often lack a domestic base of support in their own right and therefore resort to mass killing in an effort to consolidate their control on power; democratic leaders, by contrast, decreased the likelihood of state-led mass killings because democracy imposes significant barriers to government violence. Second, as demonstrated in the previous section, regime changes increase the likelihood of civil war, which in turn creates incentives for the target government to repress its population.[51] To see whether these dynamics held true for America's Cold War interventions, the following section analyzes the effects of US-backed covert regime changes on a target state's likelihood of experiencing an episode of mass killing within ten years of intervention. The measure that I use for this analysis comes from the State-Led Mass Killing dataset developed by Jay Ulfelder and Benjamin Valentino. It defines an episode of state-led mass killing as "any episode in which the actions of state agents result in the intentional death of at least 1,000 noncombatants from a discrete group in a period of sustained violence."[52]

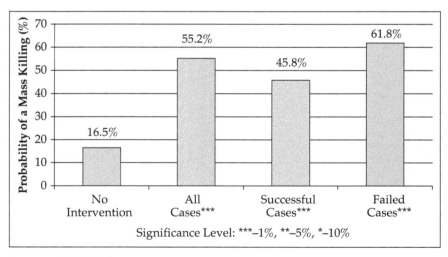

Figure 4.6. US-backed covert regime change and mass killings: bivariate correlations. Significance level: *–10%, **–5%, ***–1%.

Figure 4.6 shows bivariate correlations between US-backed covert regime changes and episodes of mass killing during the Cold War. The results show that baseline probability that a foreign country would experience an episode of mass killing within a given ten-year period during the Cold War was roughly 16.5 percent. This number grows to 55.2 percent for countries that had experienced a US-backed covert operation. Unlike in the previous analyses, whether that covert operation succeeded or failed in its short-term goal of replacing the target regime did not change the direction of this effect. States targeted in successful operations were 2.8 times more likely to experience an episode of mass killing, whereas states targeted in failed covert missions were 3.7 times more likely.

Once again, I used matching to control for the possibility of selection bias, using the same variables as in the preceding analysis of civil war. Table 4.4 reports the results of three probit models. Overall, the results are similar to the bivariate correlations and confirm my theoretical predictions. Failed covert regime changes had a positive and statistically significant effect on the likelihood that the target state would experience an episode of mass killing within the ten years following intervention. Successful operations had a positive but insignificant effect after matching, although additional tests reported in the online appendix show that the significance of this effect was contingent on whether the United States promoted democracy or authoritarianism during the operation.

Taken together, these results suggest that covert regime changes can have disastrous consequences for civilians within the target states. Countries that were targeted by the United States for a covert regime change during the Cold War were more likely to experience a civil war or an episode of mass killing afterward, and some states were less democratic as well. From the perspective of American leaders, however, these costs might be justified if

Table 4.4 US-backed covert regime change and mass killing: Probit analysis

Variable	Model 1	Model 2	Model 3
Polity score	−0.04	−0.04*	−0.02
Wealth	−0.70***	−0.59***	−0.60***
Population	0.20**	0.18**	0.19**
Ethnic fractionalization	−1.00**	−0.83*	−0.90**
Mountainous terrain	0.01	0.01	0.01
Civil war (20 yrs)	0.59**	0.58**	0.62**
Defeat interstate war (20 yrs)	0.13	0.06	0.09
New state	1.09*	0.97*	1.01*
Political instability	−0.49*	−0.38	−0.45
US Covert, all	1.03***		
US Covert, Successes		0.50	
US Covert, Failures			1.02***
Constant	3.00*	2.63*	2.22

Significance: *−10%, **−5%, ***−1%.

covert regime changes actually achieved the policy goals that they had set for them. Here too, however, my analysis paints an unpromising picture.

Washington launched its covert regime changes to resolve intractable security disputes by installing leaders with similar policy preferences to their own in the hopes that their relationship with the target state would improve afterward. Although the theoretical appeal of regime change is understandable, its record in practice was far less impressive. To begin, more than 60 percent of covert operations failed to replace their targets, and because most operations did not remain covert, these failed attempts further soured Washington's already negative relationship with the target state. Even nominally successful covert regime changes—where US-backed forces came to power—seldom delivered on their promise to improve interstate relations. Newly installed leaders may have intended to pursue Washington's preferred policies, but once in power, they found that they are constrained by the same domestic and international pressures as their predecessors. Thus, even when a covert regime change succeeded in its short-term objective of replacing the target regime, the target state's relationship with Washington was unlikely to significantly improve in the long term.

One important thing to remember though is that the effectiveness of any foreign policy must also be judged in the context of its likely foreign policy alternatives.[53] Regime changes are unique in that they are often attempted in response to particularly intractable interstate disputes. Indeed, part of the appeal of regime change is that it offers the possibility of transforming interstate relations when in situations where coercion-based strategies, such as economic sanctions or threatening to use military force, are unlikely to succeed; the logic being that if the United States could not bribe or coerce a foreign leader into pursuing America's preferred policies, regime change enabled Washington to replace that leader with someone who would. Nevertheless, this chapter suggested that the transformative appeal of regime change is overstated. Simply installing a new leader will not resolve the underlying conflict between the two states if the intervener's preferred policies cut against the target state's enduring national interests or are opposed by powerful domestic opposition forces. Only in the relatively rare situations where the intervening state's policy preferences align with those of the majority of the target state's population does regime change offer the potential of changing the target state's behavior over the long term. Paradoxically, however, regime change may be overkill in these situations. If the majority of the target state's population agrees with the policy preferences of the intervener, then these forces may be able to change their government's behavior without outside assistance, or the target government may be susceptible to coercive diplomacy. In sum, my analysis suggests that states have recurrently overestimated the benefits of covert regime change and underestimated its costs. Policymakers would therefore be wise to think twice before launching such operations in the future.

CHAPTER 5

Overview of US-Backed Regime Changes during the Cold War

> As the international situation develops, every day makes more
> evident the importance of the role which will have to be played by
> covert operations if our national interests are to be adequately
> protected.
> —George Kennan, Memorandum to Frank Wisner, January 6, 1949

Whereas the preceding three chapters introduced several theories regarding the causes, conduct, and effectiveness of regime change, this chapter puts those theories in context by providing a historical overview of America's experience with regime change during the Cold War. Looking at the broad trends in America's regime change policy highlights the shifting security interests driving US behavior over this period, the reasons why leaders preferred covert conduct, and the general utility of covert operations. The case studies in chapters 6 through 8 then test my theories in greater detail by analyzing several covert regime changes in depth.

In broadest terms, as figure 5.1 shows, each administration had at least three covert regime changes ongoing during its time in office. Variation in the frequency of these operations over time, however, suggests that US behavior was governed more by international dynamics than differences in domestic party ideology. In fact, many ongoing covert operations continued from one administration to another, across party lines, without interruption. Eisenhower's Republican administration had the greatest total number of ongoing interventions, but Democratic President Kennedy had the highest ratio of ongoing covert operations per year in office. All told, Democratic presidents authorized at least fifty-six regime changes during the eighteen years that they were in power during the Cold War (1947–89), compared to at least sixty-two missions by Republican presidents during their twenty-five years in charge. Operations against states in the Western Hemisphere remained relatively constant throughout the era; however, US interventions against the Soviet bloc and its allies mirrored Cold War dynamics. The early Cold War was the heyday of US-backed covert regime changes as Truman and Eisenhower sought to overthrow pro-Soviet regimes in Eastern Europe and prevent communist and socialist political parties from winning democratic elections in Western Europe and Japan. A second wave in the late 1950s–1960s aimed to prevent the emergence of Soviet-allied regimes in newly decolonized states in the Middle East, Africa, and Southeast Asia. The frequency of US interventions dipped during the 1970s because of post-Vietnam fatigue and heightened scrutiny of covert actions following the Watergate scandal and Church Committee investigations. As US-Soviet relations soured in the late 1970s, however, Carter launched multiple covert missions, including those in Afghanistan and Nicaragua, which were then expanded under Reagan and Bush during the so-called "Second Cold War."

The chapter is split into three sections, corresponding to the three types of security interests motivating these operations: offensive, preventive, and hegemonic. Each section outlines the motives behind that type of regime change, followed by a discussion of how each type of operation fulfilled the two prerequisites for intervention introduced in chapter 2: namely, that they were in response to a chronic, security-oriented interstate dispute and that the intervening state must have identified a plausible political alternative to the target regime. Although this chapter deals with both covert and overt cases, the six overt cases receive closer individual attention because they pose

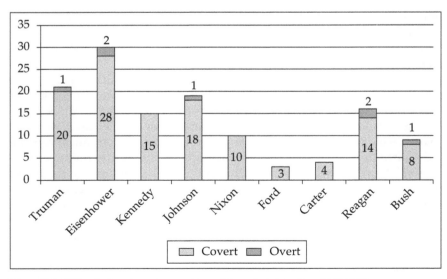

Figure 5.1. US-backed regime change attempts by administration, 1947–1989.

a stronger challenge to my assertion that states generally prefer to conduct their regime changes covertly.

Offensive Regime Change: Rollback

The United States conducted twenty-three covert and two overt offensive operations against the USSR and its allies during the Cold War. These missions were part of a larger US strategy to roll back Soviet influence by replacing Soviet-backed regimes with nationalist governments friendly to Washington or, at the very least, unwilling to cooperate with Moscow. By fracturing the Soviet bloc, the United States hoped to increase its relative military power and gain access to crucial territory in the event of war.[1] At the same time, however, US planners assiduously sought to avoid direct military conflict. They understood that war with the Red Army would be extremely costly and potentially catastrophic after Moscow acquired nuclear weapons.

How did these operations fulfill the two prerequisites for intervention? First, by the time the United States decided to pursue rollback, the conflict between the superpowers had reached a stage of chronic mutual mistrust. Although scholars continue to debate whether the Cold War was inevitable, both sides in the debate agree that the superpowers' mutually incompatible postwar aims were bound to cause a series of major disagreements.[2] On the one side, the Soviet Union's primary concern was to protect itself against another invasion. Toward this end, Stalin sought "to consolidate Soviet territorial gains, establish a Soviet sphere of influence in eastern Europe, and have a voice in the political fate of Germany and—if possible—of Japan."[3] The United States, by contrast, feared that "if Eurasia came under Soviet domination, either through military conquest or political and economic 'assimilation,' America's only potential adversary would fall heir to enormous natural resources, industrial potential and manpower."[4] Further complicating their dispute, each side wanted the states in Eastern Europe to adopt its preferred system of government—capitalist liberalism or communist authoritarianism. Yet, these political systems require radically different institutional arrangements, which prevented political compromise.

The bipolar international system that emerged out of WWII ensured that neither superpower had a sufficient military advantage to unilaterally force its opponent to submit to its demands. At the war's end, the Soviet Union had approximately 12.5 million mobilized troops compared to America's 12 million.[5] By 1948, these numbers had dropped to 2.87 and 1.36 million, respectively, but the Soviet numerical advantage was offset by the fact that the United States had a nuclear monopoly until 1949.[6] Because neither side could impose their position by force, it was clear that the two states would have to negotiate over the management of postwar Europe. But negotiations stalled due to the commitment problem inherent in their dispute: Neither super-power believed that it could acquiesce to the other's demands without jeopardizing its future security. Stalin feared that if he relinquished control over Eastern Europe, the United States or a resurgent Germany could then use this territory for an attack on the Soviet Union. Instead, he reasoned, "we cannot achieve anything serious if we begin to give in to intimidation or betray uncertainty. To get anything from this kind of partner, we must arm ourselves with the policy of tenacity and steadfastness."[7] For their part, US officials feared that once the USSR recovered from its wartime losses, it would be positioned to overrun Western Europe. The feeling in Washington at the time was summarized in the influential Clifford-Elsey report, which argued, "Soviet leaders believe a conflict is inevitable between the U.S.S.R. and capitalist states, and their duty is to prepare the Soviet Union for this conflict."[8] Therefore, "it is highly dangerous to conclude that the hope of international peace lies only in 'accord,' 'mutual understanding' or 'solidarity' with the Soviet Union."[9]

The first prerequisite—a chronic and irreconcilable security-based dispute—remained largely constant between the United States and the USSR throughout the Cold War. However, the second prerequisite—the existence of a plausible alternative government—varied by country over time, and US behavior varied with it. As this project would predict, the United States only launched offensive operations in countries when policymakers believed that widespread opposition to the Soviet-backed regime was available to support. As early as 1949, Policy Planning Staff Paper 59 pointed out, "Considerations of the relative vulnerability of the various satellites must enter into our calculations. . . . Obviously our policy both with regard to methods and tempo must differ among the several orbit countries."[10] For this reason, America's rollback operations can be grouped into two waves corresponding to periods when Moscow could not contain opposition movements within its satellites. The first wave came early in the Cold War as the USSR tried to consolidate its hold over the territory it had gained during WWII. Once Moscow secured control over these regions, however, rollback in Eastern Europe came to a halt for the next twenty years, only to resume in the 1980s when the Soviet Union's economic woes and domestic problems limited its ability to project power internationally, allowing domestic opposition movements to reemerge within several of its satellite states.

OFFENSIVE: COVERT CASES

America's first covert offensive operations sought to roll back Soviet influence in Eastern Europe by toppling the regimes that the USSR had established following WWII. In February 1946, Deputy Chief of Mission to the Soviet Union George Kennan laid the foundation for these operations in an influential 5,500-word telegram to Washington, commonly known as the "long telegram," wherein he argued that the Soviet Union's "neurotic view of world affairs" and "instinctive Russian sense of insecurity" prevented long-term cooperation with the United States. Instead, he argued, the Soviets "have learned to seek security only in patient but deadly struggle for total destruction of rival power, never in compacts and compromises with it."[11] In July 1947, Kennan expanded on these ideas in an influential *Foreign Affairs* piece, "The Sources of Soviet Conduct," which was published under the pseudonym "X" so as not given the impression that it reflected the government's official policy. The "X Article" identified several vulnerabilities within the Soviet system. For one, Kennan noted that the Soviet Union was deeply insecure about its grasp on power and that Moscow relied on draconian policies, such as forced collectivization and purges, to maintain control. Moreover, internal divisions within the Soviet Communist Party prevented it from forming a cohesive plan of action. Consequently, he warned, if "anything were ever to disrupt the unity and efficacy of the Party as a political instrument, Soviet Russia might be changed overnight from one of the strongest to one of the weakest and most pitiable of national societies."[12]

Hoping to facilitate that collapse, Truman authorized a variety of initiatives developed by Kennan in his new position as director of the State Department's Policy Planning Staff, including "economic warfare" to inhibit economic growth, as well as psychological warfare "to influence attitudes in foreign countries in a direction favorable to the attainment of its objectives and to counteract effects of anti-US propaganda."[13] America's most aggressive tactic, however, was to "develop underground resistance, and facilitate covert and guerrilla operations" to overthrow the Soviet-backed regimes.[14] Concurrent with these rollback missions in Eastern Europe, the United States launched offensive regime changes against communist governments in China and North Korea.[15] Beginning in 1949 and increasing after the 1950 Soviet-Sino Treaty of Friendship, Washington launched several ill-fated covert operations to aid various anti-communist resistance movements within China. These included Muslim Hui clans under the direction of General Ma Pu-fang in northwest China, Chiang Kai-Shek's nationalist forces, anti-communist guerillas in Manchuria, nationalist guerillas in Burma under the direction of Li Mi, and Tibetan independence movements.[16] None of these operations made significant headway.

US planners strongly preferred covert conduct during offensive regime changes, to minimize the likelihood that these actions could lead to direct conflict with the Soviet Union, understanding that failure to do so "would in all probability start a global war."[17] Chapter 6 shows that all early covert operations failed calamitously, and hundreds of men died in poorly conceived operations to incite rebellion behind the Iron Curtain. Once Washington finally came to grips with the fact that all plausible political alternatives to the Soviet-backed regimes had disappeared, the first wave of offensive operations came to a halt. Although the United States continued a major propaganda campaign, including covertly creating and funding Radio Liberty and Radio Free Europe to broadcast anti-Soviet propaganda into the Soviet Union and its satellites as part of an orchestrated bid to undermine Moscow and keep the hopes of Eastern European dissidents alive until a later date.[18]

Carter revived rollback twenty years later to reverse several perceived Soviet advances on the world stage—the invasion of Afghanistan as well as the Iranian and Nicaraguan revolutions in 1979. Hoping to reverse these trends, Carter launched a limited offensive operation in Afghanistan and paved the way for operations in Cambodia and Nicaragua.[19] Reagan expanded these operations and initiated a covert mission to support the Solidarity movement in Poland, and in 1983, NSDD 75 revived rollback by calling on the United States "to contain and over time reverse Soviet expansionism by competing effectively on a sustained basis with the Soviet Union in all international arenas. . . . U.S. policies should seek wherever possible to encourage Soviet allies to distance themselves from Moscow in foreign policy and to move toward democratization domestically."[20] Although these operations were less aggressive than their 1950s counterparts, the United States was once again willing to pursue offensive missions in Eastern Europe because Moscow had lost its ability to neutralize anti-Soviet movements within its sphere of influence, thus once again allowing US officials to find plausible opposition groups to support.

As table 5.1 shows, all covert offensive operations employed similar tactics: The United States supported armed, anti-Soviet dissident movements in their bids to overthrow the central government and establish an independent regime. Other covert tactics simply could not achieve this goal. Assassinating a country's leader would only have brought another Soviet puppet to power, and any group of plotters small enough to secretly launch a coup d'état would, once in power, have been no match for Soviet forces. At the same time, the limited size of these operations hindered their likelihood of success. Eighty-seven percent of covert offensive regime changes failed because overthrowing a powerful Soviet ally required a level of support that the United States could not achieve covertly. Indeed, only three of the twenty-three covert offensive operations replaced their target. However, the Kremlin knew of America's involvement in all three cases—Poland, Afghanistan, and Nicaragua—and each allied the United States with a relatively powerful preexisting movement.[21]

OFFENSIVE: OVERT CASES

The United States pursued overt offensive regime change twice during the Cold War. The first occasion was during the Korean War. Although the war was not launched for the purposes of regime change, a series of early victories persuaded US policymakers to expand their war aims to include regime change. This situation met the rare standards for an overt intervention for

Table 5.1 US-backed offensive covert regime change attempts during the Cold War

Date	Target State	Target Government(s)	Tactics	Objective Achieved
1949–56	Albania	Single-party: Hoxha	Dissidents	–
1949–56	Belarusian SSR	Single-party: Stalin and Khrushchev	Dissidents	–
1949–56	Bulgaria	Single-party: Dimitrov and Cherenkov	Dissidents	–
1949–68	China	Single-party: Mao	Dissidents	–
1949–56	Czechoslovakia	Single-party: Gottwaldov and Zapotocky	Dissidents	–
1949–56	East Germany	Single-party: Pieck	Dissidents	–
1949–56	Estonian SSR	Single-party: Stalin and Khrushchev	Dissidents	–
1949–56	Hungary	Single-party: Rakosi	Dissidents	–
1949–56	Latvian SSR	Single-party: Stalin and Khrushchev	Dissidents	–
1949–56	Lithuanian SSR	Single-party: Stalin and Khrushchev	Dissidents	–
1949–56	Poland	Single-party: Bierut and Zawadzki	Dissidents	–
1949–56	Romania	Single-party Personal: Gheorghiu-Dej	Dissidents	–
1949–59	Soviet Union/ Russian SSR	Single-party: Stalin and Khrushchev	Dissidents	–
1949–56	Ukrainian SSR	Single-party: Stalin and Khrushchev	Dissidents	–
1950–53	North Korea	Single-party Personal: Kim	Dissidents	–
1958–68	Tibet	Single-party: Mao	Dissidents	–
1961–64	North Vietnam	Single-party: Ho	Dissidents	–
1961–68	Cuba[1]	Single-party Personal: Castro	Assassination, Dissidents	–
1979–89	Afghanistan	Soviet-occupied: Karmal and Najibullah	Dissidents	Yes
1980–89	Nicaragua[2]	Single-party: Ortega	Democracy promotion, Dissidents	Yes
1981–89	Poland	Single-party: Jaruzelski	Democracy promotion	Yes
1982–89	Cambodia	Single-party: Samrin	Dissidents	–
1982–89	Libya	Personal: Qaddafi	Coup, Dissidents	–
Total	**23**			**3**

[1]Classified as a hegemonic operation until 1961, when Cuba's alliance with the Soviet Union was solidified.
[2]Classified as a hegemonic operation until 1980, when Nicaragua's alliance with the Soviet Union was solidified.

two reasons. First, US planners were confident that they could achieve a quick and decisive victory. Following his successful Inchon campaign, MacArthur believed that he could exploit temporary North Korean weaknesses to achieve "a decisive and crushing blow" without the Soviet Union or China entering the war, and that if he failed to do so, "a return to the status quo ante bellum would not promise security."[22] Second, a short time horizon for intervention following North Korea's invasion precluded a purely covert approach. Although the CIA pursued a covert paramilitary mission to support North Korean dissidents throughout the war, the covert operation was woefully underequipped for the task.[23] The CIA relied primarily on South Korean intelligence and lacked the connections and resources to carry out the covert operation on its own.[24]

After several bloody border clashes along the 38th parallel, North Korea invaded South Korea on June 25, 1950, rapidly overwhelming its opponents and sweeping south. US policymakers were caught off guard by the invasion but quickly called on the UN Security Council to denounce the invasion and organize an armed response to repel the North.[25] In July, a UN coalition comprised primarily of American troops and under the unified command of US General Douglas MacArthur entered the war with the limited aim of preventing North Korea from conquering South Korea. The State Department's Policy Planning Staff, now headed by Paul Nitze, warned of the dangers of trying to pursue regime change at this point: "The risks of bringing on a major conflict with the U.S.S.R. or Communist China, if U.N. military action north of the 38th parallel is employed in an effort to reach a 'final' settlement in Korea, appear to outweigh the political advantages that might be gained from such further military action."[26] However, this calculus changed in September 1950 after McArthur launched a successful amphibious assault, known as the Inchon campaign, that dramatically reversed the situation on the ground and allowed UN forces to recapture the South Korean capital, Seoul. Afterward, MacArthur urged Truman to follow up on these gains and oust Kim Il-Sung's government in Pyongyang.

Truman agreed, provided that certain conditions were met—namely, that "at the time of the operation there was no entry into North Korea by major Soviet or Chinese communist forces, no announcements of intended entry, nor a threat to counter our operations militarily."[27] He was assured that these conditions would be fulfilled. CIA analysts doubted that the Soviets would overtly enter the war because their public statements and propaganda showed "no indication that it intends to intervene directly."[28] Military planners felt similarly toward China despite a warning from Chinese premier Zhou Enlai that China was prepared to enter the war if the United States crossed the 38th parallel. One CIA intelligence estimate from mid-October declared, "Their domestic problems are of such magnitude that the regime's entire domestic program and economy would be jeopardized by the strains and the material damage which would be sustained by a war with the U.S."[29]

Truman's decision to escalate in Korea was also likely bolstered by the fact that the US public appeared to support regime change. An October 1950 Gallup poll found that 64 percent of Americans agreed that the United States should fight past the 38th parallel until the North Korean regime surrendered (27% disagreed; 9% had no opinion).[30] The confluence of these circumstances suggested that the United States could score a quick and decisive victory with low potential security costs and public support—a rare occurrence for an offensive regime change.

These predictions soon proved false. Within a month, Chinese troops launched a surprise attack across the Yalu River into Korea, scoring a heavy blow against MacArthur's forces. Soon after, the United States canceled its plans for overt regime change, although it did continue its covert efforts to overthrow the North Korean regime throughout the war. These too failed, because, at least in part, of a lack of reliable intelligence within North Korea. The end result, as a declassified history by the CIA describes, was that these missions were "not only ineffective but probably morally reprehensible in the number of lives lost."[31]

America's second overt offensive mission of the Cold War in Libya (1986) is a more complicated case. Debate continues as to whether the Reagan administration intentionally targeted Libyan leader Muammar Qadaffi during the air strikes, sought to induce his overthrow, or pursued a more limited aim during the intervention, such as to discourage his support for terrorism. Some observers claim that American officials did not explicitly seek regime change but that it would have been a welcome side effect. Others, however, argue these claims are merely cover for what was essentially an assassination attempt all along. For instance, Seymour Hersh concluded in 1987 "that the assassination of Qaddafi was the primary goal of the Libyan bombing is a conclusion reached after three months of interviews with more than 70 current and former officials in the White House, the State Department, the Central Intelligence Agency, the National Security Agency, and the Pentagon."[32] Declassified documents from the time reveal that the CIA had prepared several studies on possible successors to Qadaffi, and NSC memos before the attack note that "DOD is planning strikes against targets that play a key role both in maintaining Qadaffi in power and in directing terrorist operations abroad."[33] Likewise, during deliberations for the attack, National Security Advisor Poindexter asked CIA director William Casey, "What are the prospects for political alternatives to Qadaffi should we get lucky?"[34] Similarly, Oliver North reflected, "By law, we couldn't specifically target him. But if Gaddafi happened to be in the vicinity of the Aziziyah Barracks in downtown Tripoli when the bombs started to fall, no one would have shed any tears."[35] Considering that CIA documents identify the Aziziyah Barracks as "Qadafi's principal personal residence," this likelihood appeared high.[36] In the end, however, this speculation was irrelevant. A phone call alerted Qadaffi, and he fled the compound minutes before the US bombing.

Assuming these actions constitute an overt regime change attempt, it is consistent with the theory put forth in this study. Reagan believed a surprise attack could "be successful in minimizing American losses and maximizing chances of the operation's success."[37] He was also confident that these actions would not provoke the Soviet Union because their alliance was "based on common short-term interests."[38] Public opinion was also on his side. Before the raid, 61 percent of Americans agreed that the United States should "covertly assassinate known terrorist leaders."[39] Consistent with a rally around the flag effect, 76 percent of Americans supported the bombing afterward.[40] Although the operation's timing is consistent with this study's theory, the motive differs somewhat from other offensive operations. Washington intervened not to weaken the Soviet bloc, but rather to prevent Qadaffi from continuing a variety of "anti-Western activities," including sponsoring several terrorist organizations that targeted the United States and its allies, providing aid to radical regimes, targeting Libyan expatriates and moderate Arab leaders for assassination, and supporting leftist guerilla movements throughout the world. In fact, one 1986 State Department report determined, "Qaddafi's commitment of political, economic and military resource in anti-Western activities worldwide may be surpassed only by the Soviet Union, its European allies, and possible North Korea or Cuba."[41] By replacing Qadaffi with a leader who would cease this campaign, US planners hoped to decrease the security threat posed by the Libyan regime.

Preventive Regime Change: Containment

Preventive regime change is closely tied to a second strategy that emerged early in the Cold War and remained the guiding force behind US policy for the next 45 years: containment. As with rollback, influential diplomat George Kennan is often considered the intellectual father of the strategy. In many ways, however, Kennan merely put a name to numerous policies that the United States pursued following World War II.[42] Kennan's "X article" outlined the logic behind containment in July 1947:

> In these circumstances, it is clear that the main element of any United States policy toward the Soviet Union must be that of a long-term, patient but firm and vigilant containment of Russian expansive tendencies. . . . Soviet pressure against the free institutions of the Western world is something that can be contained by the adroit and vigilant application of counterforce at a series of constantly shifting geographical and political points, corresponding to the shifts and maneuvers of Soviet policy.[43]

Kennan called on the United States to pursue a "strongpoint defense" that would "restrain and confine" Soviet advances into areas of vital strategic importance to the United States—namely, North America, Great Britain, Central Europe, and Japan.[44] Truman embraced the policy, and the United States began to pursue containment along a variety of fronts. Early containment initiatives include providing financial aid to Greece and Turkey to fight communist insurgencies in their countries, authorizing $13 billion in Marshall Plan aid to revitalize the economies of Western Europe, establishing the North Atlantic Treaty Organization (NATO), constructing a "strategic frontier" of US military bases in the countries neighboring the Soviet Union, and developing a nuclear deterrence doctrine.[45]

Where these actions seemed insufficient to prevent a state from joining the Soviet camp, however, preventive regime change offered a potential solution. In 1947, Truman launched the first preventive regime changes of the Cold War to ensure that communist parties would not win democratic elections in Italy and France. It was his successor, Eisenhower, however, who elevated these covert missions "to a position of unprecedented prominence as a tool of American foreign and defense policy."[46] While Eisenhower scaled back the offensive operations in Eastern Europe, he embraced preventive regime change throughout the world. Unlike Kennan, who thought the United States should focus its containment efforts solely on "strongpoint defense" of areas of major strategic importance, later policymakers saw a broader role for regime change more in line with the idea of "perimeter defense," wherein the United States would try to prevent Soviet moves wherever they tried to expand—even in weak states in the third world.[47] One National Security report, NSC 162/2, warned, "Their vast manpower, their essential raw materials, and their potential for growth are such that their absorption within the Soviet camp would greatly, perhaps decisively, alter the world balance of power to our detriment." To prevent this, Eisenhower ordered the United States to "take all feasible diplomatic, political, economic, and covert measures to counter any threat of a party or individuals responsive to Soviet power to achieve dominant control in a free world country."[48] This expansive conception of the national interest resonated with Eisenhower's successors, each of whom launched at least one preventive regime change in the third world.

How do preventive operations meet this study's two necessary conditions for intervention? First, both superpowers believed that any gains for their rival's alliance system constituted a direct threat to their security. The bipolar international system made the fight for allies a zero-sum game, and each side viewed the other's moves with apprehension. As the 1949 Clifford-Elsey Report emphasized, "Beyond the borders now under her control, the Soviet Union is striving to penetrate strategic areas, and everywhere agents of the Soviet government work to weaken the governments of other nations and achieve ultimate isolation and destruction."[49] Compounding these direct threats, American officials throughout the Cold War accepted the domino theory—the belief that the 'loss' of an allied or neutral state into the Soviet sphere would make that state's neighbors more likely to ally with the Soviets as well.[50] In Eisenhower's words, "You have broader considerations that might follow what you would call the 'falling domino' principle. You have a row of dominoes set up, you knock over the first one, and what will happen to the last one is the certainty that it will go over very quickly. So you could have a beginning of a disintegration that would have the most profound influences."[51] Once US policymakers accepted the logic of domino theory, they could no longer evaluate the strategic value of any potential target state in isolation; instead, any loss to the Soviet camp was seen to "seriously endanger in the short term, and critically endanger in the long term, United States security interests."[52]

The bipolar system constrained the superpowers' ability to resolve conflicts in the third world through actions short of regime change.[53] Caught in a security competition that neither state could win by simply building up its own military, each had to rely on external balancing—allying with other states—to protect its security.[54] This meant that allies were in high demand. As such, both superpowers rejected neutrality as a feasible position for countries in the developing world, and each side viewed the Non-Aligned Movement skeptically.[55] Eisenhower's secretary of state, John Foster Dulles, explained, "The principle of neutrality . . . has increasingly become an obsolete conception, and, except under very exceptional circumstances, it is an immoral and short-sighted conception."[56] This left few options for leftist leaders in the developing world who faced the threat of a US-instigated regime change. Neutrality was unfeasible, and although they could renounce their leftist political agenda, this would mean abandoning their core beliefs and base of political support.

This study's second condition for intervention—a plausible alternative to the target regime—was easy to find in most cases. Many preventive missions occurred either in the context of a heated election or during a civil war. Consequently, the United States could simply throw its weight behind the leftists' preexisting opponents. The Soviet Union frequently did the reverse, and the local dispute would escalate into a pseudo-covert proxy conflict between the superpowers.

PREVENTIVE: COVERT CASES

All told, Washington conducted twenty-five covert preventive operations in Western Europe, the Middle East, Southeast Asia, and Africa to provide "assistance to underground resistance organizations, guerillas and refugee liberation groups; support of indigenous and anti-communist elements in threatened countries of the free world."[57] As table 5.2 shows, the timing and location of these missions shifted over the course of the Cold War as the superpowers fought for control over different geographic regions.

The earliest covert preventive operations followed shortly after World War II as the United States worked to consolidate anti-Soviet strongholds in

Table 5.2 US-backed preventive covert regime change attempts during the Cold War

Date	State	Target Government(s)	Tactic(s)	Objective Achieved
1947–52	France	Democracy: Leftist parties	Election interference	Yes
1947–68	Italy	Democracy: Leftist parties	Election interference	Yes
1952–53	Iran	Democracy/Monarchy: Mossadegh	Coup	Yes
1952–68	Japan	Democracy: Leftist parties	Election interference	Yes
1954–58	Indonesia	Democracy/Personal: Sukarno & Pro-Sukarno parties	Coup, Dissidents, Election interference	–
1955–57	Syria	Democracy: Multiple targets	Assassination, Coup	Aborted[1]
1957–58	Lebanon	Democracy: Leftist and Arab parties	Election interference	Yes
1959–73	Laos	Democracy/Personal/Warlord	Dissidents, Election interference	–
1960	Congo	Democracy: Lumumba	Assassination, Coup	Yes
1963	South Vietnam	Personal: Diem	Coup, (Inadvertent Assassination)	Yes
1964–72	Angola	Leftists forces/ Colonial authorities[2]	Dissidents	–
1964–68	Mozam-bique	Leftists forces/ Colonial authorities[3]	Dissidents	–
1964–67	Somalia	Democracy: Leftist parties	Election interference	–
1965–69	Thailand	Military-personal: Leftist parties	Election interference	–
1967–71	South Vietnam	Military: Leftist parties	Election interference	Yes
1972–75	Iraq	Single-party Personal: Hussein	Dissidents	–
1972–73	Italy	Democracy: Leftist parties	Election interference	Yes
1974–75	Portugal	Provisional: Leftist parties	Election interference	Yes
1975–76	Angola	Single-party: Neto	Dissidents	–
1979–80	South Yemen	Single-party: Ismail	Dissidents	–
1981–82	Chad	Warlord: Libyan-backed forces	Dissidents	Yes
1981–83	Ethiopia	Military-personal: Mengistu	Dissidents	–
1983–88	Liberia	Personal: Doe	Democracy promotion	–
1984–86	Philip-pines	Personal: Marcos	Democracy promotion	Yes
1986–88	Angola	Single-party: Dos Santos	Dissidents	–
Total	**25**			**12**

[1]The United States and the United Kingdom developed a plan to pursue covert regime change in Syria that was aborted before implementation. See Jones, "The 'Preferred Plan.'"
[2]Angola is omitted from Geddes's dataset because it was a Portuguese colony until 1975. In this case, the United States was backing the pro-American forces against their leftist competitors during their fight for independence from Portugal.
[3]Mozambique is the same as Angola (above).

Western Europe and Japan. The war had killed millions in both regions; most major cities lay in rubble; and their economies had been decimated. Under these bleak conditions, US officials feared that a surplus of frustrated workers might pave the way for Communist victories in postwar democratic elections.[58] Washington had some reason to worry. In 1945, communists received around 20 percent of the vote in France, Italy, and Finland; and approximately 10 percent of the vote in Belgium, Denmark, Norway, Holland, and Sweden.[59] One 1951 CIA analysis indicated that "economic aid alone and even improvement in the standard of living was by no means an adequate answer to the internal threat. It was felt therefore that consideration should be given to new techniques to deprive the French and Italian communists of their power, recognizing that these parties constituted a continuing threat to democratic government and the NATO forces in Western Europe."[60] The problem of communism's spreading appeal was compounded by the fact that "both the Italian and French governments have evidenced over reluctance to proceed forthrightly against their local communist parties."[61]

If these governments would not act, Deputy Director of Central Intelligence Allen Dulles urged the United States to do so: "There should be substantial increases in the covert support given to measures to be carried out by individuals and groups of patriotic citizens, by the press, radio, motion pictures and like media, with financial and other aid from us."[62] Toward these ends, Truman authorized two covert missions to fund center-right parties in Italian and French elections while also using propaganda and sabotage to destabilize each country's communist party and minimize leftist influence within their labor unions.[63] For similar reasons, Eisenhower approved several covert interventions to support center-right candidates in Japanese elections, which continued until at least 1968.[64]

A second wave of preventive operations began in the Middle East in the early 1950s. On account of the region's strategic value, Kennan argued that the United States "cannot permit [it] to fall into hands hostile to us, and . . . we [should] put forward, as the first specific objective of our policy and as an irreducible minimum of national security, the maintenance of political regimes in those areas at least favorable to the continued power and independence of our nation."[65] Truman authorized a covert plan to overthrow Iranian prime minister Mohammad Mossadegh in 1952 out of fear that the Iranian communist party, Tudeh, was growing in influence under his government. However, it was under his successor, Eisenhower, that Mossadegh was ousted during a 1953 US-backed coup.[66] The perceived success of the 1953 Iranian coup, in turn, inspired further interventions, and Eisenhower's "New Look" grand strategy identified "covert operations" as a major tool to prevent Soviet advances in the region.[67] Afterward, Eisenhower conspired with the British to overthrow Syria's president, Shukri al-Quwalti, and helped fix parliamentary elections in Lebanon.[68] For similar reasons, Nixon and Ford supported Kurdish dissidents in their bids for secession during the mid-1970s, and Carter covertly intervened in South Yemen in 1979.[69]

Washington further expanded its use of covert preventive operations in the late 1950s when Eisenhower sought to counter Soviet advances in Asia. In Indonesia, he ordered the United States to "employ all feasible covert means to strengthen the will, determination and cohesion of anti-Communist forces."[70] Chapter 7 shows that Eisenhower set the groundwork for covert interventions in North and South Vietnam, Laos, and Thailand that came to fruition under Kennedy and Johnson.[71] By the late 1950s, the superpowers also drew Africa into their Cold War battle. Both Moscow and Washington feared that regimes friendly to their rival could assume power in the newly decolonized nations, thereby shifting the balance of power and world opinion against them. To prevent this, Eisenhower launched as least two assassination plots against Congo's democratically elected prime minister, Patrice Lumumba.[72] Johnson launched covert missions in Mozambique, Angola, and Somalia;[73] Ford revived the covert operation in Angola;[74] and Reagan intervened covertly into Chad, Ethiopia, Liberia, Libya, and Angola.[75]

America's covert preventive operations succeeded 48 percent of the time. Twelve out of twenty-five operations brought the US-backed regime to power. America's preventive missions succeeded more often than its offensive operations because they targeted significantly weaker states. Offensive interventions pitted the United States directly against the Soviet bloc's military and state capacity. Preventive operations, by contrast, targeted regimes that did not pose a direct military threat to the United States on their own. Because the target states were not yet Soviet allies, the United States could pursue more aggressive covert tactics with less risk that their actions would spark a military confrontation with Moscow. Consequently, the United States was able to pursue a wider variety of covert strategies depending on whom in the target state they were trying to support.

PREVENTIVE: OVERT CASES

Despite their preference for covert conduct, American officials only escalated to overt conduct once during this period: Lebanon (1958). In line with this study's predictions, Washington was willing to escalate to overt conduct in Lebanon because US policymakers believed that, with the support of the American public, they could achieve a quick victory in an area of geostrategic importance.

The 1958 Lebanese intervention marked the first military action by the United States to uphold Eisenhower's new strategy, known as the Eisenhower Doctrine, which sought to prevent the Soviet Union from gaining influence within the Middle East and to sideline the growing Pan-Arab nationalist movement led by Egypt's Abdel Gamal Nasser.[76] To protect independent Arab regimes that felt threatened by the growing influence of Nasser and the Soviet Union, the doctrine stipulated, "The United States is prepared to use armed forces to assist any such nation or group of such nations requesting assistance against armed aggression from any country controlled by international communism."[77]

One of the leaders believed to be under threat was Lebanese president Camille Chamoun, who US policymakers viewed "an important asset . . . to Western stability in the area" because of his staunch anti-communism.[78] Chamoun's pro-American position brought him into conflict with leftists and Arab nationalists during parliamentary elections in 1957, and in response Eisenhower initiated a covert program "to distribute 'campaign contributions' to pro-western Lebanese politicians to help defeat anti-American candidates backed by Nasser."[79] These efforts were successful, and Chamoun supporters won 80 percent of their elections. Nevertheless, America's covert support was not enough to turn the tide of the conflict.[80] Domestic opposition to Chamoun continued to rise, and in May 1958, tensions boiled over following the assassination of an anti-Chamoun journalist. It was "a rebellion," according to US Ambassador Richard Parker, "which we had helped arrange by helping him rig the election the previous year in a scandalous way."[81] Within days, Chamoun requested that the United States land "a division of Marines" to support his regime.[82] Washington was skeptical; policymakers feared that these actions would be viewed as "gunboat diplomacy" and weighed the relative merits of intervening on behalf of an unpopular ruler against the relative costs to American credibility of not upholding the Eisenhower Doctrine.[83] Faced with these unpleasant alternatives, Eisenhower sought a middle ground. Rather than overt intervention, the United States increased its covert support for Chamoun's regime and attempted to broker a behind-the-scenes political solution with his domestic rivals.[84]

Following a leftist coup against a pro-Western regime in Iraq, however, Chamoun again appealed for British and American intervention on July 14, 1958. Interpreting the Iraqi coup as an ominous sign for all pro-American rulers in the region, US officials acquiesced to Chamoun's request, and sent 14,000 troops ashore to ensure the continuation of a pro-Western regime in Beirut. State Department reports indicate policymakers feared that if they did not intervene, "the United States would lose influence not only in the Arab States of the Middle East but in the area generally. . . . The dependability of United States commitments for assistance in the event of need would be brought into question throughout the world."[85] The need to demonstrate resolve on the international stage, combined with the fact that the mission required a rapid response and covert action had already proven insufficient, meant that US policymakers were willing to overtly intervene.[86] Eisenhower's willingness to directly intervene was likely further bolstered by the fact that the US public appeared to support the idea. For instance, a Gallup poll after the intervention found 59 percent approval and 27 percent disapproval.[87] Unlike the disastrous overt intervention in North Korea, the Lebanese operation was widely viewed as a success. American troops remained in Lebanon for four months and left after successfully backing the parliamentary election of a pro-American Christian candidate, General Fuad Chehab.[88]

Hegemonic Regime Change: Monroe Doctrine

The United States conducted eighteen covert and three overt hegemonic regime changes during the Cold War. Unlike during preventive operations, in most hegemonic cases US officials were less concerned with direct Soviet encroachment into the target country than they were worried about maintaining a hierarchical regional order. Although US leaders often framed hegemonic operations in terms of the era's superpower conflict, they pursued a foreign policy goal that both predated and survived the Cold War. As such, it makes sense to first view these missions in terms of that overall strategy before looking at its specific Cold War form.

For nearly two centuries, US foreign policy in the Western Hemisphere has been dominated by one goal: the pursuit of regional hegemony.[89] This task, Mearsheimer explains, "involved building a powerful United States that could dominate the other independent states of North and South America and also prevent the European great powers from projecting their military might across the Atlantic Ocean."[90] President James Monroe first articulated this strategy during a speech to Congress in 1823. The "Monroe Doctrine," as his speech became known, declared that "the American Continents are henceforth not to be considered as subjects for future colonization by any European power." He went on to warn the European powers that the United States would consider "any attempt on their part to extend their system to any portion of this hemisphere as dangerous to our peace and safety." These "attempts" included forming alliances with any of the sovereign states within the region because "we could not view any interposition for the purpose of oppressing them, or controlling in any other manner their destiny, by any European power in any other light than as the manifestation of an unfriendly disposition toward the United States."[91]

Later presidents fortified the Monroe Doctrine. Theodore Roosevelt added the "Roosevelt Corollary" in 1904, expanding America's right to intervene in Latin America in the case of "chronic wrongdoing, or an impotence which results in a general loosening of the ties of civilized society."[92] Roosevelt and other early twentieth-century presidents were quick to follow through on these threats. As a result, Greg Grandin notes that "by 1930, Washington had sent gunboats into Latin American ports over six thousand times, invaded Cuba, Mexico (again), Guatemala, and Honduras, fought protracted guerilla wars in the Dominican Republic, Nicaragua, and Haiti, annexed Puerto Rico, and taken a piece of Colombia to create both the Panamanian nation and the Panama canal."[93]

It took a second Roosevelt coming to the presidency in 1933 to put an end to America's interventionist behavior in Central and South America. In his first inaugural address, Franklin D. Roosevelt (FDR) announced a "good neighbor" policy toward the region in an effort to reverse the interventionist behavior promoted by the Roosevelt Corollary. He asserted, "I would dedicate this Nation to the policy of the good neighbor—the neighbor who resolutely respects himself and, because he does so, respects the rights of others—the neighbor who respects his obligations and respects the sanctity of his agreements in and with a world of neighbors."[94] FDR followed up on this promise by signing a number of international agreements rejecting regime change. At the Seventh International Conference of American States in 1933, American officials agreed that "no state has the right to intervene in the internal or external affairs of another."[95] The Charter of the Organization of American States, the United Nations Charter, and the 1975 Helsinki Agreement all reinforced this principle.[96]

Although Roosevelt did not intervene in Latin America during the twelve years of his presidency (1933–45), every Cold War president except for Ford authorized hegemonic regime changes in pursuit of Monroe Doctrine goals. Historian Melvyn Leffler explained that immediately following World War II, "The need to predominate throughout the Western Hemisphere was not a result of deteriorating Soviet-American relations but a natural evolution of the Monroe Doctrine, accentuated by Axis aggression and new technological imperatives. Patterson, Forrestal, and Army Chief of Staff Dwight D. Eisenhower initially were impelled less by reports of Soviet espionage, propaganda, and infiltration in Latin America than by accounts of British efforts to sell cruisers and aircraft to Chile and Ecuador; Swedish sales of anti-aircraft artillery to Argentina; and French offers to build cruisers and destroyers for both Argentina and Brazil."[97] Later, as the Cold War escalated, the Soviet Union came to be seen as the primary threat in the region. John Foster Dulles explained in 1947, "Soviet policy in South America subjects the Monroe Doctrine to its severest test. There is a highly organized effort to extend to the South American Countries the Soviet system of proletariat dictatorship."[98] The Truman administration's final national security document (NSC 141) summarized US postwar objectives:

> In Latin America we seek first and foremost an orderly political and economic development which will make the Latin American nations resistant to the internal growth of communism and to Soviet political warfare. Second, we seek hemisphere solidarity in support of our world policy and the cooperation of the Latin American nations in safe-guarding the hemisphere through individual and collective defense measures against external aggression and internal subversion.[99]

Numerous presidential statements confirm the importance of Monroe Doctrine principles throughout the Cold War. For instance, in response to a reporter's question about whether the Monroe Doctrine still stood in 1960, Eisenhower replied, "I think that the Monroe Doctrine has by no means been supplanted. It has been merely extended. When the Monroe Doctrine was written and enunciated, it had in mind such things as happened when the Austrians and the French—or an Austrian Emperor with some French troops—came into Mexico. Times have changed, and there are different kinds of penetration and subversion that can be very dangerous to the welfare of the OAS [Organization of American States]."[100] Later, Kennedy justified his administration's interventions in Cuba by explaining, "The Monroe Doctrine means what it has meant since President Monroe and John Quincy Adams enunciated it, and that is that we would oppose a foreign power extending its power to the Western Hemisphere."[101] Likewise, Ronald Reagan explained, "Our commitment to a Western Hemisphere safe from aggression did not occur by spontaneous generation on the day that we took office. It began with the Monroe Doctrine in 1823 and continues our historic bipartisan policy."[102]

Academic studies of US interventions in Latin America during the Cold War are often framed as a debate between whether national security or economic interests were paramount to US policymakers. In a certain sense, however, both sides are correct. It is easy to find both security and economic rationales for most interventions. In terms of security interests, US officials worried that leftist groups in the region would ally with the Soviet Union and considered control of certain geographic regions to be crucial to American security, particularly Caribbean sea lanes and the Panama Canal.[103] Economic interests were also present during many interventions: in some cases, US officials discussed protecting the foreign investments of American corporations; in others, policymakers discussed the importance of open access to Caribbean Sea lanes for US trade policy. Indeed, Reagan estimated that nearly half of US trade and two-thirds of its oil imports passed through these sea lanes.[104] Yet, both sides in the security versus economics debate struggle to explain the motives behind specific US interventions. Given the power asymmetry between the United States and states targeted in Latin America, regime change often seemed disproportionate to either the security or economic interests at stake for most countries. The US government did not have significant economic interests in most target states. None posed a direct military threat to American interests, and only two—Cuba and Nicaragua—received significant military aid from the Soviet Union; however, in both cases, American regime changes predated their governments' formal alliance with Moscow.[105]

To understand why the United States would intervene, it is therefore necessary to situate these individual cases in the context of America's overarching objective of maintaining its position of regional hegemony. US officials believed that the key to upholding this hegemony was to ensure that Latin American states were run by individuals who actively or tacitly acquiesced to the US-led order. If actively anti-American governments were allowed to assume power, US officials worried that other states would be emboldened to defect from the region's hierarchical order. Every Castro-like leader that came to power paved the way for the next, which, in turn, could eventually lead to foreign intervention into the hemisphere. As Lars Schoultz explains, "Instability per se is not the issue, of course. Few US policymakers would be concerned if Salvadorans or Guatemalans or Haitians spent their time shooting one another were it not for the fact that one possible consequence of this instability might be to provide hostile forces with the opportunity to seize territory in Latin America and then use it to threaten US security."[106] Given this, the proximate motives for these operations varied. Sometimes the United States wanted to block the election of a leftist candidate; at other times, Washington worried that the target state's government would not protect US political or military interests. The unifying characteristic of all the disputes, however, was that American officials believed that the target state was asserting authority in an area where it previously was subordinate.

With this link between insubordination and US interests in mind, it is easier to see how these operations met the two prerequisites for intervention. For one, once US leaders accepted a domino theory logic of regional integration, then every disagreement with a subordinate state could potentially be viewed as a significant problem. Fearing a potential cascade of negative repercussions, policymakers came to view small disputes as major threats to US interests. For instance, Grow's analysis of eight US interventions found that "the incumbent administration's top leaders opted for intervention in the belief that the international image of the United States would be weakened if they failed to take aggressive action—and that by moving forcibly against an unfriendly regime in the U.S. sphere of influence they would increase respect for U.S. power in the eyes of the international community."[107] From the perspective of the target governments, their dispute with Washington placed them in a catch-22. To appease the United States, they would have had to abandon their political beliefs and base of support, without which, however, they would be unable or unwilling to rule.[108]

The second precondition for intervention—a plausible alternative to the target regime—was easy to satisfy in most hegemonic cases. Frequently, these individuals actually lobbied for American support. For instance, Grow's analysis found that

> in every episode of U.S. intervention members of the local elites—Guatemalan conservatives, Cuban exiles, Dominican military officers, wealthy Chilean businessmen, opposition Guianese and Panamanian politicians, the conservative leaders of Nicaragua's and Grenada's regional neighbors—were actively at work promoting intervention in their own self-interest, helping to shape White House perceptions and U.S. strategies in the process.[109]

As Table 5.3 shows, the United States initially conducted 85.7 percent of its hegemonic operations covertly to minimize costs and conceal America's

Table 5.3 US-backed hegemonic covert regime change attempts during the Cold War

Date	Target State	Target Government(s)	Tactic(s)	Objective Achieved
1952–54	Guatemala	Democracy: Arbenz	Coup, Dissidents	Yes
1960–61	Cuba	Single-party Personal: Castro	Assassination, Dissidents	–
1960–61	Dominican Republic	Personal: Trujillo	(Inadvertent Assassination), Coup	Yes
1961–71	British Guiana/ Guyana	Colonial/Democracy: Leftist parties[6]	Coup, Election interference	Yes
1961–62	Dominican Republic	Democracy: Leftist parties	Election interference	Yes
1962–73	Chile	Democracy: Allende & Leftist parties	Coup, Election interference	Yes
1963	Haiti	Personal: Duvalier	Dissidents	–
1963–66	Bolivia	Single-party: Leftist parties	Election interference	Yes
1964	Brazil	Democracy: Goulart	Coup	Yes
1965–68	Dominican Republic	Foreign-occupied/ Personal: Leftist parties	Election interference	Yes
1965–69	Haiti	Personal: Duvalier	Dissidents	–
1971	Bolivia	Military: Torres	Coup	Yes
1979	Grenada	Personal: Bishop[7]	Democracy promotion	Aborted[8]
1979–80	Nicaragua	Single-party: Ortega	Democracy promotion, Dissidents	–
1982–85	Suriname	Military: Bouterse	Democracy promotion	–
1984–89	Chile	Military-personal: Pinochet	Democracy promotion	Yes
1986–89	Haiti	Multiple: Military/ Military-personal	Democracy promotion	–
1987–89	Panama	Military-personal: Noriega	Coup	–
Total	**18**			**10**

[1]British Guiana is excluded from Geddes's dataset because it is a British colony. After achieving independence in 1966, however, its successor state, Guyana, was also excluded.

[2]Beyond describing it as a "non-democracy," Geddes's dataset does not code the type of Authoritarian regime in Grenada because the country is too small. I have coded it as "personal."

[3]Carter authorized plans to covertly promote democratic reform in Grenada. However, the operation was aborted before its implementation after the Senate Intelligence Committee objected to the mission. See Robert M. Gates, *From the Shadows: The Ultimate Insider's Story of Five Presidents and How They Won the Cold War* (New York: Simon and Schuster, 2011), 143.

role in operations that often violated norms of justified intervention.[110] Some operations supported leaders known to have committed human rights abuses. Other missions targeted democracies, thus violating liberal norms for mutual respect between democracies. Because of these normative violations, US planners feared that their actions would undermine what David Lake describes as the region's "social contract," namely, that "dominant states must demonstrate that they cannot or will not abuse the authority that subordinates have entrusted to them. Subordinates will not enter or remain within a social contract unless they are assured that the authority they grant to the dominant state will not be used against them."[111] Henry Kissinger aptly summarized these dilemmas in a secret memorandum to President Nixon:

> We are strongly on record in support of self-determination and respect for free elections; you are firmly on record for non-intervention in the internal affairs of the hemisphere and of accepting nations 'as they are.' It would therefore be very costly for us to act in ways that appear to violate those principles, and Latin Americans and others in the world will view our policy as a test of the credibility of our rhetoric. On the other hand, our failure to react to this situation risks being perceived in Latin America and in Europe as indifference or impotence in the face of clearly adverse developments in a region long considered our sphere of influence.[112]

HEGEMONIC: COVERT CASES

Washington conducted eighteen covert hegemonic operations during the Cold War. These operations came in two forms. The first type sought to replace foreign leaders that the United States considered sympathetic to communism with rightwing regimes. The second type promoted democracy—but only for the parties and candidates that policymakers felt would act in US interests.

Many of the early hegemonic regime changes developed in a similar manner: American analysts would identify a rising socialist or communist movement in the target country, and although this regime did not pose a direct military or economic threat, officials worried that if they passively allowed it to assume power, then its very existence could foster further instability in its neighbors. This, in turn, would encourage the emergence of other communist regimes and pave the way for a Soviet beachhead in the Western Hemisphere. Thus to protect US credibility and "hemispheric solidarity," Washington would opt to replace the left-wing regime with a right-wing authoritarian leader who could contain communist subversion.[113]

Eisenhower launched America's first covert hegemonic mission to overthrow Guatemalan president Jacobo Arbenz in 1954. This mission is representative of many early US interventions. In fact, it directly served as the model for many. As such, it is worthwhile to analyze the operation in detail: Arbenz won Guatemala's 1950 presidential election on a platform of reforming Guatemala's oligarchic economy. During his inauguration speech, Arbenz promised to "transform Guatemala from a backward country with a semi-feudal economy into a modern capitalist economy."[114] Toward this end, he launched a major agrarian land reform "to liquidate feudal property . . .

in order to develop capitalist methods of production in agriculture."[115] These laws gave the Guatemalan government the right to expropriate land on estates larger than 223 acres. The brunt of this reform was born by an American corporation, the United Fruit Company (UFCO), which ultimately lost 70 percent of its 566,000 acres, amounting to one-seventh of Guatemala's arable land.[116] UFCO retaliated by lobbying the Truman and Eisenhower administrations for help.[117]

American officials considered Arbenz sympathetic to communism, although the Guatemalan leader never publicly identified himself as such. As a result, intelligence analysts watched with alarm when Arbenz appointed several communists to his cabinet, legalized the communist Guatemalan Party of Labor (PGT), and maintained close ties to PGT's leader, Jose Manuel Fortuny.[118] The US Ambassador to Guatemala aptly summarized the consensus at the time, when he declared that Arbenz "talked like a communist, he thought like a communist, he acted like a communist, and if he is not one . . . he will do until one comes along."[119]

Scholars continue to debate whether economic or security interests drove America's decision to intervene in Guatemala. Although both positions have merit, neither provides a wholly convincing account on its own because policymakers often saw the two as intertwined. UFCO's lobbying efforts helped put Guatemala on Washington's radar, but there is no direct evidence that the United States acted specifically to protect UFCO's interests.[120] As one secret State Department telegram declared, "While every important US interest in Guatemala including UFCO is under attack, our concern about communist penetration would be just as great if this were not true."[121] At the same time, American analysts did not think that Guatemala posed a direct security threat on its own, and they could not find any direct links to the Soviet Union. Secretary of State Dulles privately admitted that it was "impossible to produce evidence clearly tying the Guatemalan government to Moscow; that the decision must be a political one and based on our deep conviction that such a tie must exist."[122]

Instead, the plethora of declassified documents on this operation suggests that US officials were most concerned with the threat posed by "communist subversion" to America's regional hegemony. One typical State Department statement declared, "Communist success in Guatemala thus far does not constitute a direct military or economic threat to the United States." Rather, "the underlying Communist objectives in Guatemala are to prevent collaboration of that country with the United States in event of future international crisis, and to disrupt hemisphere solidarity and weaken the United States position."[123] Another Top Secret Policy Planning Staff document asserted that

> the real and direct threat that Guatemala poses for her neighbors is that of political subversion through the kind of across-the-borders intrigue that is a normal feature of the Central American scene. The danger is of Communist

contagion and is most immediate with respect to Guatemala's immediate neighbors. The Communist infection is not going to spread to the U.S. but if it should in the fullness of time spread over much of Latin America it would impair the military security of the Hemisphere and thus of the U.S.[124]

During the planning of the operation, policymakers expressed a strong preference for covert action, even though they understood they could easily defeat the Arbenz regime overtly. For instance, one 1953 National Security Council strategy paper determined that "Militarily, Guatemala would be defenseless against direct United States action. . . . If direct unilateral action should become necessary in a future emergency, the Arbenz regime could easily and quickly be overthrown."[125] Nevertheless, US officials feared that

> direct military or economic sanctions on Guatemala would violate solemn United States commitments and under present circumstances would endanger the entire fund of good will the United States has built up in the other American Republics through its policies of non-intervention, respect for juridical equality, and abnegation of a position of privilege. Loss of this good will would be a disaster to the United States far outweighing the advantage of any success gained in Guatemala.[126]

The CIA first developed a plan to overthrow Arbenz in 1951. A year later, Truman approved this mission, code-named PBFORTUNE. However, he called it off shortly afterward, fearing that its cover had been blown. Eisenhower revived the operation, this time renamed PBSUCCESS, in 1953. The operation itself involved two main tactics. First, the United States used several "psychological warfare" techniques—including propaganda, mass mailings to army officers, fake radio programming, and sabotage—to convince the Arbenz regime of an impending attack by a major "liberation army."[127] Second, the CIA would create a liberation army of mercenaries and Guatemalan exiles led by a disaffected Guatemalan colonel, Carlos Castillo Armas. Once Arbenz's regime had been undermined by months of psychological warfare, the CIA operational plan then envisioned "Constitutional leader [Armas] claims capability to seize power by force and issues [an] ultimatum to [the] target regime to capitulate to avoid needless bloodshed."[128] Remarkably, the plan went off largely as expected.[129] Armas and 480 followers invaded on June 17th, and fearing a major confrontation with Armas and a potential invasion by the US military, the Guatemalan Army refused to fight. Instead, they demanded that Arbenz resign, which he did on June 27, 1954.[130] US policymakers were enormously pleased with the intervention, and they revived some of its techniques during subsequent missions in Brazil, Bolivia (twice), British Guiana/Guyana, Chile, Cuba, the Dominican Republic, Haiti, and Panama.[131]

A second wave of covert hegemonic operations began during the Reagan administration. Although several first-wave operations targeted democratic governments in favor of authoritarian regimes, second-wave operations typically tried to do the opposite. Instead, they used a variety of covert tactics to promote democracy within the target state. Reagan was the first American president to employ both covert and overt efforts at foreign democracy promotion as a key component of a US grand strategy. He argued, "I have a vision of a democratic Western Hemisphere where the United States has warm and solid relations with all of the countries of the hemisphere. . . . It's in our national interests that we do so. So I'm glad that we are meeting to make sure we are doing all we can to support, protect and preserve democracy in South America."[132] Using the democracy promotion techniques discussed in chapter 3, the Reagan administration provided semi-covert financial aid via the National Endowment for Democracy and Project Democracy to pro-American democratic parties and candidates in Chile, Haiti, Nicaragua, and Suriname.[133] Although it is impossible to say whether US aid was instrumental in bringing about these results, Chile and Nicaragua each underwent a democratic transformation at the end of the Cold War.

In summary, the United States employed a variety of tactics during its covert hegemonic operations—assassination, coup d'état, covertly influencing democratic elections, and supporting dissident movements. Because the United States was so much stronger than the target states, it could adjust its tactics according to the situation. Many operations were also helped by the fact that most target states had weak state institutions and poor civil-military relations. This meant that the United States could often readily identify a military leader in the target country who was eager for their assistance in launching a coup. As a result, 55.5 percent of America's covert hegemonic operations succeeded—ten out of eighteen operations brought Washington's preferred government to power.

HEGEMONIC: OVERT CASES

The United States escalated to overt conduct in two cases (the Dominican Republic, 1965, and Panama, 1989) and conducted one (Grenada, 1983) overtly from the beginning. All three cases are consistent with the claim put forth in chapter 3 that states will escalate to overt conduct when they believe they can score a quick, decisive victory, with public support, in the context of an ongoing political crisis wherein policymakers wished to signal resolve on the international stage.

The first operation occurred in 1965 when Johnson launched Operation Power Pack in the Dominican Republic days after the start of a civil war. In this case, investigated in more detail in chapter 8, America's main objective was to prevent Dominican Constitutionalists—considered sympathetic to communism—from gaining power. However, Johnson's advisors understood that international audiences would find this motivation normatively inappropriate. UN Ambassador Adlai Stevenson explained that an "intervention to 'restore order' and prevent a communist victory would almost certainly involve the United States in pro-Loyalist activities likely to be condemned throughout the hemisphere as a return to gunboat diplomacy in support of a military regime."[134] At the same time, however, rapidly unfolding events on the ground precluded a purely covert approach. The Constitutionalists had already gained a significant advantage within days of the start of the civil war, and Johnson feared that if he did not act quickly, the Constitutionalists would soon establish a "second Cuba" in the Dominican Republic. Nevertheless, Johnson understood that international observers were unlikely to accept these rationales for intervention. Instead, his administration publicly justified intervention by claiming that "American lives are in danger," going so far as to demand an invitation from the regime's leader requesting US intervention for this purpose.[135] The US public was sympathetic to these arguments, and 76 percent of Americans supported intervention.[136] Following the successful overt operation, however, American officials reverted to covert tactics to guarantee that a pro-American conservative party would win the first elections in the post–civil war era.

The United States did not attempt another overt hegemonic operation until the Reagan administration. In 1983, Reagan ordered the invasion of Grenada amid a bloody political crisis following the execution of Maurice Bishop as part of a military coup led by Hudson Austin. Unlike America's previous hegemonic operations, Reagan did not prefer to conduct this operation covertly. To the contrary, he believed that a quick and decisive victory in Grenada would create domestic support for the fight against communism and signal America's resolve to its foreign adversaries—a particularly important objective at time considering the invasion came just two days after Hezbollah bombed US Marine barracks in Beirut, killing 241 American servicemen.[137] As Secretary of State Shultz argued, "We must win this one. It is terribly important not just for the outcome in Grenada, but the precedent it sends all over the world, from Moscow to Korea, to European capitals."[138] In his address to the American public, Reagan highlighted the need for a rapid response to protect American students in Grenada and the mission's moral legitimacy:

> First, and of overriding importance, to protect innocent lives, including up to 1,000 Americans, whose personal safety is, of course, my paramount concern. Second, to forestall further chaos. And third, to assist in the restoration of conditions of law and order and of governmental institutions to the island of Grenada where a brutal group of leftist thugs violently seized power, killing the Prime Minister, three cabinet members, two labor leaders and other civilians, including children.[139]

Reagan's case was bolstered by requests for US assistance "to restore order and democracy" from the island's governor general and the Organization of Eastern Caribbean States (OECS), drafts of which were written by the US State Department.[140] The mission, code-named Urgent Fury, was a remarkably easy victory with only nineteen American lives lost. The US public supported intervention 71 percent to 22 percent.[141]

The final overt hegemonic regime change occurred in December 1989, when the George H. W. Bush administration overthrew Panamanian leader Manual Noriega. Although once a US ally, Noriega's relationship with the United States soured in the mid-1980s after the *New York Times* publicly exposed his drug and arms trafficking and the fact that he had been receiving roughly $200,000 per year in covert pay from the CIA.[142] Shortly afterward, Reagan initiated a campaign to oust Noriega through a combination of covert political action and overt economic sanctions.[143] However, Reagan did not invade. He feared this would have negative repercussions for Vice President Bush's 1988 presidential campaign.[144] In October 1989, however, US policymakers learned of a potential coup by Panamanian major Moises Giroldi. President Bush decided to help, arguing, "You've had me out there for the last couple of months begging these guys to start a coup. If someone's actually willing to do one, we have to help them."[145] Toward this end, the United States offered minor logistical support to the plotters by establishing several roadblocks.[146] Nevertheless, the coup was badly mangled, and soon after, American officials decided to opt for an overt intervention instead. Two months later, Reagan launched Operation Just Cause, in his words, to "safeguard the lives of Americans, to defend democracy in Panama, to combat drug trafficking and to protect the integrity of the Panama Canal treaty."[147] The operation was successful, quickly overthrowing Noriega, with 80 percent approval from the American public.[148]

This chapter compared the theories introduced in the preceding four chapters to America's overall historical record during the Cold War. It put forth four main arguments. The first was that states use regime change to pursue three types of security interests. *Offensive operations* corresponded to the Cold War strategy of rollback; *preventive operations* corresponded to the strategy of containment; and *hegemonic operations* pursued a strategy that both predated and survived the Cold War—that is, achieving regional hegemony in the Western Hemisphere. In the context of the Cold War, this meant that the United States tried to prevent left-wing regimes from assuming power, out of fear that such takeovers would spark a series of defections from the American-led regional order. Second, I argued that states only conduct regime changes in response to interstate disputes when the disputes are (1) driven by incompatible security policy preferences and (2) when policymakers in the intervening state can identify a plausible political alternative to the target regime. I then discussed how and when each of the three types of operations met those two prerequisites for intervention. Third came the argument that the United States had a clear preference for covert conduct to minimize the missions' potential military, economic, and reputational costs. Depending on the type of operation, different costs became more salient. For example, policymakers wanted to conduct offensive operations covertly to avoid the potential security costs of war with the Soviet Union, whereas they preferred to conduct hegemonic operations covertly to minimize economic costs and avoid the reputational costs associated with violating the sovereignty of states within the Western Hemisphere. Finally, I maintained that US policymakers intervened overtly on six occasions when a covert mission was either impossible to carry out within a short time horizon or because policymakers believed they could achieve an easy victory that would demonstrate US resolve.

CHAPTER 6

Rolling Back the Iron Curtain

> The political warfare initiative was the greatest mistake I ever
> made. . . . It did not work out at all the way I had conceived it.
> —George Kennan testifying before the US Senate in 1975

Most accounts of America's covert Cold War activities focus on a few well-known cases, such as Iran, Guatemala, and Chile. Far less well known are American covert operations in Eastern Europe and the Soviet Union, which the United States launched to roll back Soviet influence following the Second World War. Building on an array of declassified data, this chapter explores the causes, conduct, and consequences of these understudied missions. It proceeds as follows: In the first section, I explain why these cases were selected and compare this project's predictions to the alternative explanations. Next, I describe the collective context and objectives of these missions. Third, I ask why the Truman and Eisenhower administrations opted for covert—rather than overt—conduct. I then offer a comparative historical analysis of three cases: Albania, the Ukrainian Soviet Socialist Republic, and Yugoslavia. I ask why the United States intervened in the first two cases, but not in Yugoslavia, even though all were communist regimes. The case studies also address the reasons the missions in Albania and Ukraine failed, and discuss the pros and cons of covert conduct. Finally, I conclude by drawing out the theoretical lessons of these cases.

Case Selection and Alternative Hypotheses

The United States launched thirteen offensive rollback operations in Eastern Europe and the USSR during the 1940s and 1950s. The operations continued in the same manner across Truman's Democratic and Eisenhower's Republican administrations. All thirteen US missions were conducted covertly, and all thirteen failed at overthrowing their target.

CHAPTER 6

Of all the places where the United States intervened behind the Iron Curtain, I chose to focus on the Albanian, Ukrainian, and Yugoslavian cases for three reasons. First, although at first glance they seem to share much in common, they also vary in important ways that allow me to test the competing explanations. For instance, Washington only halted its regime change operations in Albania and the Ukrainian SSR after years of failure finally convinced US planners that the missions would not succeed. By contrast, after some initial debate, American policymakers decided that it was not in America's interests to overthrow the Yugoslav government. If ideology alone drove American behavior, this variation should not exist, because all three states had communist governments. Instead, I argue that realpolitik considerations drove US actions. After Stalin expelled Yugoslavia from the Cominform in 1948, Washington saw an opportunity to drive a wedge into the Soviet bloc by supporting Tito's government as a model of a non-Soviet-aligned communist regime in the hopes that other states would follow Yugoslavia's example and withdraw from the Soviet bloc. Second, I have selected cases that had a wide variety of high-quality primary source information available. To accomplish this, I acquired archival records from the National Archives and Records Administration (NARA), National Security Archive (NSA), and Truman and Eisenhower presidential libraries, as well as a plethora of data made available through the Nazi War Crime Disclosure Act of 2007. Thousands of primary source documents were identified for each operation, verifying its planning and implementation. Finally, cases were selected that are representative of the covert offensive operations conducted by the United States during this time. Indeed, each of the other eleven missions launched in Eastern Europe shared the same objective, used the same tactics, and ultimately suffered the same failure.[1]

ALTERNATIVE EXPLANATIONS

The four major competing explanations of regime change cannot adequately explain America's offensive missions in Eastern Europe. The normative, economic, regime type, and "rogue CIA" explanations each make specific predictions for US behavior that do not match the historical record. Instead, US officials focused on national security concerns while deciding if, when, and how to intervene.

Normative theories argue that international norms of justified intervention govern state behavior and predict that the United States should not promote illiberal regimes or leaders likely to commit human rights abuses. In practice, however, I argue that when a state wants to do something that violates these norms, it simply does so covertly. This dynamic is reflected in America's behavior during its rollback operations, wherein the United States not only promoted authoritarian regimes but also collaborated with many normatively unacceptable groups in the process, including numerous former

126

Nazis, multiple groups of Nazi collaborators, and other groups known to have committed mass killings.

Liberal theories of regime change predict that the United States should attempt to replace communist governments with liberal democracies. While US policymakers undoubtedly opposed communism, I found little evidence that the United States used regime change to promote either liberal values or liberal regimes. On the contrary, the United States knowingly backed illiberal nationalist groups, many of whom had ties to the Nazis during WWII. It is possible that US policymakers felt that it was pragmatic to support illiberal nationalist regimes in the short term in order to make democratization in the region possible later on. Because these operations failed, however, it is impossible to say for sure. However, it is worth noting that this is a different mechanism than is laid out in existing ideological accounts, and shows that, in the short term at least, security interests trumped ideological ones. Moreover, and contrary to the predictions of ideological accounts, I show that the United States actually backed Tito's communist regime, following the Yugoslav-Soviet split, in an effort to create "two opposing blocs in the Communist world, a Stalinist group and a non-conformist faction, either loosely allied or federated under Tito's leadership."[2] National Security Council Directive 58 explained the reasons why Washington actively supported Yugoslavia's communist government:

> None of the Eastern European countries, except Czechoslovakia, has ever known anything but authoritarian government. Democracy in the western sense is alien to their culture and tradition. . . . Were we to set as our immediate goal the replacement of totalitarianism by democracy, an overwhelming portion of the task would fall on us, and we would find ourselves directly engaging the Kremlin's prestige and provoking strong Soviet reaction, possibly in the form of war or at least in vigorous indirect aggression. . . . The more feasible immediate course, then, is to foster a heretical drifting-away process on the part of the satellite states. . . . And when the final breaks occur, we would not be directly involved in engaging Soviet prestige; the quarrel would be between the Kremlin and the Communist Reformation.[3]

There is also no evidence for the "rogue CIA" hypothesis. Instead, the executive branch carefully oversaw the planning and implementation of these missions. Both Truman and Eisenhower were involved in their planning and authorization, and the National Security Council continuously monitored the operations. Kennan, in particular, worked to protect his oversight, arguing that as the State Department's representative, he "would want to have specific knowledge of the objectives of every operation and also of the procedures and methods employed in all cases where those procedures and methods involve political decisions."[4]

Economic accounts also fare poorly. There is no evidence for hypothesis 3a, that the missions sought to protect the interests of American multinational corporations. Contrary to what these theorists would predict, the United States had virtually no direct investments in the region at the time. However, the case for hypothesis 3b—that the United States uses regime change to promote its position as the head of the global capitalist order—is more nuanced. One of America's top foreign policy objectives during the era was to establish a global capitalist economic order open to US trade and investment, particularly in Western Europe and Japan. Nonetheless, economic interests were not salient during the policymaking process for these operations. Although US officials undoubtedly would have liked to see the collapse of the region's communist regimes, for the time being they were more concerned about strengthening Western Europe's capitalist bloc. In fact, some policymakers argued that these operations would actually run counter to America's economic interests. For instance, the Clifford-Elsey Report argued, "Cooperation by the Soviets can result in increased trade. The United States government must always bear in mind, however, that the questions of the extent and nature of American trade should be determined by the overall interests of this country."[5] Thus, to the extent that US planners discussed economic interests, it was usually in the context of how economic warfare could help facilitate the collapse of these regimes.

In contrast to these accounts, I find that national security concerns drove US behavior. Specifically, I argue that the United States employed regime change to decrease the military threat posed by the Soviet bloc and to secure a buffer zone in Eastern Europe.[6]

Historical Background

Because each of this chapter's cases emerged from the same initiative, it makes sense to look first at their collective context; and to understand the origin of rollback, one must consider the condition of Eastern Europe in the 1940s. At the time of the first intervention, much of Eastern Europe had been wrecked by more than a decade of conflict. In the Eastern European regions occupied by both the USSR and Nazi Germany, 14 million civilians died between 1933 and 1945 from intentional mass killings and the forced imposition of catastrophic agricultural policies.[7] An additional 28 million Soviet citizens are estimated to have died during World War II.[8] After turning the tide of the war by destroying the German 6th Army at the Battle of Stalingrad in the winter of 1942–43, the Red Army spent the next twenty-eight months ferociously driving the Wehrmacht back to Berlin, leaving the Soviet Union in control of most of Eastern Europe at the war's end. Stalin took advantage of these conquests to install pro-Soviet communist regimes throughout the region in an effort to increase the Soviet sphere of influence and create a buffer zone against a resurgent Germany.[9] Stalin pointed out that the USSR had compelling reasons to want to do so:

> The Germans made their invasion of the USSR through Finland, Poland, Rumania, Bulgaria, and Hungary. The Germans were able to make their invasion through these countries because at the time, governments hostile to the Soviet Union existed in these countries. . . . What can be surprising about the fact that the Soviet Union, anxious for its future safety, is trying to see to it that governments loyal in their attitude to the Soviet Union should exist in these countries?"[10]

Although Stalin may have felt that his actions were justified, British and American policymakers were more skeptical. Nonetheless, at the Yalta Conference in February 1945, Roosevelt and Churchill agreed to grant Stalin a sphere of influence within Eastern Europe in exchange for a promise that the newly liberated countries would hold free and fair elections following the war.[11] After the war, however, the Soviet Union struggled to consolidate its control over a region devastated by war, massive ethnic relocations, and roaming partisan organizations. Over 60 million Europeans had been displaced from their homes.[12] In the USSR alone, Russian historian Dmitri Volkogonov recounts, "Thousands of centres of population lay in ruins . . . virtually the entire western part of the country was engulfed in partisan warfare which threatened to spread to the surrounding territory."[13]

It was during this period that the British launched the first covert operations against the Soviet Union. Indeed, despite their wartime alliance, the United Kingdom began preparing for a postwar confrontation with Moscow, before the end of hostilities, by establishing contact with anti-Soviet partisan bands in the Baltic states. These groups were comprised of tens of thousands of dissidents, known as the "Forest Brothers," who had organized themselves into armed bands to fight for the independence of Latvia, Lithuania, and Estonia.[14] From 1945 through 1954, British intelligence maintained extensive connections with these groups, providing them with arms, intelligence, and training for penetration missions against the Soviet Union in the hopes of inciting a major rebellion. However, little came of these operations. Unbeknownst to the British at the time, these operations "were in fact compromised in an elaborate Soviet design to turn agents from the West into deep-covert agents of the East."[15]

Shortly after the war, US Army Intelligence (G-2) and the Army's Counter Intelligence Corps (CIC) encountered similar partisan groups as Eastern European refugees poured into the US occupation zone in Bavaria. Displaced persons (DP) camps were particular hotbeds, and the American zone of Germany alone housed 2.3 million refugees.[16] It was in these camps that the United States first encountered many of the groups they would later use in covert operations, including the Organization of Ukrainian Nationalists (OUN) and a far-right Russian émigré group known as the Narodno-Trudovoy Soyuz (NTS).[17] US intelligence agents encountered similar dissident groups throughout Soviet-controlled Eastern Europe. In Romania, the Office of Strategic Services (OSS) identified "guerilla warfare cadres to commit acts of sabotage behind enemy lines in the event of war between the Anglo-Americans and the USSR."[18] In Hungary, intelligence officials made contact with right-wing organizations and secretly helped politicians threatened by communists escape from the country. In Austria, Czechoslovakia, and Soviet-occupied Eastern Germany, the US Army CIC operated clandestine intelligence networks to identify potential intelligence assets.[19]

Meanwhile, Washington's alliance with Moscow began to fray after a series of crises in late 1945 and 1946. Although Stalin wanted to consolidate a sphere of influence in Eastern Europe, officials within the Truman administration worried that his real aims were far greater. It was into this apprehensive environment that the US Deputy Chief of Mission in Moscow, George Kennan, sent his famous "long telegram" outlining his opinion of Soviet ideology and postwar strategy. In the words of Clark Clifford, this dispatch would become "probably the most important and influential message ever sent to Washington by an American diplomat."[20] Kennan warned that Soviet policy sought "to advance relative strength of USSR as [a] factor in international society."[21] Cooperation with the Soviet Union was virtually impossible because its leaders were "committed fanatically to the belief that with the US there can be no permanent *modus vivendi*, that it is desirable and necessary that the internal harmony of [American] society be disrupted . . . [and] the international authority of our state [must] be broken, if Soviet power is to be secure."[22] Further amplifying this threat were "governments or governing groups willing to lend themselves to Soviet purposes in one degree or another, such as present Bulgarian and Yugoslav Governments, North Persian regime, Chinese Communists, etc. Not only propaganda machines but actual policies of these regimes can be placed extensively at disposal of USSR."[23]

To evaluate Kennan's assessment, President Truman ordered Clark Clifford and George Elsey to "prepare a summary of American relations with the Soviet Union."[24] The resulting report—officially titled "American Relations with the Soviet Union," but also known as the "Clifford-Elsey Report"—amassed the collective opinion of America's foreign policy elite and was resolute in its findings. It declared that

> unless the United States is willing to sacrifice its *future security* for the sake of 'accord' with the U.S.S.R. now, the government must, as a first step toward world stabilization, seek to prevent additional Soviet aggression. The greater the area controlled by the Soviet Union, the greater the military requirements of this country will be.[25]

The Long Telegram and the Clifford-Elsey Report convinced Truman of the seriousness of the Soviet threat. Consequently, over the course of the next two years, the United States developed a two-pronged strategy to deal with the USSR. The first part of this strategy was known as "containment," and sought to contain the Soviet threat by balancing Soviet power, preventing third parties from allying with Moscow, and rehabilitating the economies of Western Europe. The second major strategy was known as "rollback," and aimed to reverse Soviet territorial gains through a program of covert economic and psychological warfare.

Kennan, who had since been appointed the director of the State Department's Policy Planning Staff (PPS), began to design a foreign policy to achieve rollback. If a Soviet-American conflict was in the making, however, he realized that the United States would require three things: the infrastructure to carry out the operations, far better intelligence on the Soviet Union, and a steady flow of covert funds. Kennan began by building an infrastructure capable of carrying out large covert missions. During WWII, the CIC and OSS had maintained covert contact with anti-Nazi resistance groups, most famously the French Resistance and the Polish Home Army.[26] Following the war, however, Truman shut down the OSS, opting instead for a new peacetime agency known as the Central Intelligence Group (CIG). However, the CIG quickly proved too small to handle the task.[27] In an effort to reform America's national security apparatus to handle the challenges of the new era, Congress passed the National Security Act of 1947. The act created many of the relevant policymaking bodies of the post-WWII era, including the National Security Council (NSC), the Department of Defense, and the Central Intelligence Agency (CIA) to run "espionage and counter-espionage operations abroad."[28] To carry out "political warfare" initiatives, the Office of Policy Coordination (OPC) was established in September 1948 "to undertake the full range of covert activities incident to the conduct of secret political, psychological, and economic warfare together with preventive direct action (paramilitary activities)—all within the policy direction of the Departments of State and Defense."[29] For the next four years, the OPC, under the leadership of Frank Wisner, carried out America's covert missions behind the Iron Curtain. In 1952, however, the OPC officially merged with the CIA, which took over the handling of covert operations for the rest of the Cold War.

The second necessary component to launch rollback operations was better intelligence on Soviet activities in Eastern Europe.[30] After the war, the US Army's G-2 intelligence unit and the CIC set about collecting this data by interviewing German prisoners of war and Eastern European refugees. In May 1945, they received a major break when the former head of Nazi military intelligence for the Eastern Front, Reinhard Gehlen, approached US Army officials in the Wörgl POW camp. According to a declassified CIA history:

> [Gehlen] indicated that he had—long prior to the end of the war—seen its inevitable conclusion and he had discussed with some key members of his

organization not only the preservation of his files—with the ultimate object in mind of turning them over to us—but that he had also arranged with some of his key personnel to attempt to contact them for the purpose of securing their cooperation with him in presenting us with as clear a picture of the Soviets as possible.[31]

In addition to this intelligence, Gehlen also offered ties to anti-Soviet groups behind the Iron Curtain. A major part of the Nazi war effort on the Eastern Front had been the use of local collaborators to police Nazi-held territory and infiltrate behind Soviet lines. Émigré groups on the German payroll included the Russian Liberation Movement (aka the "Vlasov Army" after its leader, Andrei Vlasov), the Russian Narodno-Trudovoy Soyuz (NTS), the Organization of Ukrainian Nationalists (OUN), the Latvian Daugavas Vanagi, and the Albanian Balli Kombëtar (BK).[32] Each of these groups has been implicated in mass killings. In fact, according to Holocaust expert Raul Hilberg, "The importance of these auxiliaries should not be underestimated. Roundups by local inhabitants who spoke the local language resulted in higher percentages of Jewish dead."[33]

US Army officials agreed not to charge Gehlen or his associates with war crimes in exchange for his expertise, his files, and access to his contacts. Although some officials found collaborating with "that bunch of Nazis" to be morally reprehensible, others argued he provided crucial intelligence when they needed it most.[34] Ultimately, strategic concerns trumped moral ones. Gehlen's organization grew to include hundreds of ex-Nazis, who provided key intelligence, contacts to right-wing émigré groups throughout Eastern Europe, logistical support, and labor for America's covert rollback missions.[35] Over the next decade, the US government spent at least $200 million and employed around 4,000 staff to rebuild Gehlen's organization.[36]

The final requirement for interventions was a covert source of funding for these operations. According to some accounts, the Marshall Plan gave 5 percent of its funds to the OPC—roughly $685 million in total—to gather intelligence and covertly fund, train, and arm resistance fighters.[37] As a result, between 1948 and 1952, the OPC's budget grew from $4.7 million to over $200 million, of which more than half went to rollback operations in Eastern Europe.[38] To conceal the fact that this money came from the US government, Kennan devised a plan to launder the money through "private intermediaries." One NSC directive explained this process:

General direction and financial support would come from the Government; guidance and funds would pass to a private American organization or organizations (perhaps "business" enterprises) comprised of private citizens of the approximate caliber of Allen Dulles; these organizations, through their field offices in Europe and Asia, would establish contact with the various national underground resistance representatives in free countries and through these intermediaries pass on assistance and guidance to the resistance movements behind the Iron Curtain.[39]

By November 1948, American policymakers identified regime change as one goal of these covert interventions. NSC 20, written by Kennan, declared that although the United States could not overtly overthrow the Soviet Union during peacetime, covert action could be used to make it difficult for the "present Soviet leaders . . . to retain their power in Russia."[40] NSC 20/4 elaborated: "To counter the threats to our national security and well-being posed by the USSR, our general objectives with respect to Russia, in time of peace as well as in time of war, should be . . . to encourage and promote the gradual retraction of undue Russian power and influence from the present perimeter areas around traditional Russian boundaries and the emergence of the satellite countries as entities independent of the USSR."[41] A NSC Staff Study explained the strategic importance of the satellites in the context of the Cold War: "The satellites are important in the current balance of power in Europe because they augment the political, military and economic power of the Soviet Union and extend Soviet power into the heart of Europe. The permanent consolidation of Soviet control in this area would represent a serious threat to the security of Western Europe and the United States. . . . The elimination of Soviet domination of the satellites is, therefore, in the fundamental interest of the United States."[42]

A top-secret 1949 Policy Planning Staff (PPS) Paper, "U.S. Policy Toward the Soviet Satellite States in Eastern Europe," further delineated the steps necessary to fracture the Soviet bloc. PPS 59 argued, "Our overall aim with respect to the satellite states should be the gradual reduction and eventual elimination of preponderant Soviet power from Eastern Europe without resort to war." To this end, it continued, "We should, as the only practical immediate expedient, seek to achieve this objective through fostering Communist heresy among the satellite states, encouraging the emergence of non-Stalinist regimes as temporary administrations, even though they be Communist in nature. It must, however, be our fixed aim that eventually these regimes must be replaced by non-totalitarian governments desirous of participating with good faith in the free world community."[43]

America's early rollback missions were timed to take advantage of the period before Moscow had consolidated control over its satellites, by helping anti-Soviet dissident groups incite underground rebellions that would replace the fledgling Soviet-backed regimes with independent national governments. Interestingly, US policymakers explicitly modeled these operations on those conducted by Nazi Germany during WWII. One declassified memo remarked, "A psychological offensive to subvert the Red Army is considered a primary objective. This type of offensive, as attempted by the German Army in World War II, was known as the 'Vlasov Movement' [sic]."[44] To reinforce these efforts, the United States simultaneously launched a major propaganda effort using pamphlet drops, sponsored publications, and radio broadcasts on Radio Free Europe, Radio Liberty, and the Voice of America.[45] Many propaganda operations supported émigré groups—often identified and vetted by the Gehlen organization—radioing messages into their home states to incite resistance.

Why Did Policymakers Conduct Rollback Operations Covertly?

Washington preferred to conduct these early rollback operations covertly to minimize the danger that American actions could inadvertently spark a war with the Soviet Union. American planners understood that trying to overthrow Soviet allies was an inherently provocative action. For instance, NSC 20/1 warned, "We cannot say, of course, that the Russians will sit by and permit the satellites to extricate themselves from Russian control in this way. We cannot be sure that at some point in this process the Russians will not choose to resort to violence of some sort: i.e., to forms of military reoccupation or possibly even to major war, to prevent such a process from being carried to completion."[46] Consequently, Kennan argued that the United States "should do everything possible to keep the situation flexible and to make possible a liberation of the satellite countries in ways which do not create any unanswerable challenge to Soviet prestige."[47]

US planners calibrated their actions to maximize the likelihood of success while minimizing the possibility of military retaliation. In theory, covert conduct minimized security costs in multiple ways. First, if the Soviets uncovered an operation, they would hold the foreign dissidents responsible, and the US government could "plausibly deny" its role. Second, covert conduct allowed the United States to avoid any entangling alliance commitments to the foreign actors on the ground. If the Kremlin decided to crack down on one of these movements, American credibility was not on the line to come to their aid. Third, covert conduct allowed the United States to avoid publicly challenging the credibility or prestige of the Soviet Union—even when the Soviets were aware of the operations—which decreased the likelihood that Soviet leaders would feel forced to respond in order to save face in front of domestic and foreign audiences.

In addition to these strategic rationales for covert conduct, American policymakers also had powerful normative reasons to keep their role secret. In this regard, there was an obvious divergence between America's public statements and private actions. On the one hand, Truman publically called for the dissolution of the Soviet bloc. For instance, during his speech to Congress on what became known as the "Truman Doctrine," he declared, "I believe that it must be the policy of the United States to support free peoples who are resisting attempted subjugation by armed minorities or by outside pressures."[48] Yet at the same time, Truman understood that the legitimacy of this endeavor would be undermined if the American public became aware of the details of these operations, specifically the fact that, in many cases, the United States was supporting authoritarian groups known to have collaborated with the Nazis and committed mass killings.

Given the cost differences between covert and overt operations, policymakers never seriously considered the possibility of intervening overtly. In fact, NSC 58, "United States Policy toward the Soviet Satellite States in Eastern Europe," dismissed it out of hand: "Resort to war as a course of action is raised in this paper solely for the purpose of making clear that it should be rejected as a practical alternative. This course is rejected, if for no other reason, because it is organically not feasible for this Government to initiate a policy of creating a war."[49] Still, policymakers understood that all covert operations "must be carried out with the full acceptance of the risk of war."[50] Immediately after WWII, US planners considered this risk low, given America's preponderance of power and nuclear monopoly.[51] Kennan argued, "The danger of war is vastly exaggerated in many quarters. The Soviet Government neither wants nor expects war in the foreseeable future."[52] By 1949, however, many in Washington feared that America's relative power had declined as it demobilized its wartime armies, while the Soviet Union's power had grown as it consolidated control over Eastern Europe and acquired atomic weapons. The Joint Chiefs of Staff estimated that the Soviet Union possessed 175 Red Army divisions and 75 Eastern European divisions, compared to only a handful of battle-ready American divisions.[53] Analysts even warned that the Soviet Union could possess a first-strike nuclear capability against the United States by 1954.[54]

To reverse this trend, the Truman administration released NSC Directive 68 in April 1950. Although scholars often consider NSC 68 to be a pivotal point in the escalation of the Cold War, in terms of America's covert operations, it simply reaffirmed previous policy. Toward that end, it called for the "intensification of affirmative and timely measures and operations by covert means in the fields of economic warfare and political and psychological warfare with a view of fomenting and supporting unrest and revolt in selected strategic satellite countries."[55] Following NSC 68, there was little change in US strategy in Eastern Europe between the Truman and Eisenhower administrations. Although Eisenhower had criticized the Democrats for not taking a hard enough line against the Soviets during the 1952 presidential election, after taking office, he was impressed to learn the scale of Truman's covert initiatives.[56] Eisenhower's incoming secretary of state, John Foster Dulles, was also one of the earliest and most ardent proponents of covert warfare. This was reflected by the fact that the CIA conducted six times as many covert operations (of all types, not just regime change) in January 1953 compared to January 1951.[57]

With more covert efforts came greater risks of Soviet retaliation, which in turn meant that the United States was under greater pressure to keep its actions covert while trying to overthrow increasingly powerful regimes. As Soviet-backed forces consolidated control within the target states, American policymakers struggled to find plausible political alternatives to the targeted regimes. For instance, The CIA's European director, Frank Lindsay, argued in a declassified memo in 1952, "The instruments currently advocated to reduce Soviet power are both inadequate and ineffective against the Soviet political system. The consolidated Communist state . . . has made virtually impossible the existence of organized clandestine resistance capable within the foreseeable future of appreciably weakening the power of the state."[58] In a similar vein, NSC 174 noted in December 1953, "Despite the widespread popular opposition to communism in each of the satellites, known underground groups capable of armed resistance have survived only as scattered remnants in a few areas, and are now generally inactive."[59] Thus, officials in the Eisenhower administration began to accept that rollback in Eastern Europe was a lost cause.

Although many of America's covert operations behind the Iron Curtain continued for several years—many still explicitly with the objective of regime change—in practice, the objectives for these interventions may have fallen short of regime change and instead sought to raise the costs for the Soviet Union of its continued domination of the region. For instance, NSC 174 explained, "Policy within that field would be determined with a view to contributing toward the eventual elimination of dominant Soviet power over these people, but its usefulness need not depend on its effectiveness in achieving this purpose within any given period of time." Instead, the report continues, "the more immediate criteria for judging the desirability of any particular measures would be their effectiveness in slowing down Soviet exploitation of the human and material resources of the satellites, in maintaining popular resistance to and non-cooperation with Soviet policies, and in strengthening those forces which would minimize Soviet assets and maximize Soviet liabilities in this area in case of war."[60] In July 1956, NSC 5608 officially scaled backed the objectives of America's covert operations along these lines:

> U.S. policy should be directed toward the weakening and the eventual elimination of dominant Soviet power over these peoples, although the accomplishment of this goal in the near future cannot be expected. The more immediate criteria for judging the desirability of any particular measures would be their effectiveness in promoting and encouraging evolutionary change toward the weakening of Soviet controls and the attainment of national independence by the countries concerned.[61]

While the United States continued to run clandestine espionage and propaganda missions in Eastern Europe throughout the Cold War, it was not until the 1980s, when declining Soviet power once again enabled new opposition groups to emerge, that the United States launched another covert regime change mission in the region.

Case Study: Albania

Operation BGFIEND—America's plan to overthrow the government of Albania—was one of the largest covert offensive missions of the early Cold War. Beginning in 1949, the OPC and CIA sought to topple the Soviet-backed regime of Enver Hoxha by infiltrating small groups of dissidents into the country so that they could incite a nationwide revolt. It was, in the words of OPC director Frank Wisner, "a clinical experiment to see whether larger roll-back operations would be feasible elsewhere."[62] This section first provides a brief historical background of Albania, followed by a discussion of the regime change mission and the reasons why it failed.

At the time of America's intervention, Albania was considered the least developed country within the Soviet bloc. Before WWII, Albania had been a monarchy led by the dictatorial King Zog I.[63] After Fascist Italy conquered Albania in April 1939, however, King Zog fled to London in exile, and Italian forces established a puppet regime led by the Albanian Fascist Party in his place. Italian rule was unpopular and provoked the emergence of numerous Albanian dissident groups seeking to overthrow the fascist regime. Of these groups, three were most influential: (1) the National Liberation Movement (NLM), a communist group led by Enver Hoxha;[64] (2) the Balli Kombëtar (BK), a nationalist group led by Midhat Frashëri, which opposed both communism and monarchy; and (3) the Legaliteti, a pro-monarchist group led by Abas Kupi, seeking the return of King Zog.[65] In addition to their conflicting political views, the three groups differed along a variety of other fronts. The communist NLM was led by leftist intellectuals, and the group was comprised primarily of followers from Islamic or Eastern Orthodox backgrounds in southern Albania, who spoke the Tosk dialect of Albanian. Both the BK and Legaliteti, by contrast, were led by conservative business and landowning elites, and their followers included individuals from Roman Catholic backgrounds from the northern part of the country, who spoke the Gheg dialect of Albanian.[66]

When Italy surrendered in July 1943, the NLM and Balli Kombëtar joined forces to topple Italy's puppet regime in Albania.[67] However, this collaboration quickly broke down after the two groups disagreed over their conflicting political aims and the postwar status of Kosovo. (The NLM wanted to return Kosovo to Yugoslavia, whereas the BK wanted to incorporate it into Albania.)[68] Soon after, NLM and BK forces began to clash openly. In October 1943, Hoxha ordered NLM forces to "attack and destroy the force of the Balli Kombëtar wherever they may find them, even if it should mean suspending operations against the Germans."[69] Midhat Frashëri gave similar instructions to his BK followers, and when Nazi Germany invaded Albania in September 1943, many Ballist (BK) units opted to collaborate with the German occupiers against the NLM. Afterward, many BK members held prominent positions in the new fascist government. By early 1944, twenty Ballist battalions were fighting alongside Nazis against Hoxha's partisans.[70] Some Ballists also joined the Nazi-organized Albanian SS Skanderbeg Division—a group known to have committed anti-Semitic purges.[71] Over the course of 1944, however, Hoxha's NLM slowly gained the upper hand. By November, the Nazi-backed regime fell, and the communists assumed power, with Hoxha serving as prime minister. The following spring, communists won seventy-seven out of a possible eighty-two seats during elections for a national assembly.[72]

As in the Baltic States, the British launched the first covert efforts to overthrow the new communist government. Although the British Special Operations Executive (SOE) had covertly backed the NLM's effort to expel Nazi forces during WWII, they objected to their creation of a communist state afterward. Anglo-Albanian relations deteriorated even further after Albania fired on British warships conducting a minesweeping mission in the Corfu Channel, claiming that the ships had invaded Albanian territorial waters.[73] Consequently, as early as 1946, British forces tried to destabilize Hoxha's regime in favor of the exiled King Zog.[74] However, as postwar Britain struggled to rebuild its economy, it lacked the resources to fund large overseas operations.[75] Thus, in 1949, MI6 and the British Foreign Office (BFO) lobbied American policymakers to collaborate and finance their mission, codenamed Operation Valuable.

American policymakers were intrigued by the possibility. The operation meshed with the more aggressive rollback policies proposed in PPS 59, and offered the added benefit of indirectly supporting US objectives in Greece. OPC Deputy Frank Lindsay explained, "The Communists were supplying their guerrillas in Greece out of their bases in Macedonia, Bulgaria, and Albania. The requirement came essentially out of State: we have to do something to relieve the pressure on Greece by stirring up a little trouble in their own back yard."[76] As a result, Secretary of State Dean Acheson later recalled that the British Foreign Minister Ernest Bevin "asked me if we would basically agree to bring down the Hoxha (Communist) government . . . I said yes."[77]

In June 1949, the OPC formally approved the operation, which they codenamed BGFIEND.[78] On July 1, 1949, the CIA Office of Confidential Funds approved $900,000 for the project through the end of 1950, broken down into $126,500 for personnel expenses, $100,000 for supplies, and $500,000 for equipment.[79] A CIA report from October 1949 outlined Washington's objectives for intervention:

Current U.S. policy with regard to Albania has as its objective the restoration of Albanian independence through the overthrow of the Moscow-controlled regime and its replacement by an enlightened government acceptable to the people of Albania. Such a government would enjoy the support of the United

States as long as it remains friendly to the U.S. and its objectives and hostile to the Soviet Government and its objectives.[80]

To oversee the operation, an Anglo-American Special Policy Committee was set up with James McCarger and Frank Lindsay representing the OPC, Robert Joyce representing Kennan's Policy Planning Staff, Lord Earl Jellicoe representing the BFO, and MI6's Kim Philby acting as liaison between the British and American intelligence agencies.[81]

Albania made an appealing target. The state was diplomatically isolated compared to other Soviet-backed regimes, and after the Soviet-Yugoslav split of 1948, it no longer bordered the Soviet bloc. In addition, Albania's mountainous terrain facilitated guerilla operations, and opposition to Hoxha was considered widespread.[82] Indeed, one State Department official estimated that the opposition "included almost everyone not directly involved in the regime."[83] As a result, American analysts predicted that "under proper circumstances, a successful revolt could be initiated by the United States with a force introduced from abroad of only 1000 to 2000 men."[84]

At the same time, however, US planners acknowledged that Moscow's control of Hoxha's regime was "the most open and direct of any in the Soviet orbit."[85] In addition, Hoxha had numerous Russian advisors overseeing his 65,000-man army and 15,000-man security force. Thus, they feared that the mission could spark Soviet retaliation, and possibly even "risk starting World War III inadvertently by placing the USSR in a position she feels she cannot accept."[86] Nevertheless, US planners considered that unlikely. One 1949 analysis stated, "The USSR will probably not use Soviet or Satellite Armed Forces to put down a revolution in Albania" nor would they "attack any western nation or Yugoslavia as a result of an overthrow of the present Albanian regime."[87]

National security concerns were paramount throughout the deliberations. If successful, the operation would secure numerous national security interests. For one, toppling Hoxha's regime would result in a "worldwide loss of USSR prestige," which would help the United States to win the ideological contest of the Cold War. Second, US planners believed it would deny the Soviets access to the Adriatic Sea, thereby increasing the security of the US Navy's Sixth Fleet, which operated in the area.[88] Third, the mission would rid America's newfound ally, Yugoslavian president Josip Broz Tito, of a potential adversary and pave the way for a regional alliance of Albania, Yugoslavia, and Italy.[89] Fourth, it would also "greatly aid the activation of widespread resistance in other satellites and in the Soviet Union as it would be proof that it is possible for an underground resistance group to throw off successfully a communist regime."[90] Finally, US policymakers believed that the operations could succeed at a low cost, some sources even claiming that "for peanuts the US could get a friendly government in Albania."[91]

None of the alternative theories offers a convincing account of American actions. For one, there is no evidence that planners foresaw either short-term or long-term economic gains from intervening. On the contrary, some US policymakers thought that the prospect of providing economic aid to a newly liberated Albania was an argument *against* intervention. In the words of one OPC document, the "economic value of Albania is practically negligible. In fact, Albania is more a detriment than an asset."[92] Likewise, there is no evidence that the United States was trying to create a liberal regime within Albania. The operational plans do not mention establishing a democracy, and the groups supported by the United States were not democratic. In fact, OPC director Wisner admitted, "Albania is not, nor was it, a democracy. It is only beginning to emerge from a tribal era. A new Albanian regime probably could not provide a workable democracy; military dictatorship would probably result."[93] Finally, as discussed below, the United States violated norms of justified intervention by promoting illiberal groups known to have committed war crimes.

The first phase of the plan was to develop "a refugee Albanian Committee to serve both as a front and as a rallying point for subsequent activities."[94] The OSS had identified fifty-five different active resistance groups in Albania at the end of WWII.[95] Of these, the two most influential were the Balli Kombëtar and King Zog's Legaliteti. However, each group presented major problems. The BK had collaborated with both the Italian and German occupying governments, and numerous Ballist leaders could be tied to massacres as a result.[96] Analysts also doubted their reliability and competency. One CIA report remarked that the "Balli Kombëtar was at all times so poorly organized and so confused by its own concurrent double-dealings with Axis and Ally that it never became aware of its primary patriotic duty."[97] Conversely, members of the Legaliteti had collaborated with the Nazis, and their entire political agenda seemed to only amount to restoring the monarchy.[98] In addition, the groups had problems with one another.[99] Even so, after extensive negotiations, OPC/CIA agents persuaded the groups to join forces to form a new organization seated in New York, known as the National Committee for a Free Albania (NCFA). They agreed that the BK and Legaliteti would each comprise 40 percent of the NCFA's membership while the remaining 20 percent could come from other groups.[100] Midhat Frashëri, the BK leader, was selected to be the NCFA's first leader.

On August 26, 1949, the NCFA made its debut in a press conference in Paris. The NCFA's first proclamation declared, "A Committee for Free Albania is created to represent all those Albanians who wish to establish a government representative of the fundamental human rights in their country. . . . All activities of the committee aim at the restoration of the full independence, sovereignty and territorial integrity of the Albanian nation."[101] Soon after, NCFA leaders were invited to visit the United States at the behest of the

Committee for Free Europe, an OPC-funded cover organization. However, many members of the NCFA had difficulty acquiring US visas, given their wartime collaboration with Nazi Germany.[102] The State Department turned down their visas, ruling that the "political backgrounds of many of the Albanian exiles in Italy are somewhat checkered and . . . might sooner or later occasion embarrassment."[103] Thus, the OPC found itself in the uncomfortable position of promoting foreign leaders whom another branch of the US government did not even want in the country.[104] Declassified documents from the Nazi War Crimes Act show that the United States conspired with numerous known war criminals as a part of this endeavor. For instance, they encouraged Hasan Dosti to become head of the NCFA following Frashëri's death, despite knowing that he "served as a Cabinet Minister under the fascists."[105] Likewise, the CIA collaborated with Xhaver Deva despite his behavior during WWII as "a German agent and 'prize quisling'" who had started "a pro-German movement."[106]

The second stage of the plan called for a major psychological warfare initiative to "bolster the morale of the Albanian people and give them a sense of direct participation in a dynamic resistance movement supported by the West through the National Committee for Free Albania" and "stimulate passive resistance and active sabotage."[107] Toward this end, the CIA's Psychological and Paramilitary Staff funded NCFA publications, launched high-altitude balloon drops of anti-Hoxha leaflets, and created Radio Free Albania.[108] According to a CIA report, the propaganda's main objective was to "exacerbate Albania's already difficult political and economic situation and consequently to weaken the present regime's hold on the people. Propaganda activities therefore should be geared to create among the Albanian population—and in some instances among the present regime—feelings of insecurity, chaos, resentment, and fear, keeping the hope for eventual liberation alive."[109]

The third phase of the operation involved covertly infiltrating local anticommunist dissidents into Albania to incite a rebellion that would topple Hoxha's government. With the help of the Gehlen Organization, the OPC/CIA and British SIS began to recruit Albanian émigrés from within displaced persons camps in 1949. One Albanian dissident, Vasil Andoni, recalled, "Those were the golden days. They promised us the moon. They were going to protect us from our greedy neighbors and free us from the communists at the same time."[110] These dissidents—known as "pixies"—were to form the backbone of Albania's anti-communist resistance. OPC case officer Michael Burke explained the process:

Each member committed himself to find among his political followers in the refugee camps and elsewhere suitable men who would volunteer to be pathfinders, who would parachute into their country in pairs, establish initial contacts and form the first resistance cadres. If the results were positive, a larger body of men would be recruited for paramilitary training and would be infiltrated in commando-like units at some propitious time.[111]

Although Wisner initially wanted to train the émigrés at a US base in Libya, he agreed to switch to Malta, observing, "Whenever we want to subvert any place, we find that the British own an island within easy reach."[112] Each state had a preferred means to infiltrate the pixies. The British liked to use MI6 and SIS boat incursions along Albania's southern coast and overland missions from Greece. The Americans preferred OPC parachute drops into northern and central Albania.

In 1949, the joint Anglo-American team infiltrated three groups of pixies into Albania by sea with varying levels of success. Two missions successfully infiltrated their pixies into the country only for them to find that Albanian security forces were hot on their trail, forcing them to cross over into Greece without having established a base of resistance.[113] The third mission was a disaster. On September 16, 1949, nine pixies were dropped on the Karaburu Peninsula. Five men were killed shortly afterward, and four escaped to Greece.[114] Other infiltrations had similar results throughout 1950 and 1951.[115] One Albanian dissident later recalled, "I parachuted into the Mati in 1950. . . . Others came to join us. Some across the frontier and some by sea. But the ones who came by sea never found us. They landed and the police were always there."[116] Discouraged by the operation's poor record, the British government decreased its role, and from 1952 onward, the mission was an almost exclusively American affair.[117]

To replace their losses, the United States established a training camp for 250 émigrés on a base near Heidelberg, Germany.[118] These men, known as Company 4000, were involved in America's first unilateral airdrop on November 11, 1950.[119] Over the next year and half, Company 4000 launched over a dozen major pixie infiltrations. During these airdrop operations, the pixies were loaded onto C-54 cargo planes piloted by Polish exiles at a military airfield outside of Athens and then parachuted into the Albanian countryside under the cover of darkness. Almost every mission failed. On November 19, for instance, two groups of pixies were dropped into the country. Albanian security forces immediately captured the first group while the second group struggled to survive because they could not locate the supplies dropped for them by the Polish pilots. Halil Nerguti, one of the pixies dropped in the operation, later complained, "We had received instructions that as soon as we landed we had to signal to the pilot in order for him to throw the material. But the pilot did not wait for the signal and threw the material in the darkness, without us knowing where it had fallen. . . . We looked in vain. The next day, the material was caught by the forces of Sigurimi and the frontier guards."[120] Eventually, the group fled to Yugoslavia.[121]

In January 1951, Hoxha's security forces gunned down twenty-nine out of forty-three pixies that were smuggled into northern Albania to stir up resistance among the Catholic population; the remainder were arrested.[122] A group dropped the following month was arrested en masse by Albanian security forces.[123] During another mission in July, the OPC dropped three groups of pixies, of which "one was obliterated on landing, one was surrounded in a house and burned alive, while two pixies of the last group of four were killed and the other two captured, with an embarrassing public trial in Albania that fall."[124] On October 24, Radio Tirana reported the "annihilation of thirteen spies dropped by parachute on Albanian territory by the United States Espionage services" and correctly identified seven OPC agents by name.[125] The next day, the station followed up by announcing the elimination of "seven spies and diversionists parachuted into Albania by the British Intelligence Services."[126] Indeed, one study found that of forty-nine Albanian agents that had been infiltrated by the United State between November 1950 and October 1951, only two were still alive and in contact with the control center in Athens by the end of 1951.[127]

Given this poor record, or what the CIA euphemistically described as "adverse developments in the infiltration program," US planners began to worry that Albanian security forces were being forewarned of the operations and patrolling the pixie drop sites in advance.[128] In July 1951, suspicion settled on Kim Philby, a member of the Special Policy Committee that had been established to oversee rollback operations, who had served as the British liaison in Washington to the FBI, CIA, and OPC.[129] Thanks to his strategic position, Philby had been able to reveal to his Soviet handlers the coordinates of OPC/CIA infiltrations into Albania.[130] After two of his close associates defected to the Soviet Union in spring 1951, Philby was unable to shake the cloud of suspicion enveloping him and was dismissed from his position within the SIS in late July 1951.[131]

At the same time that US planners realized that the operation had been compromised, however, they also received word of growing unrest within Albania. "There is mounting evidence of active opposition to the Hoxha regime," one optimistic 1951 intelligence report declared. "A German POW who was repatriated from Albania in June 1950 had heard that the Balli Kombëtar had an active underground organization and said its members rarely fell into the hands of the police and they nearly always received prior warning from the population."[132] A small group of pixies, infiltrated in early 1952, began to radio back to their OPC handlers that they had recruited Albanians who were sympathetic to their cause, and requested money, weapons, and additional training to help spread the growing rebellion.[133] Inspired by similar reports, the CIA and OPC decided to continue the infiltration operations. 1952 operational plans called for two types of agent operations: "penetration operations" with the goal of "the subversion of key figures so that the required degree of neutralization of the army and other vital branches of the Hoxha government is achieved at such time as the moment seems appropriate for the overthrow of the regime" and "harassment operations" with the "objective of maintaining the passive resistance of the Albanian people against the regime and developing dormant resistance potential."[134] Policymakers continued running covert operations of this nature into Albania until 1954.[135]

Despite these positive signs, however, Hoxha's forces continued to intercept the pixie drops. In December 1953, US analysts discovered the reason why: the broadcasts were a ruse by the KGB and Hoxha's secret police, the Sigurimi, to entrap additional partisans. Hoxha later claimed in his memoirs:

> We force the captured agents to make radio contact with their espionage centers in Italy and elsewhere, hence to play our game, totally deceiving these centers, which showed themselves to be completely incompetent and shortsighted. Things went so far that they dropped us whatever we dictated to their agents who had fallen into the trap. The bands of the criminals, who were dropped in by parachute or infiltrated across the border at our request, came like lambs to the slaughter, while the armaments and other materials which they dropped or brought with them went to our account. In a word, they came and we were waiting for them.[136]

In 1954, Hoxha's administration launched a major show trial of eight of the captured pixies, revealing the American operation in remarkable detail.[137] Finally, on April 16, 1956, the CIA cancelled its remaining support for the NCFA due to "budgetary reasons and because of the relative ineffectiveness for political purposes of the existing arrangement."[138]

Even without Philby's espionage, however, there are many reasons to suspect that Operation BGFIEND/Valuable was never going to succeed. Indeed, Philby resigned from his intelligence role years before the operation was finally cancelled, suggesting that there were deeper reasons for its failure. To begin, policymakers undermined the credibility of their endeavor by ignoring the alleged past crimes of the NCFA leadership. For instance, Hasan Dosti, the second leader of the NCFA and a BK member, had served as Minister of Justice during the Italian fascist regime. As a result, Hoxha's government was able to undermine the NCFA's legitimacy by labeling Dosti a "war criminal" and tying him to "large-scale massacres, imprisonments and confinements of the people."[139] Second, planners underestimated the difficulty of inciting a mass nationalist uprising in a state whose population lacked a strong sense of national identity. In this regard, Albania was a particularly poor target for intervention. In the words of one CIA analysis, "Albania as an independent, national state is more an artificial creation of power than an expression of national will."[140] Instead, the Albanian population was split into two major ethnic groupings (the Gheg and Tosk) and across three major religions (70% Muslim, 20% Greek Orthodox, and 10% Catholic).[141] This, in turn, complicated Anglo-American efforts to unify disparate anti-communist groups and create propaganda messages with widespread appeal. Third, Albania's underdevelopment hindered America's psychological warfare initiatives. Written propaganda was ineffective in a country where 80 percent of the population was illiterate.[142] Likewise, Radio Free Albania struggled because the population largely did not have radios or electricity.[143] Fourth, and perhaps because it was one of the OPC's first missions, US planners repeatedly made amateurish mistakes, such as misdirecting their high-altitude weather balloons and accidentally dropping anti-Hoxha propaganda in Yugoslavia, Bulgaria, and over the sea.[144] On other occasions, they air-dropped émigrés into Albania without having given them proper parachute training.[145] One Albanian recruit later recalled, "We asked for parachute training but the Americans refused. They said that one of us might break a leg. We replied that we would rather break a leg in Germany than while landing in Albania."[146] The lack of country-specific expertise also led to easily avoidable mistakes. For example, few in Albania heard the NCFA's first radiobroadcast into Albania because it went on the air at 4:00 p.m., and Albanian authorities did not switch on electricity in the country until 6:00 p.m.[147]

Most importantly, policymakers consistently overestimated their ability to keep the US role secret. Wisner lamented, "An operation that was supposed to be kept under the wraps of secrecy was known in all relevant details by anyone in the region that had an interest in Albania."[148] The operation's cover was likely blown as soon as OPC and SIS agents began contacting Albanian émigrés to form the NCFA. Indeed, as early as September 1949, OPC analysts warned, "It is apparent that U.S. (OPC) intentions in Albania are no longer secret and that Soviet Intelligence is undoubtedly aware of contemplated U.S.-British intervention in Albania. As a result the successful accomplishment of all the phases of project BGFIEND will become increasingly difficult."[149] The mission's cover was certainly blown by March 1950, when the *New York Times* reported that the United States was attempting to covertly destabilize Hoxha's regime.[150] The result, as CIA director Walter Bedell Smith explained in 1951, was that "somewhere in the process it becomes pointless to attempt to deceive the enemy on US participation, just as it would have been naïve for the USSR to expect the United States to believe it had no part in supporting and directing the Greek Communist guerillas."[151] Consequently, the United States could not muster the requisite forces to overthrow the regime while maintaining plausible deniability. OPC agent Michael Burke lamented: "In the end, it was not possible to do without overt air and military support from England and the United States or somewhere. You couldn't do it with just the locals."[152] OPC agent and future head of the CIA's European division, Frank Lindsay, agreed: "The Kremlin wasted Philby on Albania. The operation went down the drain because we couldn't maintain security in the DP camps and because the communist security apparatus was so damn strong."[153]

Case Study: Ukrainian Soviet Socialist Republic

America's covert efforts to overthrow the Ukrainian Soviet Socialist Republic unfolded in a similar manner to its mission in Albania, despite the fact that the Ukrainian partisan groups supported by the United States were older, larger, and more established than their Albanian counterparts. The origin of the Ukrainian partisans dates back to the Ukrainian War of Independence (1917–21), when Ukrainian nationalists fought Russian, Bolshevik, and Polish forces in an effort to establish an independent nation-state. By 1921, however, the Soviet Union had conquered most of Ukraine, and Poland annexed the western regions of Galicia and Volhynia. Ukrainian nationalists formed several independent underground movements in response, and in 1929, these groups merged to form the Organization of Ukrainian Nationalists (OUN), with the goal of reclaiming the lost territories and overthrowing the Soviet regime. The 1930s, however, proved disastrous for their movement. Stalin's first Five-Year Plan, implemented between 1928 and 1932, devastated millions of lives through a policy of forced industrialization, deportation, and collectivization, and created the largest human-created famine in history, with an estimated 3.3 million Ukrainians deliberately starved to death in 1932 and 1933.[154] The Great Terror of 1937–38 killed an additional 300,000 Polish and Ukrainian Soviet citizens within the region.[155] Given the brutality of Soviet rule, many Ukrainian nationalists began to look toward Nazi Germany as potential liberators.

In September 1939, Germany and the USSR invaded Poland following a secret agreement, known as the Molotov-Ribbentrop Pact, between the two countries to divide Poland between them. Afterward, Soviet Ukraine reincorporated the territories of Galicia and Volhynia. As a result, many Ukrainian fighters who had been arrested by the Polish government were freed and then reunited with Ukrainian nationalists from within Soviet Ukraine. Two of these nationalists, Mikola Lebed and Stepan Bandera—hard-line members of the OUN who had been serving life sentences for their alleged role in the assassination of the Polish minister of the interior in 1934—would later become prominent.[156] Within the OUN, however, tension grew between its established leadership and the more radical younger generation of Galician nationalists. In August 1940, Bandera split from the group, forming a new revolutionary faction (OUN-B).[157]

In the months leading up to Germany's surprise attack against the Soviet Union, OUN-B leader Bandera met with Nazi leaders to establish two Ukrainian battalions to assist the German Army during its invasion, codenamed Operation Barbarossa, and accepted 2.5 million marks to fund covert operations against the USSR.[158] Consequently, two Ukrainian battalions fought alongside Nazi forces during Germany's invasion on June 22, 1941. The Ukrainian auxiliaries proved to be willing and ready collaborators for the

Nazi mass killing program in Eastern Europe. In April 1941, OUN-B propaganda had declared, "Jews in the USSR constitute the most faithful support of the Bolshevik regime and vanguard of Muscovite imperialism in Ukraine."[159] Likewise, at a July 1941 meeting, OUN-B forces ruled that Jews "have to be treated harshly. . . . We must finish them off. . . . Regarding the Jews, we will adopt any methods that lead to their destruction."[160] In the days following the German invasion, OUN-B troops launched pogroms throughout East Galicia, killing an estimated 12,000 Jewish civilians.[161]

On June 30, 1941, OUN-B proclaimed an independent Ukrainian state, with its capital in Lvov. However, Hitler had never intended for Ukrainian "subhumans" to actually achieve independence, and he promptly ordered a crackdown on the OUN-B within twenty-four hours.[162] Bandera was sent to the Sachsenhausen concentration camp.[163] Despite their leader's imprisonment, OUN-B continued to survive underground, and consolidated control in Western Ukraine and Galicia. During this period, Lebed, OUN-B fighters, and other partisan groups around Galicia consolidated their forces into the Ukrainian Insurgent Army (UPA) to fight for Ukrainian independence from both the Nazi and Soviet regimes. To create a homogenous Ukrainian state, the UPA engaged in widespread terrorism, mass killing, and ethnic cleansing against the Polish, German, Soviet, and Jewish populations in the region. Their manifesto declared, "Long live greater independent Ukraine without Jews, Poles and Germans: Poles behind the San [River], Germans to Berlin, Jews to the gallows."[164]

One of the UPA's major targets was the Polish population in Western Ukraine. In April 1943, UPA leader Lebed declared that they should "cleanse the entire revolutionary territory of the Polish population."[165] The diary of a Ukrainian Jew who survived the war by hiding in an attic, Moshe Maltz, recounts that "Bandera men . . . are not discriminating about who they kill; they are gunning down the populations of entire villages. . . . Since there are hardly any Jews left to kill, the Bandera gangs have turned on the Poles. They are literally hacking Poles to pieces. Every day . . . you can see the bodies of Poles with wires around their necks, floating down the river Bug."[166] In the first half of 1943, UPA partisans and Ukrainian peasants murdered 40,000 Poles in Volhynia. On a single day, July 11, 1943, the UPA killed 10,000 Poles in 167 separate locations.[167]

By July 1944, however, the Red Army returned to the region during its westward offensive against Nazi forces. Using arms and munitions left behind by the retreating Germans, the UPA redirected their attacks toward the Soviets.[168] Maltz's diary notes, "Most of the Bandera gangs, men and women, from the villages . . . are still hiding out in the woods, armed to the teeth, and hold up Soviet soldiers. The Soviets may be the rulers of the towns, but the Bandera gangs reign supreme in the surrounding countryside, especially at night. The Russians . . . have their hands full. . . . Hardly a day passes without a Soviet official being killed."[169] That same month, members of the UPA, OUN-B, and several other nationalist groups came together to form the Supreme Ukrainian Liberation Council (UHVR), with the UPA acting as its military branch. The UHVR's manifesto called for the unity of "all leading political elements, irrespective of their ideological convictions or political affiliation, who uphold the political sovereignty of the Ukrainian state."[170] By the end of 1945, Soviet sources estimate that the Ukrainian nationalists had killed over 30,000 Soviet soldiers and collaborators.[171]

After the Soviet front passed through Ukraine, approximately 40,000 UHVR partisans retreated into the Carpathian Mountains—forces that the United States would later look to as the potential source for a major anti-Soviet rebellion.[172] American officials first came into direct contact with the UHVR in April 1946.[173] Over the next few months, the US Strategic Services Unit (SSU) and CIC gathered information on the Ukrainian resistance by interviewing Ukrainian émigrés within American displaced persons camps.[174] Owing to the wartime collaboration between Nazi Germany and the Ukrainian partisans, the Gehlen Organization played a decisive role in making many of the introductions. One 1947 CIC report notes, "The German Underground [aka Gehlen Organization], composed of former HJ [Hitler Youth] Leaders, SS [Schutzstaffel paramilitary forces] Officers and other high ranking NSDAP [National Socialist German Workers' Party] members, are working in close connection with the Bandera movement, because he holds excellent connections through his network of agents and informants which are spread throughout all four zones of occupied Germany, Austria, Czechoslovakia, Russia and Poland."[175] Another December 1946 analysis declared that "after a thorough study of the Ukrainian problem and a comparison of information from several sources in Germany, Austria and Rome, source believes that UHVR, UPA and OUN-Bandera are the only large and efficient organizations among Ukrainians."[176] Beginning in 1946, American intelligence forces began to use Ukrainians in Germany for espionage and counterespionage projects.[177]

One partisan introduced to American intelligence agencies was Mikola Lebed, the leader of the UHVR and chief of the Sluzba Bezpeka (SB), the security branch of the OUN-B. As mentioned earlier, Lebed had been an early and influential member of the OUN-B, had served time for the assassination of the Polish minister of the interior, and had encouraged the ethnic cleansing of Polish civilians in 1943. Indeed, one 1947 CIC report cites sources labeling Lebed a "well-known sadist and collaborator of the Germans."[178] Nevertheless, in February 1947, Lebed approached the CIC about the possibility of collaboration. According to the CIC report,

> The SB would be willing to offer the CIC the use of its nets in Germany and is prepared, upon request, to send agents into Soviet Occupied Europe. In support, the SB would expect guarantee of financial aid, assistance in solving of housing and transportation problems. . . . The fact that the SB was being used by U.S. authorities would be known only to BANDERA, no more

than three top agents of the SB, and the U.S. authorities making the contact. The agents in the net would continue to work as before, and would not know that their information was being forwarded to a U.S. agency.[179]

The CIC accepted the deal, and US officials moved Lebed and his family to Munich to avoid extradition by the Soviet Union.

The CIC got another major break on September 10, 1947, when German police alerted them to the presence of foreign fighters near Passau.[180] Fearing a Soviet invasion, the CIC formed a search party and located a band of men with Soviet uniforms and equipment. According to a CIA history of the event, "American troops disarmed and interned a detachment of thirty-five soldiers of the Ukrainian Insurgent Army (UPA) in the area of Passau. This UPA detachment, equipped with machine guns and automatic pistols, succeeded in forcing its way from the Carpathians through Czechoslovakia via Linz (Austria), to Wildernraan near Passau, in four weeks' time."[181] After interviewing the men for over three weeks, the CIC determined that they were members of the UPA that had been sent west to make contact with American forces. Along the way, the group reported twenty-two separate military engagements, including one that killed the Polish vice minister of defense.[182]

At the same time that the CIC was cultivating these ties with the Ukrainian partisans, Kennan and other American policymakers back in Washington were developing the doctrine of rollback. In April 1948, a top-secret CIA report to the NSC, "Utilization of the Mass of Soviet Refugees in US National Interest," suggested a more aggressive role for these groups:

> During the past three years, CIA (and its predecessors) has systematically explored the potential intelligence value of numerous anti-Communist and anti-Soviet groups in Central and Eastern Europe. Contacts have been developed with the leading groups of the mass of Soviet émigrés, e.g. Ukrainians, Georgians, Balts and White Russians. Although these contacts were established primarily for the purposes of procuring intelligence on Eastern Europe and USSR, sufficient overall information on these groups has been inevitably gathered to permit a sound evaluation of their possible value to the US Government for the purposes of propaganda, sabotage and anti-Communist political activity.[183]

Toward this end, the CIA launched Operation AERODYNAMIC in 1948. The first stage of AERODYNAMIC involved "the successful establishment of courier contact with the resistance movement in the Ukrainian S.S.R."[184] The first covert airdrop into Ukraine occurred on September 5, 1949, when two Czech pilots in an unmarked C-47 flew from an American airfield in West Germany through East Germany, Poland, and into Soviet Ukraine. Although detected by Soviet radar, they dropped two partisans into Lvov. Soon after, in the words of a declassified CIA history, "The Soviets quickly eliminated the agents." Nevertheless, the report goes on to note that the "operation sparked considerable interest at headquarters and resulted in expanded CIA exploitation of the ZPUHVR [Ukrainian Supreme Council of Liberation]."[185]

Subsequent airdrops proved more successful. Indeed, one CIA report found that "the pouches received from the Ukrainian resistance movement as late as October 1950 comprise the largest single green of intelligence reports received from inside the USSR in recent years."[186] In October 1950, the CIA reported that these couriers had revealed three things:

a. A well established and secure underground movement is active today in the Ukrainian SSR under the direction of the Ukrainian Supreme Council of Liberation (UHVR).
b. The UHVR's Ukrainian Insurgent Army (UPA) is still capable of ensuring the physical security of the underground's headquarters and centers of political and propaganda activity. In addition, it carries out retaliation raids on MVD/MGB and Communist Party installations for morale, harassment and propaganda purposes.
c. Anti-Soviet activities conducted by the civilian elements of the movement include the distribution of a wide variety of printed propaganda material, and the expansion of resistance cells throughout the Western and Eastern Ukraine.[187]

With this evidence of a plausible political opposition to support, the CIA determined that "the support, development and exploitation of the Ukrainian Underground movement for resistance and intelligence purposes will be increased on a priority basis."[188] OPC director Wisner noted, "In view of the extent and activity of the resistance movement in Ukraine, we consider this to be a top priority project."[189]

One month later, policymakers drew up operational plans calling for "the exploitation and expansion of the Ukrainian resistance movement for the following purposes, either now or in time of war: a. political and psychological warfare; b. resistance and guerrilla warfare."[190] To establish a unified anti-Soviet émigré front, the United States provided Lebed's UHVR with financial support to create propaganda leaflets, newspapers, radio programs, and books. At the same time as these American operations, British forces ran complementary missions to support Bandera's OUN.[191] Washington also worked to develop widespread anti-Soviet propaganda aimed at creating a unified Ukrainian nationalist movement. For example, one CIA proposal was to create an English-language periodical, tentatively titled *The Nationalist*, "to promote Nationalism as an ideological issue designed to counter the ideological drive of Soviet Communism." Toward that end, the memo continues:

> The Ukrainian nationalist movement in this country and in the world in general could be utilized to serve as a spearhead of a drive to counter the Soviet

Communist ideology and to rally the forces of true nationalistic ideals on the side of the free world. The ideological and social forces behind nationalism represents an antithesis of the Soviet Communist ideology which is totalitarian and international in its political philosophy. True nationalism puts the emphasis on the individual character, of the nation and the country, it represents the centrifugal forces inherently opposed to the maxims and ideas of the Soviet Communist, and for this reason, could be effectively used in countering the Soviet drive to subvert and alienate the underdeveloped nations of the world.[192]

The second component of AERODYNAMIC was an aggressive offensive effort to support UHVR partisans within Ukraine. To do so, the OPC would "provide support through air drop to enable the resistance to expand its organization and potential for OPC-type clandestine activities. This support will include provision of such items as medical supplies, sabotage equipment, limited supplies of specialized arms, printing presses, throw-away radios, etc."[193] Like the Albanian operation, America's covert airdrops into Ukraine were disastrous, and many partisans lost their lives as a result. Kim Philby also played a role in the collapse of this operation. In March 1951, he notified Soviet forces that the United States planned to airdrop three teams of six men into Ukraine.[194] However, as with Albania, Ukrainian partisans continued to be killed in missions following Philby's dismissal in July 1951. A letter from one of the Ukrainian dissidents in September 1952 explains why:

> I regret very much that all my efforts to contact the Leadership have so far failed; the efforts to make contact have cost many lives. I am sure you can understand my despair when I see couriers returning without success or sometimes not returning at all. In the time we have been fighting, the enemy has been able to discover the points in the structure of our organization which are most vulnerable to attack, and has used every means to paralise [sic] contact between different groups of the organization with the purpose of neutralizing the organization's activities. These tactics were well known to us but, of course, strength is on the side of the enemy.[195]

By 1954, the CIA had lost all contact with UHVR forces in Ukraine, and after five years of "abortive missions," the CIA ended AERODYNAMIC's paramilitary efforts.[196] A CIA history of the operation concluded, "In the long run, the Agency's effort to penetrate the Iron Curtain using Ukrainian agents was ill-fated and tragic."[197]

As in Albania, US planners found that the Soviet security forces in Ukraine always seemed to be one step ahead of them. Indeed, they were. Archival evidence shows that Soviet intelligence officials knew of the Anglo-American connections to Ukrainian nationalists as early as 1946. For instance, Historian Jeffrey Burds uncovered a top-secret letter from the Soviet Deputy Minister of Internal Affairs from December 1946 that states,

The character and direction of OUN espionage demonstrates that their re-connaissance activity has been incited by foreign intelligence services. Other OUN documents and materials [obtained] by intelligence-investigative operations of the MVD SSSR provide grounds for supposing that in its espionage the OUN presently is oriented toward the English and Americans.

I hereby order: 1. Notify all operations personnel in the organs of the Ukrainian MVD that work in the struggle against the OUN rebels is simultaneously a struggle against agents of foreign intelligence services.[198]

This order is noteworthy because it shows that any hope of "plausible deniability" was blown before the mission began, and that Soviet officials already associated nationalist movements with American espionage in 1946. This provides some support for the claims made by Soviet spymaster Pavel Sudoplatov that "the origins of the Cold War are closely interwoven with Western support for nationalist unrest in the Baltic areas and Western Ukraine."[199] It also highlights the difficulty of maintaining the secrecy of a covert operation against a powerful state like the Soviet Union. In addition to their agents in Ukraine, the Soviet Union also maintained an extensive spy network in the American displaced persons camps and among the Ukrainian émigré community at large. In the words of Sudoplatov, "There was nothing we didn't know about Ukrainian emigrant organizations and the Bandera movement."[200] Owing to these connections, the Soviet NKVD had largely eliminated many partisan forces within Ukraine by the time AERODYNAMIC got off the ground, suggesting that the covert mission never stood a chance of success.

Case Study: Yugoslavia

In the context of the early Cold War, American behavior toward Yugoslavia seems like an anomaly. US policymakers never tried to "roll back" Tito's government—unlike every other communist regime in Eastern Europe. What was different about Yugoslavia? Contrary to the predictions of the ideological and normative theories of regime change, the United States actually *supported* Tito in a strategic effort to fracture the Soviet bloc. This section first provides a brief background on Yugoslavia, followed by a discussion of the reasons why US officials decided not to intervene in this case.

As with Albania and Ukraine, to understand America's Cold War policy in Yugoslavia, one must first look at the political situation within the country during WWII. The Axis powers conquered Yugoslavia within two weeks in April 1941. In response, two major Yugoslavian resistance movements quickly emerged to combat the occupying forces: the Yugoslav Partisans, a communist group led by Josip Broz Tito, and the Chetniks, a Serbian nationalist and pro-monarchy movement.[201] Initially the two groups collaborated against the Axis forces; however, they split in 1941 because of their incompatible postwar aims. In their bid to establish an independent Serbian state, the Chetniks went on to collaborate with both the Italian and German occupying forces against the Partisans and other non-Serbian groups.[202] Eventually, Tito's Partisans gained the upper hand in the bloody civil war. Over the next four years, the Partisans successfully defeated their Nazi and Italian occupiers as well as the fascist puppet regimes in Croatia and Montenegro. In March 1945, Tito was appointed prime minister of the newly liberated state of Yugoslavia.

Given the covert missions that the United States launched in Albania, Ukraine, and eleven other places in Eastern Europe, it is reasonable to expect that American policymakers would want to do the same in Yugoslavia. If ideology alone drove US policy, we would expect American policymakers to have targeted Tito's Communist regime as it did the other communist states behind the Iron Curtain. Many of the prerequisites for intervention appear to be there. In the "long telegram," Kennan identified the Yugoslav government as a "propaganda machine" whose policies "can be placed extensively at the disposal of the Soviet Union."[203] Likewise, Truman denounced Tito for his covert support of communist forces in the Greek Civil War.[204] Additionally, US intelligence agencies spent the years following WWII cultivating similar contacts with anti-Communist Yugoslavian émigré groups as they had with other dissident groups throughout Eastern Europe. Declassified documents from the Nazi War Crime Disclosure Act reveal that the CIC, CIA, SIS, and the Gehlen Organization all maintained contact with the Serbian Chetniks and former members of the Croatian Ustaša regime because of their opposition to Tito's government.[205]

Why didn't American policymakers try to overthrow Yugoslavia? The answer lies in Tito's relationship with Moscow. Yugoslavia and the USSR remained allies after WWII. Over the next three years, however, tension grew between the two regimes. Stalin objected to Tito's independent foreign policy, and he criticized Tito for unnecessarily provoking Western powers by trying to incorporate Italian territory into Yugoslavia and openly supporting the Greek communists during their civil war. The rift deepened in 1948 when Tito announced that Yugoslavia would be following an independent economic plan compared to the rest of the Soviet bloc. In retaliation, the Cominform expelled Yugoslavia on June 28.[206] This came as a shock to American policymakers. Before the split, many assumed that Eastern European communist leaders would always heed Soviet orders. However, Kennan quickly realized the diplomatic opportunities that the split offered. Tito's expulsion suggested that nationalist interests could trump transnational communist forces; the Soviet bloc was not monolithic. Two days later, he wrote,

A new factor of fundamental and profound significance has been introduced into the communist movement by the demonstration that the Kremlin can

153

be successfully defied by one of its own minions. By this act, the aura of mystical omnipotence and infallibility, which has surrounded the Kremlin power has been broken. The possibility of defection from Moscow, which has heretofore been unthinkable for foreign communist leaders, will from now on be present in one form or another in the mind of every one of them.[207]

What's more, Kennan felt that the defection could be repeated. The Soviet Union was "so overbearing and so cynical" in its treatment of its satellites that "conditions are therefore favorable to a concerted effort on our part designed to take advantage of Soviet mistakes and of the rifts that have appeared, and to promote the steady deterioration of the structure of moral influence by which the authority of the Kremlin has been carried to peoples far beyond the reach of Soviet police power."[208]

For these reasons, Kennan argued that it was in America's best interest to support Yugoslavia. To do so, the United States provided Tito with sufficient aid to prevent the collapse of his regime while also trying to persuade him to abandon his support for Greek communist guerillas. The United States also relaxed its trade restrictions with Yugoslavia and offered Marshall Plan aid to Tito, war materiel, and munitions—provided they did not threaten US security.[209] Policymakers later increased their aid in response to Stalin's covert efforts to overthrow Tito's regime.[210] By demonstrating the feasibility of a non-Stalinist communist regime, US planners hoped to "foster a heretical drifting-away process on the part of the satellite states."[211] Ultimately, they felt that "such a development could conceivably grow to the point where there would be two opposing blocs in the Communist world—a Stalinist group and a non-conformist faction either loosely allied or federated under Tito's leadership."[212]

Contrary to the predictions of many ideological theories of regime change, America's decision to support Tito shows that when its strategic and ideological interests clashed, strategic interests prevailed. Policymakers clearly believed that Yugoslavia was communist. For instance, NSC 58 argued in 1949, "Yugoslavia's state philosophy, like that of the U.S.S.R. and its satellites, is Marxism-Leninism. Furthermore, Tito rose to power and retains it by sedulous application of the Leninist-Stalinist blueprint for totalitarianism. It is only in the third ideological stratum that of subservience to the interests of the U.S.S.R. that Tito openly deviates ideologically from the satellites."[213] However, as long as Yugoslavia remained an adversary to the Soviet Union, it could be a potential ally to the United States. Kennan explained, "Much as we may dislike him, Tito is presently performing brilliantly in our interests in leading successfully and effectively the attack from within the communist family on Soviet imperialism. Tito is being perhaps our most precious asset in the struggle to contain and weaken Russian expansion. He must be allowed to prove on his own communist terms that an Eastern European country can secede from Moscow's control and still succeed."[214] Subsequent

US policy reviews affirmed the utility of supporting Tito's regime. For instance, NSC 174 argued in 1953, "Tito's establishment of an independent communist regime . . . has brought valuable assets to the free world in the struggle against Soviet power. It proves a standing example of successful defiance of the Kremlin and is proof that there is a practical alternative for nationalist communist leaders to submission to Soviet control."[215]

This chapter first examined the emergence of rollback and the role of covert regime change within US grand strategy during the early Cold War. I then compared American actions in Albania, the Ukrainian Soviet Socialist Republic, and Yugoslavia, and found strong support for many of the theoretical claims developed in chapters 2, 3, and 4.

To begin, the Ukrainian and Albanian cases fulfill this study's two prerequisites for regime change. By the time of the first interventions, Moscow and Washington's conflicting visions for the region meant that Soviet-American dispute had reached an impasse. US leaders considered the dispute to be irreconcilable by means short of regime change due to the structure of the international system and the obstinacy of Soviet leaders. Nonetheless, Washington only intervened when policymakers could identify a plausible political alternative with "reasonable prospects of survival."[216] When these opposition forces disappeared in the mid-1950s, US planners scaled back the objectives of these operations. Covert regime change did not resume in Eastern Europe until the 1980s, when the emergence of the Solidarity movement in Poland once again provided policymakers with a plausible anti-Soviet group to support.

Second, US leaders opted for regime change because they believed that by installing groups with whom they shared a deep mutual interest—namely, those countries' independence from the USSR—they increased the odds that the two states would cooperate with the United States in the future. Because these groups unambiguously shared America's primary goal, officials within the Truman and Eisenhower administrations were willing to overlook their past war crimes and authoritarian tendencies. Interestingly, the extent to which US officials actively promoted nationalist groups and nationalist beliefs in their propaganda for these missions shows that, although the Cold War is often portrayed as a battle between the two great transnational ideologies—communism and liberalism—early US foreign policy was premised on harnessing the power of another powerful ideology—nationalism—in the fight against the Soviet Union.

Third, US policymakers focused on national security concerns during their deliberations, specifically the military threat posed by the combined forces of the Soviet bloc. Security concerns were paramount in each major policy-making statement discussed in this chapter: the "long telegram," the Clifford-Elsey Report, the Truman Doctrine, as well as NSC reports 10/2, 20/4, 58, 68, 74, and 5606. The main objective behind these operations was to decrease the military threat posed by the USSR by fracturing the Soviet bloc and preventing Soviet control over strategically valuable territory in Eastern Europe.

Fourth, the alternative arguments do not offer a persuasive account of these missions. Normative accounts cannot explain why the United States agreed to promote groups known to have committed human rights violations or why they were willing to collaborate so closely with former Nazis in the process. Rather, strategic concerns dominated normative ones. In the words of CIA agent Harry Rositzke, "We knew what we were doing. It was a visceral business of using any bastard as long as he was anti-Communist . . . the eagerness or desire to enlist collaborators meant that sure, you didn't look at their credentials too closely."[217] Similarly, ideological accounts cannot explain why the United States failed to promote democratic groups during these missions or why Washington supported Tito's communist regime. Instead, I argued that communist regimes did not inherently threaten American planners on their own, but Soviet control over these states did. Or in the words of CIA director Walter Bedell Smith, "The United States does not fear communism if it is not controlled by Moscow and not committed to aggression."[218] Likewise, in contrast to the rogue CIA hypothesis, Kennan worked hard to ensure that the missions had executive approval and that the NSC had "specific knowledge of the objectives of every operation and also of the procedures and methods employed."[219]

Fifth, US policymakers decided to intervene covertly to minimize costs. Covert conduct lowered security costs by allowing the United States to deflect blame for its actions onto others, eschew entangling commitments to its foreign allies, and avoid directly challenging Soviet prestige. As a result, US policymakers minimized the chance of military escalation with the Soviet Union. Moreover, covert conduct allowed the United States to avoid the reputational costs that it would have suffered had the unsavory details of these operations become publicly known.

Finally, the Albanian and Ukrainian cases illustrate the difficulty of covertly overthrowing a powerful state. All early covert rollback operations yielded similar results. The Anglo-American operations in Latvia, Lithuania, and Estonia, introduced earlier, were doomed to failure from the start. As early as October 1945, MGB (Russian Ministry for State Security) counterintelligence officers captured Latvian infiltrators carrying Secret Intelligence Service (SIS) codebooks and radios. Forcing the infiltrators to collaborate, the MGB was then able to provide false intelligence and identify the time and location of future infiltrations.[220] Ultimately, Soviet forces set up two fictional resistance movements, which the United States and the United Kingdom covertly supported until 1954. The same thing happened in Poland, where the United States ran a large covert operation to support another partisan group deeply penetrated by Soviet spies, the Freedom and Independence Movement (WIN Inside). In Bulgaria, Hungary, Romania, and the

Soviet Union, Soviet forces repeatedly intercepted covert airdrops of partisans, leading one CIA official to remark in 1957, "The path of experience in attempts at the legalization of black infiltrated bodies into the USSR has been strewn with disaster."[221] Likewise, little came from the covert operations to support Czech, Slovak, and East German émigré and dissident groups in their bids to foment popular revolutions. In summary, as CIA agent Rositzke recounted, "These cross-border operations involved enormous resources of technical and documentation support, hundreds of training officers, thousands of safe-houses, and, above all, hundreds of courageous men who preferred to fight the Russians or the communists rather than linger in DP camps or emigrate to Brazil. Scores of agents paid with their lives for our concern."[222]

Containment, Coup d'État, and the Covert War in Vietnam

> They started on me with Diem, you remember? "He was corrupt and he ought to be killed." So we killed him. We all got together and got a goddamn bunch of thugs and we went in and assassinated him. Now, we've really had no political stability since then.
>
> —Lyndon Johnson, February 1, 1966

Whereas the "rollback" operations discussed in the previous chapter aimed to weaken the Soviet bloc on its own terrain, "containment" missions sought to prevent foreign governments from joining the Soviet camp in the first place. Toward this end, Washington launched one overt and twenty-five covert regime changes. Containment was also behind America's longest and bloodiest confrontation of the Cold War—the Vietnam War, a conflict that claimed the lives of between 1.2 and 3.2 million Vietnamese as well as 58,220 Americans.[1] This chapter investigates how and why Presidents Eisenhower, Kennedy, and Johnson escalated America's role in Vietnam and the role that America's covert operations in North and South Vietnam between 1954 and 1964 played in that process. I argue that US leaders launched these operations in an effort to pave the way for an honorable withdrawal from the region. Paradoxically, however, the missions had precisely the opposite effect of their intentions: rather than strengthening the South Vietnamese state and enabling an American pullback, they destabilized the government in Saigon and complicated American military efforts in the north.

This chapter proceeds in four parts. First comes a discussion of case selection and alternative explanations. Next is an analysis of the emergence of the containment strategy in Southeast Asia and America's escalating involvement in Vietnam. The third section details how top-level US policymakers debated launching regime changes against North and South Vietnam at five key points between 1954 and 1963. Finally, the chapter concludes by investigating why policymakers preferred to conduct these operations covertly and why the United States later limited its efforts to overthrow Ho Chi Minh.[2]

Case Selection and Alternative Explanations

Over the course of the Cold War, the United States conducted over two dozen preventive regime change missions in Western Europe, the Middle East, Southeast Asia, and Africa. Although each of these operations is interesting, I have chosen to analyze the Vietnamese case in detail because it allows me to test several of this project's predictions.

The case is well suited for process-tracing American behavior because the United States gradually escalated its role in Vietnam over two decades. This is particularly useful given the potential for selection bias and the problem of identifying "negative cases" that often confronts causal arguments.[3] If this project is correct, the United States should only launch regime changes when two conditions are met: (1) It is embroiled in a security-based dispute with another state driven by irreconcilable policy preferences, and (2) it can identify a plausible alternative to the target government. If I were to look only at known instances of regime change, these two conditions may occur in every case. Logically, however, it does not follow that these two conditions were the decisive factor causing the operations. Thus, to avoid "selecting on the dependent variable," it is important that I identify cases where these necessary conditions did not occur. The Vietnamese case allows me to do so because on several occasions between 1954 and 1964, Eisenhower and Kennedy seriously considered—but ultimately decided against—regime change. What accounted for this variation? As my theory would predict, I find that the United States only intervened when the conditions on the ground precluded it achieving its objectives via means short of regime change, and policymakers believed they could identify a plausible alternative to the existing regime.

The case also allows us to analyze why American leaders preferred to intervene covertly. For instance, Kennedy preferred to covertly intervene in both North and South Vietnam because he believed that it decreased both operations' military, economic, and reputational costs. If the United States intervened overtly, Kennedy feared American prestige would be on the line, and he would be forced to further escalate America's military involvement. For these same reasons, Johnson ended the modest covert mission that Kennedy had launched against North Vietnam in 1964, after determining that the mission's low odds of success did not warrant the risk that it would complicate America's efforts to withdraw from the region.

Moreover, the Vietnamese case also allows comparison of the relative short-term effectiveness of different covert tactics and types of operations. In other words, why are some governments easier to replace than others? For instance, why did a hastily arranged coup overthrow South Vietnam's Ngo Dinh Diem in the fall of 1963, whereas covert efforts to build a resistance movement in North Vietnam never came close to succeeding? This discrepancy points to the fundamental limitations of covert action. The preventive operation in South Vietnam succeeded because the coup plotters were strong relative to Diem, and the mission was easy to conceal because Americans were welcome in the country. By contrast, the offensive operation in North Vietnam failed because the anti-communist fighters covertly backed by the United States were never any match for Hanoi's powerful security apparatus, and the United States faced a limit to the amount of covert assistance it could provide to them without committing ground troops above the 17th parallel. Consequently, more than three-quarters of the agents who the United States covertly infiltrated in the north as part of these efforts were captured or killed by North Vietnamese forces, and the remaining agents went missing in action before they could destabilize Ho's regime. The cases also reveal some of the longer-term impacts of covert interventions. Although the quantitative analyses in chapter 4 are useful for identifying the recurrent effects of regime change across many cases, often the blowback of covert operations is case specific and not easily captured by quantitative measures. For instance, although the 1963 US-backed coup in South Vietnam successfully overthrew Diem's government, it still did not produce the results that planners had hoped for. Contrary to policymakers' predictions, the leaders who took over after Diem were unstable, unpredictable, and incompetent, which in turn hampered South Vietnam's ability to defend itself without US assistance and encouraged the Viet Cong to escalate their attacks.

The cases also allow us to test the competing explanations. The intervention in South Vietnam is inconsistent with the normative, liberal, and economic hypotheses. For one, US actions in South Vietnam clearly violated norms of justified intervention by supporting a military coup that targeted a long-standing ally. The case also contradicts hypothesis 2b that the United States should promote democracy during its regime changes. Throughout its dealings with Saigon, American policymakers' primary concern was to ensure that a strong government capable of combating the growing communist insurgency ruled South Vietnam. For this reason, the United States stood by Diem's autocratic government up until the point that he was deemed too self-serving and incompetent for this task, at which point Washington switched its support to the generals who overthrew him, in the hopes that they would better manage the country's counterinsurgency efforts. Similarly, economic accounts fare poorly in this case. I found no evidence for hypothesis 3a, that the United States intervened to protect the economic interests of any specific American multinational corporation. As with all of the case studies, however, the case for hypothesis 3b, that the United States intervened to protect its position as the head of a capitalist international order, is more complicated. American leaders undoubtedly did not want South Vietnam to switch from a Western-oriented capitalist economy to a communist one, and these economic interests were part of the reason that the United

States was involved in the Southeast Asia in the first place. However, security concerns dominated policymaking deliberations, and it was a security-oriented dispute over Diem's counterinsurgency efforts—not his economic policy—that caused the United States to turn against his regime in 1963.

Scholars continue to debate America's role in the assassination of South Vietnamese Prime Minister Ngo Dinh Diem. Some argue that the coup was largely a Vietnamese affair and that the United States did not play a decisive role. Others claim that Kennedy personally did not intend to overthrow Diem, but that the CIA, State Department, and America's ambassador to Vietnam, Henry Cabot Lodge Jr., overstepped their bounds by encouraging a coup without the president's approval. Key to this argument is a cable sent by State Department officials on August 24, 1963, in which its authors—Harriman, Hilsman, and Forrestal—appear to give US approval for a coup.[4] At the time, however, Kennedy and other top policymakers were out of town on holiday and approved the cable over the phone. As a result, JFK and his top advisors appear not to have fully considered its ramifications, leading some scholars to claim that the president had not approved of the operation. If this account is true, the cable supports a variant of the "rogue CIA" hypothesis in that lower-level government officials are alleged to have launched the coup without presidential approval, although the key actors in this case were mainly State Department officials, not CIA.

Contrary to this account, however, I argue that Kennedy played a decisive role in the operation. Although mid-level State Department policymakers sent the cable, the president chose not to rescind it, and two months later he held multiple high-level meetings to debate the pros and cons of an intervention, and supported a new coup plan. As part of this new operation, US officials provided intelligence and logistics to the coup plotters, including $42,000 in covert aid through a CIA intermediary on the day of the operation. This meant that, although Vietnamese generals staged the actual coup, the United States was deeply complicit in its plot. Indeed, Robert Kennedy said to his brother days before the coup, "I mean it's different from a coup in the Iraq [sic] or [a] South American country; we are so involved in this."[5] Similarly, Robert McNamara, who served as Secretary of Defense for Kennedy and Johnson, later recalled, "The CIA has often been called a 'Rogue Elephant' by its critics, but I consider that to be a mischaracterization. During my seven years in the Defense Department (and I believe throughout the preceding and following administrations), all CIA 'covert operations' (excluding spying operations) were subject to the approval of the president and the secretaries of state and defense, or their representatives. The CIA had no authority to act without that approval. So far as I know, it never did."[6] Nonetheless, although Kennedy was actively involved in the coup plotting, I find no evidence that he supported Diem's assassination. On the contrary, JFK appears never to have considered what would happen to Diem or his brother after the coup, and he was distressed to hear of their murders.

The reasons for America's covert missions in North Vietnam are less controversial. Virtually all scholars agree that the United States intervened for strategic reasons—to contain the spread of Soviet and Chinese influence into the region, to signal American resolve, and to simply bleed their opponents. Instead, academic debate over the causes of the Vietnam War focuses on specific details of the case. For instance, some scholars argue that US involvement in the war would not have escalated if Kennedy had not been assassinated. Others debate whether Johnson knowingly or unintentionally misled the American public with the Gulf of Tonkin Resolution. This project speaks to these case-specific debates and shows how and why America's covert activities contributed to its decision to escalate America's role in the conflict.

US Foreign Policy and Regime Change in Southeast Asia

At the dawn of the Cold War, Vietnam appeared of little concern to American policymakers. Kennan, for instance, excluded Southeast Asia on his original 1948 list of the five vital areas of industrial and military power where the United States should focus its efforts to contain the Soviet Union.[7] Within six years, however, Washington would debate launching a regime change in Vietnam. A decade after that, the United States had sent over half a million troops to the region. How did this happen? The answer lies in the region's shifting power dynamics brought about by the Second World War, the "loss" of China, and the growth of communist forces in North Vietnam. This section follows US strategy in Vietnam between 1945 and 1965. After first providing a brief background on the conflict, I discuss five separate points between 1954 and 1963, when the United States debated launching either a preventive mission in South Vietnam or an offensive operation against North Vietnam. The section analyzes why US policymakers decided against intervention in three of these cases and why they opted for covert conduct in the remaining two.

HISTORICAL BACKGROUND

Vietnam had been part of the larger French colony known as Indochina from 1887 until the Second World War. Following Nazi Germany's defeat of France in June 1940, Germany installed a puppet regime to rule France, which, in turn, ordered French colonial administrators in Indochina to collaborate with Germany's wartime ally, Japan. The result of this political maneuvering was that the French colonial administration in Indochina remained intact for most of World War II, but Japan directed its policy from behind the scenes.

During the war, several groups of Vietnamese nationalists emerged to combat their Japanese occupiers and the French colonial authorities. Of these forces, the Indochinese Communist Party (ICP) was the best prepared for an armed confrontation. Under the leadership of Ho Chi Minh and Vo Nguyen Giap, ICP fighters infiltrated into the region from China to establish underground resistance networks, build secret bases, and gather intelligence. In 1941, Ho and Giap joined forces with several non-communist groups to form the "League for the Independence of Vietnam" or "Vietminh," and for the next four years, the Vietminh waged a guerilla war against the Japanese and the French colonial administration. US intelligence agents in Southeast Asia watched these developments with interest, and in early 1945, the OSS enlisted Ho to establish an underground intelligence network in Indochina and to help rescue allied pilots shot down over China.[8] In exchange for Ho's cooperation, the OSS trained Vietminh forces and provided them with equipment and weapons.[9] The collaboration was largely successful. Later, US government documents admitted, "Whatever else he was, Ho was a leader and organizer par excellence, an astute manipulator of men. . . . He came to power in North Vietnam under the aegis of the Allies, and by popular acclaim."[10]

In March 1945, as the Allies appeared poised for victory in Europe, Japan feared a direct Allied invasion of Vietnam. In an attempt to retain control, Japan expelled the remaining French advisors and established a short-lived puppet government known as the Empire of Vietnam, led by Emperor Bao Dai. After Japan surrendered in August, however, the Empire of Vietnam collapsed, and Vietminh forces quickly moved to fill the power vacuum left in its wake. The result, as the Pentagon Papers recount, was that "when the allies arrived, the Viet Minh were the de facto government in both North and South Vietnam: Ho Chi Minh and his DRV in Hanoi, and an ICP-dominated 'Committee of the South' in Saigon."[11] Nevertheless, the Vietminh's control of Vietnam was similarly short lived. In September 1945, French troops returned to reestablish France's colonial rule. Unable to reach a negotiated settlement, the French and Vietminh came to blows in November 1946. The conflict degenerated into full-scale war one month later.

Truman opposed France's bid to reestablish its colonial empire, but he hesitated to get directly involved.[12] Officials in his administration were similarly torn, and US policy during 1947 and 1948 reflects this indecision. Despite America's cooperation with the Vietminh during World War II, Truman ignored at least eight requests from Ho for US support for Vietnamese independence.[13] At the same time, however, he also rejected French calls for financial aid and pushed Paris to grant greater autonomy to Vietnamese leaders.[14] To avoid committing to either position, Washington deemed the "war as fundamentally a matter for French resolution."[15]

US policy changed abruptly in 1949 following the "loss" of China to communism, which reignited American fears of Soviet encroachment into Southeast Asia. At the time, however, US policymakers had no indication that the Soviet Union intended to intervene. For instance, a State Department report admitted that the "dept. has no evidence of direct link between Ho and Moscow."[16] Even if no direct evidence was available, however, the paper concluded that the United States should "assume it [a Soviet-Vietminh alliance] exists."[17] The Pentagon Papers would later describe American policymaking at the time as being

> dominated by the tendency to view communism in monolithic terms. The Viet Minh was, therefore, seen as part of the Southeast Asia manifestation of the worldwide communist expansionary movement. . . . This strategic perception of the communist threat was supported by the espousal of the domino principle: the loss of a single nation in Southeast Asia to communism would inexorably lead to the other nations of the area falling under communist control.[18]

For these reasons, Truman officially recognized Bao Dai's regime in February 1950, despite his wartime collaboration with Imperial Japan.[19] Afterward, US aid to the French war effort grew steadily. In March 1950, Truman approved $15 million in military aid for Indochina and $10 million for Thailand.[20] In 1952, Indochina alone received $100 million per year, and by 1953, the United States was paying a full 40 percent of France's war budget in Vietnam.[21] Nevertheless, US economic aid failed to turn the tide in Vietnam. For, as a CIA history would later recount, "No amount of material aid could compensate for anachronistic colonial policies and incompetent leadership."[22]

MARCH–JULY 1954: OVERT INTERVENTION FOLLOWING FRENCH COLLAPSE?

Eisenhower first debated regime change during the Dien Bien Phu crisis and the subsequent collapse of French rule in Indochina.[23] In late 1953, Vietminh leader Vo Nguyen Giap laid siege to a French fortress at the remote Vietnamese village of Dien Bien Phu. By February 1954, American analysts feared a French surrender and began to weigh their options. One potential was for the United States to intervene directly in support of the embattled French garrison. While seriously considering the possibility, Eisenhower feared a direct intervention would bring China into the war and therefore ruled that if the United States were to intervene, it would have to do so covertly, and "we would have to deny it forever."[24] Doubting the feasibility of such a plan, however, Eisenhower decided against a covert intervention, and on May 7, 1954, France surrendered at Dien Bien Phu. Immediately afterward, Eisenhower again faced the question of whether the United States should launch an overt regime change to reinstate French rule and prevent the Vietminh from consolidating control of the entire country. In preparation, the Joint Chiefs of Staff (JCS) developed several operational plans for intervention.[25]

The State Department also drafted a congressional resolution to permit the United States to assist its allies "to maintain their authority . . . against subversive and revolutionary efforts fomented by Communist regimes."[26]

Eisenhower, however, decided not to launch an overt regime change, fearing that such an action would involve the United States in a protracted military conflict. Indeed, as early as 1951, Eisenhower had written in his diary, "I am convinced that no military victory is possible in that kind of theater."[27] Part of his reluctance stemmed from the fact that throughout the crisis, his administration carefully monitored US public opinion, which showed 68 percent opposition to US military involvement.[28] Eisenhower therefore ruled there was "no possibility whatever of U.S. unilateral intervention in Indochina, and we had best face that fact."[29] Instead, he preferred a policy that would secure US interests "at the least cost," and argued, "There are plenty of people in Asia, and we can train them to fight well. I don't see any reason for American ground troops to be committed in Indochina."[30] In lieu of US troops, his administration instead developed a twofold plan for Vietnam: a negotiated settlement in the South and covert warfare in the North.

For the first step, Eisenhower encouraged the French and Vietnamese to reach a negotiated armistice. In July 1954, the Geneva Accords did so, by effectively partitioning Vietnam into two countries at the 17th parallel: North Vietnam (the Democratic Republic of Vietnam—DRV), controlled by the Vietminh and led by Ho Chi Minh, and South Vietnam (the Republic of Vietnam—RVN), governed by Emperor Bao Dai. The Accords envisioned this partition to be temporary and called for democratic elections in 1956 to reunify Vietnam under a single government. Publicly, US officials supported the accords; privately, they lamented their results. A Defense Department history later concluded, "Its grant of Vietnamese territory above the 17th parallel to the communist Ho Chi Minh was a painful reminder of the scarifying French defeat by the Viet Minh, the first defeat of a European power by Asians (Asian communists at that), a defeat shared by the United States to the tune of more than $1.5 billion in economic and military assistance granted France and the Associated States of Indochina."[31]

While the CIA had been covertly aiding the French war effort since 1950, after the accords, Eisenhower escalated covert missions into North Vietnam.[32] On January 21, 1954, Eisenhower shifted the CIA mission to include anticommunist guerilla warfare in North Vietnam.[33] To direct the program, the NSC dispatched General Edward Lansdale to South Vietnam to head a team known as the Saigon Military Mission (SMM).[34] Lansdale's mission was barely off the ground, however, when French colonial rule collapsed, and in August 1954, he received a new order. NSC 5429/2 called on the United States to "make every possible effort, not openly inconsistent with the U.S. government position as to the armistice agreements, to defeat Communist subversion and influence and to maintain and support friendly non-Communist governments" including to "conduct covert operations on a large and effective scale in support of the foregoing policies."[35] Three months later, NSC 5429/3 again ordered the United States to "utilize all feasible overt and covert means, consistent with a policy of not being provocative of war, (at the risk of but not provocative of war) to create discontent and internal divisions within each of the Communist-dominated areas of the Far East, and to impair their relations with the Soviet Union and with each other."[36]

Toward these ends, Eisenhower ordered Lansdale and the SMM to develop a spy ring and underground guerilla network in North Vietnam.[37] As part of the Geneva Accords, North and South Vietnam had agreed to allow a three-hundred-day period where Vietnamese civilians could resettle to their preferred region. Lansdale's first objective was to exploit this period and "train, equip, and infiltrate a handful of small paramilitary teams into North Vietnam."[38] To establish these networks, the CIA turned to two anticommunist nationalist groups: the Dai Viet and the Vietnam Nationalist Party [aka Viet Nam Quoc Dan Dang—VNQDD].[39] Each group had a questionable past. The Dai Viet had collaborated with Japan during World War II, and the CIA suspected that members of the VNQDD were reporting US actions to the French and Chinese.[40] Little came of these initial covert operations. CIA agent Lucien Conein later recounted:

I recall having about twenty paramilitary stay-behind agents from the North . . . I continued to send more agents into the North until as late as 1956. . . . Very few of them returned. Several stay-behind agents did transmit by radio from the North, but then, suddenly, everything went silent up North. It was as if the bottom had fallen out. This was in 1956. It became obvious that our agents had been captured, but I never figured out who talked.[41]

By 1956, Washington's first round of covert missions into North Vietnam ended in failure. Unfortunately for US policymakers, the same cannot be said of the Vietminh's covert efforts in South Vietnam. During the resettlement period, Ho ordered 10,000 Vietminh fighters to form an underground network in South Vietnam to "destabilize the fledgling South Vietnamese nation through political agitation and propaganda, and provide the seeds of an 'indigenous' southern insurgency should Ho order one."[42] These "stay-behind" fighters later formed the backbone of the Viet Cong that would wage an insurgency in South Vietnam from 1959 onward.

Simultaneous with these early covert forays in the North, Eisenhower took several steps to strengthen the South Vietnamese state. This was a tall order. According to one CIA report, in South Vietnam "there existed neither a sense of nationhood nor an indigenous administration."[43] To help overcome these problems, the United States pressured Emperor Bao Dai to assume a more ceremonial leadership role and to appoint Ngo Dinh Diem as the acting premier of South Vietnam.[44] US planners preferred Diem to Bao Dai because of his staunch anti-communism, nationalist credentials, and ability to speak fluent English. Once in power, the US plan called for "Diem to establish a government of national union representative of [the] dominant elements on the political scene. After bringing some stability to the nation, a Constituent Assembly would be called and a constitution drafted to herald the legal de-throning of Emperor Bao Dai and inauguration of democracy."[45] To protect Diem's new regime, the United States joined several Western states, the Philippines, and Thailand in forming a mutual defense pact—the Southeast Asian Treaty Organization (SEATO)—"to prevent further losses to communism" in the region and approved a huge political, military, and economic aid program for South Vietnam.[46] Consequently, the Pentagon calculated, "in the years 1955 through 1960, more than $2 billion in aid flowed into Vietnam, and more than 80% of that assistance went toward providing security for the Government of Vietnam."[47]

DECEMBER 1954–MAY 1955: COVERTLY OVERTHROW SOUTH VIETNAM?

Despite American policymakers' initial hopes for Diem, US support for his regime waned during the first months of his rule. Shortly after assuming office, Diem moved to exclude potential rivals from influential roles in his regime. However, these moves proved insufficient, and it soon became clear that he would face major opposition from various military elites, the Cao Dai and Hoa Hao religious sects, and the Binh Xuyen—a group that the Pentagon Papers described as "a fairly sophisticated organization of 6000 big-time gangsters and river pirates."[48] In November, America's ambassador to Vietnam wrote to the State Department, "Diem, despite his integrity and intense patriotism, may not be up for the job. His lack of personality, his stubbornness, his narrowness, and dislike of bold action may be greater than all support and guidance we give him and a possible successor must be sought."[49]

In December 1954, US officials first began to call for Diem's removal. Sent to Saigon "to coordinate and direct a program in support of Diem's government,"[50] US General J. Lawton Collins wrote to Eisenhower, warning of the "lack of unity among Vietnamese and lack of decisive leadership on [the] part of Diem."[51] Thus, Collins argued the United States should "consider urgently, as [a] possible alternative, the early return of Bao Dai."[52] However, State Department officials were reluctant to do so, writing, "We recognize the dangers posed by the above policy, but [given] the lack of more useful alternatives that we will continue to support Diem, because there is no one to take his place who would serve US objectives any better."[53] Secretary of State Dulles explained, "We have accepted him because we knew of no one better. Developments have confirmed our fear as to his limitations but no substitute for him has yet been proposed."[54] Given these conditions, US planners decided to "maintain flexible policy and proceed carefully" with respect to Diem, and in January 1955, they began to investigate alternatives to his rule.[55]

The situation reached a breaking point in the spring of 1955. In March, Cao Dai and Hoa Hao leaders joined forces, forming a group called the "United Front of National Forces" and calling on Diem to form a more representative government. Meanwhile, armed clashes broke out between the Binh Xuyen and paratroopers loyal to Diem. The two sides reached a strained ceasefire on March 31, but US officials in Vietnam seriously doubted Diem's ability to maintain stability. Once again, Collins requested that the United States consider alternatives to Diem. On April 25, Dulles replied to Collins that the matter was being debated "at the highest level," and that Collins "should be prepared for [the] possibility that this might involve some changes in relations to Diem."[56] Two days later, Dulles acquiesced, agreeing that the "U.S. will consider a change in regime."[57]

Before the United States could put any plans in place, however, Diem moved against his opponents. On April 28, Diem ordered the National Army to attack the Binh Xuyen, and after a nine-hour battle that claimed hundreds of lives, he emerged victorious. According to the Pentagon Papers, "Washington responded with alacrity to Diem's success, superficial though it was. Saigon was told to forget Dulles's earlier message about US willingness to see a change in government. Policy had not changed after all: the United States supported Diem. The Saigon embassy burned the first message."[58] Dulles informed Collins on May 1, "For us at this time to participate in a scheme to remove Diem would not only be domestically impractical but also highly detrimental [to] our prestige in Asia."[59]

Dulles's rationale for reversing his position on regime change is consistent with my theory. After Diem reestablished control, neither of my theory's two necessary conditions were present. For one, Washington's grievances with Diem at this point were not rooted in him having irreconcilable policy differences with the United States—just that he appeared to be losing power to those who did. Although American policymakers would have preferred a stronger leader, this project's second condition—a plausible alternative to Diem—also did not exist at the time. As a result, as Dulles concluded:

> Diem is the only means US sees to save South Vietnam and counteract the revolutionary movement underway in Vietnam. US sees no one else who can. Whatever US view has been in past, today US must support Diem wholeheartedly. US must not permit Diem to become another Karensky [sic].
>
> Bao Dai . . . had irretrievably lost capacity to be anything but titular head of government. . . . Cao Dai and Hoa Hao could be used but not Binh Xuyen. . . . With support (of France and US), Diem could sit on top of revolution. Diem is only force of moderation. . . . US was giving funds to support Vietnamese army and could not see anyone else to give funds to but Diem for that purpose.[60]

With regime change off the table, the United States continued to back Diem's government for the rest of the decade. For his part, Diem took the opportunity to consolidate his power, and cancelled the 1956 national election that had been mandated by the Geneva Accords to reunify the country. Contrary to common belief, however, Diem did not cancel the elections on Washington's orders. Instead, the Pentagon Papers note, "The U.S. did not— as is often alleged—connive with Diem to ignore the elections. U.S. State Department records indicate that Diem's refusal to be bound by the Geneva Accords and his opposition to pre-election consultations were at his own initiative."[61] Nevertheless, the cancelled elections served US interests. The 1956 elections had long been a source of anxiety in Washington because policymakers believed that communists were likely to win. If South Vietnam cancelled the election, however, the communists would be able "to pose as the sole champions of national unification," and "world public opinion and, for that matter, domestic opinion would have difficulty in understanding why the United States should oppose in Vietnam the democratic procedures which it advocated for Korea, Austria, and Germany."[62] Given these conflicting interests, the Eisenhower administration struggled to form a coherent policy throughout 1954 and 1955. Before a decision in Washington was made, according to Kathryn Statler, "Diem made the choice for the United States by refusing to cooperate and ignoring the July 1955 deadline to begin consultations with the North. The Eisenhower administration considered using the threat of cutting American aid in order to force Diem to consider consultations, but in the end chose not to. Against its better political instincts, but fearful above all of the collapse of the anticommunist government in the South, the Eisenhower administration decided to support Diem."[63]

With the challenges to his rule temporarily overcome, Diem became an increasingly autocratic and unpopular ruler. Not only was he a Catholic in a predominantly Buddhist country, he was also, as the CIA noted, "a hopelessly incompetent administrator who always lost the forest in the trees."[64] General Collins lamented that Diem suffered from an "apparent incapacity for creative thinking and planning."[65] Further exacerbating things, Diem was deeply suspicious of all elites outside of his immediate family. Instead, he turned almost exclusively to family members for advice. Chief among these were his brother, Ngo Dinh Nhu, and sister-in-law, Madame Nhu—both of whom had made many enemies on their own.

Lacking domestic support himself, Diem relied heavily on US aid to retain power. "Up to 1960," the Defense Department calculated, "Vietnam was one of the largest recipients of U.S. economic and military assistance in the world: the third ranking non-NATO recipient of aid, [and] the seventh ranking worldwide."[66] A key part of this aid was assistance through the US Military Assistance Advisory Group (MAAG) to strengthen the Army of the Republic of Vietnam (ARVN) and an internal South Vietnamese security force, the Civil Guard. Despite the massive aid, however, South Vietnam's position continued to deteriorate, and Diem continued to face significant internal threats to his rule.[67] He barely survived a military coup attempt in November 1960, which left him shaken, increasingly paranoid, and even more reliant on his brother and sister-in-law for advice.

Hoping to capitalize on Diem's weakness, the Communist Lao Dong (or Vietnamese Workers Party) met in Hanoi in early 1959 and announced its intention "to overthrow the ruling power of the imperialists and the feudalists and establish a revolutionary government of the people." The group understood the potential costs of such actions, warning that "because the U.S. imperialists are the most warmongering of the imperialists, the uprisings of the people in the south has the possibility of becoming a protracted armed struggle."[68] In June 1959, communist forces began to smuggle weapons and supplies into South Vietnam, using an elaborate camouflaged supply network through Vietnam, Laos, and Cambodia, known as the "Ho Chi Minh Trail." The consequences were felt immediately. US intelligence reports recorded, "2,500 assassinations took place in 1959, more than double the previous year" and "sabotage, previously localized, became widespread."[69] Ho also ordered the Vietminh fighters who had remained behind in South Vietnam following the Geneva Accords to unite. On December 20, 1960, they did so, forming the National Liberation Front (NLF), or Viet Cong, with the aim of launching a "people's war" to win independence from the "U.S. Imperialists" and "Diem and his clique."[70]

JANUARY 1961–JANUARY 1964: COVERT OPERATIONS IN NORTH VIETNAM

As one of his last duties in office, Eisenhower's secretary of defense, Thomas Gates Jr., sent General Lansdale back to Vietnam on a fact-finding mission to assess the NLF insurgency. Lansdale wrote a twelve-page report on the matter, warning that Vietnam was in "critical condition" and in need of "emergency treatment."[71] Shortly after Kennedy's inauguration, JFK's new deputy national security advisor, Walt Rostow, passed this report to Kennedy. JFK was stunned. "Walt, this is going to be the worst one yet," he reflected. "I'll tell you something. Eisenhower never mentioned the word Vietnam to me."[72]

Kennedy was quick to act. Within the week, he convened his administration's first National Security Council meeting and asked Lansdale to brief the council on his findings. Lansdale recommended that the NSC authorize a "Basic Counterinsurgency Plan for Vietnam," which the US embassy in Saigon had recently submitted to deal with the rise in Viet Cong attacks. This plan called for the United States to train an additional 20,000 men for the ARVN and 38,000 for the Civil Guard.[73] Kennedy supported the counterinsurgency plan but wanted to know what the United States could do to weaken the North Vietnamese regime.

In fact, plans to do that were already underway. Since late 1960, the CIA had begun training paramilitary teams to infiltrate North Vietnam. CIA Station Chief of Saigon (1959–62) and Chief of the Far East Division (1962–67) William Colby later described the objective of these missions: "Our strategy had been to just get the framework up there. Just get some kind of framework up there upon which you can build resistance or sabotage, or whatever you need to do, psychological or whatever."[74] By the time of JFK's inquiry, however, the mission had made little progress. Only four out of eight proposed teams had been formed, and none were yet deployed.[75] Kennedy was dissatisfied. On January 28, he ordered the CIA to send "guerrillas to operate in the North."[76] One month later, he checked on the CIA's efforts and once again was displeased with their progress. To speed things up, JFK issued NSAM 28 to the director of Central Intelligence, instructing "that we make every possible effort to launch guerilla operations in Viet Minh territory at the earliest possible time."[77]

In early 1961, the CIA initiated a program to insert Vietnamese operatives into North Vietnam to create an espionage and resistance network. Colby modeled the missions after ones that he had run in Norway as an OSS agent during the Second World War.[78] Colby explained:

> Flights left Danang in the dusk headed north with Vietnamese trained and equipped to land in isolated areas, make cautious contact with their former home villages and begin building networks there. Boats went up the coast to land others on the beaches, and we started leaflet drops and radio programs designed to raise questions in North Vietnamese homes about their sons being sent to South Vietnam to fight and about the vices of communist rule.[79]

To maintain plausible deniability of America's role in the operations, agents were airdropped into the country from a small airline created by the CIA and manned by Nationalist Chinese aircrews known as Vietnamese Air Transport.[80] Yet, not everyone on the American side was convinced of the wisdom of such operations. In spring 1961, for instance, Robert Myers, who headed the Far East Division's North Vietnam Task Force, questioned Colby whether the US-backed forces stood a chance against Ho Chi Minh's regime, having seen similar operations fail in China in the 1950s.[81] According to a CIA history, "Colby disagreed, arguing that suitable safe areas could be found, at last in lightly populated areas where black teams could set up reasonably secure bases."[82]

The CIA's first infiltrations succeeded—to an extent. In March and February 1961, the CIA infiltrated two singleton agents into North Vietnam by sea, and a team of four, code-named ATLAS, by air. According to CIA records, the singleton agent infiltrated by sea in March "stayed four days, observing communist police controls and 'various minor military installations.' Still using fabricated documentation, he took a bus south to Vinh Linh, then walked to the Ben Hal River, crossing back into South Vietnam, apparently again under cover of darkness."[83] Encouraged by this initial success, the CIA inserted another Vietnamese agent in April 1961. After recruiting his brother, this agent "dispatched the first of an initial series of 23 messages that inaugurated the longest and most prolific radio correspondence from any penetration of the North run either by CIA or by its successor, the Special Operations Group of the Military Assistance Command Vietnam (MACV)."[84] Unfortunately for the CIA, however, these early infiltrations would be the high point of the program.

Subsequent air and sea drops failed entirely. Agent after agent was killed in action, went missing, or was captured by North Vietnamese forces. By the end of 1963, four teams—code-named REMUS, TOURBILLON, BELL, and EASY—and the singleton agent inserted in February 1961, code-named ARES, were still reporting from North Vietnam. However, the reporting from these groups was sporadic, and some of their CIA handlers began to question whether North Vietnamese forces had compromised them.[85] Indeed, these suspicions were confirmed by a 1968 MACVSOG study that found that all of the groups still reporting from North Vietnam had been captured by North Vietnamese forces and were acting as double agents.[86] Of the at least 250 individuals sent into North Vietnam between 1961 and 1963, records suggest that the CIA only exfiltrated one (and that agent had completed only four days of cursory intelligence collection).[87] All others failed. Of those whose records are available, North Vietnamese security forces captured roughly two-thirds; 20 percent disappeared without explanation; and 10 percent died in action.[88] This pattern continued for America's infiltration missions into the North until they were eventually cancelled in 1968. All told, over five hundred agents were lost in the fiasco.[89]

Given this poor record, it did not take long for US officials began to question the wisdom of the infiltrations. In October 1961, Lansdale complained that the entire CIA effort lacked cohesion and purpose, writing:

> Consideration should be given to a longer-range policy towards North Vietnam. If the Communists can wage subversive war to capture a country, then it is high time that we paid them in the same coin. Admittedly, it is a long and arduous task to free a country behind the Iron or Bamboo Curtain. But, if our objective was to create a situation akin to that in Hungary, and then be prepared to help, with the end objective of uniting Viet-Nam again under a Free Government, there would be a considerably larger program to be planned for actions against North Vietnam.[90]

After several more failures, CIA headquarters began to demand that its agents in Saigon improve operational security. Despite their poor record, however, some CIA field agents were optimistic that the mission could be salvaged. A typical CIA cable to headquarters from this time declared:

We [are] not locating, recruiting, training, dispatching and directing . . . teams [merely] to obtain low level or even high level [order of battle intelligence]. . . . [We] have emphasized potential resistance, contacts with families to build up Intel assets, examination of potential harassment targets such as roads, reports of political controls, attitude of population, etc.[91]

As the infiltration effort was getting off the ground in the spring of 1961, however, events back in Washington brought the future of the CIA program into question. In April 1961, the CIA launched the ill-fated Bay of Pigs invasion of Cuba. The mission's disastrous results incensed Kennedy, who had campaigned heavily on Cuba during the 1960 election, and he blamed the CIA in large part for the invasion's failure. CIA Director Allen Dulles, Deputy Director Charles Cabell, and Deputy Director of Plans Richard Bissell were forced to resign, and in June 1961, Kennedy signed three executive orders—NSAMs 55, 56, and 57—curtailing the CIA's role in paramilitary operations by shifting responsibility for the conduct of large unconventional covert programs from the CIA to the Pentagon.[92] This process, known as Operation Switchback, gradually transferred control of various CIA operations in Vietnam to a newly created DOD joint-service command known as Military Assistance Command Vietnam (MACV). In practice, this meant that the CIA would continue to run its covert programs in North Vietnam during the 1961–63 period, at which point they would be handed over to the Pentagon.

With the infiltrations making little progress, in December 1962, Colby decided to shift the focus of US efforts to psychological warfare. He explained, "The agent operations did not work. It was my thesis that if we worked reasonably hard on psychological operations, which included radios and things like that, you could have an impact because the communists are so hyper about the danger of resistance that if you suggest that there was any opposition group within their ranks, it would drive them crazy."[93] Toward this end, US agents launched an extensive effort to use leaflets, fake radio programming, forged documents, and the creation of a fictitious resistance movement, the Sacred Sword of the Patriots League (SSPL) to convince North Vietnamese civilians that there was an active resistance movement within their country and to serve as a cover for US and South Vietnamese actions.[94] In March 1963, CIA officer Herbert Weisshart was sent to Saigon to help establish the SSPL based on his experiences running psychological warfare operations in China during the 1950s.[95] According to declassified reports, the back story for the SSPL was that they were "a group of dissident, nationalistic Vietnamese striving to free their beleaguered country from the grip of all that oppress her" and that the group was formed in April 1953 by a group of former Vietminh led by Le Quoc Hung, who opposed both communist and foreign rule for their country and sought its eventual liberation.[96] As part of this effort, the CIA airdropped a variety of leaflets and small gifts emblazoned with the SSPL logo into North Vietnam.[97] Psychological warfare infiltration teams were also airdropped into the country in the second half of 1963 to "spread SSPL leaflets while collecting intelligence and hitting sabotage targets."[98] As with the early infiltration efforts, however, most teams were never heard from again.[99] Thus, the situation by the end of 1963, when the CIA was to turn operations over to the Pentagon as part of Operation Switchback, was bleak. After three years of operations, the CIA had not made any significant progress toward establishing guerilla resistance in the country.

What accounts for the persistence of the failed CIA covert campaign in North Vietnam between 1961 and 1963? A subsequent CIA review points to three things. First, "the short, easy answer—and one with a good deal of force—is that the CIA had to do something to respond, first to the original Kennedy mandate in the spring of 1961, and then to pressures that increased in proportion to the decline of South Vietnamese fortunes in 1963."[100] Second, the CIA had few alternatives. Without a large resistance group in North Vietnam to support, and facing tight border security, air and sea infiltrations were the only way to get into the north. Further complicating efforts, the CIA relied on South Vietnamese intelligence to recruit the agents to be infiltrated north, which raised questions about their reliability.[101] Weisshart later explained this failure: "[We] were never invited in, there was no resistance up there. . . . There was no one to hook up with and start a resistance operation. Certainly it was not possible in terms of the way we were trying to do it."[102] Finally, the report notes that infiltrations were simply standard practice in the CIA. Colby and others in the agency had gotten their positions of leadership based on their experience on OSS paramilitary operations against Nazi Germany. As a result, a CIA history recounts, there existed, "a managerial mindset in the Directorate of Plans (DDP) that almost reflexively applied the techniques of World War II partisan warfare to denied-area operations in the Cold War. . . . [Many agents] were aware of the slim results produced by the teams infiltrated into Eastern Europe and the Soviet Union, in the early years of the Cold War, and then into China and North Korea, but they accepted this modus operandi as 'the way we do things.'"[103] In that regard, the failure of the infiltration missions should not have surprised the CIA. Indeed, Colby would later acknowledge, "You know we got involved in supporting a Polish resistance organization that turned out to be totally manipulated. The East Germans have said that many of our so-called agents were really being run by them. The Cubans have recently said the same. So [North Vietnam] isn't a novel situation."[104]

JANUARY–DECEMBER 1961:
COVERTLY OVERTHROW SOUTH VIETNAM?

Kennedy took office during a period of growing turmoil in South Vietnam. The Viet Cong, multiple political factions, religious sects, and disgruntled military officers all had Diem in their sights. Many US planners considered Diem stubborn and inept, but they could not identify a better alternative. As a result, Kennedy continued Washington's tense but supportive relationship with Saigon. Shortly after taking office, JFK authorized $28.4 million to expand the South Vietnamese Army (ARVN) and $12.7 million to increase the size of Diem's Civil Guard.[105] He increased this support on April 29 by approving NSAM 52, which called for "a series of mutually supporting actions of a military, political, economic, psychological and covert character" to bolster South Vietnam's internal security.[106] As part of this program, JFK ordered additional US military advisors sent to Vietnam to help train the ARVN, the Civil Guard, and Special Forces, causing the number of US advisors to grow from 685 in 1959 to more than 11,000 in 1962.[107] During this same period, US aid grew from $59 million to $140 million.[108]

As US aid to South Vietnam grew, however, many US officials began to question the wisdom of backing Diem. He was seen as unpopular, aloof, and incompetent. One CIA report noted, "Diem never placed real importance on winning the voluntary allegiance of the peasantry, and his own sporadic efforts with Nhu to mobilize the population against the Communists were clumsy and halfhearted."[109] Moreover, Diem's efforts to insulate himself from another coup were inhibiting the MAAG-ARVN's fight against the Viet Cong insurgency.[110] A declassified CIA history recounted, "Like any authoritarian ruler, Diem fully understood the potential of his security services to be used against him by ambitious or disgruntled underlings, and he chose their leaders with attention more to personal loyalty than to competence."[111] This frustrated US military planners, who argued that Diem's actions were reducing ARVN effectiveness and thus aiding the Viet Cong insurgency.

In Washington, calls to overthrow Diem mounted throughout 1961. Kennedy's trusted advisor John Kenneth Galbraith reasoned, "The only solution must be to drop Diem. . . . It is a cliché that there is no alternative to Diem's regime. . . . This is an optical illusion arising from the fact that the eye is fixed on the visible figures. It is a better rule that nothing succeeds like successors."[112] Likewise, Rostow warned, "Diem's practices, intended to guard him against a military coup, thus help create frustrations driving the military to stage one. The vicious circle needs to be broken. It could be broken by a successful coup against Diem, but for us to encourage one would involve grave risks."[113] To prepare for the possibility of a coup, the State Department asked the embassy in Saigon to provide it with a list of the plausible alternatives to Diem.[114]

Even so, Diem survived these challenges. Faced with the choice of launching a coup or increasing the US support to Diem, the president chose the latter. Kennedy based this decision, in mid-November 1961, on recommendations provided to him by General Maxwell Taylor, whom he had sent on a fact-finding mission to Vietnam. Taylor made several arguments against the coup. For one, he did not believe the United States had identified a plausible alternative to Diem, and thus "it would be dangerous for us to engineer a coup under present tense circumstances, since it is by no means certain that we could control its consequences and potentialities for Communist exploitation."[115] Furthermore, he wrote, "Engineering or backing a coup involves large risks in both the local situation and in the broader framework of world opinion. It is not something we do well."[116] Additionally, Taylor did not believe that America's dispute with Diem was irreconcilable. Instead, he maintained, "We are convinced that a part of the complaint about Diem's administrative methods conceals a lack of first-rate executives who can get things done. . . . The proposed strategy of limited partnership is designed both to force clear delegation of authority in key areas and to beef up Vietnamese administration until they can surface and develop the men to take over."[117] The logical end of these arguments was that rather than overthrowing Diem, the United States increased its support for his government.

On November 22, 1961, Kennedy ordered the United States "to join the Viet-Nam government in a sharply increased joint effort to avoid a further deterioration of the situation in South Vietnam."[118] One month later, Washington launched "Operation Beef-Up," dramatically increasing US financial and military aid to Diem. Paradoxically, every time Kennedy increased America's involvement in South Vietnam, he asserted that his ultimate objective was to withdraw US forces. The result, according to one CIA memo in January 1963, is that "the war remains a slowly escalating stalemate."[119] As the president fumbled to find a way out of Vietnam, one potential pathway appeared on January 19, 1963, when US military planners submitted the "Comprehensive Three Year Plan for South Vietnam" to the Joint Chiefs of Staff. It called for a temporary buildup of US military assistance to enable the "Vietnamization" of the war effort. To strengthen the ARVN, the United States would prove $405 million in military aid in 1963 and 1964, and $673 between 1965 and 1968. Strengthening the ARVN, in turn, would allow the United States to reduce the number of US military advisors in Vietnam from 12,200 in 1965 to 1,500 in 1968.[120]

MAY–NOVEMBER 1963: COVERTLY OVERTHROW SOUTH VIETNAM?

American plans to draw down forces were overtaken by events. Two days after Kennedy's foreign policy team met to settle the details of the "U.S. Comprehensive Plan South Vietnam," a major crisis broke out in South Vietnam.[121] On May 8, 1963, ARVN forces opened fire on Buddhist civilians protesting against a governmental ban on flying religious flags. Nine Buddhists died. Diem, a staunch Roman Catholic, denied the government's role, instead blaming the Viet Cong for the attack.[122] The claim was implausible, and tension rose between Diem's regime and the predominantly Buddhist population. "By June it was clear that the regime was confronted not with a dissident religious minority, but with a grave crisis of public confidence," the Pentagon Papers explained. "The Buddhist protest had become a vehicle for mobilizing the widespread popular resentment of an arbitrary and often oppressive rule."[123]

The Buddhist uprising caught Kennedy off guard. International audiences overwhelmingly sided with the Buddhists, particularly after the *New York Times* published disturbing images of a monk self-immolating in protest of Diem's anti-Buddhist policies. Washington urged Diem to address the situation. The Pentagon Papers note, "The U.S. made repeated attempts to persuade Diem to redress the Buddhist grievances, to repair his public image, and to win back public support. The Ngos were unwilling to bend. Diem, in true mandarin [sic] style, was preoccupied with questions of face and survival—not popular support."[124] US planners viewed Diem's brother, Ngo Dinh Nhu, as one of the main obstacles to resolving the crisis, as noted in a July 1963 CIA report:

> In the negotiations with the Buddhists, Nhu urged his brother to take a firm line and is, by his own statement, wholly out of sympathy with the concessions made. On the basis of past performance, we think it unlikely that he will help to implement the settlement; his influence on Diem will be rather in the direction of delaying and hedging on commitments, a tendency to which Diem himself is already disposed.[125]

The behavior of Diem's sister-in-law, Madame Nhu, was perhaps even more problematic. A CIA history noted, "If Nhu's behavior suggested paranoia, his wife showed signs of megalomania."[126] Known as the "Dragon Lady," Madame Nhu stirred tensions further after writing that she would "clap hands at seeing another monk barbecue show, for one cannot be responsible for the madness of others."[127]

Frustrated with Saigon's intransigence, the United States decided to take a harder line with Diem. Kennedy replaced America's ambassador to South Vietnam, Fredrick Nolting, whom he viewed as too conciliatory toward Diem, with Henry Cabot Lodge Jr., a hard-line Republican. During Lodge's introductory tour, however, the already tenuous situation in South Vietnam unraveled. On August 21, Diem declared martial law, allegedly in response to Buddhist protests. The next day, his brother Nhu launched a major synchronized attack, using ARVN troops, against Buddhist pagodas throughout South Vietnam. Nhu's forces arrested 1,400 monks and wounded at least 30.[128] These attacks, the Pentagon Papers recount, were "a direct, impudent slap in the face for the U.S. Nhu expected that in crushing the Buddhists he could confront the new U.S. Ambassador with a fait accompli in which the U.S. would complainingly acquiesce, as we had in so many of the regime's actions which we opposed."[129] For many US policymakers, these acts were the final straw.

Disgruntled Vietnamese military leaders had first told CIA agent Lucien Conein on July 8 that there was discussion of a military coup against Diem.[130] Washington's response at the time, however, was noncommittal, and the coup plotters backed down.[131] Following the pagoda raids, however, several Vietnamese generals approached their American contacts again to ask what the US position would be toward a military coup. Seeking advice, Ambassador Lodge cabled Washington on August 24: "Suggestion has been made that U.S. has only to indicate to 'Generals' that it would be happy to see Diem and/or Nhus go, and deed would be done."[132] Nevertheless, he was hesitant. "Situation at this time does not call for that, in my judgment, and I believe we should bide our time, continuing to watch situation closely."[133]

Lodge's cable arrived in Washington on Memorial Day weekend, when many top policymakers were out of town. As a result, mid-level State Department officials—W. Averell Harriman, Roger Hilsman, and Michael Forrestal—drafted a cable in reply. Afterward, Forrestal called Kennedy, who was vacationing at the time, for approval. "Can't we wait until Monday, when everybody is back?" Kennedy asked.[134] Forrestal replied that they "really want to get this thing out right away." Kennedy replied, "Well, go and see if you can get it cleared." With this go-ahead, Harriman and Hilsman contacted George Ball, Dean Rusk, Roswell Gilpatric, and representatives of the Defense Department and CIA for their approval. Each agreed. Rusk replied, "Well, go ahead. If the president understood the implications, [I] would give a green light." According to historian Howard Jones, "The most noteworthy feature of this bizarre decision-making process was that no one made a decision but merely signed off on one that they all thought someone else had made."[135] Consequently, many cite this message, Cable 243, as the key piece of evidence that Kennedy was not intimately involved in the coup. It stated:

> It is now clear that whether military proposed martial law or whether Nhu tricked them into it, Nhu took advantage of its imposition to smash pagodas with police. . . . Also clear that Nhu has maneuvered himself into a commanding position. U.S. government cannot tolerate position in which power lies in Nhu's hands. Diem must be given chance of removing Nhu and his coterie and replace them with best military and political personalities available. If, in spite of all your efforts, Diem remains obdurate and refuses, we must face the possibility that Diem himself cannot be preserved. . . . We must at the same time tell key military leaders that U.S. would find it impossible to continue to support GVN [government of South Vietnam] militarily and economically unless above steps are taken immediately which we recognize requires removal of the Nhus from the scene.[136]

Harriman, Hilsman, and Forrestal sent Cable 243 on Saturday, August 24, 1963. At a White House meeting the following Monday morning, Kennedy was surprised to find his top foreign policy staff at odds over the weekend's developments. Neither Secretary of Defense Robert McNamara nor Director of Central Intelligence John McCone had seen Cable 243. Secretary of State Dean Rusk and Chairman of the Joint Chiefs of Staff General Maxwell Taylor had each signed off on it, but based on the assumption that the president had already approved it.

Although Kennedy was displeased with the State Department for its handling of Cable 243, he chose not to retract it. Before the United States proceeded, however, he wanted more information on the plot.[137] JFK reiterated these points during meetings on Wednesday: "We should ask Ambassador Lodge and General Harkins how we can build up military forces which would carry out a coup."[138] The next day, Lodge and Harkins each indicated that they thought the war was unwinnable with Diem as premier. "Any course is risky, and no action at all is riskiest of all," Lodge replied.[139] "We are launched on a course from which there is no respectable turning back: The overthrow of the Diem government. There is no turning back in part because U.S. prestige is already publicly committed to this end in large measure and will become more so as facts leak out. . . . We should proceed to make all-out effort to get Generals to move promptly."[140] Harkins was more hesitant. He preferred simultaneously supporting the generals' plans and giving Diem an ultimatum to remove Nhu from power. However, he noted that the generals would "not move without U.S. support and until detailed practical plans are drawn, and forces aligned."[141]

When deciding whether to support the coup, US policymakers focused on two things: (1) the probability that the coup plotters' plan would succeed, and (2) whether the generals offered a plausible political alternative to Diem. For example, in a cable to Saigon, Rusk told Lodge, "The USG [United States government] supports the movement to eliminate the Nhus from the government, but that before arriving at specific understandings with the Generals, General Harkins must know who are involved, resources available to them and overall plan for coup. The USG will support a coup which has good chance of succeeding."[142] To evaluate the plausibility of Diem's alternatives, Kennedy asked for biographies of the Vietnamese generals and an official assessment of which ARVN military units would likely side with the generals during the coup.[143]

In contrast to the rogue CIA hypothesis, Kennedy was intimately involved throughout the deliberations. In fact, he personally cabled Lodge that night, saying, "I have approved all the messages you are receiving from others today, and I emphasize that everything in these messages has my full support. We will do all that we can to help you conclude this operation successfully."[144] He continued, "Until the very moment of the go signal for the operation by the Generals, I must reserve a contingent right to change course and reverse previous instructions. While fully aware of your assessment of the consequences of such a reversal, I know from experience that failure is more destructive than an appearance of indecision."[145]

Despite support from Washington, the coup was losing momentum. CIA agents reported that the Vietnamese generals were being noncommittal during meetings throughout the last week of August.[146] For their part, the generals feared that the United States would sell them out to Nhu, and they therefore wanted the United States to demonstrate its commitment by cutting off aid to Diem's regime.[147] US policymakers were reluctant to do so, fearing that if they cut aid prematurely, Nhu would recognize the signal and move against the plotters.[148] Kennedy instead authorized Lodge to cut US aid when he saw fit.[149] Still, the generals hesitated. The National Security Council concurred on August 30: "All agreed that from the evidence now available it looked as if the Generals were either backing off or were wallowing."[150] Rusk told Lodge the plotters seemed to have "no plan and little momentum" and recommended that the United States develop contingency plans. "Obviously, an abortive effort inspired by or attributed to the United States will be disastrous."[151] Finally, on August 31, CIA agents in Saigon cabled Washington: "This particular coup is finished. . . . Generals did not feel ready and did not have sufficient balance of forces."[152]

After the August coup flamed out, policymakers were divided about how to proceed. According to the Pentagon Papers, "a month-long policy review took place in Washington and in Vietnam. It was fundamentally a search for alternatives." On the one side, "the military and the CIA both in Saigon and Washington" saw no "realistic alternatives to Diem." On the other side, the White House staff, embassy staff, and State Department felt "the war against the VC would not possibly be won with Diem in power and preferred therefore to push for a coup of some kind."[153] To overcome this impasse, Kennedy authorized two fact-finding missions to South Vietnam. The first, headed by General Victor Krulak and the State Department's Joseph Mendenhall, was inconclusive; Krulak and Mendenhall came to diametrically opposed conclusions about the situation in Vietnam.[154] The second, headed by Secretary McNamara and General Taylor, was more consistent.

The McNamara-Taylor Report, submitted on October 2, evaluated the viability of a coup. While agreeing that Diem had been a major impediment to the US war effort, the report noted, "The prospects that a replacement regime would be an improvement appear to be about 50–50."[155] Thus, the lack of a plausible alternative to Diem led them to advise against a coup:

Obviously, clear and explicit U.S. support could make a great difference to the chances of a coup. However, at the present time we lack a clear picture of what acceptable individuals might be brought to the point of action, or what kind of government might emerge. We therefore need an intensive clandestine effort, under the Ambassador's direction, to establish necessary contacts to allow the U.S. to continuously appraise coup prospects. If and when we have a better picture, the choice will still remain difficult whether we would prefer to take our chances on a spontaneous coup (assuming some action by Diem and Nhu would trigger it) or to risk U.S. prestige and having the U.S. hand show with a coup group which appeared likely to be a better alternative government.[156]

In place of a coup, McNamara and Taylor recommended several measures to pressure Diem into complying with US wishes. Of these, "the most powerful instrument at our disposal is the control of military and economic aid."[157] Kennedy quickly adopted the recommendations, and issued a press release announcing the withdrawal of 1,000 US personnel.[158]

The next day, the generals approached their CIA contacts about the possibility of a coup.[159] Kennedy's foreign policy team once again met on October 5 to debate whether to support the generals' plans.[160] Ultimately, they decided to stick with the McNamara-Taylor plan, wiring to Lodge, "President today approved recommendation that no initiative should now be taken to give any active covert encouragement to a coup. There should, however, be urgent covert effort . . . to identify and build contacts with possible alternative leadership as and when it appears."[161] That same day, CIA agent Lucien Conein met with the leader of the plotters, General Duong Van Minh, who requested clarification of the US position.[162] Washington obliged him, saying, "U.S. will not thwart such a move if it offers prospects of a more effective fight against the VC. Security and deniability of all contacts is paramount."[163]

On October 23, CIA agent Conein once again met with the generals, who informed him that the coup was imminent. Two days later, Ambassador Lodge cabled Washington in support of the plan. Lodge argued that no new government could "bungle and stumble as much as the present one has."[164] Even if the coup failed, he said, "our involvement to date through Conein [makes the US role] within the realm of plausible denial."[165] Kennedy, however, was hesitant to support the coup unless it would succeed. He had Bundy cable Lodge, "We are particularly concerned about hazard that an unsuccessful coup, however carefully we avoid direct engagement, will be laid at our door by public opinion almost everywhere. Therefore, while sharing your view that we should not be in position of thwarting coup, we would like to have option of judging and warning on any plan with poor prospects of success."[166]

Lodge cabled back, "We believe balance would tip in favor of coup group in event. . . . Chances of this would be greatly enhanced if at critical juncture U.S. publicly announced that all aid through the Diem government had ceased. . . . However, believe I should have standby authority to make declaration to this effect, implying termination of aid to present GVN [government of Vietnam] if in my judgment it is necessary to success coup."[167] Once again, on October 29, Kennedy's team met to debate the coup. Key to the debate was the balance of forces between the coup plotters and Diem. Based on CIA estimates, Colby noted, "The key units come out about even. There's enough, in other words, to have a good fight."[168] Kennedy hesitated, saying, "The burden of proof should be on the coup promoters to show that they can overthrow the Diem government."[169]

Although still expressing reservations, Kennedy made the crucial decision to defer authority to Lodge. On October 30, Bundy cabled Lodge, "We do not accept as a basis for US policy that we have no power to delay or discourage a coup. In your paragraph 12 you say that if you were convinced that the coup was going to fail you would of course do everything you could to stop it. We believe that on this basis you should do everything you can to stop or delay any operation, which in your best judgment, does not give better than even prospect of success."[170]

With this action, Kennedy effectively approved the coup. He knew that the coup was imminent and that Lodge strongly favored it. Thus, by leaving the decision up to Lodge to estimate whether the coup's odds of success were sufficiently high to justify continued US support, he essentially gave Lodge permission to proceed. Indeed, Kennedy acknowledged this point four days after the coup: "While this was a Vietnamese effort, our own actions made it clear that we wanted improvements, and when these were not forthcoming from the Diem Government, we necessarily faced and accepted the possibility that our position might encourage a change of government."[171] Two subsequent US governmental investigations confirmed Washington's responsibility for the operation. In 1976, the Church Committee determined that "American officials offered encouragement to the Vietnamese generals who plotted Diem's overthrow, and a CIA official in Vietnam gave the generals money after the coup had begun."[172] In a similar vein, the Pentagon Papers concluded:

> For the military coup d'état against Ngo Dinh Diem, the U.S. must accept its full share of responsibility. Beginning in August of 1963, we variously authorized, sanctioned and encouraged the coup efforts of the Vietnamese generals and offered full support for a successor government. In October, we cut off aid to Diem in a direct rebuff, giving a green light to the generals. We maintained clandestine contact with them throughout the planning and execution of the coup and sought to revise their operational plans and proposed new government. Thus, as the nine-year rule of Diem came to a bloody end, our complicity in his overthrow heightened our responsibilities and our commitment in an essentially leaderless Vietnam.[173]

The generals launched their coup on November 1. Although they had promised the United States two days' warning, they gave only a few hours' notice. Shortly afterward, CIA agent Lucien Conein delivered $42,000 in American currency to one of the generals.[174] The CIA had planned this action one week earlier, by authorizing "inducements (financial, political or otherwise) to opportunists or recalcitrants in support of coup group."[175]

By late afternoon, the plotters had cornered Diem and Nhu in the presidential palace. Hoping to summon US support, Diem telephoned Lodge, asking, "What is the attitude of the U.S.?" Lodge was noncommittal. "I do not feel well enough informed to be able to tell you," he replied. "I have heard the shooting, but am not acquainted with all the facts. Also it is 4:30 a.m. in Washington and the U.S. government cannot possibly have a view." Pressed further by Diem, he added, "As I told you only this morning, I admire your courage and your great contributions to your country. For no one can take away from you the credit for all you have done. Now I am worried about your physical safety. I have a report that those in charge of the current activity offer you and your brother safe conduct out of the country if you resign. Had you heard this?" Diem replied, "No." After a pause, "You have my telephone number." This would be Diem's last recorded conversation with an American.[176]

Two hours later, someone in the palace waved a white flag. Believing that this signaled that the brothers wanted to peacefully surrender, General Duong Van Minh—the head of the coup plotters—and his forces descended on the palace. To their surprise, however, they learned that Diem and Nhu had fled the compound. Unbeknownst to either the generals or the Americans, Diem had secretly built tunnels beneath the palace to allow for an easy escape in the event of an emergency. The brothers fled, first to the home of a supporter and later to a Catholic church. However, their luck soon ran out. Minh's forces were hot on their trail and apprehended the brothers the next morning. Diem and Nhu were arrested; their hands were tied behind their back; and they were placed in the back of an armored car. Then, for reasons that are still unclear, Minh's personal aide and bodyguard, Captain Nhung, murdered the brothers en route to headquarters. According to another Vietnamese officer present:

> As we rode back to the Join General Staff Headquarters, Diem sat silently, but Nhu and the [captain] began to insult each other. I don't know who started it. The name-calling grew passionate . . . [Nhung] lunged at Nhu with a bayonet and stabbed him again and again, maybe fifteen or twenty times. Still in a rage, he turned to Diem, took out his revolver and shot him in the head. Then he looked back at Nhu, who was lying on the floor twitching. He put a bullet into his head too. Neither Diem nor Nhu ever defended themselves. Their hands were tied.[177]

In an effort to cover up the murders, the generals announced that the brothers had committed suicide. However, it quickly became clear that this was not the case. That night, the CIA station in Saigon cabled Washington to announce the brothers' deaths. They noted that there were reports of a dual execution.[178]

Kennedy was shocked to learn of their deaths. According to Taylor, who was present at the time, "Kennedy leaped to his feet and rushed from the room with a look of shock and dismay on his face which I had never seen before. He had always insisted that Diem must never suffer more than exile and had been led to believe or had persuaded himself that a change in government could be carried out without bloodshed."[179] Shortly afterward, Bundy cabled Lodge: "Deaths of Diem and Nhu, whatever their failings, has caused shock here and there is danger that standing and reputation of incoming government may be significantly damaged if conviction spreads of their assassination at direction of one or more senior members of incoming regime."[180] Any remaining doubt as to the cause of the brothers' deaths was removed on October 4 when the CIA obtained photographs of their bodies, shot in the head, with their hands tied behind their backs.[181] A summary of that day's National Security Council meeting notes, "Bundy said this was not the preferred way to commit suicide, and regretted that the coup leaders still insisted that it was."[182]

Meanwhile, back in Saigon, the generals dismissed Diem's cabinet, and on November 5, they announced a new government, led by General Minh as president and chief of the Military Committee. Despite the fact that his personal aide had murdered the Diem brothers, US officials in Saigon were initially quite optimistic about the possibility of working with General Minh. MACV commander Harkins cabled to Washington, "The hope is for early upsurge in tempo and effectiveness of the military counterinsurgency efforts."[183] Shortly afterward, the State Department declared, "There is better assurance than under Diem that the war can be won."[184] Likewise, Lodge wrote, "We should not overlook what this coup can mean in the way of shortening the war and enabling Americans to come home."[185] Although he was deeply upset by Diem's death, Kennedy was also optimistic about working with the new regime. He wrote back to Lodge, "Your own leadership in pulling together and directing the whole American operation in South Vietnam in recent months has been of the greatest importance, and you should know that this achievement is recognized here throughout the Government. . . . With renewed appreciation for a fine job, John F. Kennedy."[186]

JOHNSON ADMINISTRATION: CONSEQUENCES

Diem's death preceded Kennedy's own assassination by just three weeks. It is therefore impossible to say what long-term effects the 1963 Vietnamese coup would have had on Kennedy's foreign policy. By the time Johnson assumed office, however, US planners began to realize the drawbacks of their actions.

The first major problem was that the coup had upended the existing political power structure in South Vietnam. Minh's government suffered from a "lack of decisiveness and vigor . . . [and] general uncertainty as to their authority."[187] What's more, the Pentagon Papers note, "As efficient as the military coup leaders appeared, they were without a manageable base of political support."[188] However corrupt and incompetent Diem's regime had been, it at least possessed a system for delegating authority. A declassified CIA history recounts:

> Seeing the government's failure solely in terms of Diem's weaknesses as a leader, both the Americans and the generals had concentrated exclusively on the mechanics of the coup, giving no attention to the structure or policy direction of a successor government. . . . Had the effort been made, it would have revealed that Diem and his coterie were only part of the problem. An ill-led army and a sclerotic bureaucracy, both still practicing the authoritarian style of their decayed dynastic and colonial predecessors, presided over a body politic divided along religious, ethnic, and class lines.[189]

Minh's government did not improve South Vietnam's political stability, as US policymakers had predicted. On the contrary, the Pentagon Papers state, "[T]he GVN did not succeed in achieving political stability. Its military forces did not stem the pattern of VC successes. Rather, a series of coups produced 'revolving door' governments in Saigon."[190] In January 1964, General Nguyen Khanh ousted General Minh. The result, McNamara noted, was "a sharp drop in morale and organization, and Khanh has not yet been able to build these up satisfactorily. There is a constant threat of assassination or of another coup, which would drop morale and organization nearly to zero."[191] Not surprisingly, additional coups in September 1964, January 1965, and February 1965 further exacerbated the deteriorating situation.

A second problem, compounding the first, was that the NLF decided to take advantage of the confusion caused by Diem's demise to increase its attacks against the regime. After learning of the coup, NLF leader Nguyen Huu Tho described it as "a gift from Heaven for us."[192] Five days after Diem's assassination, the NLF issued a manifesto, demanding, "The U.S. government must end its armed aggression against South Vietnam."[193] Viet Cong attacks increased steadily over the next few months. CIA intelligence analyst George Carver explained:

> When Diem was overthrown, his overthrow came as a surprise to the Communists. . . . [They were] faced with a great opportunity and a great risk. The risk was that after the inevitable period of shake-up, they would get a post-Diem government that had Diem's strengths without his weaknesses and that to them spelled disaster. The opportunity was to strike while the iron was hot and before [the successor government] could get settled. They began in 1963 really escalating their level of military activity.[194]

Although Johnson had inherited a rapidly deteriorating situation in South Vietnam, US planners hoped to reverse that trend by escalating their covert operation in the North. On November 20, 1963, just two days before JFK's assassination, Kennedy's top advisors—including McNamara, Rusk, Ball, Bundy and McCone—met with high-level military and CIA officials working on Vietnam at a conference in Honolulu to discuss the recent developments. High on the agenda was the question of CIA covert missions in North Vietnam, which were scheduled to be handed over to the Pentagon as part of Operation Switchback. Three years of failed infiltrations had convinced CIA leaders of the futility of such actions given the strength of Ho's regime and the lack of significant organized indigenous resistance in the country, and the CIA planned to shut down the infiltration and sabotage operations by 1965. Speaking to the group, Colby admitted, "It isn't working, and it won't work any better with the military in charge."[195] Secretary of Defense McNamara disagreed with Colby's assessment. He believed the failure of the CIA operation resulted from its small scale, and hoped that with the additional resources that MACV could provide, they would get a "bigger bang for the buck."[196]

Four days later, President Johnson—newly sworn into the job following Kennedy's assassination—met with Kennedy's advisors in Washington to be brought up to date on the situation in Vietnam, and concurred that the United States "would pursue the policies agreed to in Honolulu adopted by the late President Kennedy."[197] As part of this meeting, US military planners briefed Johnson on Operation Plan 34A (OPLAN 34A), which the Pentagon Papers described as "an elaborate program of covert military operations against the state of North Vietnam."[198] OPLAN 34A called for "progressively escalating pressure" of four types of missions over a "12-month period under conditions short of limited war." First were "harassing" missions including "small unspectacular demolition operations, moderate level psychological operations, [and] small-scale intelligence collection actions." Next were "attritional" missions including "small-scale resistance operations, airborne and seaborne raids by small forces on important military and civilian installations." Third were "punitive" attacks including "raids by company and battalion size forces, covert where possible, but attributable to Republic of Vietnam (RVN) if they became overt." Last were "aerial attacks" against "DRV installations."[199] OPLAN 34A also intensified America's ongoing covert regime change effort in North Vietnam. Toward that end, the plan called for a "continuation of the already approved . . . covert programs" with "an expansion of that effort" to "include a buildup to support resistance movement operations (both real and notional)."[200]

Johnson was initially excited about the covert program. McNamara later wrote, "Grasping for a way to hurt North Vietnam without direct US military action, President Johnson wanted the covert action strengthened."[201] McNamara agreed, arguing that the plans "present a wide variety of sabotage and psychological operations against North Vietnam from which I believe we should aim to select those that provide maximum pressure with minimum risk."[202] On November 26, he signed NSAM 273, which authorized increased covert operations against North Vietnam while also declaring, "The objectives of the United States with respect to the withdrawal of U.S. military personnel remain as stated in the White House statement of October 2, 1963."[203]

By December, however, LBJ's enthusiasm for escalating the covert war in North Vietnam began to wane. He feared that OPLAN 34A would interfere with his ability to withdraw US forces, by provoking North Vietnam to "retaliate by stepped-up activity against SVN [South Vietnam]" or that the actions might "evoke a strong international reaction."[204] Thus, on December 21, 1963, LBJ ordered Viktor Krulak and the 303 Committee to evaluate OPLAN 34A and "select from it those actions of least risk."[205]

Krulak's committee dramatically reduced OPLAN 34A. In mid-January 1964, they submitted a "Program of Actions" to LBJ that "contained a total of 72 [categories of] actions which if implemented over a 12-month period, would produce a total of 2,062 separate operations. Out of the 72 [categories of] actions proposed . . . 33 were ultimately approved for implementation during Phase 1."[206] Krulak's committee suggested that OPLAN 34A exclude any covert efforts to topple Ho Chi Minh by creating a resistance movement in North Vietnam, judging such actions too dangerous. According to historian Robert Gillespie, "Thanks to the intervention of the State Department's representative (a protégé of W. Averell Harriman named William H. Sullivan) on the interdepartmental committee, the most controversial aspects of the plan had been toned down or eliminated. Gone was any mention of creating a resistance movement with North Vietnam, notional or otherwise. The possibility of destabilizing the communist regime in Hanoi brought nasty visions of Chinese intervention and a repeat of the Korean stalemate."[207] Instead, the committee recommended focusing its efforts on strengthening South Vietnam and dissuading the North from continuing its attacks against the South. On January 19, 1964, Johnson approved the Krulak committee's revised version of OPLAN 34A. With this action, Johnson ended the CIA's modest covert effort to overthrow the North Vietnamese regime.

Nonetheless, the CIA and MACV would each continue to run large covert operations north of the border with goals short of regime change. Their objective, according to OPLAN 34A, was "to convince the DRV leadership that its current support and direction of war in the Republic of Vietnam and its aggression in Laos should be reexamined and stopped."[208] In a reversal of its previous policy, OPLAN 34A also ordered that US agents "develop special psychological operations designed to assure that the DRV correctly evaluates operations carried out under the plan as being primarily retributional in nature and not as an attempt by the United States or RVN to invade or conquer the DRV."[209] Somewhat ironically, this meant that the same agencies that had used psychological operations to convince Hanoi that it faced serious internal threats to its rule were now using psychological operations to assure Hanoi that its rule was secure. The result was that although the United States continued to run major covert missions into North Vietnam, it did not do so for the purpose of regime change. This continued even after MACV assumed control over America's paramilitary operations.

Not everyone agreed with the administration's decision to end the regime change efforts against Hanoi. On several occasions, the Special Operation Group (SOG) of MACV requested permission from LBJ's administration to create a covert resistance movement in North Vietnam. According to a 1970 MACVSOG study, "the authors of OPLAN 34A intended that the formation of resistance groups in NVN [North Vietnam] would be fundamental to the success of the program."[210] Consequently, MACSOG "made three concert efforts in the years following the promulgation of 34A to gain acceptance of the resistance concept."[211] The first of these efforts sought to create a resistance movement comprised of "country and hill tribal groups."[212] It was disapproved in September 1965 over concerns that the "operation might be outside the power of our government to control" and "that if they got into trouble, there would be no way to help them and they would be left to be slaughtered."[213] The Joint Chiefs of Staff rejected a second proposal in 1966, arguing, "The formation of the front would almost inevitably be attributed to the US and because its aims are contrary to US policy, would result in embarrassment to the U.S. government."[214] A final attempt in 1968 sought to "broaden base and increase viability, as well as credibility, of notional resistance group (SSPL)."[215] This proposal too was rejected because "the bombing halts and negotiations commencing 1 April 1968, brought all serious proposals for increased action against the North to a standstill."[216]

Johnson's rationale for cancelling the covert efforts to create a resistance movement was fourfold. First, by the time of its cancellation, it was clear that America's covert effort to create an indigenous resistance movement in North Vietnam was neither effective nor something the United States could plausibly deny. Second, the United States did not have a viable alternative to Ho Chi Minh. Even if it could somehow topple Ho, without a non-communist alternative party, his replacement would almost certainly also come from his party, the Lao Dong. Ambassador Lodge explained, "I welcome exerting increased pressure on North Vietnam with the double aim of bringing about a cease-fire by the VC and Pathet Lao and neutralizing North Vietnam, turning it into an oriental Yugoslavia. I do not think it profitable to try to overthrow Ho Chi Minh, as his successor would undoubtedly be tougher than he is."[217] Third, Johnson's overall strategy in Vietnam had two main objectives: to create stability in South Vietnam and to force North Vietnam to halt its support of communist insurgents. Regime change was counterproductive to both of those tasks because it increased Hanoi's incentives to escalate the conflict and decreased the likelihood of a negotiated settlement. Fourth, the plan was incoherent. Even if the United States could have somehow created an indigenous resistance movement that threatened Ho Chi Minh, this development would only have encouraged China and/or the Soviet Union to enter the war to protect the DRV, thereby hindering Johnson's ability to withdraw US troops.

Johnson's foreign policy during 1964 reflects his desire to find a middle way in the conflict. On the one hand, he feared a conservative backlash if he withdrew US advisors from Vietnam. A retreat from Vietnam, he feared, would jeopardize his "Great Society" domestic agenda, which he viewed as the most important goal of his presidency. Thus, he declared, "I'm not going to lose Vietnam. I am not going to be the President who saw Southeast Asia go the way China went."[218] At the same time, however, Johnson did not want to escalate America's role in Vietnam. He lamented, "Losing 190 lives in the period that we have been out there is bad, but it is not like the 190,000 that we might lose the first month if we escalated that war."[219] Faced with two undesirable options, Johnson sought to avoid both escalation and withdrawal. "We are not," he said, "about to start another war and we're not about to run away from where we are."[220]

Believing himself to be in a lose–lose situation, Johnson's lesser evil was to continue to support South Vietnam in the hope that they could regain enough stability to fight off the Viet Cong insurgents. Toward this end, he continuously increased American aid to Saigon throughout 1964. Nevertheless, as the Pentagon Papers point out:

> It is clear with the advantage of hindsight that these steps were grossly inadequate to the magnitude of the tasks at hand. . . . But such hindsight misses the policymakers' dilemma and the probable process by which the approved actions were decided upon. President Johnson had neither a congressional nor a popular mandate to Americanize the war or to expand it dramatically by 'going north.' U.S. hopes were pinned on assisting in the development of a GVN strong enough to win its own war.[221]

Johnson believed that his only hope for victory was to re-stabilize the South Vietnamese government that the United States had destabilized when it encouraged the generals to overthrow Diem. By the summer of 1964, however, it was clear that Saigon was not up to the task. McNamara wrote, "It is now necessary to add further US military assistance to counter the Viet Cong offensive. We have never made the statement since September 1963, that we believed that we could bring the bulk of the training forces out by the end of 1965, because the actions in November [1963] and January [1964] made it quite clear that would not be possible."[222]

Perhaps the ultimate irony of LBJ's policy is that congressional approval to escalate America's overt role in Vietnam may have come thanks to a covert US operation gone awry. This authorization, known as the Gulf of Tonkin Resolution, was made after a series of events that began on August 2, 1964, when two North Vietnamese torpedo boats attacked an American destroyer, USS *Maddox*, in international waters in the Gulf of Tonkin. Unbeknownst to Congress at the time, however, was the fact that the North Vietnamese assault had probably been provoked by an earlier attack on two DRV facilities by South Vietnamese raiders who were working with the United States as part of OPLAN 34A, using boats supplied by the US Navy and attacking targets selected by the CIA.[223] Further complicating the question of culpability, the North Vietnamese boats had been ordered to attack at a time when the USS *Maddox* was still in North Vietnamese territorial waters on an intelligence mission. The situation deteriorated further two days later when another US warship, the USS *Turner Joy*, reported a similar North Vietnamese attack. However, military officials soon began to doubt whether the second attack actually occurred or whether the USS *Turner Joy* had misinterpreted radio signals. Nevertheless, even after Johnson received word of this confusion, he still used both attacks as justification to seek congressional authorization "to take necessary steps, including the use of armed force, to assist any member or protocol state of the South Asia Collective Defense Treaty requesting assistance in defense of its freedom."[224] On August 7, 1964, the Gulf of Tonkin Resolution passed 416–0 in the House and 88–2 in the Senate, thereby paving the way for Johnson to rapidly escalate the number of US troops in Vietnam and commit the US to open warfare against North Vietnam.

Why Did the United States Prefer Covert Conduct?

In Vietnam and elsewhere, US officials clearly preferred covert conduct during preventive operations because, in the words of William Colby, it "held out the promise of frustrating Soviet ambitions without provoking conflict."[225] Covert action thus became the preferred middle option between doing nothing and sending in the Marines. As a result, Washington initially attempted every preventive operation covertly for three mutually reinforcing reasons.

First, although the states targeted in preventive regime changes did not pose a direct military threat to the United States, US policymakers understood that a war with them was still potentially costly—especially if it escalated to involve the USSR or China. In the Vietnamese case, a 1961 National Intelligence Estimate predicted that if the United States overtly intervened, North Vietnam would "begin to receive increasing military assistance from the Soviet Union and Communist China openly and in unconcealed violation of the [Geneva] Agreements, and to build up an air force which would include jets."[226] Not surprisingly, security considerations were central in the policymaking debates over whether the United States should intervene covertly or overtly. For instance, the JCS pointed out to Kennedy in 1961:

> Formal commitment of United States forces in this [overt] manner would probably generate Communist Chinese overt countermeasures, the magnitude of which would be determined by the degree to which Communist China desired to become openly committed to aggression in Southeast Asia and subject herself to further countermeasures.

> In [the] event the United States does not desire to commit its own forces openly to interdiction, there are covert, unconventional and guerrilla-type operations, as well as other measures, which can be made more effective.[227]

Because direct conflict with either the Soviet Union or China was Kennedy's worst-case scenario, it is not surprising that he preferred to intervene covertly to decrease the likelihood of escalation. Covert conduct also fit nicely into Kennedy's overall defense policy, which was based on the principle of "flexible response." Unlike Eisenhower, who sought to deter Soviet expansion by threatening "massive retaliation" using nuclear weapons in response to conventional Soviet attacks, Kennedy believed that America's deterrent threats would be more credible if the United States could retaliate proportionately to any aggressive move by the Soviets. Consequently, he saw covert and unconventional warfare as attractive tools to combat the unconventional tactics used by the communist insurgents.[228]

A second reason why the United States preferred to conduct its preventive operations covertly is that covert conduct lowered the missions' material costs significantly. Compared to the billions of dollars that the United States spent in Vietnam between 1950 and 1975, the costs of America's covert regime change missions were negligible. For instance, Lansdale's "Basic Counterinsurgency Plan for Vietnam" listed under costs for covert operations: "There may be small amounts required annually for the continuation of ongoing activities; these amounts would not be significant in terms of the overall magnitude of costs of the plan."[229] Indeed, these costs were so low that Kennedy wrote "Why so little?" in the margin of the plan next to the $660,000 that it allocated for "Psychological Operations" in North Vietnam.[230] America's direct costs in the coup that toppled Diem came to the $42,000 that Conein delivered to the generals on the day of the coup. Tellingly, however, this amount could have been higher, but Conein could only fit $42,000 into his bag, and thus he left an additional $28,000 behind in his safe.[231]

The third reason why American policymakers favored covert conduct is that it allowed the United States to pursue actions that third parties were unlikely to view as normatively acceptable. For instance, Kennedy preferred to conduct the operation against North Vietnam covertly because it allowed him to avoid international criticism for undermining the Geneva Accords by sending in "combat troops in the generally understood sense of the word."[232] Indeed, the CIA had estimated that overt "action would cause the DRV to try to gain 'compensation' in some manner, such as possibly declaring the 1954 Geneva Agreements, or certain articles of the Agreements, abrogated."[233] Similarly, Kennedy worried about the international backlash following Diem's death. For instance, on the day of the coup, he requested "that a paper be prepared on the subject" of "how we can square recognition of the Vietnamese rebel government which had overthrown a constitutional government with our position of not recognizing the rebel government which had overthrown the constitutional government in Honduras."[234]

This chapter put forth three main arguments. First, I argued that security considerations drove American decision-making in Vietnam. Washington turned against Diem because he was seen as too incompetent to combat the growing NLF insurgency in his country, and feared that if he remained in power, the entire region would fall to communism. Similarly, US policymakers targeted the North Vietnamese regime to prevent it from reunifying the country under communist rule, to contain the spread of Soviet and Chinese influence in the region, and to deter other potential aggressors. At the same time, I found that the major alternative arguments could not explain the case. Normative and liberal accounts cannot explain US behavior. Contrary to what these theorists would predict, the United States first promoted a colonial regime, then an authoritarian one, and repeatedly collaborated with the groups with poor human rights records as part of its covert interventions. Likewise, the argument that Kennedy did not personally approve the 1963 coup is overstated. Although mid-level State Department officials may have overstepped their bounds by sending the infamous Cable 243 in August 1963, Kennedy had plenty of time to retract the cable, which he did not. Instead, his administration decided to pursue the cable's objectives two months later.

Second, the chapter investigated five separate periods—three negative and two positive cases—when the United States debated launching a regime change in North or South Vietnam and showed that the United States was only willing to intervene when this project's two preconditions for intervention were met. In the case of South Vietnam, Washington's inability to find a plausible alternative to Diem explains why Washington stuck by its problematic ally for so long and rejected multiple earlier calls for his ouster. In the case of North Vietnam, Lansdale, Colby, and other high-level CIA officials appear to have dramatically overestimated the plausibility of opposition forces in North Vietnam during the 1961–63 period. According to Colby's deputy, Robert Myers, "The totality of communist control measures made such operations impossible. The reason for our failure lay in the thinking of our superiors that it was World War II all over again."[235] Once policymakers came to grips with this fact in 1964, however, the goals of America's covert missions in North Vietnam were explicitly limited to exclude regime change.

Finally, neither of the covert regime changes worked as US policymakers intended. Operations in the North, which shared much in common with America's earlier rollback operations, demonstrated the difficulty of overthrowing a consolidated communist state. Overthrowing Diem was far easier, but it too ultimately proved counterproductive. Instead of bringing stability to South Vietnam, Diem's assassination weakened the South Vietnamese regime, thereby leading the United States to escalate its involvement. It is impossible to say how differently the situation in Vietnam would have turned out if the United States had not launched its covert regime change operations. What is clear is that top US policymakers—including Johnson, Taylor, Harkins, Lansdale, and McNamara—have each pointed to these covert operations as one of the main reasons for America's failed strategy in Vietnam. After the 1963 coup, for instance, White House adviser William Bundy wrote, "Americans in both public and policy circles were bound henceforth to feel more responsible for what happened in South Vietnam."[236] Colby agreed: "I consider the worst mistake of the Vietnam War: the American-sponsored overthrow of Diem."[237]

Dictators and Democrats in the Dominican Republic

Any unilateral American intervention, in the absence of an external attack upon ourselves or any ally, would have been contrary to our traditions and to our international obligations. But let the record show that our restraint is not inexhaustible. If the nations of this hemisphere should fail to meet their commitments against outside Communist penetration then I want it clearly understood that this government will not hesitate in meeting its primary obligations which are to the security of our nation.

—John F. Kennedy, April 20, 1961

Located only five hundred miles off the coast of Florida, the Dominican Republic has always conducted its political affairs in the shadow of the United States. In fact, Congress nearly annexed the country in 1870, and US troops twice occupied it in the early twentieth century.[1] To combat the country's chronic political volatility, Washington backed General Rafael Trujillo's authoritarian regime after he seized power in a 1930 coup. By the late 1950s, however, US leaders began to question Trujillo's increasingly erratic and brutal rule. Concerned that his regime might spark a popular revolt similar to the one that had recently toppled Fulgencio Batista in Cuba, Eisenhower authorized a covert campaign to overthrow Trujillo in 1960. But the operation misfired. Trujillo was assassinated in 1961, but his fall brought his equally cruel son to power, which in turn led to a series of coups. Fearful that communists could come to power amid this mayhem, Kennedy and Johnson launched multiple covert and one overt regime change operation in the Dominican Republic in hopes of creating a stable, pro-US regime. This chapter analyzes the causes, conduct, and consequences of those interventions. Unlike in the previous case studies, I argue that Eisenhower, Kennedy, and Johnson did not foresee a direct Soviet threat in the country when they decided to intervene. Instead, America pursued a goal that preceded the Cold

War and continues to this day—the maintenance of a hierarchical regional order in the Western Hemisphere. With this end in view, US policymakers feared that if a socialist or communist regime came to power in the Dominican Republic, its success could spark left-wing revolts in neighboring countries, leading to a cascade of defections from the US-led order and potentially the collapse of US regional hegemony.

Case Selection and Alternative Hypotheses

Although the United States launched eighteen covert hegemonic regime changes in twelve countries during the Cold War, the Dominican Republic is a particularly interesting case for several reasons. For one, proponents of the "rogue CIA" and economic alternative explanations have each singled out the Dominican case as good evidence for their theories, thus making it a harder test for mine. Second, covert operations in the Dominican Republic involved a variety of tactics, including assassination, coup d'état, covertly backing dissident groups, and secretly funding selected candidates in the country's democratic elections, thus allowing me to evaluate the pros and cons of each tactic. Third, the case is unique in that the United States pursued regime change covertly in 1961 and 1962, and overtly during the 1965 civil war, before returning to covert conduct to influence Dominican elections in 1966 and 1968. This within-case variation allows me to test whether my theory's prerequisite conditions for covert and overt intervention were met across time. Finally, Washington's actions in the Dominican Republic mirrored its behavior toward several other states in the Western Hemisphere, providing a clearer picture of how US leaders used covert regime change to manage the political affairs of client states.

Existing theories of regime change cannot fully explain US behavior in the Dominican Republic. There is little support for normative and liberal accounts, and though the "rogue CIA" hypothesis has some traction in explaining Trujillo's assassination in 1961, it cannot explain later covert actions in 1962, 1966, or 1968. Moreover, the evidence is against those who claim the United States acted to protect American business interests. Instead, Washington's overarching goal during each mission was to maintain its position as a regional hegemon.

Numerous normative and ideological accounts of justified intervention predict that the United States should promote democracy or, at the very least, respect democratic processes during its regime changes. In the case of the Dominican Republic, however, US leaders appeared willing to support a variety of regime types—both liberal and autocratic—as long as they served US interests: For instance, Washington worked with military strongman Rafael Trujillo from 1930 to 1960 despite his well-established record of human rights abuses. After Trujillo proved a liability, however, Eisenhower and

Kennedy supported a military coup to replace him. When these plans back-fired and Trujillo's son Ramfis seized power, Kennedy ranked his options as follows: "In descending order of preference: a decent democratic regime, a continuation of the Trujillo regime, or a Castro regime. We ought to aim for the first but we can't really renounce the second until we are sure we can avoid the third."[2] Following this ranking, Kennedy reluctantly worked with Ramfis Trujillo's autocratic regime until it began to implode in late 1961, at which time he publicly called for democratic elections while successfully us-ing coercive diplomacy to hasten the younger Trujillo's departure. Rather than actually promoting free and fair elections after Ramfis Trujillo's regime collapsed, however, JFK ordered the CIA to covertly support two moderate political parties during the 1962 elections in order to prevent a communist or socialist victory. After a US-supported candidate, Juan Bosch, won the elec-tion, Kennedy backed Bosch's government for several months before decid-ing that he was incompetent and switching US support to the military junta that overthrew him. In 1965, Johnson overtly intervened during the Domini-can Civil War to prevent a communist victory. But like Kennedy, he did not promote entirely free elections afterward. Instead, Johnson authorized the CIA to covertly support right-wing candidates in 1966 and 1968 elections. Taken as a whole, these actions suggest that although the United States was decidedly anti-communist, it was only willing to actively support democ-racy in the Dominican Republic when it brought a pro-US party to power.

The case also allows us to test the proposition that modern Western states have embraced a norm against assassinating foreign leaders.[3] I find that al-though US policymakers viewed assassination as distasteful, the normative constraint against launching this type of operation was not sufficiently strong to prevent Washington from supporting the 1961 Dominican plot to oust Rafael Trujillo, even though they understood that Trujillo was likely to be assassinated during the coup. Instead, US officials justified this action as the lesser of two evils. For instance, America's consulate general in the Domini-can Republic, Henry Dearborn, reasoned in a cable to Washington, "Politi-cal assassination is ugly and repulsive, but everything must be judged in its own context. The United States used the atom bomb on Hiroshima and that was ugly and repulsive—unless one stops to consider that it was used to save thousands of lives in the long run."[4] Still, US officials understood that international audiences would view the United States negatively for sup-porting an operation that resulted in Trujillo's death and thus preferred to do so covertly—suggesting that while the normative constraint against killing foreign leaders was not powerful enough to cause Washington to call off the regime change attempt, it was strong enough to drive the operation underground.[5]

Related to this is the question of whether Kennedy intended for Trujillo to be assassinated and whether the CIA overstepped its bounds during the operation. On the one hand, declassified documents reveal that the dissidents' assassination plot was discussed and approved in meetings with high-level officials in the Kennedy administration, including Bissell, Bowles, Bundy, Dulles, Gilpatric, McNamara, and Rusk. Although there is a lack of direct evidence that Kennedy was briefed on the assassination, officials in his administration requested that memoranda on the assassination plot "be prepared for higher authority on the subject."[6] When asked later why his briefings to Kennedy did not specifically mention assassination, CIA Deputy Director for Plans Richard Bissell testified, "I don't know whether it was because this was common knowledge and seemed to me unnecessary to include it, or as you are implying, there was an element of concealment here. I would be very surprised if it were the latter, in this case."[7] On the other hand, Kennedy's office cabled the Dominican CIA station the day before the attack that "as a general policy [the United States] could not condone political assassination," but that the US would continue to support the Dominican dissidents.[8] Despite this warning, the dissidents assassinated Trujillo the following day. Some have taken this as evidence that the CIA intentionally acted against JFK's orders by not stopping the operation. Although the historical record is still murky, available evidence suggests that the CIA did not interpret the cable as a shift in US policy, just that the US did not want to be directly involved in Trujillo's death. Moreover, although the CIA provided material goods to the coup plotters, it did not believe it had enough control over their actions to call off the operation. Given the ambiguity regarding US intentions created by the cable, I have erred on the side of caution throughout this study and classified America's involvement in Trujillo's assassination as inadvertent.

Some proponents of the economic rationale for regime change argue that the United States turned against Dominican leader Juan Bosch in 1963 to protect the economic interests of US corporations.[9] For instance, one charge is that the United States acted to protect the interests of Central Romana, an American sugar company that ran the largest agricultural complex in the Dominican Republic, La Romana. By these accounts, the management of La Romana was upset to lose the preferential treatment that it had received under the Trujillo regime, during which time the company had paid its 18,000 Dominican workers approximately $1 per day. After the Trujillos left power, La Romana employees were able to organize and demand higher wages, and by 1962, the average worker's pay had grown to $3.25 per day.[10] During Juan Bosch's seven-month term in 1963, La Romana employees went on strike, and their wages increased an additional 30 percent.[11] According to economic-oriented accounts, the final straw causing Washington to turn against Bosch came in June of that year when Bosch informed the US ambassador of his plans for land reform, which would nationalize many Central Romana holdings.[12]

Nonetheless, there is little reason to believe that the United States intervened in the Dominican Republic to protect the interests of any American corporation. For one thing, although records of executive-level policymaking meetings show a great deal of concern about the threat of communism in general, they very seldom discuss the specific holdings of any US firm. Second, US leaders repeatedly took actions that hurt the economic interests of American sugar producers in the Dominican Republic. For example, Eisenhower imposed economic sanctions on the Dominican Republic in 1960 to retaliate for Trujillo's assassination attempt on the Venezuelan president, and in 1962, Kennedy ended US subsidies on Dominican sugar, decreasing its value to the market price.[13] US policymakers were willing to take these actions—contra to the interests of American multinational corporations in the country—because sugar comprised over half of the Trujillo family's business holdings and thus offered a unique source of leverage over the regime.[14] Finally, though Bosch's plan for land reform briefly distressed US policymakers, they did not consider it a major threat. In fact, the US ambassador persuaded Bosch to drop his plans before he had a chance to make them public.[15] In sum, there is scarce evidence that US planners viewed the Dominican Republic as posing a major economic threat to its interests or that the United States acted to protect the economic interests of Central Romana or any other American firm through its covert activities.

Regime Change in the Dominican Republic, 1960–68

From its independence in 1844 until 1930, Dominican politics were a remarkably violent and volatile affair. Indeed, the country had 123 separate rulers during its first eighty-six years of existence.[16] Throughout this time, Washington's relationship with Santo Domingo was guided by two principles. First was the Monroe Doctrine of 1823, which stated that any European effort to colonize or interfere with any state in the Western Hemisphere would be considered an act of aggression by the United States and would warrant a military response.[17] The second, known as the "Roosevelt Corollary," was introduced by Theodore Roosevelt in 1904 and granted the United States the authority to intervene to enforce legitimate contractual claims made by European powers and to combat domestic political disturbances within Latin American countries.[18]

In keeping with these principles, US forces intervened in the Dominican Republic in 1904 to establish a Customs' Receivership after the Dominican government failed to repay its significant debt to European and American creditors.[19] Ten years later, amid a bloody civil war, President Wilson again ordered US Marines to occupy and stabilize the country.[20] As a part of this mission, US forces dissolved the Dominican Army and established a national guard, known as the Dominican National Police (*Policia Nacional Dominicana*—PND). In 1918, an ambitious twenty-five-year-old named Rafael Trujillo joined the PND. Despite his criminal record and having been court-martialed in 1920 (and later acquitted) for holding a man hostage and raping his teenage daughter, Trujillo made a favorable impression on the Marines who trained him.[21] Reports from the period describe him as "calm, even-tempered, forceful, active, bold, and painstaking . . . one of the best in the service."[22] By the time US forces withdrew following the election of President Horacio Vásquez in 1924, Trujillo had been promoted to the rank of major. In 1927, Vásquez reorganized the PND as the National Army and put Trujillo in command as a brigadier general.[23] With this new authority, Trujillo soon found himself in position to challenge Vásquez to become the most powerful man in the country.

THE RISE AND FALL OF RAFAEL TRUJILLO (1930–61)

Trujillo grasped his opportunity to gain power during a 1930 uprising against Vásquez. Early in the uprising, Trujillo made a deal with the rebel leader, Rafael Estrella Ureña, that his forces would not defend Vásquez's regime if Trujillo could run for president in the May 1930 elections. The deal worked as planned. For his part, Estrella Ureña captured Santo Domingo in February. After Vásquez fled, however, Trujillo sidelined his opponents and won the sham election in May with over 95 percent of the vote.[24] After taking office, Trujillo soon assumed dictatorial powers. He adopted titles like "Generalissimo," "the Benefactor," and "El Jefe." He renamed the country's capital Ciudad Trujillo and embezzled billions of dollars into family bank accounts.[25] For many years, Trujillo's political party, the Dominican Party (*Partido Dominicano*—PD) was the only party allowed to compete in elections, and the PD received 100 percent of the vote in nearly every election between 1936 and 1957.[26]

Through all of this, Washington reluctantly accepted Trujillo's rule because of his strong opposition to communism and, in 1954, even worked with the dictator to covertly overthrow Jacobo Arbenz's leftist regime in Guatemala.[27] CIA Station Chief Henry Dearborn explained the feeling during this time: "He had his torture chambers, he had his political assassinations, but he kept law and order, cleaned the place up, made it sanitary, built public works and he didn't bother the United States. So that was fine with us."[28] By the late 1950s, however, officials in the Eisenhower administration began to question America's relationship with Trujillo. "About the time I got there," Dearborn continued, "his iniquities had gotten so bad that there was a lot of pressure from various political groups, civil rights groups and others, not only in the United States, but throughout the hemisphere, that something just had to be done about this man."[29]

Two events in particular were crucial in turning Washington against the dictator. First was Trujillo's role in the 1956 disappearance of a Basque academic living in New York City, Jesús de Galíndez, who had attracted Trujillo's ire by writing his PhD dissertation at Columbia University on the regime's human rights abuses. After Galíndez turned down an offer from Dominican agents to sell his dissertation for $25,000, Trujillo allegedly ordered his kidnapping.[30] According to later CIA and FBI investigations, Dominican security agents kidnapped Galíndez on the night of March 12, 1956, from a Manhattan subway station. A twenty-three-year-old American pilot named Gerald Lester Murphy then flew a drugged Galíndez from Amityville, New York, to Ciudad Trujillo, where he was tortured and killed on arrival.[31] Although the FBI investigated Galíndez's kidnapping, it was not until the American pilot who had flown him to the Dominican Republic also disappeared nine months later that the case began to unravel. According to State Department files, "Murphy told his American fiancée that in March, 1956 he flew an apparently drugged man in a light plane non-stop from New York to Ciudad Trujillo. He later 'learned' the man was Jesus de Galíndez, anti-Trujillo Spanish exile . . . ."[32] After the FBI pressured Trujillo's regime for information on Murphy's disappearance, they announced that an internal investigation had revealed that Murphy was murdered by a Dominican pilot named Octavio de la Maza. Before US agents could interview de la Maza, however, he too died under mysterious circumstances. A US State Department inquiry into Murphy's death summarizes the explanation provided by Dominican authorities: "Our Charge was informed that de la Maza had hanged himself in his cell at 4 A.M. that morning. The charge was shown an alleged suicide note in which de la Maza said he had met Murphy the evening of December 3rd, that they went to the site near the sea where Murphy's automobile was later found, that Murphy had made 'improper advances,' that there was a struggle during which Murphy fell into the sea, and that de la Maza had decided to kill himself out of remorse."[33] US authorities were highly suspicious of the story, and the FBI later determined that de la Maza's suicide note had been a forgery.[34]

The second major event to turn the United States against Trujillo was Castro's rise to power in Cuba. Although Trujillo was avowedly anti-communist, US officials feared that his brutal regime could spark a communist revolution similar to the one that overthrew Cuba's Fulgencio Batista in 1959. The United States had good reason to worry. Long-standing dictators were falling throughout the region. In 1954, dictators ruled twelve out of twenty Latin American states. By 1961, however, only Trujillo and Paraguay's Alfredo Stroessner remained.[35] Washington's fear of a popular revolution increased after Castro declared his intention to overthrow the Dominican Republic—a threat that was taken seriously given Trujillo's unpopularity among his country's rural poor.[36] Given these concerns, Eisenhower feared that continued US support for Trujillo would encourage anti-Americanism throughout the region and undermine the US-led order. America's ambassador to the Dominican Republic, Joseph Farland, wrote, "We are under directives to seek to avoid giving any impressions that US favors dictatorships in Latin America. A part of the picture is that anti-Trujillo attitude in Latin America is considerably high."[37] Eisenhower concurred, "American public opinion won't condemn Castro until we have moved against Trujillo."[38]

American fears of "another Cuba" escalated after Castro's forces invaded the Dominican Republic on June 14, 1959. Although Trujillo quickly quashed the invasion, US policymakers criticized the regime for its brutal crackdown on its domestic opposition afterward.[39] Believing that Trujillo's indiscriminate repression had become counterproductive, Washington feared that another popular uprising was imminent. A 1959 Special National Intelligence Estimate warned: "Should Trujillo leave the scene, those remaining in the regime probably could not long control the situation and a struggle for power would result, in which pro-Communist exiles and other radicals would play a prominent part."[40] Ambassador Farland agreed: "The Dominican Communists in exile will come rushing back and will attempt to take over the reins of government during the confused period of reorganization."[41] If this revolution were to succeed, the State Department advised that it could spark communist victories in "Haiti, Nicaragua, Panama, Guatemala and other Central and Latin American countries."[42]

Numerous Latin American leaders shared Eisenhower's concern.[43] During an August 1959 meeting in Chile, for example, foreign ministers from throughout the region debated whether it might be possible to incite a democratic revolution in the Dominican Republic, similar to the one that had recently overthrown Venezuelan dictator Perez Jimenez. But US officials were skeptical. Secretary of State Christian Herter argued, "History has shown that efforts to impose democracy in a country, by force and from outside, can easily result in the mere substitution of one form of tyranny for another."[44] Assistant Secretary Roy Rubottom agreed, "One only had to consider Venezuela's experience during the past year, when the people of that nation had themselves overthrown Perez Jimenez, without outside assistance or intervention. The strict observance of non-intervention is perhaps the best way to promote democracy."[45]

Given the difficulties associated with sparking a popular democratic revolution, Eisenhower debated other ways to covertly overthrow Trujillo in early 1960. At an NSC meeting in January, Undersecretary of State Livingston Merchant argued that the time had come for the United States to replace Trujillo. But, he warned, this would not be an easy task. Trujillo had crushed all moderate opponents to his regime. As such, Merchant suggested that the United States should try to initiate a covert campaign to "coalesce non-Communist business, professional, and academic groups into an opposition."[46] Eisenhower acquiesced, and the CIA began drawing up plans to start funding these groups soon after.[47] As my theory would predict, however, Eisenhower was unwilling to attempt to oust Trujillo until he was confident that these groups could provide a plausible political alternative to the dictator. For instance, an April 1960 memo from Secretary of State Herter to the president explained, "The United States would immediately take political action to remove Trujillo from the Dominican Republic as soon as a suitable successor regime can be induced to take over with the assurance of US political, economic, and—if necessary—military support."[48] Before attempting to covertly topple the regime, however, Washington first tried to persuade Trujillo to peacefully step down in favor of a comfortable exile with a "trust fund" in Portugal or Morocco.[49] Trujillo rejected the offer, arguing, "I'll never go out of here unless I go on a stretcher."[50]

Meanwhile, a small group of Dominican elites had been secretly hashing a plan to oust Trujillo. Leading the group was Antonio de la Maza, whose brother Octavio had been framed and murdered by Trujillo's henchman during the Galíndez/Murphy scandal. In the spring of 1960, the Dominican conspirators first made contact with US Ambassador Farland during a cocktail party.[51] The plotters requested US help securing rifles with telescopic scopes, which were banned within the country.[52] Farland passed the request to Washington, and on June 16, 1960, CIA headquarters cabled its Dominican station to appoint CIA agent Henry Dearborn as a "communications link" between the dissidents and the CIA.[53] Dearborn agreed but asked for confirmation that the United States would act to "clandestinely . . . develop effective force to accomplish Trujillo overthrow."[54] CIA headquarters confirmed this proposal.[55]

Contrary to the rogue CIA hypothesis, available evidence shows that high-level Eisenhower administration officials supported the coup, despite understanding that it could result in Trujillo's death. For instance, on June 28, 1960, Assistant Secretary of State Rubottom met with CIA Station Chief J. C. King. During this meeting, King asked Rubottom, "To what extent will the US government participate in the overthrowing of Trujillo. . . . Would it provide a small number of sniper rifles or other devices for the removal of key Trujillo people from the scene?" King's handwritten note on the memo confirms that Rubottom's response was yes.[56] Likewise, a July 1, 1960, CIA memo states that the requested arms "would be used against key members of the Trujillo regime" and that "approval for delivery of these arms has been given by Assistant Secretary of State Roy Rubottom, who requests that the arms be placed in the hands of the opposition at the earliest possible moment."[57] Similarly, a July 14, 1960, letter from Dearborn to Rubottom complains that the group was "in no way ready to carry on any type of revolutionary activity in the foreseeable future except the assassination of their principal enemy."[58]

In August 1960, Washington officially cut its relations with the Dominican Republic after Trujillo was caught trying to assassinate one of his long-time rivals, Venezuelan president Rómulo Betancourt.[59] In response, Eisenhower joined the Organization of American States (OAS) in placing economic sanctions on the regime, closed the US embassy in Ciudad Trujillo, and recalled the US ambassador. In an effort to appease the United States, Trujillo announced that he would hold democratic elections in 1961. He also forced his notoriously cruel brother Héctor to resign as president, and replaced him with a moderate cabinet minister, Joaquín Balaguer.[60] These efforts were in vain. Consol General and de facto CIA Station Chief Henry Dearborn, who had become America's primary source within the Dominican Republic after the US ambassador was recalled, wrote to Washington that Trujillo would continue "his political domination whether he is President or dogcatcher" and that there was no indication that the regime would "abolish arbitrary arrests, prison tortures, or reprisals against its political opposition."[61]

On October 3, 1960, the CIA submitted a memo entitled "Plans of the Dominican Internal Opposition and Dominican Desk for Overthrow of the Trujillo Government." It declared that plans "have been developed on a tentative basis which appear feasible and which might be carried out covertly by CIA with a minimal risk of exposure." Toward this end, the CIA requested two things: "a. Delivery of approximately 300 rifles and pistols, together with ammunition and a supply of grenades . . . b. Delivery to the same cache described above, of an electronic detonating device with remote control features which could be planted by the dissidents in such a manner as to eliminate certain key Trujillo henchmen."[62] Following up a few weeks later, Dearborn wrote to Assistant Secretary of State Thomas Mann:

> One further point, which I should probably not even make. From a purely practical standpoint, it will be best for us, for the OAS, and for the Dominican Republic if the Dominicans put an end to Trujillo before he leaves this island. If he has his millions and is a free agent, he will devote his life from exile to preventing stable government in the D.R., to overturning democratic governments and establishing dictatorships in the Caribbean, and to assassinating his enemies. If I were a Dominican, which thank heaven I am not, I would favor destroying Trujillo as being the first necessary step in the salvation of my country and I would regard this, in fact, as my Christian duty. If you recall Dracula, you will remember it was necessary to drive a stake through his heart to prevent a continuation of his crimes.[63]

In November, the State Department director of Intelligence and Research warned that "the tide is now running against the United States and the longer the current impasse continues, the more unfavorable to US interests the outcome is likely to be."[64] Swayed by these accounts, Eisenhower's special task force to evaluate covert action, known as the Special Group, approved a broad plan of covert support to anti-Trujillo forces on December 29, 1960.[65] Then, on the last day of the Eisenhower administration, Dearborn was informed that his request to supply arms to the dissidents had been approved.[66]

Kennedy inherited the ongoing Dominican operation along with several others in the Congo, Cuba, and Vietnam. Even before his inauguration, Kennedy appointed a task force to evaluate US strategy in Latin America. Writing in 1960, the task force concluded, "To support the few remaining dictatorships or regimes based on plutocracies or oligarchic landowners would mean supporting doomed reactionary groups whose downfall would leave the United States in an untenable popular position." It continued, however, that there was "no group capable of undertaking the task of government" within the Dominican Republic. Therefore, the task force suggested the United States should begin covertly "choosing and training cadres."[67] Secretary of State Dean Rusk concurred with the assessment, writing to Kennedy a few weeks after his inauguration: "Account must be taken of the adverse effect on our position of leadership in the hemisphere if we support tyranny in the Dominican Republic. Our ability to marshal Latin American support against the Castro dictatorship would be impaired."[68] Consulate General Dearborn agreed, "Our theme has been that the longer Trujillo continues to dominate the D.R. the more susceptible the country is becoming to leftist extremists, and that, therefore, Trujillo's overthrow in the near future would be in the interest of the U.S."[69]

Based on these assessments, Kennedy authorized a covert effort to train new potential leaders on the moderate left.[70] The president hoped that by raising the standard of living for average citizens and providing a left-wing alternative to communism, he could offer a "third way" between right-wing dictatorship and communist revolution.[71] The mission fit well within his overall strategy for the region, known as the Alliance for Progress, a $20 billion development plan designed to improve US relations and economic cooperation throughout the region.[72]

Simultaneous with his covert efforts to develop moderate left leaders in the Dominican Republic, Kennedy continued to support the ongoing coup and assassination plot against Trujillo. On February 10 and 15, US officials met with dissidents in New York City who debated multiple ways of killing Trujillo, including guns, fragmentation grenades, poison, and bombs.[73] Afterward, Secretary of State Dean Rusk wrote to Kennedy:

> Our representatives in the Dominican Republic have, at considerable risk to those involved, established contacts with numerous leaders of underground opposition. These leaders look to the United States for assistance. They believe in a free enterprise economic system, plan the nationalization of public utilities with compensation to the owners, intend to institute a land reform program based on agricultural cooperatives and the nationalization of idle agricultural land and intend to confiscate all of Trujillo's properties. They have agreed on a president to lead them, propose to prevent the re-entry of Communist and subversive agents and to hold elections within a two-year period during which they plan to carry out their program.[74]

Toward this end, Rusk continued, "The CIA has recently been authorized to arrange for delivery to them outside the Dominican Republic of small arms and sabotage equipment."[75]

Frustrated by the mission's slow progress, Dearborn pressed Washington for additional arms. On March 13, the CIA station put in a request for fifty fragmentation grenades, five rapid-fire weapons, and ten 64 mm anti-tank rockets.[76] Three days later, Dearborn sent a thinly coded message to the State Department:

> The members of our club are now prepared in their minds to have a picnic but do not have the ingredients for the salad. Lately they have developed a plan for the picnic, which just might work if they could find the proper food. They have asked us for a few sandwiches, hardly more, and we are not prepared to make them available. Last week we were asked to furnish three or four pineapples for a party in the new future, but I could remember nothing in my instructions that would have allowed me to contribute this ingredient. Don't think I wasn't tempted. I have rather specific guidelines to the effect that salad ingredients will be delivered outside the picnic grounds and will be brought to the area by another club.[77]

Nevertheless, the question of whether the dissidents really offered a plausible alternative to Trujillo remained salient. Even Dearborn admitted in a March 22 cable, "There is no well organized unitary opposition to Trujillo. On the other hand, on the basis of the judgment of our best sources 80 to 90 per cent [sic] of literate Dominicans are anti-Trujillo and would like to have a representative form of government oriented toward the west, one which would not intervene in the affairs of its neighbors and which would respect basic human rights."[78] Unsatisfied with this answer, CIA headquarters wrote that the station should not pass the weapons to the dissidents until they had developed a better plan for governing after Trujillo's fall. "We should attempt to avoid precipitous action by the internal dissidents until opposition group and HQS are better prepared to support [redacted word], effect a change of regime, and cope with the aftermath."[79] Despite this reluctance, however, CIA Headquarters apparently changed its mind and instructed the station to pass three 30-caliber M1 carbines to the dissidents on March 31.[80] They did so, passing the arms to the leader of the conspirators, Antonio de la Maza.[81]

Following the Bay of Pigs fiasco on April 17, Kennedy had second thoughts about the wisdom of the anti-Trujillo mission. Bissell later testified, "There developed a general realization that precipitous action should be avoided in the Dominican Republic until Washington was able to give further considerations to the consequences of a Trujillo overthrow and the power vacuum that would be created."[82] On April 28, Rusk wrote to Dearborn, encouraging him to develop a plausible alternative to Trujillo:

> US strongly hopes any succeeding government will be broadly acceptable to people of Dominican Republic, will be oriented toward US, and will promptly commit self to establishment democracy and firm scheduling of free elections. . . . As opportunity presents self under circumstances outlined above you should encourage formulation [of a] realistic coalition [of] civilian and military elements capable holding power as provisional government friendly toward and disposed [to] work [ing] with US.[83]

Within the Dominican Republic, however, the dissidents finally felt ready to attack. Their plan called for a group of seven men, led by Luís Amiama Tío and Antonio Imbert Barrera, to ambush Trujillo as he was traveling on a highway out of Ciudad Trujillo without his security detail. Afterward, General José "Pupo" Román Fernandez, secretary of state for the Armed Forces, would launch a military coup and arrest high-level officers loyal to Trujillo.[84] One conspirator wrote these instructions:

> Once Trujillo is dead, Pupo Román and Juan Tomás Díaz will head a civilian-military junta with Antonio de la Maza as secretary of the armed forces; all members of the Trujillo family will be arrested. Some will be permitted to leave and other will be brought to justice. . . . President Balaguer will be taken to the National Palace where he will be obliged to sign the decrees establishing the junta. The junta will ask for the intervention of the United States to prevent bloodshed.[85]

In late April, Dearborn cabled CIA headquarters that the dissidents were ready to attack.[86] Washington responded that the United States was not yet prepared to cope with the aftermath of an assassination and ordered Dearborn not to pass any additional weapons to the conspirators.[87] After speaking with the dissidents, Dearborn responded, "We doubt statements U.S. government not now prepared to cope with aftermath will dissuade them from their attempt."[88]

On May 29, the Kennedy administration sent Dearborn a top-priority cable: "We must not run risk of U.S. association with political assassination, since U.S. as [a] matter of general policy cannot condone assassination. The last principle is overriding and must prevail in doubtful situation"[89] The cable continued, however, that Dearborn should "inform dissident elements of U.S. support for their position."[90] Whether this cable was designed to stop the covert operation, delay it, or merely provide cover for the White House should America's role in the plot become publicly known cannot be determined definitively from the available declassified documents. A 1975 presidential investigation into the CIA's covert activities and its involvement in plans to assassinate foreign leaders, known as Rockefeller Commission, later determined that "the preparation of this message, and the required coordination, consumed about two weeks. There is no evidence of any efforts during this period to recover the weapons or otherwise interfere in the assassination plans."[91] Dearborn later testified that he interpreted the cable as meaning "we don't care if the Dominicans assassinate Trujillo, that is all right. But we don't want anything to pin this on us, because we weren't doing it, it is the Dominicans who are doing it."[92] As such, he did not attempt to cancel the mission. Instead, he replied, "HQ [Headquarters] aware extent to which U.S. government already associated with assassination. If we are to at least cover up tracks, CIA personnel directly involved in assassination preparation must be withdrawn."[93]

The dissidents struck the next day. After thirty-one years in power, Trujillo was shot and killed after the coup plotters ambushed his Chevrolet Bel Air on a highway outside of Ciudad Trujillo. Afterward, Dearborn telegrammed to Washington: "Have now established beyond any doubt whatever Trujillo assassinated by group desiring democratic anti-communist government . . . Trujillo [was] shot once in [his] chin, once in [the] side of [his] head, and four times in [the] back of [his] head but that he was armed and injured some of the attackers."[94] Kennedy learned of the assassination while meeting with French president Charles de Gaulle in Paris.[95]

Other than killing the dictator, however, every other part of the plot did not proceed as planned. To begin, four of the conspirators were wounded after Trujillo and his driver returned fire on their car. Moreover, Antonio de la Maza accidentally left a gun registered to another conspirator at the scene, and Trujillo's driver survived the attack. Worse still, General Pupo Román panicked under pressure and hesitated to launch the military coup.[96] After waiting for hours, Román finally ordered Trujillo's top supporters to assemble at an army base. By this time, however, they were suspicious of his motives and refused to follow orders. One of Román's colleagues at the time lamented, "He has neither the capacity nor the character to do it. He has failed to exploit the confusion. He is only proving he is no commander, confirming Trujillo's own estimation of him."[97]

Within hours, the plot began to unravel. Trujillo's notorious intelligence agency, the Military Intelligence Service (*Servicio de Inteligencia Militar*—SIM), led by Johnny Abbés García, quickly began rounding up the conspirators. Several were caught trying to receive medical help. On May 31, one of the plotters confessed, "General Román . . . would dominate the country with the support that was agreed upon with the United States government, as an agreement has been made through the American consul, Henry Dearborn, in this city."[98] Within the week, SIM agents had arrested or killed nearly all of the conspirators and hundreds of innocent bystanders. Of the core group of plotters, only two—Antonio Imbert Barrera and Luís Amiama Tío—were able to evade capture.[99] Meanwhile, Trujillo's thirty-year-old son Ramfis learned of his father's death while vacationing in France and quickly returned to the Dominican Republic to claim control.[100]

WASHINGTON'S CONFLICTED RELATIONSHIP WITH
RAMFIS TRUJILLO (1961–62)

Officials in the Kennedy administration eyed Ramfis's return and the continuing fallout from the coup with great apprehension. During a meeting of Kennedy's top aides, Undersecretary of State Chester Bowles recounted that they discussed "horror stories of assassination and retaliation which were reported going on behind the scenes at the Dominican capital."[101] Attorney General Robert Kennedy's notes from June 1 stated, "The great problem now is that we don't know what to do because we don't [*sic*] what the situation is and this shouldn't be true, particularly when we have known that this situation was pending for some time."[102] That same day, Rusk warned Kennedy that anti-American groups would try to exploit the power vacuum created by Trujillo's assassination: "Trujillo's death leaves Joaquín Balaguer in key position as continuing President and head of recognized Dominican State. Anti-US elements such as Abbés-Ramfis clique will probably attempt [to] subject him [to] their exclusive influence."[103] Kennedy's advisors split on how best to proceed. Some in the administration—including Robert Kennedy, Secretary of Defense Robert McNamara, and Chairman of the Joint Chiefs of Staff General Lyman Lemnitzer—argued that the United States should intervene overtly to prevent the situation from deteriorating further. A second group headed by State Department officials—including Secretary of State Rusk, Undersecretary of State Bowles, and Undersecretary of Political Affairs George McGhee—argued that aggressive overt action was unwarranted and would undermine America's treaty commitments and general image in the region.

Meanwhile, in the Dominican Republic the new regime sought to assuage Washington's concerns about its crackdown on political opponents in the hopes of averting an American intervention. On June 4, Dearborn met with Joaquín Balaguer, who continued in his position as the Dominican Republic's president under Ramfis Trujillo. During this meeting, Balaguer "denied [the] existence [of] violence and reign of terror in Dominican Republic" and "emphasized he was eminently anti-Communist and would fully support western democracies."[104] On June 12, Ramfis followed up by personally writing to Washington, expressing his willingness to do "anything reasonable" to improve US-Dominican relations, and asked the United States to "take leadership in specifying what should be done."[105]

Balaguer and Ramfis's claims were met with skepticism. Many policymakers had hoped that the elder Trujillo's assassination would create an opening for a popular, pro-American democracy. Ramfis's power grab threatened this vision, and many believed that he would follow his father's example. Dearborn, in particular, was adamant in his opposition, having warned months earlier that "Ramfis is most unstable, ruthless, US-hating, untrustworthy and cynical occupant of whole Trujillo nest and we should avoid him like bubonic plague."[106] At the same time, however, thirty years of dictatorship had stripped the country of its democratic forces, and US officials feared that communists would be able to exploit the power vacuum caused by a weak regime. On July 10, Kennedy wrote, "If we could not have a democracy with some hope of survival I would rather continue the present situation than to have a Castro dictatorship. That is our policy and we want to make sure that in attempting to secure democracy we don't end up with a Castro-Communist island."[107] A July 17 memo explained:

> The basic political problem facing the U.S. is how to encourage and foster a stable government, resistant to Castroism, constructed from Balaguer's mod-

erate wing of the existing government, the middle-of-the-road opposition elements and the armed forces. An effort to prolong the control of unreconstructed Trujillista elements beyond an adequate transition period would be to invite revolution and disorder at a time when there is no one to exercise the controlling role formerly played by the Generalissimo. To act precipitately to remove the Trujillos before firm foundations are established for a more representative government would be to invite a collapse of authority if not civil war.[108]

Seeing no other options, US officials decided to try to work with Ramfis and Balaguer in the hopes that they could promote "a smooth and orderly transition from the previously repressive regime to a more liberal and enlightened regime."[109] Through gradual reform, US planners hoped to create a "political climate and system, which would allow free elections" and include "all non-Castro, non-communist elements who adhere to the Dominican constitution."[110]

Over the next few months, Ramfis and Balaguer took several small steps to liberalize the Dominican political system and grant civil liberties. Washington, however, was impatient with the slow pace of reform. On October 3, the president's special assistant, Richard Goodwin, wrote to Kennedy:

> The opposition is well-meaning but as yet has not displayed any capacity for effective government. No political figure, around which activity could be centered, has emerged from the opposition ranks. . . . There is no pleasant answer to this problem. But I believe we should do the following: Accept the fact of Ramfis remaining in power and bargain to create an acceptable democratic facade which will win the confidence—if reluctant confidence of the opposition—and create the conditions under which future democratic government may be possible.[111]

In other words, the United States would continue to work with Ramfis's authoritarian regime for political expediency, but would also press the regime to gradually liberalize with the hopes of eventually creating suitable conditions for democratic rule in the country. Toward this end, Balaguer and Ramfis agreed to hold democratic elections in 1962, in which no member of the Trujillo family would be allowed to participate.

Ramfis Trujillo's reign came to an abrupt halt in November 1961. Under pressure from the Dominican military to quash street uprisings, Ramfis recalled his uncles, Héctor and Arismendi Trujillo, from exile on November 15, 1961. Outraged, Kennedy was determined not to let the Trujillos consolidate their power during this "behind-the-scenes national crisis."[112] On November 17, he ordered a flotilla of fourteen ships to wait off the coast of the Dominican Republic and gave the Trujillos twenty-four hours to leave the country, or else he would order the Marines to occupy it. The show of force worked, and Ramfis immediately fled the country. Soon afterward, Dominican

Air Force General Rafael Rodriguez Echevarria declared his support for Balaguer and launched an attack that successfully ousted the remaining Trujillos.[113]

With the Trujillos gone, President Balaguer found himself heading a highly unstable country. A loosely allied group of business and landed elites, known as the National Civic Union (*Unión Cívica Nacional*—UCN), formed to protest Balaguer's rule and organized a general strike in late November. By December, Kennedy had decided Balaguer's situation was untenable. On December 16, the White House wrote to its embassy in Santo Domingo, "We believe that the following suggested course of action will bring final success, after which we are confident President Balaguer can return to an important official position of some prestige. . . . Balaguer should also announce—on his own initiative—his intention to create a Council of State, a representative cabinet, and to take other measures necessary to assure a government of national unity with elections."[114] Toward this end, Washington suggested that Balaguer resign in February 1962.[115] Without US support, however, Balaguer saw little reason to wait and resigned the following day.[116]

On January 1, 1962, the Council of State was sworn in as the Dominican Republic's interim government and announced its intention to hold democratic elections within the year. The council included Balaguer as president, several representatives from the UCN, and the two surviving conspirators of the plot against Trujillo. Soon afterward, the OAS lifted its sanctions, and the United States reestablished full diplomatic relations with the country.[117] Unfortunately, the arrangement failed to resolve the military's opposition to the UCN, and after only two weeks, Air Force General Echevarria launched a military coup.[118] Kennedy quickly warned the military that the United States would withdraw its aid if the Council were overthrown. The threat worked, and several air force officers arrested Echevarria. Soon after, Captain Elías Wessin y Wessin reconstituted the Council of State and announced democratic elections in December 1962. After seven months of turmoil, US policymakers were relieved. A March 4 memo from the US embassy notes, "Government of this country is now in hands of moderate, anti-dictatorial and anti-Communist group which if anything is over-friendly to and dependent on US in this age of nationalism. It is accepted or supported by vast majority of politically conscious elements of population as transition to elections at end of year."[119]

1962 PRESIDENTIAL ELECTIONS

In the eleven-month run-up to the elections, two political parties emerged as the frontrunners. The first was the National Civic Union (*Unión Cívica Nacional*—UCN), representing the country's business sector. The United States had played "a key role in encouraging the business and professional leaders to establish the UCN" the previous summer, and the party had gained popular support, given its role in Ramfis Trujillo's downfall.[120] The UCN candidate, Viriato Fiallo, was a medical doctor with no previous political experience, but some political legitimacy for having been jailed by Trujillo.

The second party was the Dominican Revolutionary Party (*Partido Revolucionario Dominicano*—PRD), a left-wing group formed by Dominican exiles in Cuba in 1939. The PRD candidate was Juan Bosch, a writer and well-known opponent of Trujillo's regime. US planners viewed the PRD as a plausible left-wing alternative to communism. A CIA report described Bosch as "most accurately cataloged as belonging to the reformist, nationalistic, democratic left."[121] A Special 1961 National Intelligence Estimate noted, "At recent rallies the party has demonstrated some drawing power among city workers, other elements of the lower class, and poorer segments of the middle class. However, the majority of the middle class, which suffered most under the tyranny, is critical of PRD leaders as men who have remained out of the country for decades and escaped hardship and abuse."[122]

To prevent communists or groups affiliated with the previous regime from winning the 1962 election, Kennedy authorized a covert operation to fund the UCN and PRD. A CIA memorandum explained, "The primary objectives of clandestine activity are to prevent the accession to power in the Dominican Republic of a Communist/Castro controlled government, to create an atmosphere which will foster democratic evolution, and to obtain reliable and timely intelligence needed to formulate effective overt and covert action programs."[123] Toward this end, the plan called for the United States to

> support democratic non-Communist political groups in their efforts to achieve victory in the 1962 elections and to maintain their political viability thereafter. Currently, support is being given to the *Unión Cívica Nacional* (National Civic Union—UCN) and the *Partido Revolucionario Dominicano* (Dominican Revolutionary Party—PRD). Generally, equal support should be authorized in the future for both the UCN and PRD to provide particular support for the services of non-American political advisors and for party conventions in May 1962 and other organization efforts. [124]

By covertly supporting both the UCN and PRD, US officials hoped to prevent the victory of several far-left groups as well as parties tied to the previous regime, including Balaguer's Reformist Party, the Democratic Revolutionary Nationalist Party, the Social Democratic Alliance, and the Authentic Dominican Revolutionary Party.[125]

Several CIA-backed nonprofit organizations played a key role in Washington's covert plan. Kennedy authorized covert aid to the groups in the hope that they could "organize and support anti-Communist front groups capable of conducting militant action and propaganda against Communist/Castro individuals and groups."[126] Toward this end, the Institute for International

Labor Relations (IILR) provided literature to Dominican opposition groups. The Institute for Political Education (IPE) sought "to train high and medium level cadres for the Latin American left-of-center political parties, in both ideological and tactical fields."[127] The Inter-American Center for Political Training (*Centro Interamericano de Política Aprendizaje*—CIDAP) helped to organize Dominican peasants into the National Federation of Peasant Brotherhoods (*Federación Nacional de Hermandades Campesinas*—FENHERCA), a group that supported the PRD and eventually grew to 150,000 members.[128]

On December 20, 1962, the Dominican Republic held its first open democratic election since 1924. Bosch's PRD won heartily, receiving 648,000 out of the roughly 1 million votes cast, and beating the UCN by a margin of two to one. In addition to taking the presidency, PRD won twenty-two out of twenty-eight seats in the Senate and forty-eight out of seventy-four seats in the Chamber of Deputies.[129] Kennedy was pleased with the PRD's victory, authorized $100 million in aid to support the new regime, and sent his trusted advisor John Bartlow Martin to be ambassador.[130] On April 29, Bosch unveiled the new Dominican constitution, which granted basic civil liberties to the population, prohibited the deportation of dissidents, and legalized divorce.

On assuming office in February, Bosch and the PRD inherited a variety of major problems, including a large government deficit, a currency crisis, and a distrustful military. Unfortunately, the PRD had no experience running a country, and within months Bosch had disappointed virtually every political constituency in the Dominican Republic. To balance the budget, he cut public spending, and unemployment rose to over 30 percent.[131] Dominican peasants complained that Bosch did not follow through on his 1962 election campaign promises to divide Trujillo's vast estates and resettle landless peasants on sixteen-acre plots. Meanwhile, the landed elite feared that Bosch planned to redistribute their land, and created a new party, the Dominican Independence Association (*Asociacion Dominicana Independiente*—ADI) in response. The Catholic Church opposed legalizing divorce as well as Bosch's efforts to separate church and state, and the military complained that communists and socialists had been given too much leeway to organize under Bosch's new constitution.[132]

Washington soon lost faith in Bosch as well. Johnson later explained, "We continued to hope that Bosch would be able to do for his people what President Rómulo Betancourt had done for Venezuela after dictatorship had been overthrown there. But Bosch was no Betancourt. While his aspirations were admirable, his performance was weak."[133] Undersecretary of State George Ball was more blunt, describing Bosch as "unrealistic, arrogant and erratic. I thought him incapable of running even a small social club, much less a country in turmoil. He did not seem to me a communist . . . but merely a muddle-headed, anti-American pedant committed to unattainable social reforms."[134] US policymakers were even more displeased after Bosch laid out his plan for land reform to Ambassador Martin during a June meeting: "Estates larger than the prescribed limit would be seized over a five-year period. A 20 percent tax, to be paid in land only, would be levied. Thus all land over the legal limit would be transferred to the state without compensation by the end of five years, and then distributed to landless peasants."[135] However, Martin quickly dissuaded Bosch from enacting the reform. Instead, a CIA-backed group, the Inter-American Center for Social Studies (*Centro Interamericano de Estudios Sociales*—CIDES) took over "the major share of national planning in the Dominican Republic" during Bosch's term.[136]

By September, however, the situation had reached its crisis point. On September 19, the ADI launched a general strike to protest "the growing communist infiltration in the country."[137] On September 22, Martin cabled Washington, recommending that the United States "should recognize Bosch is not much of a president, that we should recognize most of his opposition is almost equally incompetent, and that we should attempt to take his government away from him, insofar as possible." Therefore, he continued, the United States should "use every means—or almost every means—to get rid of those whom we cannot control; exert every pressure to put our own people close to him and the other levers of power and, to the extent possible, though these people run his government without his knowing it."[138] As part of this effort, Martin wanted the CIA to "get control clandestinely" of several left-wing parties in order "to keep the far left split."[139]

Before Washington could formulate a strategy, however, General Wessin y Wessin launched a coup on September 24. In a last ditch effort to protect his regime, Bosch asked Martin for an aircraft carrier to come to his aid. Martin forwarded Bosch's request and publicly opposed the coup, but wrote to Washington, "I have no desire to return him, or his Cabinet or PRD to power."[140] Undersecretary of State Ball responded, "We cannot contemplate either serious use of carrier or implied threat against a coup in the present circumstances . . . little more can be done to maintain [Bosch] in office against the forces he himself has generated in opposition." Given Bosch's troublesome tenure as president, US policymakers decided they could no longer hold back the Dominican military, which moved to oust him.[141] After only seven months in power, Bosch fled into exile in Puerto Rico on September 25.

REID CABRAL ERA

Once in power, the military dissolved Congress, voided Bosch's constitution, banned communist groups, and promised to hold democratic elections at some point in the future. Soon afterward, the military installed a three-man junta, known as the Triumvirate, and invited "six minority parties, only one of which has a significant popular following" to join their coalition.[142] Bosch, Balaguer, and the PRD were "given no role or representation in the present government."[143] US policymakers were split on how best to proceed. On the one hand, as Secretary of State Rusk wrote to the embassy, the United States did not want to support the military, which was "seen in [the] US as arbitrary perpetrators of endless series of coups against elected civilian government."[144] On the other hand, no one in Washington wanted to see Bosch return to power. Thus, Rusk wrote, the

> U.S. should not seek to impose unacceptable—or any single—solution in DomRep. We recognize Communist dangers; we will insist on its being curbed, in our own interests as well as DomRep's. But we must ensure in so far as realistically possible that would-be *golpistas* [Spanish for leader of a coup] in other LA [Latin American] countries take no encouragement from Dom coup, and we must ensure that any solution to present impasses takes fully into account the desire of Dom people (and US people) that control over their destiny shall be returned to hands of a government responsive to their will.[145]

The only way for the United States to do this was to "remember that all PRDers, just like all military, not bad per se, and not 'brainwashed' . . . we must stop thinking in labels and bogeymen, face realities and individuals."[146] Seeing no plausible political alternative to the Triumvirate, Kennedy decided in mid-October to recognize the junta, but he was assassinated before he could.[147] After assuming office, President Johnson recognized the junta in December 1963.

Within months, Reid Cabral dominated the Triumvirate, and the other two members later stepped down. US policymakers were cautiously optimistic about these developments. A State Department paper praised Cabral as "by far the best Chief of State to appear on the Dominican scene."[148] At the same time, however, officials warned he could be "erratic and impulsive; when things are going well his self-confidence sometimes indulges itself in a form of cockiness, which irritates those whom it would be in his interest to cultivate."[149] Yet, seeing no better alternative, US policymakers decided to support Cabral. Toward this end, the CIA made covert attempts "to divide the PRD and bribe people in high level positions in the party."[150] Washington believed that if the opposition could be split, Cabral might have a chance in the coming elections.

Within the Dominican Republic, however, Cabral was widely unpopular. The fact that he had risen to power via a military coup left a permanent "stain of political illegitimacy" on his regime.[151] What's more, the US embassy reported, Cabral appeared to be "in no hurry to begin the electoral process."[152] In early 1964, he banned political protests and postponed elections until September 1965. Cabral also appeared to be doing little to help his country's severe economic recession. One-third of the population was estimated to be unemployed, and US officials feared that "the poor and the unemployed, most of whom scrape through on a minimum subsistence diet and have trouble even getting water, while not active politically, appear to be steadily drifting leftward in their sympathies."[153] As a result, the State Department admitted, "Although honest, and perhaps the closest thing to a patriot that the Dominican Republic has produced," Cabral "has no political sex appeal."[154] Indeed, a spring 1965 CIA poll found that Cabral had only 5 percent public approval compared to Bosch's 25 percent and Balaguer's 50 percent.[155]

OPERATION POWER PACK

On April 24, 1965, a group of junior military officers, led by Lt. Col. Francisco Caamaño, ousted Cabral. The officers, calling themselves the Constitutionalists for their support of Bosch's 1963 constitution, declared their intention to restore a democratic regime led by Juan Bosch. In support of this effort, a group of rebels captured Radio Santo Domingo and called for nationwide protests to support Bosch. The Constitutionalists were a diverse group, including PRD members, military officers, democratic socialists, and communists. Their plan, code-named Enriquillo, was to rapidly capture the National Police Headquarters and San Isidro Air Force base before the military could properly respond, thereby forcing General Wessin to concede defeat and paving the way for Bosch to return to power. But General Wessin had no intention of surrendering. Under his command, a group of anti-rebel forces, known as the Loyalists for their allegiance to the Cabral regime, gathered at the San Isidro Air Force base. Thus, the situation on April 26, as the State Department explained to Johnson, was that "the Wessin group and the Air Force are in one camp; a large part of the Army that is in Santo Domingo, the capital itself, is supporting the rebel government and the loyalties of the troops outside the capital are still uncertain."[156]

All of these developments took US planners completely by surprise. Indeed, US Ambassador W. Tapley Bennett was not even in the country at the time. In his absence, William Connett was acting as *Charge d'affairs*, and Connett proceeded to send a series of alarming highest priority messages to Washington. Part of the reason for America's lack of forewarning was that throughout the Reid Cabral era, the embassy had made no contacts within the PRD or among the disgruntled military officers.[157] One embassy employee noted, "Tap [Bennett] did not know anyone to the left of the Rotary Club," and Connett "seemed to be ill at ease with people who were not correctly dressed."[158] As a result, the embassy relied heavily on its conservative contacts within the Dominican military for information on the rebel movement. Those contacts, however, had strong incentive to exaggerate the communist threat so that US forces would come to their aid. Consequently, the embassy greatly misjudged the Constitutionalist's aims and their strength. For that reason, the embassy encouraged the Loyalists to act decisively in order to prevent what was perceived as a likely communist takeover.[159]

On April 27, the crisis heated up. Loyalists and Constitutionalists clashed outside Santo Domingo. By the end of the day, it appeared that the Constitutionalists had gained the upper hand. In response, Johnson ordered US Marines to evacuate as many as possible of the 1,172 US nationals believed to be in the Dominican Republic to Puerto Rico.[160] Meanwhile, the CIA reported to Rusk:

> Should the forces of General Elías Wessin y Wessin, supported by the major elements of the air force and elements of the navy over the next several hours or days be unable to defeat that revolution that started last Saturday, the Dominican Republic . . . will be so far on the way to becoming another Cuba that the tide may well not be able to be turned back unless the US takes prompt and strong action. Pro-Communist—if not communist—people are emerging as members of the 'cabinet' of 'provisional president' Molina Ureña. Communists are gathering arms and reportedly have a real "in" with at least one arsenal. They set up strong points within the city.[161]

In response, Rusk wrote to the embassy, "Our primary objectives are restoration of law and order, prevention of possible Communist takeover, and protection of American lives. . . . Believe you should contact military leaders of contending forces and suggest to them establishment of military junta to act as provisional government."[162] With US approval, Wessin then ordered P-51s to attack the presidential palace where the PRD's temporary leader, Molina Ureña, was working.[163] Not realizing America's complicity in the attack, Ureña went to the US embassy to ask for help. After meeting with Bennett, however, he soon realized that the rebels would not have Washington's approval. Giving up hope, he and other top PRD leaders sought asylum in a friendly embassy.[164]

The constant stream of alarming updates coming from the US embassy disturbed Johnson. In a telephone conversation with Mann, he declared, "We're going to have to really set up that government down there and run it and stabilize it some way or other. This Bosch is no good." If he were to return from exile, Johnson asked, "Does that mean, you think, that this is another Castro government?" Mann responded, "Not yet, no. Hard to tell what comes out of one of these messes, who comes out on top. We don't think that this fellow Bosch understands that the communists are dangerous. We don't think that he is a communist. What we are afraid of is that if he gets back in, he'll have so many of them around him—and they're so much smarter than he is—that before you know it, they would take over."[165]

The following day, April 28, Loyalist commanders followed American advice and formed a military junta led by Colonel Pedro Bartolomé Benoit. Given Ureña's defection on the previous day, it appeared that the pro-Bosch forces were on the brink of collapse. In a stunning turn of fortune, however, the Constitutionalists launched a surprise attack that enabled them to defeat Wessin's troops and go on the offensive. The US embassy reported:

> While I regret as much as anyone that, once again, we have to rely on military solution for political crisis engendered by confused democratic left, all valid elements of which now either in asylum or hiding, as much from extremists who have come to dominate rebel situation, as well as from opposing military forces. However, plain fact of situation is that while leftist propaganda naturally will try to fuzz situation as fight between military and people, issue here now is fight between Castro-type elements and those who oppose it. We should be clear as to situation.[166]

Soon after, Bennett requested that Washington send 1,200 Marines "to help restore peace to this country."[167] On April 28, Johnson ordered five hundred Marines ashore "to establish secure point or points for evacuation [of] U.S. nationals and other foreigners."[168]

Two days later, Johnson ordered the 82nd Airborne to occupy Santo Domingo. This mission, known as Operation Power Pack, would be America's first overt intervention for military purposes in the Western Hemisphere in over thirty years. The orders given by the Joint Chiefs of Staff to Lt. General Bruce Palmer Jr., the operation's commanding officer, stated, "Your announced mission is to save U.S. lives. Your unannounced mission is to prevent the Dominican Republic from going Communist. The President has stated that he will not allow another Cuba—you are to take all necessary measures to accomplish this mission."[169] Toward this end, 14,000 Marines arrived in Santo Domingo on May 1 to support the Loyalists and restore order within the occupied zone.

On May 2, Johnson delivered a speech to justify the invasion to the American public. His address introduced a revision to FDR's Good Neighbor Policy—sometimes dubbed the "Johnson Doctrine"—arguing that the United States would intervene into the domestic affairs of states within the Western Hemisphere to prevent "the establishment of a communistic dictatorship."[170] Both Congress and the public initially supported the mission. House Resolution 124 declared, "Any such subversive domination or threat of it violates the principles of the Monroe Doctrine, and of collective security as set forth in the acts and actions heretofore adopted by the American Republics."[171] A US public opinion poll in May found that 76 percent of those surveyed supported Johnson's decision to send troops to Santo Domingo.[172]

Throughout May, US forces continually escalated their attack on the Constitutionalists. Meanwhile, Johnson sent America's ambassador to Mexico, Thomas Mann, to create a provisional government led by technocrats and business leaders who could restore stability and eventually pave the way for elections. Mann sought to find a negotiated solution that would appease both the rebels and military but would not upset the existing military hierarchy or try to push through difficult social reforms. Not surprisingly, neither the rebels nor military could be satisfied with the other's proposals. Meanwhile, the CIA initiated a covert mission to discredit the rebel leadership. One aspect of this plan sought to bribe Colonel Caamaño to defect. If he refused, the CIA would then discredit him by leaking that he sought US financial support.[173] Before this could occur, however, Loyalist forces defeated the Constitutionalists on June 15, 1965. Seeing no alternative, the rebels accepted Mann's proposal for an interim government with a neutral president and elections the following year. Then on September 3, Héctor Garcia Godoy was sworn in as provisional president. Most US forces withdrew soon after, but a small contingent remained to oversee the transition to democratic elections the following year.

Did the US government overestimate communist involvement in the uprising? Johnson was acutely anxious at the time that the United States would misjudge the situation. The possibility of a rebel victory was extremely worrisome at a time when the Bay of Pigs fiasco was only beginning to dim.[174] If the United States underestimated the communist influence, Johnson feared it might soon have a "second Cuba." If the situation were overestimated, on the other hand, Johnson worried that the United States might be responsible for a military crackdown reminiscent of the Soviet invasion of Hungary in 1956.[175] The available evidence suggests that several small communist groups were involved in the fighting, specifically the 14th of June Movement and the Dominican Popular Movement (*Movimiento Popular Dominicano*— MPD). At the same time, however, previous CIA studies of these groups had estimated that they had a few hundred members at best.[176] It is unclear where the US embassy got the figure that there were 12,000 communists fighting in Santo Domingo.[177] Testifying before a closed session of Congress on April 30, Rusk stated, "We have identified eight well-known Communist leaders who are very active at the present time in leading armed groups. We know there are about 40 to 50 Dominicans in the Dominican Republic who have been trained by Castro."[178] Johnson rejected these numbers: "For all we know there are 800 leaders . . . no one on earth knew if this was a pro-Castro or Communist affair."[179]

Although it seems implausible in hindsight that a couple dozen communists could have overthrown a country of 4 million people, it is important to consider the historical context: six years earlier, Castro had invaded Cuba, a country of 7 million, with only twenty men. Even if it was unlikely that a few dozen communists could somehow take over the Dominican Republic, Johnson was unwilling to take that chance. On April 28, he told an advisor, "I think the worst domestic political disaster we could suffer would be for Castro to take over."[180] At the same time, Johnson was mired in the escalating South Vietnamese crisis, and he feared that if the United States lost credibility by failing to prevent a communist victory in the Dominican Republic, it would encourage communist advances elsewhere. Early in the crisis,

Johnson worried aloud, "What can we do in Vietnam if we can't clean up the Dominican Republic?"[181]

What is certain is that at the time of the intervention, US policymakers simply did not have reliable intelligence on the number of communists in the country. During an April 30 meeting, Johnson asked "if the CIA could document Castro's involvement." McNamara replied "that he didn't think so. He thought the CIA might show that certain people were trained in Cuba, but not that Castro was directing the training."[182] Given this ambiguity, according to the operation's Commanding Officer, Lt. General Bruce Palmer Jr., "All civilian advisers, including Rusk and McNamara, and Wheeler (the only military adviser), had recommended against immediate intervention."[183] Palmer later admitted, "The truth was that no one had a handle on what was going on in Santo Domingo."[184] Indeed, three days after the Marines landed, Washington encouraged the US embassy to produce "additional material available on the President's statement that the revolutionary movement has been taken over by a band of Communist conspirators."[185] The embassy was unable to do so.[186]

1966 AND 1968 ELECTIONS

With Héctor Garcia Godoy acting as provisional president and the fighting temporarily subdued, US policymakers debated what to do next. Despite tens of millions of dollars in US aid, the "provisional government has proven weaker than feared."[187] Indeed, on two separate occasions during the fall of 1965, US forces had to put down a military coup against Godoy.[188] In October, the CIA issued a special report on the Dominican Republic, which warned, "We think, for example, that the expansion in size of the electorate—those who have politically awakened during the past few years and the large additional number of young people now qualified to vote—will strongly favor the left. . . . If such a candidate won the election, his government would probably be anti-US and Communist-influenced."[189]

By December 1965, however, Godoy appeared stronger, and US planners had confidence that the provisional government would endure and hold elections as promised.[190] Former presidents Balaguer and Bosch had each returned from exile, making them the presumptive candidates for the *Partido Reformist* and PRD, respectively. Washington now faced the dilemma of how to ensure that a moderate pro-US candidate would win the election without provoking left-wing parties to withdraw from it. On December 30, Johnson's oversight committee for covert actions, the 303 Committee, met "to determine whether the US Government should engage in a covert operation designed to support the presidential candidate most likely to be able to establish and maintain a stable government in the Dominican Republic which is friendly to the US and which is capable of carrying out essential domestic reforms."[191] During a 303 Committee on January 6, the group decided that

Balaguer would be the best candidate for the United States to support, and started planning covert support for his election campaign.[192]

On January 11, 1966, the National Security Council released its "Contingency Plan for the Dominican Elections." It declared:

> The purpose of the projected operation is to provide essential support to Balaguer's campaign; its implementation must be guided by certain basic considerations. First, it is essential that the operation be carried out in such a way that United States sponsorship cannot be proven in any way. . . . Second, while Balaguer will need financial help as well as assistance in other forms in order to overcome certain handicaps, the amount of assistance given him must be controlled to avoid overweight.[193]

Toward this end, the CIA would provide Balaguer with three types of support: "(1) funds to be provided [*two lines of source text redacted*]; (2) information, expertise and political guidance relayed through reliable intermediaries whom Balaguer trusts; (3) development of media and other assets having a natural bias toward Balaguer or toward his platform."[194]

Over the next few months, the operation went smoothly, and Balaguer slowly gained support. At the same time, however, US planners worried that unless the PRD participated in the election, Balaguer's victory would be considered illegitimate and could usher in another period of instability. To prevent the PRD from withdrawing, embassy officials met with Bosch to convince him that the United States would "recognize and support a freely elected government."[195] In March, the CIA discussed approaching "Venezuela, Oduber, Figueres, the Mexican Government and possibly Frei to ask them to urge Bosch to stay in the race."[196] By April, Bosch was persuaded, and the PRD agreed to participate in the elections.[197]

Despite America's covert support for Balaguer, a National Intelligence Estimate warned that the United States "cannot predict the outcome with any confidence."[198] Although Balaguer was leading in the polls, Bosch was still a major threat given "his ability to appeal to the Dominican masses in terms they find understandable and attractive."[199] What's more, planners feared that "extremists of the right or left may attempt to disrupt them by undertaking terrorist acts or, in the case of the far left, trying to provoke incidents."[200] Given this, the 303 Committee authorized additional covert "funds into the campaign to ensure that Balaguer does not lose momentum at a critical point in the race because of shortage of cash."[201] CIA polls on May 10 found Balaguer leading Bosch, 46.1 percent to 34.8 percent, but also reported that more Dominicans expected Bosch to win than Balaguer.[202] Days before the election, the US embassy considered the election "a toss-up, with Bosch probably being right now the man to beat."[203]

On June 1, Balaguer's PR won with 57 percent of the vote compared to Bosch's PRD's 39 percent.[204] The pro-Castro 14th of June Movement received less than 1 percent of the vote.[205] Although Bosch and other left-wing candidates complained that the United States had covertly supported Balaguer, UN and OAS electoral observers found the election to be "free and fair."[206] Seven in ten American liberals agreed.[207] Balaguer's landslide victory "helped create a honeymoon period for his administration, and he moved quickly to establish a strong degree of control over the bureaucracy and to dominate the Congress."[208] Before long, however, Balaguer struggled to cope with the dire economic and social problems facing the Dominican Republic. By November, the CIA warned that growing dissatisfaction with Balaguer was creating "a trend toward political polarization . . . which, if left unchecked, could produce a dangerous situation in the next 6–9 months."[209] To reverse this trend, the CIA began a small covert campaign to "assist moderate PRD members to increase their influence on party affairs and encourage them to remain in or rejoin the PRD to counter radical influences" and "diminish [the] influence on PRD affairs of the more extreme radicals and any Communist infiltrators."[210]

As Balaguer worked to assert his political control within the Dominican Republic, his critics began to fear that he would return the country to authoritarian rule. An April 1967 National Intelligence Estimate reported, "A major weak point for Balaguer is his vulnerability to charges of neo-Trujillismo."[211] As evidence, his critics pointed to "his former chief military aide, Colonel Neit Nivar Seijas, and several other Presidential advisors, who are trusted Balaguer colleagues from Trujillo days. They also cite police excesses— specifically the roundup in late January of 500–800 'leftists' suspected of plotting."[212]

After the PRD withdrew from municipal elections in 1968 and other left-wing groups threatened to follow suit, Johnson debated providing covert aid to the Social Christian Reformist Party (*Partido Reformista Social Cristiano*— PRSC) to "keep them in the municipal elections as a validating force for the elections."[213] The 303 Committee later clarified, "The objective is not to make the PRSC a major party but to insure [*sic*] its active participation in the municipal elections."[214] On February 16, Johnson approved the covert operation: "The basis for this decision was that, with the abstention of the Dominican Revolutionary Party (PRD) and other opposition parties from the elections, the Balaguer government was in danger of being deprived of the psychological impact which a contested election would have in the Dominican Republic."[215]

On May 15, Balaguer's PR won sixty-six out of seventy-seven Dominican municipalities, including Santo Domingo. The PRSC won two, and independent parties won the remaining nine.[216] The 303 Committee determined the covert operation had been a success. A June memorandum states, "The covert passage of funds to the PRSC had its desired effect. The party withstood heavy pressure from the PRD and other abstentionists— including some of its own young militants—and participated in the May elections."[217] Now exercising control at the executive, legislative, and municipal levels, Balaguer's PR remained in power for more than a decade. Although he continued to hold elections, Balaguer's regime tended toward authoritarianism. A 1968 CIA intelligence report, noted, "Balaguer's style of governing bears many of the hallmarks of Trujillo, in whose government he served for many years."[218] Nevertheless, the report accurately predicted, "Balaguer will probably be able to continue to hold a firm grip on power without having to resort to extreme authoritarian measures."[219] Finally, in 1978, Balaguer lost an election to Antonio Guzman, prompting the military to intervene on his behalf. Under intense pressure from US president Jimmy Carter, however, the military backed down, and Guzman's assumption of the presidency marked the Dominican Republic's first peaceful democratic transition.

Why Did the United States Intervene Covertly versus Overtly?

Eisenhower, Kennedy, and Johnson all strongly preferred covert conduct during their regime change missions in the Dominican Republic. Unlike the previous case studies, however, they preferred covert conduct primarily because it minimized each mission's reputational costs, rather than its security costs. Despite these actions occurring during the Cold War, US leaders had no fears that the Soviets might come to the Dominican Republic's defense, and the USSR was barely mentioned during policy debates. Instead, US leaders preferred covert conduct so that they could uphold an image consistent with the "Good Neighbor Policy."

As discussed in chapter 5, President Franklin D. Roosevelt introduced the Good Neighbor policy in 1934 as a corollary to the Monroe Doctrine. It stated that the United States would no longer intervene in the domestic political affairs of states within the hemisphere. FDR hoped that by respecting the sovereignty of Latin American states, they would be more willing to accept America's position as regional hegemon.[220] Problems arose, however, when Latin American countries acted against US interests, and Washington could no longer use gunboat diplomacy to coerce them into submission. Covert regime change offered a solution to this dilemma by allowing the United States to look like it was still upholding the doctrine, while secretly subverting it. Early in the Cold War, the National Security Council cited the Good Neighbor policy as a reason for the United States to develop its covert psychological warfare capabilities:

> It is to be noted that Latin America is an area unique for the United States, because of the overt Good Neighbor and non-intervention policies of long standing, and the powerful reasons necessitating those overt policies. The security of covert operations and the further development of policy and man-

agement systems which protect such security both in Washington and in the field are of peculiar importance for this area.[221]

Because Washington had staked its reputation on nonintervention, any regime change in the Western Hemisphere could harm US credibility. Even when targeting Trujillo's brutal authoritarian regime, a NSC report warned that

> while it is highly desirable in the present Dominican situation for the US to be identified with and to support democratic elements seeking to overthrow Trujillo, we necessarily run some risks in doing so. If Trujillo is overthrown with US support, we may well be criticized by world opinion for subverting an existing government, albeit a highly unpopular one. A miscalculation of the capabilities of the moderate group could mean that U.S. support for an unsuccessful attempt against the Trujillo regime would be exposed, and following on the recent Cuban experience U.S. prestige would plummet.[222]

Likewise, it is not surprising that Johnson reverted to covert conduct to influence Dominican elections in 1966 and 1968. In addition to violating the Good Neighbor policy, Johnson had both normative and practical reasons to conduct these operations covertly. For one, many prominent American liberals, including Robert Kennedy, J. William Fulbright, and Mike Mansfield, viewed Bosch and the PRD favorably, and they had strongly criticized Johnson for his heavy-handed response to the Dominican crisis in 1965.[223] Given the domestic turmoil that Johnson faced at home and the escalating crisis in Vietnam, he could not risk further alienating his liberal base by overtly targeting Bosch again. In addition, Johnson worried that if the United States overtly supported Balaguer's campaign, the PRD would withdraw from elections, thus rendering them illegitimate and potentially reigniting the Dominican Civil War. Consequently, plans for the 1966 covert operation note, "Since the United States is already believed to favor Balaguer and will probably be accused of supporting him regardless of its actions, it is more than ever essential that any support provided to Balaguer be sophisticated, and entirely covert."[224]

Although Johnson would have preferred to resolve the 1965 Dominican crisis covertly, he was willing to overtly intervene because he felt that the situation necessitated a rapid response and that he could secure a quick and easy victory with public support. Throughout the crisis, both the CIA and US embassy continually warned the president that he had only "hours or days" to intervene, or else the country "will be so far on the way to becoming another Cuba that the tide may well not be able to be turned back unless the U.S. takes prompt and strong action."[225] Given this short window for action, a covert operation was simply unfeasible. The decision to overtly intervene was made easier by the fact that Johnson felt that a US victory was inevitable and that the US public would support the mission. Indeed, he remarked to congressional leaders on April 28, "I want you to know that I have just taken an action that will prove that Democratic presidents can deal with Communists just as strong as Republicans."[226]

This chapter investigated America's covert and overt regime change operations in the Dominican Republic between 1960 and 1968. It put forth four main arguments. First, the main alternative explanations do not explain US behavior. There is little evidence that the United States intervened to protect the economic interests of Central Romana or any other corporation. On the contrary, Washington actively worked against American business interests on several occasions, and US officials rarely discussed specific corporate interests during their policy debates. Likewise, although there may be some evidence to support the rogue CIA argument in the case of Trujillo's assassination, these claims have been overstated, and the argument cannot explain America's covert regime change operations in 1962, 1966, or 1968. Second, the United States intervened in the Dominican Republic to protect its position as regional hegemon. US policymakers feared that if a communist government came to power there, their success could inspire a series of defections from the US-led regional order. Third, US planners preferred covert conduct to minimize the reputational costs associated with violating the Good Neighbor policy and manipulating democratic elections. Finally, Johnson overtly intervened during the Dominican Civil War because he felt that the situation required a rapid response and that he could achieve a quick and easy victory by employing open US support.

CHAPTER 9

Covert Regime Change after the Cold War

The vast majority of America's covert and overt regime changes during the Cold War did not work out as their planners intended. Washington launched these regime changes to resolve security-oriented interstate disputes by installing foreign leaders with similar policy preferences. American experiences during the Cold War, however, illustrate that this was often quite difficult in practice. Thirty-nine out of sixty-four covert regime changes failed to replace their targets and because America's role in most of these failed interventions generally did not remain a secret, they further soured Washington's already negative relationship with the target state. Even nominally successful covert operations—where the US-backed forces assumed power—failed to deliver on their promise to improve America's relationship with the target state. Washington soon learned that changing the policy preferences of another state is more difficult than simply replacing that state's leadership, because a government's policy preferences have deeper roots than the beliefs of any individual leader. Consequently, once in power, many leaders installed via regime change found that they were caught in a catch-22: if they pursued Washington's orders, they risked alienating domestic audiences, who may then attempt to remove them from power, such as was the case following US interventions in Iran (1953) or Guatemala (1954). If they sided with their domestic audiences against the United States or found themselves constrained from pursuing Washington's interests once in office by the political realities of their position, however, disputes between the two states may soon reemerge, such as in the Dominican Republic (1962) or South Vietnam (1963).

Despite the prominent role that covert regime change played in US foreign policy during the Cold War, there is little reason to believe that they played a decisive role in America's ultimate victory. Reviewing the cases, there are only a handful of clear-cut successes where the target state became a reliable ally of the United States afterward, such as Italy (1947–68), France (1947–52), and Japan (1952–68). In these cases, however, there is good reason to doubt that the covert intervention was ultimately responsible for these states' close relationship with Washington. For one, it is quite possible that many of the political parties covertly backed by the United States during these missions would have won their elections without American support. Indeed, most enjoyed significant leads over their rivals before the intervention. In addition, each of these early Cold War covert operations were accompanied by massive overt efforts to democratize the political systems of the target states, integrate them into liberal international institutions, and to bind them to Washington via powerful security alliances, such as NATO.[1]

What role did the remaining covert operations play in America's victory in the Cold War? Interviewed in 1997, Director of Central Intelligence R. James Woolsey reflected, "Two covert actions helped change the course of history and the Cold War. First, Radio Free Europe; Walesa and Havel both have said it was the most important thing the United States did during the Cold War. And the aid to the Mujahedeen that stopped the Soviets in Afghanistan. When people talk about covert actions, they ought to talk about those two first and foremost."[2] Twenty years later, Woolsey's assessment still seems accurate, although many have come to question the longer-term utility of the operation in Afghanistan. Woolsey's 1997 statement reflects the conventional view at the time that Operation Cyclone—America's covert effort to back Afghan Mujahedeen forces against their Soviet occupiers from 1979 to 1989—helped the United States win the Cold War by forcing the Soviet Union to commit substantial resources to maintain their puppet in Kabul at a time when their authority was crumbling at home. Supporting this view, some have estimated that by the late 1980s, Moscow had sent 120,000 troops into the country and was spending over $5 billion per year on its counterinsurgency efforts there.[3] After the September 11, 2001, attacks, however, many began to second-guess the wisdom of the intervention. Countless journalists, scholars, and pundits have repeated the claim that the United States was partially responsible for 9/11 by funding and training Bin Laden and other Arab fighters in Afghanistan during the 1980s. For these reasons, Operation Cyclone is often cited as the quintessential example of how covert operations can result in blowback on their creators.

Despite the prevalence of this belief, the story is not that simple. Although Bin Laden did fight in Afghanistan during the 1980s, there is little evidence that he received any direct support from the CIA.[4] For his part, Bin Laden denied these allegations,[5] as did Al-Qaeda leader Ayman al-Zawahiri and numerous US officials associated with the mission, including the CIA's station chiefs Bill Peikney and Milton Bearden, who oversaw aid disbursement to the Mujahedeen; Vincent Cannistraro, who ran the Afghan Working Group; and Marc Sageman, who worked with the Mujahedeen as a foreign service officer in Islamabad.[6] Although the CIA's links to Bin Laden may have been exaggerated, that is not to say that Washington is entirely faultless in the affair either. In order to maintain plausible deniability, the CIA delegated responsibility for aiding and arming the Afghan fighters to Pakistan's Inter-Services Intelligence (ISI), which used its position to support Islamist—as opposed to nationalist—militant groups within Afghanistan. The effect, according to Michael Rubin, was that "by delegating responsibility for arms distribution to the ISI, the United States created an environment in which radical Islam could flourish. And with the coming of the Taliban, radical Islam did just that."[7] One could thus argue that Operation Cyclone, combined with Washington's declining interest in the country following the Soviet withdrawal, helped to create a power vacuum that was filled with militant Islamists, thereby setting the stage for Bin Laden to seek sanctuary in Taliban-controlled Afghanistan in 1996.

Does this mean that Operation Cyclone was ultimately not in America's best interest? Not necessarily. On the one hand, the operation clearly demonstrates the potential danger of covertly arming militant groups and working with intermediaries with their own interests. At the same time, however, the mission must be placed in its historical context. President Carter had good strategic reasons to intervene in 1979: acquiescing to a Soviet invasion could have paved the way for further Soviet incursions into Afghanistan's neighbors, Pakistan and Iran, where America's longstanding ally, Shah Pahlavi, had recently been overthrown. President Reagan too had good incentive to continue the mission to further bleed Soviet forces at a time when they were already strained by domestic upheaval throughout the Soviet bloc.[8]

As the above example illustrates, weighing the pros and cons of covert interventions is tricky. Equally difficult to measure is the erosion in trust that the United States has suffered internationally on account of its exposed covert regime changes. Because of its reputation for covertly meddling in the domestic affairs of other states, the CIA has become fodder for conspiracy theorists and a favorite scapegoat of unpopular leaders throughout the world. Indeed, the agency has been blamed for everything from President Kennedy's 1963 assassination,[9] to his son's accidental death in a 1999 airplane crash,[10] to John Lennon's 1981 murder,[11] Princess Diana's death in a 1997 car accident,[12] and the 2007 suicide attack on Pakistani prime minister Benazir Bhutto.[13] Other polls have found that 12 percent of African Americans believe that the CIA created and spread the Human Immunodeficiency Virus (HIV) in an attempt to wipe out African Americans and homosexuals;[14] 14 percent of American voters believe that the CIA created the crack cocaine epidemic during the 1980s;[15] and 7 percent believed that it helped to fake the moon landing.[16] Internationally, a 2008 poll of seventeen nations found that 15 percent of respondents believed that the US government was behind the 9/11 attacks.[17] Even within the United States, a 2007 survey found that 29 percent of Americans believed that the CIA knew about the attacks in advance and 22 percent believed that President Bush personally knew.[18]

These examples highlight one of the ironies of covert action: Washington pursued many regime change operations covertly to protect its reputation as the leader of the free world on the international stage. Yet, many covert interventions led to precisely the opposite result. Why? Because secrecy seems sinister, which means that revealed covert operations have a tendency to get blown out of proportion. In some cases, the United States has been accused of single-handedly overthrowing a foreign government, when, in reality, it played a secondary role to foreign actors. In other cases, relatively benign covert actions appeared much more malevolent when Washington's role was uncovered. Today, suspicion seems to fall on the CIA whenever something unseemly happens throughout the world, whether or not there are plausible reasons to believe that the United States had anything to do with it. These allegations not only help fuel anti-Americanism, they also undermine the credibility of Washington's treaty commitments and diplomatic negotiations. For these reasons, Director of Central Intelligence William Webster lamented, "[Covert action] is an activity that has been assigned to us and accounts for less than three percent of our resources but which attracts the most heat, the most confusion, and generates the most ill ease and suspicion."[19]

Covert Regime Change in the Post–Cold War Era

The end of the Cold War did not mean the end of America's aggressive pursuit of regime change. In the twenty-seven years since the fall of the Soviet Union, Washington has continued to habitually intervene both covertly and overtly throughout the world. Although US policymakers' appetite for regime change has not diminished, America's post–Cold War interventions have taken on new forms. For one, America's objectives for pursuing regime change have shifted to reflect its new security environment. During the Cold War, most US interventions aimed either to weaken the Soviet bloc or to prevent states from allying with Moscow. Its post–Cold War interventions, by contrast, have focused less on great power politics and more on preventing security threats from emerging from minor powers, particularly terrorism and nuclear proliferation.[20]

Second, the shift from a bipolar to a unipolar international system lowered the costs of overt intervention. Following the collapse of the USSR, America's relative advantage in the global distribution of power grew to unprecedented levels.[21] The United States spends nearly the same amount on its military expenditures as the other major powers combined—many of which are US allies.[22] It also possesses the world's best navy and other unrivalled power-projection capabilities, spends far more on military research and development than any other major power, and is home to the world's largest high-technology economy.[23] With no peers to challenge its expansions, Washington is freer to pursue regime change without fear of becoming entangled in a proxy war with another superpower.[24] Given this shift in the balance of power, many politicians and pundits contended that the United States should take advantage of its preeminent position to promote pro-American regimes throughout the world. For instance, Charles Krauthammer in his influential 1990 *Foreign Affairs* piece, "The Unipolar Moment," argued that Washington needed to find "the strength and will to lead in a unipolar world, unashamedly laying down the rules of world order and being prepared to enforce them."[25]

Third, democracy promotion has taken on a larger role in US foreign policy.[26] I argued in chapter 2 that policymakers pursue regime change to install political leaders who they believe share similar policy preferences to their own. During the Cold War, America's main concern was preventing the growth of the Soviet alliance system, and the individuals most likely to share this preference were right-wing autocrats. Despite their liberal rhetoric, US leaders feared that promoting democracy in many countries would lead to the election of socialist or communist parties, which Washington would have a hard time opposing without appearing hypocritical. With the collapse of the Soviet Union and communism's declining appeal as a viable alternative, however, Western-style liberalism appeared to have gained worldwide popularity and promoting democracy became a more attractive option. Francis Fukuyama's famous 1989 essay "The End of History" captured the spirit at the time: "What we may be witnessing is not just the end of the Cold War, or the passing of a particular period of postwar history, but the end of history as such: that is, the end point of mankind's ideological evolution and the universalization of Western liberal democracy as the final form of government."[27] If foreign populations shared this commitment to liberal values, policymakers reasoned, then spreading democracy could lead to the election of US-oriented regimes, predisposed toward cooperating with Washington.

In particular, the rapid collapse of communist regimes throughout Eastern Europe led many to believe that the Reagan administration had struck a winning formula for regime change with its "Project Democracy" efforts that used quasi-governmental agencies, like the National Endowment for Democracy (NED), to support the growth of democratic civil institutions and pro-American political parties. As such, US government funding to NED increased roughly fivefold, from $31.3 million in 1984 to $153.2 million in 2015.[28] Today, NED programs run in more than ninety countries.[29] Although the number of US-backed democracy promotion programs has grown, most of today's programs pursue less aggressive objectives than their Cold War counterparts. In an extensive analysis of the subject, for instance, Sarah Bush found that "in the 1980s, prominent donors such as the United States' National Endowment for Democracy frequently challenged autocrats by supporting dissidents, political parties, and unions overseas via the majority of their programs. Now they are more likely to support technical programs, such as efforts to improve local governance, that do not disturb the status quo in other countries."[30] Specifically, she found that "Relatively tame programs increased from around 20 percent of NED's grants in 1986 to around 60 percent in 2009."[31]

Whereas Americans may view these democracy promotion programs as the lawful behavior of an admirable NGO, America's adversaries see these actions as illegitimate covert meddling by the US government. Russia, in particular, has been highly critical of America's democracy promotion efforts after pro-Russian governments were removed from power during the "color revolutions" in Georgia (2003), Ukraine (2004), and Kyrgyzstan (2005) as well as the Ukrainian Euromaidan protest (2013–14)—all places where the United States had funded significant democracy initiatives. In Ukraine, for instance, Assistant Secretary of State for Eurasian Affairs Victoria Nuland estimated that the United States invested over $5 billion to help Ukrainians build "democratic skills and institutions" between 1991 and 2013.[32] In 2016 alone, the NED spent $4.46 million funding seventy-two democracy assistance programs in Ukraine.[33] These actions have not gone unnoticed in Moscow. In a 2014 speech, the Russian defense minister, Sergei Shoigu, warned that these uprisings were "used as an excuse to replace nationally oriented governments with regimes controlled from abroad."[34] Putin agreed, arguing in November 2014, "In the modern world, extremism is being used as a geopolitical instrument and for remaking spheres of influence. We see what tragic consequences the wave of so-called color revolutions led to. For us this is a lesson and a warning. We should do everything necessary so that nothing similar ever happens in Russia."[35] In July 2015, Russia banned the NED from operating within its borders, thereby ending seventy-four ongoing NED programs in the country offering $4.7 million in US assistance.[36]

These three trends—a focus on terrorism and nuclear proliferation, lowered cost for overt intervention, and democracy promotion—gained momentum throughout the 1990s. During the Persian Gulf War in 1990–91, President George H.W. Bush opted not to go to Baghdad and remove Saddam Hussein from power, in part because it would undermine the tacit consent that the Soviet Union—still intact and sufficiently formidable at that point— had given to the operation.[37] Even at the time, however, many in Washington questioned this decision, arguing that the United States should capitalize on its newfound position of strength to replace chronically troublesome regimes like Saddam's with friendlier, democratic governments.

Following the collapse of the USSR, however, the idea that the United States should forcefully promote democracy abroad gained traction. Clinton's official national security strategy "Engagement and Enlargement" asserted "All of America's strategic interests—from promoting prosperity at home to checking global threats abroad before they threaten our territory— are served by enlarging the community of democracy and free market nations."[38] Toward this end, US democracy promotion aid grew from $100 million at the end of the Cold War to $700 million in 2000.[39] Nevertheless, Clinton's support for democracy was not uniform. In keeping with its Cold

War behavior, the United States only promoted democracy where it fit with America's broader security and economic interests, such as in Colombia and Ukraine. Where democratization clashed with US security interests or was likely to bring to power groups opposed to the United States—as in Egypt or Saudi Arabia—it was eschewed.[40]

The idea that the United States should capitalize on its preeminence to pursue regime change against rogue states also gained ground under Clinton. For instance, in a 1994 *Foreign Affairs* piece, National Security Advisor Anthony Lake advocated for an assertive policy toward "backlash states" like "Cuba, North Korea, Iran, Iraq and Libya."[41] Lake argued that these states shared certain characteristics, namely, that they were "ruled by cliques that control power through coercion, [and] they suppress human rights and promote radical ideologies. While their political systems vary, their leaders hare a common antipathy toward popular participation that might undermine the existing regimes . . . they are embarked on ambitious and costly military programs—especially in weapons of mass destruction (WMD) and missile delivery systems."[42] He concluded, "As the sole superpower, the United States has a special responsibility for developing a strategy to neutralize, contain, and through selective pressure, perhaps eventually transform these backlash states into constructive members of the international community."[43] This set the stage for President Clinton to authorize Operation Uphold Democracy in 1994 to restore Jean-Bertrand Aristide to power following a military coup in Haiti;[44] to sign the Iraqi Liberation Act in 1998, officially making it the "policy of the United States to remove the regime headed by Saddam Hussein from power in Iraq";[45] and to pursue a variety of overt and covert efforts designed to remove Slobodan Milosevic from power in 1999 and 2000.[46]

During the 2000 presidential election, George W. Bush campaigned against the nation-building efforts associated with the Clinton era. On the day before the election, for instance, Bush warned in his final rebuke of Al Gore, "I'm worried about an opponent who uses nation building and the military in the same sentence."[47] However, as he put it bluntly in his memoir, "After 9/11, I changed my mind."[48] Immediately after the attacks, influential Neoconservatives from within and outside of the administration argued that the only way to end the threat posed by radical Islamic terrorism was to transform the region from a hotbed of violence and dictatorship into a bulwark of democracies.[49] Krauthammer, for instance, wrote in late September 2001, "The overriding aim of the war on terrorism is changing regimes. . . . Afghanistan is just stage one. A logical stage two is Syria. . . . Stage three is Iraq and Iran, obviously the most difficult and dangerous. . . . Changing regimes in Kabul and changing policy in Damascus, however, would already have radically changed the regional dynamic by demonstrating American power in a region where power, above all, commands respect."[50] Converted to this line of reasoning, Bush embraced a policy of unilateral and preemptive regime changes to democratize rogue states that became known as the "Bush Doctrine."

The first example of the Bush Doctrine in action came in Afghanistan. Contrary to popular belief, however, policymakers in the Bush administration had debated overthrowing the Taliban before 9/11. In fact, it was on the day before the attacks, September 10, 2001, that the National Security Council first authorized a three-stage plan to oust the regime in Kabul: First, Washington would give Taliban leaders an ultimatum to hand over Bin Laden. If they refused, the United States would begin to covertly arm anti-Taliban groups. If those groups failed to topple the regime, the United States would seek "to overthrow the Taliban regime through more direct action."[51] Following the next day's attacks, the White House quickly adopted an accelerated version of this plan. After Kabul rejected Washington's ultimatum, Bush launched Operation Enduring Freedom, which employed small numbers of US Special Forces, Marines, and CIA operatives working with the Northern Alliance and other indigenous groups to direct heavy airstrikes against Taliban positions.[52] The operation appeared to be a wild success. Within weeks, the US-backed coalition conquered the country and installed a pro-American leader, Hamid Karzai, at a cost of one dozen US fatalities.[53] In January 2004, an assembly of Afghan delegates approved a constitution, and in October, Karzai became the first democratically elected head of the country, with 55 percent of the vote.[54]

Despite this auspicious beginning, however, the operation soon fell victim to the familiar problems associated with foreign-imposed regime change, and Washington's relationship with Karzai soured over the next decade. Although Karzai shared many US policy preferences, he failed to make them a reality. As my theory would predict, Karzai struggled to balance the demands of pacifying his external patrons and maintaining the allegiance of his internal supporters.[55] Beginning in 2005 as the Afghan civil war heated up and domestic support for his regime waned, Karzai turned to publicly vilifying his American backers.[56] US efforts to restore cooperative relations with his regime through off-the-books payments did little to improve relations, especially after Karzai began to suspect that the United States was trying to remove him from power.[57] As one European diplomat recounted, "Never in history has any superpower spent so much money, sent so many troops to a country, and had so little influence over what its president says and does."[58] Indeed, by March 2014, US-Afghan relations had reached the point that Karzai told the *Washington Post*: "To the American people, give them my best wishes and my gratitude. To the U.S. government, give them my anger, my extreme anger."[59]

Much ink has already been spilled about the Iraq war. However, to put the war in the context of Washington's broader post–Cold War foreign policy, two points are worth repeating. First, although more than half of Americans now claim to have opposed the war in 2003, this may be selective amnesia.[60] In fact, polls from the time found 72 percent of Americans supported the invasion.[61] Popular support for the war is not surprising considering how well it fit into the foreign policy consensus of Washington elites at the time, namely, that American preeminence enabled the United States to pursue foreign interventions at low cost, that terrorism and WMD posed majority security threats, and that spreading liberalism was the answer to these problems. As Michael MacDonald writes, "The Bush administration is accused of using high-minded claptrap about freedom, democracy, and markets to sell the war, but the accusation gets the decision exactly wrong. The key to explaining the choice for regime change is that the Bush administration, and most American political and foreign policy elites too, subscribed to the shibboleths, euphemisms, and platitudes."[62] Second, the Iraq War went wrong for the same predictable reasons that regime changes—both covert and overt—usually do. Removing Saddam Hussein from power destabilized the entire region, and promoting democracy at the point of bayonets quickly proved far more difficult than anticipated.

Like Bush in 2000, Barack Obama campaigned on the promise to avoid the dangers of nation building and foreign military adventurism. Throughout his presidency, Obama remained consistently skeptical of the utility of regime change operations, warning, for instance, in a 2016 interview, "We have history. We have history in Iran, we have history in Indonesia and Central America. So we have to be mindful of our history when we start talking about intervening, and understand the source of other people's suspicions."[63] Nevertheless, on at least two occasions, Obama was persuaded by members of his administration to initiate covert regime changes. In 2011, Washington launched a joint covert and overt effort to remove Libyan dictator Muammar Qaddafi from power.[64] Two years later, Obama authorized a CIA-run covert program, code-named Timber Sycamore, to support "moderate" opposition fighters associated with the Free Syrian Army in their efforts to oust Syrian president Bashar al-Assad.[65] Neither of these interventions turned out as anticipated. Rather than creating an opportunity for democracy to flourish, both countries descended into prolonged, multisided civil wars.

Donald Trump is the first American president to be elected amid allegations of covert foreign meddling in the US election process. According to declassified versions of a joint CIA, FBI, and National Security Administration report on Russian activity during the 2016 election, "Moscow's influence campaign followed a Russian messaging strategy that blends covert intelligence operations—such as cyber activity—with overt efforts by Russian Government agencies, state-funded media, third-party intermediaries, and paid social media users or 'trolls.'" Russia's goals, the authors continue, "were to undermine public faith in the U.S. democratic process, denigrate Secretary Clinton and harm her electability and potential presidency. . . . Putin and the Russian government developed a clear preference for President-elect Trump."[66]

That the Kremlin preferred Trump over Clinton is not surprising. Trump repeatedly praised Putin on the campaign trail, calling him "very smart" and a "strong leader."[67] He also celebrated Russian strategy in Syria as the best way to defeat ISIS, voiced his misgivings about defending America's NATO allies in the Baltic, and said that he "would be looking into" recognizing Crimea as Russian territory.[68] He was, as Representative Adam Schiff (D-California), the top Democrat on the House Intelligence Committee, put it, the "most ostentatiously pro-Russian candidate in history."[69] Putin, by contrast, is said to bear a personal grudge against Clinton for her having asserted during her tenure as secretary of state that Russia's 2011 parliamentary elections were rigged.[70]

Whether Clinton would have won the 2016 election if not for Russia's covert meddling is arguable. Although Clinton undoubtedly had many strikes against her—high unfavorability ratings at the start of her campaign, an ongoing and high-profile FBI investigation during the campaign into her use of a private email server during her tenure as secretary of state, and her share of questionable campaign decisions—Russia's covert campaign certainly did not help. Thanks to WikiLeaks's continual release of hacked emails throughout October 2016, the news cycle in the weeks leading up to the election was flooded with embarrassing anti-Clinton stories, which were then amplified and exaggerated online in a coordinated campaign by paid Russian trolls, and she was unable to produce sufficient turnout in key battleground states. However, as the CIA's head of the Directorate of Intelligence, Ray S. Cline, once explained, the key to a successful covert mission is "supplying just the right bit of marginal assistance in the right way at the right time."[71] Considering that Clinton won the popular vote by 2.86 million but lost the electoral college due to 77,193 voters in Wisconsin, Michigan, and Pennsylvania, did Russia's covert campaign amount to "just the right bit of marginal assistance" to tip the scales to Trump? It is possible. If Clinton had been able to replicate Obama's 2012 turnout in these states, she would have won them by more than half a million votes.[72]

Russia's covert interference in the 2016 election appears to be a harbinger of things to come. In January 2017, the CIA, FBI and National Security Administration warned, "We assess Moscow will apply lessons learned from its campaign aimed at the US presidential election to future influence efforts in the United States and worldwide, including against US allies and their election processes."[73] Moscow's penchant for covert action is not surprising considering that technological advances have made covert operations far easier to orchestrate today compared to during the Cold War. The widespread adoption of cyber communication has made states and politicians vulnerable to espionage on scales previously unthinkable, and organizations like WikiLeaks allow state actors to conceal their role in massive data dumps of hacked material. The internet has also made it far easier to covertly move money across borders, as anyone with a few hundred dollars can now establish an offshore shell corporation to quickly and anonymously launder money.[74] At the same time, the barrier to entry for news and entertainment outlets has also been lowered, allowing intelligence services to generate and spread propaganda at rates that would dumbfound their Cold War counterparts.[75] Meanwhile, online social networks—like Facebook, Twitter, Reddit, and Instagram—offer the perfect platform to distribute propaganda to sympathetic American audiences. The Kremlin could not have designed a better propaganda-distribution mechanism if they had done it themselves. Conservative estimates find that 126 million Americans—40 percent of the population—were exposed to Russian propaganda on Facebook as part of the Russian interference campaign in 2016, including 10 million people on Election Day alone.[76] Likewise, Twitter has acknowledged the existence of two hundred accounts linked to Russia's covert efforts, but researchers working on this topic say that this is just a tiny fraction of the total number of Russian-backed fake accounts on Twitter.[77] Unfortunately, neither organization has much incentive to substantially address these problems. Facebook earned $27.6 billion in 2016 alone, predominately from advertising revenue, based on its promise to cheaply and efficiently deliver targeted ads to amenable audiences.[78] Similarly, one of the key drivers of Twitter's stock value is its total number of "monthly active users," which means that the company has little incentive to cull the huge number of fake accounts within its network used to disseminate propaganda.[79]

The problems raised by the new technology may very well get worse in future elections. Although there is no evidence, to date, that Russia was able to alter voting results in 2016, experts warn that America's voting systems remain vulnerable to hacking.[80] Also alarming is the emergence of new technologies that allow users to create fake audio and video footage of real people that is difficult to distinguish from reality, suggesting that, in the near future, propagandists will be able to create persuasive videos of politicians doing or saying whatever they would like.[81] Given the low cost of this type of covert meddling, if US policymakers want to deter Russia from launching similar operations in future elections, they would have to impose significant costs to penalize states for such behavior. Unfortunately, as of this writing, President Trump has shown no willingness to do so, and, in stark opposition to the consensus view of the US intelligence community, has repeatedly stated that he believes Putin's claim that he did not meddle in the US election.[82]

Whether Trump will embrace the regime change policies of his predecessors remains to be seen. On the one hand, he repeatedly bemoaned America's overreliance on regime change and criticized Clinton for her support of the Iraq War and the Libyan and Syrian interventions. Arguing, for instance, at a rally in Cincinnati, he stated, "We will pursue a new foreign policy that finally learns from the mistakes of the past. We will stop looking to topple regimes and overthrow governments. . . . Our goal is stability, not chaos."[83]

On the other hand, there is reason to believe that Trump may become an active proponent of regime change. For one, despite his claims to the contrary, Trump is on tape having supported both the Iraq War and the Libyan intervention.[84] His cabinet is also filled with advisers on record in support of regime change, particularly against Iran.[85] In addition, as a Washington outsider, Trump may seek out the unique executive powers that covert interventions provide. Finally, it is worth remembering that we have heard this story before. Both Obama and Bush campaigned against regime change only to change their mind after assuming office.

Should President Trump change his position on covert regime change, he would be with good company. The allure of covert action has long seduced skeptical US leaders. Perhaps the most remarkable feature of America's Cold War behavior is that despite having been warned time and again, policymakers continued to pursue covert regime changes. A typical 1961 review, for instance, warned, "We have been unable to conclude that, on balance, all of the covert actions programs undertaken by the CIA up to this time have been worth the risk or the great expenditure of manpower, money, and other resources involved."[86] Just as this warning was insufficient to dissuade Kennedy from launching several covert interventions within months, subsequent warnings to his successors were ignored. It is true that, at times, US leaders tried to minimize the potential risks associated with covert interventions by decreasing their size or trying to maintain vigilant oversight over them. Nevertheless, the problem, as National Intelligence Council Chair Gregory Treverton explained, is that "once covert interventions begin, no matter how hesitantly or provisionally, they can be hard to stop. Operation realities intrude, with deadlines attached. New stakes are created, changing the balance of risks and rewards as perceived by political leaders . . . the burden of proof switches from those who would propose covert action to those who oppose it."[87] Taken together, this suggests that policymakers should think twice before launching covert regime changes. Although, on occasion, these missions have succeeded, more often than not they have backfired on their creators. President Trump would thus be wise to heed Director of Central Intelligence Richard Helms's warning: "We must realize that today's world is far too sophisticated to permit covert action to be wielded about like an all-purpose political chain saw. At its best, covert action should be used like a well-honed scalpel, infrequently, and with discretion lest the blade lose its edge."[88]

Notes

1. The False Promise of Covert Regime Change

1. John M. Owen IV, *The Clash of Ideas in World Politics: Transnational Networks, States, and Regime Change, 1510–2010* (Princeton, NJ: Princeton University Press, 2010); Alexander B. Downes and Jonathan Monten, "Forced to be Free? Why Foreign-Imposed Regime Change Rarely Leads to Democratization," *International Security* 37, no. 4 (2013): 90–131; Nigel Lo, Barry Hashimoto, and Dan Reiter, "Ensuring Peace: Foreign-Imposed Regime Change and Postwar Peace Duration, 1914–2001," *International Organization* 62, no. 4 (2008): 717–36. See Owen, 165–66, for discussion of America's covert Cold War interventions. Based on their coding rules, Downes and Owen's dataset includes five successful covert cases.

2. Sima Qian and Raymond Dawson, *The First Emperor: Selections from the Historical Records* (New York: Oxford University Press, 2007), chap. 2.

3. Hans Morgenthau, *Politics among Nations: The Struggle for Power and Peace* (New York: McGraw-Hill Companies, 2006 [1948]), 241.

4. Thomas Ward, "Norms and Security: The Case of International Assassination," *International Security* 25, no. 1 (2000): 110.

5. Ward, "Norms and Security," 110.

6. David S. Foglesong, *America's Secret War against Bolshevism: US Intervention in the Russian Civil War, 1917–1920* (Chapel Hill: University of North Carolina Press, 2001).

7. The most expansive existing analysis is a 2013 study by Berger et al., which looks at CIA interventions in fifty-one countries during the Cold War. Definitional differences drive this discrepancy in the total number of cases. This current analysis differs from theirs in five ways. Their dataset includes thirty-five covert efforts to "support an existing regime" defined as "CIA interventions that did not install the current regime, but begin to provide significant support to the regime and helped it maintain power," and twenty-six covert efforts to "install and support" a new government. This study, by contrast, is only concerned with the latter category. Second, this study includes both successful and failed operations, whereas their study looks only at successful missions. Third, this study uses primary sources, but theirs relies on secondary sources. Fourth, based on information in those primary sources as well as variations in their definitions of a "CIA intervention" versus my definition of a "U.S.-backed covert regime change," I have come to different conclusions regarding the characterization of seven of their twenty-six CIA interventions to "install and support" leaders, because I believe that the available primary evidence

indicates that the United States was not actively involved in promoting the regime change. Finally, I classify Grenada 1983 as an overt intervention. Daniel Berger, William Easterly, Nathan Nunn, and Shanker Satyanath, "Commercial Imperialism? Political Influence and Trade during the Cold War," *American Economic Review* 103, no. 2 (2013): 863–96. Data on the categorization of their cases is from the replication material for their project, "Documentation for CIA intervention dataset for 'Commercial Imperialism, US Influence and Trade during the Cold War,'" http://scholar.harvard.edu/files/nunn/files/cia_kgb_intervention_data_documentation.zip.

8. Bruce Bueno De Mesquita and George W. Downs, "Intervention and Democracy," *International Organization* 60, no. 3 (2006): 627–49; Lo, Hashimoto, and Reiter, "Ensuring Peace," 717–36; Dan Reiter, *How Wars End* (Princeton, NJ: Princeton University Press, 2009); Elizabeth Nathan Saunders, *Leaders at War: How Presidents Shape Military Interventions* (Ithaca, NY: Cornell University Press, 2011); Alexander B. Downes and Lindsey A. O'Rourke, "You Can't Always Get What You Want: Why Foreign-Imposed Regime Change Seldom Improves Interstate Relations," *International Security* 41, no. 2 (2016): 43–89.

9. Analogous to James D. Fearon, "Domestic Political Audiences and the Escalation of International Disputes," *American Political Science Review* 88, no. 3 (1994): 577–92; Melissa Willard-Foster, "A Peace Too Costly to Keep: Why Major Powers Overthrow Foreign Governments" (paper prepared for the American Political Science Association 2012 Annual Meeting, New Orleans, LA, September 2012).

10. Bruce Bueno De Mesquita, James D. Morrow, Randolph M. Siverson, and Alastair Smith, "An Institutional Explanation of the Democratic Peace," *American Political Science Review* 93, no. 4 (1999): 791–807; Robert Powell, "War as a Commitment Problem," *International Organization* 60, no. 1 (2006): 169–203; Alexander B. Downes, "The Causes of Foreign-Imposed Regime Change in Interstate Wars" (paper prepared for delivery at the 2008 Annual Meeting of the American Political Science Association, Boston, MA, August, 28–31, 2008); Scott Wolford, Dan Reiter, and Clifford J. Carrubba, "Information, Commitment, and War," *Journal of Conflict Resolution* 55, no. 4 (2011): 556–79.

11. Downes and O'Rourke "You Can't Always Get What You Want," 43–89.

12. W. Michael Reisman, "The Manley O. Hudson Lecture: Why Regime Change Is (Almost Always) a Bad Idea," *American Journal of International Law* 98, no. 3 (2004): 516–25; Andrew J. Enterline and J. Michael Greig, "Perfect Storms? Political Instability in Imposed Polities and the Futures of Iraq and Afghanistan," *Journal of Conflict Resolution* 52, no. 6 (2008): 880–915; Downes, "The Causes of Foreign Imposed Regime Change"; Alexander Downes, "Catastrophic Success: Foreign-imposed Regime Change and Civil War" (paper prepared for delivery at the 2010 Annual Meeting of the American Political Science Association, Washington, DC, September 2–5, 2010).

13. George Bush, "Full Text: George Bush's Speech to the American Enterprise Institute," *Guardian*, February 27, 2003.

14. Martha Finnemore, *The Purpose of Intervention: Changing Beliefs About the Use of Force* (Ithaca, NY: Cornell University Press, 2004), 77; Casualty estimates from Benjamin A. Valentino, *Final Solutions: Mass Killing and Genocide in the 20th Century* (Ithaca, NY: Cornell University Press, 2013), 139.

15. Patrick James, "Structural Realism and the Causes of War," *Mershon International Studies Review* 39, no. 2 (1995): 181–208.

16. Robert Jervis, "Cooperation under the Security Dilemma," *World Politics* 30, no. 2 (1978): 167–214; Kenneth Waltz, *Theory of International Politics* (Boston: Addison-Wesley, 1979); John J. Mearsheimer, *The Tragedy of Great Power Politics* (New York: Norton, 2001), chap. 3

17. Owen, *Clash of Ideas in World Politics*, 8.

18. My theory therefore best fits within the Neoclassical strain of Realism. Gideon Rose, "Review: Neoclassical Realism and Theory of Foreign Policy," *World Politics* 51, no. 1 (October 1998): 144–72.

19. Easton, Gunnell, and Stein find that political scientists define *regime* as "consisting of three basic elements: institutions, operational rules of the game, and ideologies (goals, preferred rules, and preferred arrangements among political institutions)." David Easton, John G.

Gunnell, and Michael B. Stein, *Regime and Discipline: Democracy and the Development of Political Science* (Ann Arbor: University of Michigan Press, 1995), 8–9.

20. Territorial conquest, colonization, and annexation all imply direct rule by the intervening state. Although a change of government occurs in these scenarios, it is a consequence of the larger political objective to eliminate the target state or incorporate its territory and resources into the intervening state. By contrast, regime change aims to exercise indirect rule over the target state by allowing the target government to retain de jure authority over its territory. As a result, the motives and causal logics behind each type of operation are likely to vary significantly.

21. Two types of operations can be described as "covert": (1) operations designed to remain secretive through their planning and implementation phases as well as after completion, and (2) operations designed to maintain operational security and/or enable a surprise attack, but for which the state does not try to conceal its role after completion. This project concerns only the former category.

22. Some propaganda efforts involve calls to overthrow a foreign government. However, I exclude these operations from my data unless the intervening state also attempted other direct efforts at regime change. American use of anti-communist propaganda during the Cold War was so ubiquitous that including all cases would stretch the definition of *regime change* beyond what I consider reasonable limits.

23. National Security Council Directive 10/2, May 12, 1948, "Draft Report by the National Security Council," *Foreign Relations of the United States (FRUS), 1945–1950, Emergence of the Intelligence Establishment*, ed. C. Thomas Thorne Jr. and David S. Patterson (Washington, DC: US Government Printing Office [GPO], 1996), Doc. 274.

24. John M. Owen and Roger G. Herbert, "Intervention and Regime Change," in *Emerging Trends in the Social and Behavioral Sciences: An Interdisciplinary, Searchable, and Linkable Resource*, ed. Robert A. Scott and Marlis C. Buchmann (Somerset, NJ: John Wiley & Sons, 2015), https://onlinelibrary-wiley-com.proxy.bc.edu/doi/pdf/10.1002/9781118900772.etrds0194. See Berger et al., "Commercial Imperialism?," 863–96, for a study combining regime change and regime maintenance efforts.

25. Berger et al., "Commercial Imperialism?," 863–96.

26. Quoted in Evan Thomas, "Counter Intelligence," review of *Legacy of Ashes: The History of the CIA*, by Tim Weiner, *New York Times*, July 22, 2007.

27. Stephen D. Krasner, *Sovereignty: Organized Hypocrisy* (Princeton, NJ: Princeton University Press, 1999), 20.

28. Greg Grandin, *Empire's Workshop: Latin America, the United States, and the Rise of the New Imperialism* (New York: Metropolitan Books, 2006), 19.

29. Central Intelligence Agency (CIA), "Memorandum for: Executive Secretary, CIA Management Committee, Subject: Family Jewels," May 16, 1973, National Security Archive, https://nsarchive2.gwu.edu/NSAEBB/NSAEBB222/family_jewels_full_ocr.pdf; Church Committee, *Alleged Assassination Plots Involving Foreign Leaders* (Washington, DC: US GPO, 1975); Church Committee, *Final Report of the Senate Select Committee to Study Governmental Operations with Respect to Intelligence Activities* (Washington, DC: US GPO, 1976); Pike Committee "Hearings before the Committee on Intelligence," Parts 1–4 (1975–76), Psychological Strategy Board, December 19, 1951, "The Development of American Psychological Operations, 1945–1951," Central Intelligence Agency (CIA), Freedom of Information Act (FOIA) Electronic Reading Room, https://www.cia.gov/library/readingroom/document/cia-rdp86b00269r000900020001-9; and Allen E. Goodman, Bruce D. Berkowitz, and the Twentieth Century Fund, *The Need to Know: The Report of the Twentieth Century Fund Task Force on Covert Action and American Democracy; With a Background Paper* (New York: Century Foundation Press, 1992).

30. On the dangers of selecting on the dependent variable, see Barbara Geddes, "How the Cases You Choose Affect the Answers You Get: Selection Bias in Comparative Politics," *Political Analysis* 2, no. 1 (1990): 131–50; Gary King, Robert O. Keohane, and Sidney Verba, *Designing Social Inquiry: Scientific Inference in Qualitative Research* (Princeton, NJ: Princeton University Press, 1994); Scott Ashworth, Joshua D. Clinton, Adam Meirowitz, and Kristopher W. Ramsay,

"Design, Inference, and the Strategic Logic of Suicide Terrorism," *American Political Science Review* 102, no. 2 (May 2008): 269–73.

31. James Mahoney and Dietrich Rueschemeyer, eds., *Comparative Historical Analysis in the Social Sciences* (Cambridge: Cambridge University Press, 2003); Alexander George and Andrew Bennett, *Case Studies and Theory Development in the Social Sciences* (Cambridge, MA: MIT Press, 2004), 181–204; John Gerring, *Case Study Research: Principles and Practices* (New York: Cambridge University Press 2007), 217.

32. Timothy McKeown, "Case Studies and the Statistical Worldview: Review of King, Keohane, and Verba's *Designing Social Inquiry: Scientific Inference in Qualitative Research*," *International Organization* 53, no. 1 (2003): 161–90; Gerring, *Case Study Research*; Dan Slater and Daniel Ziblatt. "The Enduring Indispensability of the Controlled Comparison," *Comparative Political Studies* 46, no. 10 (2013): 1301–27.

33. Slater and Daniel Ziblatt. "Enduring Indispensability," 1312.

34. McKeown, "Case Studies," 161–90.

2. Causes

1. Michael MacDonald, *Overreach: Delusions of Regime Change in Iraq* (Cambridge, MA: Harvard University Press, 2014).

2. Nina Tannenwald, *The Nuclear Taboo: The United States and the Non-Use of Nuclear Weapons Since 1945* (Cambridge: Cambridge University Press, 2007), 4.

3. Stephen D. Krasner, *Sovereignty: Organized Hypocrisy* (Princeton, NJ: Princeton University Press, 1999), 20.

4. For historical accounts about the spread of Westphalian sovereignty, see Charles Tilly, *Coercion, Capital, and European States, AD 990–1992* (Oxford: Blackwell, 1992); Hendrik Spruyt, *The Sovereign State and Its Competitors: An Analysis of Systems Change* (Princeton, NJ: Princeton University Press, 1996); Derek Croxton, "The Peace of Westphalia of 1648 and the Origins of Sovereignty," *International History Review* 21, no. 3 (1999): 569–91.

5. Norms can have a positive effect on state behavior by motivating states to launch certain types of interventions, or a negative effect by constraining states from launching others. On the positive side, some scholars argue that norms can motivate foreign interventions to protect minority rights or to prevent humanitarian disasters. W. Michael Reisman, "The Manley O. Hudson Lecture: Why Regime Change Is (Almost Always) a Bad Idea," *American Journal of International Law* 98, no. 3 (2004): 516–25. See also Jack Donnelly, "State Sovereignty and International Intervention: The Case of Human Rights," in *Beyond Westphalia: State Sovereignty and International Intervention*, ed. G. M. Lyons and M. Mastanduno (Baltimore, MD: Johns Hopkins University Press, 1995), 115–46; Martha Finnemore, "Constructing Norms of Humanitarian Intervention," in *The Culture of National Security: Norms and Identity in World Politics*, ed. Peter J. Katzenstein (New York: Columbia University Press, 1996), 153–85; Martha Finnemore and Kathryn Sikkink, "International Norm Dynamics and Political Change," *International Organization* 52, no. 4 (September 1998): 887–917; Martha Finnemore, *The Purpose of Intervention: Changing Beliefs about the Use of Force* (Ithaca, NY: Cornell University Press, 2004); Nicholas Rengger, "The Judgment of War: On the Idea of Legitimate Force in World Politics," *Review of International Studies* 31, Supplement S1 (December 2005): 143–61. However, proponents do not claim to explain the motives behind all regime changes. Instead, their work highlights the emergence of a new motive for intervention that they expect to be more prevalent in the post–Cold War era. Thus, the fact that Washington did not launch any regime change to promote human rights norms during the Cold War does not contradict their theory. At the same time, these theories cannot be used to explain America's Cold War interventions. For a more on how human rights norms evolved over time, see Janne Haaland Matláry, *Values and Weapons: From Humanitarian Intervention to Regime Change?* (Basingstoke, UK: Palgrave Macmillan, 2006), chaps. 8 and 9; Beth A. Simmons, *Mobilizing for Human Rights: International Law in Domestic Politics* (Cambridge: Cambridge University Press, 2009). For a skeptical view, see David L. Cingranelli

and David L. Richards, "Respect for Human Rights after the End of the Cold War," *Journal of Peace Research* 36, no. 5 (September 1999): 511–34.

6. Stephen C. Ropp and Kathryn Sikkink, *The Power of Human Rights: International Norms and Domestic Change* (Cambridge: Cambridge University Press, 1999), chaps. 1 and 6; Ernest R. May, Philip Zelikow, Kirsten Lundberg, and Robert David Johnson, eds., *Dealing with Dictators: Dilemmas of US Diplomacy and Intelligence Analysis, 1945–1990* (Cambridge, MA: MIT Press, 2006); Finnemore, *The Purpose of Intervention*.

7. Krasner, *Sovereignty*, 20; Finnemore, *The Purpose of Intervention*, 3.

8. On the normative prohibition of conquest and annexation in the Post-WWII era, see Tanisha M. Fazal, *State Death: The Politics and Geography of Conquest, Occupation, and Annexation* (Princeton, NJ: Princeton University Press, 2007), chap. 3. On the norms against assassination, see Thomas Ward, "Norms and Security: The Case of International Assassination," *International Security* 25, no. 1 (2000): 105–33. On norms against preventive war, see Scott Silverstone, *Preventive War and American Democracy* (Abingdon, UK: Routledge, 2012).

9. Michael W. Doyle, "Kant, Liberal Legacies, and Foreign Affairs," *Philosophy and Public Affairs* 12, no. 3 (1983): 213. See also Michael W. Doyle, "Kant, Liberal Legacies, and Foreign Affairs, Part 2," *Philosophy and Public Affairs* 12, no. 4 (1983): 323–53; Michael W. Doyle, "Three Pillars of the Liberal Peace," *American Political Science Review* 99, no. 3 (2005): 463–66.

10. Thomas Risse-Kappen, *Cooperation among Democracies: The European Influence on U.S. Foreign Policy* (Princeton, NJ: Princeton University Press, 1997), 33.

11. On the emergence and expansion of democratic peace norms, see Bruce Russett, *Grasping the Democratic Peace: Principles for a Post–Cold War World* (Princeton, NJ: Princeton University Press, 1994). For accounts focusing on norms of nonviolent conflict resolution and respect for the rule of law, see Doyle, "Kant, Liberal Legacies, and Foreign Affairs," 213; Doyle, "Kant, Liberal Legacies, and Foreign Affairs, Part 2," 323–53; William J. Dixon, "Democracy and the Management of International Conflict," *Journal of Conflict Resolution* 37, no. 1 (1993): 42–68; Zeev Maoz and Bruce Russett, "Normative and Structural Causes of Democratic Peace, 1946–1986," *American Political Science Review* 87, no. 3 (1993): 624–38; William J. Dixon, "Democracy and the Peaceful Settlement of International Conflict," *American Political Science Review* 88, no. 1 (1994): 14–32; John M. Owen, "How Liberalism Produces Democratic Peace," *International Security* 19, no. 2 (1994): 87–125; Gregory A Raymond, "Democracies, Disputes, and Third-Party Intermediaries," *Journal of Conflict Resolution* 38, no. 1 (1994): 24–42; Kurt Taylor Gaubatz, "Democratic States and Commitment in International Relations," *International Organization* 50, no. 1 (1996): 109–39; Bear F. Braumoeller, "Deadly Doves: Liberal Nationalism and the Democratic Peace in the Soviet Successor States," *International Studies Quarterly* 41, no. 3 (1997): 375–402; William J. Dixon, "Dyads, Disputes and the Democratic Peace," in *The Political Economy of War and Peace*, ed. Murray Wolfson (New York: Springer, 1998), 103–26; Spencer R. Weart, *Never at War: Why Democracies Will Not Fight One Another* (New Haven, CT: Yale University Press, 1998); Alexander Wendt, *Social Theory of International Politics* (Cambridge: Cambridge University Press, 1999); William J. Dixon and Paul D. Senese, "Democracy, Disputes, and Negotiated Settlements," *Journal of Conflict Resolution* 46, no. 4 (2002): 547–71; Paul K. Huth and Todd L. Allee, *The Democratic Peace and Territorial Conflict in the Twentieth Century* (Cambridge: Cambridge University Press, 2002); Vesna Danilovic and Joe Clare, "The Kantian Liberal Peace (Revisited)," *American Journal of Political Science* 51, no. 2 (2007): 397–414. For accounts focusing on internalized norms of individual freedom, see Doyle, "Kant, Liberal Legacies, and Foreign Affairs," 213; Doyle, "Kant, Liberal Legacies, and Foreign Affairs, Part 2," 323–53; Maoz and Russet, "Normative and Structural Causes of Democratic Peace," 1993; Owen "How Liberalism Produces Democratic Peace," 87–125; Raymond, "Democracies, Disputes, and Third-party Intermediaries," 24–42; Gaubatz, "Democratic States and Commitment in International Relations"; Braumoeller, "Deadly Doves," 375–402; Wendt, *Social Theory of International Politics*; Danilovic and Clare, "The Kantian Liberal Peace (Revisited)," 397–414. For more on how shared democratic identities prevent democracies from perceiving one another as threats, see Jarrod Hayes, "Securitization, Social Identity, and Democratic Security: Nixon, India, and the Ties That Bind," *International Organization* 66, no. 1 (January 2012): 68; see also Thomas Risse-Kappen, "Democratic Peace—Warlike Democracies? A

Social Constructivist Interpretation of the Liberal Argument," *European Journal of International Relations* 1, no. 4 (1995): 491–517; Jarrod Hayes, "Review Article: The Democratic Peace and the New Evolution of an Old Idea," *European Journal of International Relations* 18, no. 4 (2012): 767–91.

12. Church Committee, *Alleged Assassination Plots Involving Foreign Leaders* (Washington, DC: US Government Printing Office [GPO], 1975).

13. James H. Doolittle, William B. Franke, Morris Hadley, and William D. Pawley, "Report on the Covert Activities of the Central Intelligence Agency," September 30, 1954, CIA Freedom of Information Act (FOIA) Electronic Reading Room, https://www.cia.gov/library/readingroom/docs/CIA-RDP86B00269R000900010003-8.pdf, 3. For Kennan's thoughts, see Gordon A. Christenson, "Kennan and Human Rights," *Human Rights Quarterly* 8, no. 3 (1986): 345–73.

14. Stephen Van Evera, "The Case Against Intervention," *Atlantic Monthly* 266, no. 1 (1990): 72–80; Krasner, *Sovereignty*, 20; Tarak Barkawi and Mark Laffey, *Democracy, Liberalism, and War: Rethinking the Democratic Peace Debate* (Boulder, CO: Lynne Rienner, 2001); Dan Reiter and Allan C. Stam, *Democracies at War* (Princeton, NJ: Princeton University Press, 2002); Jaechun Kim, "Democratic Peace and Covert War: A Case Study of the US Covert War in Chile," *Journal of International and Area Studies* (2005): 25–47; David Kinsella, "No Rest for the Democratic Peace," *American Political Science Review* 99, no. 3 (2005): 453–57; Alexander B. Downes and Mary Lauren Lilley, "Overt Peace, Covert War? Covert Intervention and the Democratic Peace," *Security Studies* 19, no. 2 (2010): 266–306; Anna Geis and Wolfgang Wagner, "How Far Is it from Königsberg to Kandahar? Democratic Peace and Democratic Violence in International Relations," *Review of International Studies* 37, no. 4 (2011): 1555–77.

15. The six democratic regimes that were replaced by authoritarian governments are Iran (1952–53), Guatemala (1953–54), Congo (1960), British Guiana/Guyana (1961–71), Brazil (1964), and Chile (1964–73). Historians continue to debate the level of direct US involvement in the 1973 coup in Chile that replaced Salvador Allende, although most agree (and declassified documents support) that the US had a long history of covert action in Chile, including direct involvement in a failed 1970 coup and an ongoing covert campaign to destabilize the regime. Peter Kornbluh, *The Pinochet File: A Declassified Dossier on Atrocity and Accountability* (New York: New Press, 2013). For a skeptical view, see Kristian Gustafson, *Hostile Intent: US Covert Operations in Chile, 1964–1974* (Washington, DC: Potomac Books, 2007).

The United States was also involved in an aborted covert regime change operation against the democratic government of Syria (1955–57) and unsuccessfully supported a coup against Sukarno's "guided democracy" regime in Indonesia (1954–58).

16. Sebastian Rosato, "The Flawed Logic of Democratic Peace Theory," *American Political Science Review* 97, no. 4 (2003): 591.

17. Quoted in Kim, "Democratic Peace and Covert War," 40; Tarak Barkawi, "Scientific Decay," *International Studies Quarterly* 59, no. 4 (December 1, 2015): 116.

18. Quoted by Barkawi, "Scientific Delay," 116.

19. David P. Forsythe, "Democracy, War, and Covert Action," *Journal of Peace Research* 29, no. 4 (1992): 393. See also Maoz and Russett, "Normative and Structural Causes of Democratic Peace, 1946–1986," 14–32.

20. Indeed, Doyle includes seven of these states as liberal members of the "pacific union" in his foundational piece on the subject. Doyle, "Kant, Liberal Legacies, and Foreign Affairs," 213.

21. Forsythe, "Democracy, War, and Covert Action," 386.

22. Michael Poznansky, "Stasis or Decay? Reconciling Covert War and the Democratic Peace," *International Studies Quarterly* 59, no. 4 (2015): 1.

23. Doyle, "Kant, Liberal Legacies, and Foreign Affairs," 213.

24. Kim, "Democratic Peace and Covert War," 40; Downes and Lilley, "Overt Peace, Covert War?," 266–306.

25. Other DPT critics have expanded on this susceptibility of leaders to change their perceptions of regime type based on their strategic interests. See, for instance, Ido Oren, "The Subjectivity of the 'Democratic' Peace: Changing U.S. Perceptions of Imperial Germany," *International Security* 20, no. 2 (1995): 147.

26. Barkawi, "Scientific Decay," 827–29.

27. Rosato, "Flawed Logic," 593.

28. Suzanne Werner, "Absolute and Limited War: The Possibility of Foreign-Imposed Regime Change," *International Interactions* 22, no. 1 (1996): 78. Werner's conception of political authority is not synonymous with regime type. Because she saw significant variation in the exercise of political authority within states nominally of the same regime type, her measure aims to capture variation in the competitiveness and openness of executive power. Nevertheless, a broader implication of her work is that states are more likely to attempt regime change following a war, when their opponent has dissimilar political institutions. Supporting this position, Mark Peceny, Caroline Beer, and Shannon Sanchez-Terry found that democracies and personalist dictatorships clashed during more militarized interstate disputes than their numbers alone would have suggested. Mark Peceny, Caroline C. Beer, and Shannon Sanchez-Terry, "Dictatorial Peace?," *American Political Science Review*, March 2002, 15–26.

29. Alexander B. Downes, "The Causes of Foreign-Imposed Regime Change in Interstate Wars" (paper prepared for delivery at the 2008 Annual Meeting of the American Political Science Association, Boston, MA, August, 28–31, 2008), 39.

30. Barbara Geddes, Joseph Wright, and Erica Frantz, "Autocratic Breakdown and Regime Transitions: A New Data Set," *Perspectives on Politics* 12, no. 2 (June 2014): 313–31. Regime types for all operations are coded based on the regime type of the target government during the first year of the US intervention. I have adapted this dataset in several places to be able to test the hypotheses. First, the dataset does not include democratic states, which I have added. (The omission of these states from the dataset signifies their democratic coding.) Second, the dataset includes several subsets of party-based and military regimes, which I have collapsed into two categories according to the conventions that they suggest in their codebook. Third, operations in the Dominican Republic in 1961–62 and 1965–68, as well as Portugal in 1974 are coded as democratic, rather than personal or military, because Washington's operations were aimed to influence the results of upcoming democratic elections. Fourth, Iran in 1953 is coded as a democracy, rather than a monarchy, because Washington's covert operation targeted the democratically elected leader of Iran, not the Shah. Fifth, Guyana and Suriname are omitted from their dataset because of their small population size. I have coded these states as a democracy and military regime, respectively. Sixth, operations to support pro-Western independence forces in colonial Angola and Mozambique during the 1960s are coded according to the regime type of their colonial power, Portugal.

31. Doyle, "Kant, Liberal Legacies, and Foreign Affairs," 213; Doyle, "Kant, Liberal Legacies, and Foreign Affairs, Part 2," 323–53; David A. Lake, "Powerful Pacifists: Democratic States and War," *American Political Science Review* 86, no. 1 (March 1992): 24–37; Nils Petter Gleditsch and Håvard Hegre, "Peace and Democracy: Three Levels of Analysis," *Journal of Conflict Resolution* 41, no. 2 (1997): 283–310; Arvid Raknerud and Håvard Hegre, "The Hazard of War: Reassessing the Evidence for the Democratic Peace," *Journal of Peace Research* 34, no. 4 (1997): 385–404; Lars-Erik Cederman and Kristian Skrede Gleditsch, "Conquest and Regime Change: An Evolutionary Model of the Spread of Democracy and Peace," *International Studies Quarterly* 48, no. 3 (September 1, 2004): 603–29.

32. Doyle, "Kant, Liberal Legacies, and Foreign Affairs, Part 2," 324–25.

33. Owen identifies three long waves of regime promotion. These include Catholicism and Protestantism in Europe from 1520 to the 1700s; Republicanism, Constitutional Monarchy, and Absolute Monarchy in Europe and the Americas from 1770 to the 1800s; and Communism, Liberalism, and Fascism from 1910 to 1990. John M. Owens IV, *The Clash of Ideas in World Politics: Transnational Networks, States, and Regime Change, 1510–2010* (Princeton, NJ: Princeton University Press, 2010); Downes, "Causes of Foreign-Imposed Regime Change in Interstate Wars," 39, also finds some empirical support for this argument.

34. Owen, *Clash of Ideas in World Politics*, 182–83.

35. Tony Smith, *America's Mission: The United States and the Worldwide Struggle for Democracy* (Princeton, NJ: Princeton University Press, 2012).

36. Susan B. Epstein, Nina M. Serafino, and Francis T. Miko, "Democracy Promotion: Cornerstone of U.S. Foreign Policy," (Washington, DC: Congressional Research Service, December 26, 2007).

37. Joshua Muravchik, *Exporting Democracy: Fulfilling America's Destiny* (American Enterprise Institute, 1992), 20.

38. Owen, *Clash of Ideas in World Politics*. These are South Korea (1950), Lebanon (1958), Laos (1964), Vietnam (1965), the Dominican Republic (1965), Cambodia (1970), Grenada (1983), and Panama (1989).

39. Owen, *Clash of Ideas in World Politics*, 19–20, for coding.

40. Bruce Bueno de Mesquita and George Downs find that US military interventions between 1946 and 2001 did not increase the democratization of their target. Bruce Bueno de Mesquita and George W. Downs, "Intervention and Democracy," *International Organization* 60, no. 3 (2006): 627–49. Other studies have found that America's overt interventions only had a positive impact on democratization when US policymakers were publicly committed to promoting democracy. Because most interventions did not aim to democratize their target, however, the net effect of US interventions was either neutral or negative. James Meernik, "United States Military Intervention and the Promotion of Democracy," *Journal of Peace Research* 33, no. 4 (November 1996); In a similar vein, Margaret Herman and Charles Kegley determined that "interventions with the intent of protecting or promoting democracy led to the desired outcome, interventions with other purposes resulted in the target states becoming more autocratic." Margaret G. Hermann and Charles W. Kegley Jr., "The U.S. Use of Military Intervention to Promote Democracy: Evaluating the Record," *International Interactions* 24, no. 2 (June 1, 1998): 98. Looking at US military interventions between 1898 and 1992, Mark Peceny found that such an intervention "in and of itself does not have a positive impact on democracy," but that Washington could play a positive democratizing role in cases when it promoted free and fair elections. Mark Peceny, "Forcing Them to Be Free," *Political Research Quarterly* 52, no. 3 (September 1999): 549. Scott Walker and Frederic Pearson replicated Peceny's finding that most US military interventions did not bring about democratization, but argue that he overestimated the long-term democratizing effects of US missions to promote free and fair foreign elections. Scott Walker and Frederic S. Pearson, "Should We Really 'Force Them to Be Free?' An Empirical Examination of Peceny's Liberalizing Intervention Thesis," *Conflict Management and Peace Science* 24, no. 1 (April 1, 2007): 37–53. Finally, analyzing the effect of all foreign-imposed regime changes (FIRCs) between 1816 and 2008, Alexander Downes and Jonathan Monten conclude, "U.S. FIRCs thus brought democracy in three out of twenty-eight cases (11 percent). . . . Other democracies were similarly unsuccessful. . . . [This] suggests that the identity of the intervener— whether the United States or some other democracy—has little effect on targets' chances of becoming consolidated democracies." Alexander B. Downes and Jonathan Monten, "Forced to be Free? Why Foreign-imposed Regime Change Rarely Leads to Democratization," *International Security* 37, no. 4 (2013): 129.

41. Proponents of ideological theories of regime change counter that Washington's interventions to promote authoritarian regimes need to be considered within their Cold War context. Owen writes, "It is important that most of these non-forcible interventions entailed support for *anti-communist* authoritarians." Owen, *Clash of Ideas in World Politics*, 166. The implication of this argument is that although US interventions may have promoted authoritarian leaders in the short term, these illiberal regime changes were ultimately in pursuit of a long-term liberal goal—namely, defeating communism and winning the ideological struggle of the Cold War. Reagan's influential adviser, Jeane Kirkpatrick, famously articulated a version of this argument in her 1979 piece "Dictatorships and Double Standards." Kirkpatrick argued that US interventions to support anti-communist dictators was justified because "although there is no instance of a revolutionary 'socialist' or Communist society being democratized, right-wing autocracies do sometimes evolve into democracies—given time, propitious economic, social, and political circumstances, talented leaders, and a strong indigenous demand for representative government." Jeanne Kirkpatrick, "Dictatorships and Double Standards," *Commentary* 65, no. 8 (November 1, 1979): 37. The biggest problem with this argument is that there was no evidence at the time that right-wing dictatorships are any more likely to become liberal democracies in the end than their left-wing counterparts. Another challenge facing this argument is that because the Cold War was simultaneously a geostrategic competition between two military superpowers and an ideological battle between two systems of gov-

ernment, it is often difficult to say whether the United States supported right-wing dictators in the third world because they opposed communism as an ideology or the Soviet Union as a military threat. Throughout the case studies, these two factors have been disentangled by careful analysis of the statements of US leaders during policy deliberations over intervention. Overall, more evidence exists that the United States supported right-wing dictators because they were militarily opposed to the Soviet Union than because they were ideologically anticommunist.

42. Melissa Willard-Foster, "A Peace Too Costly to Keep: Why Major Powers Overthrow Foreign Governments" (paper prepared for the American Political Science Association 2012 Annual Meeting, New Orleans, LA: September 2012), 32.

43. James D. Morrow, Bruce Bueno de Mesquita, Randolph M. Siverson, and Alastair Smith, "Selection Institutions and War Aims," *Economics of Governance* 7, no. 1 (January 2006): 47. For supporting arguments, see Bruce Bueno De Mesquita, James D. Morrow, Randolph M. Siverson, and Alastair Smith, "An Institutional Explanation of the Democratic Peace," *American Political Science Review* 93, no. 4 (1999): 791–807. Nevertheless, there are methodological concerns about this study that bring into question their results. To begin, their dataset's coding of regime change skews their sample: 382 victorious states in militarized interstate disputes where both sides used force and where at least one side had goals relating to their opponent's regime. Morrow et al. use the Correlates of War (COW) dataset (2006), 45–46. As Downes points out, "Roughly 18 percent of the cases are composed of North Korea versus South Korea, another 11 percent consist of intervention in the Russian Civil War, and 7 percent comprise the overthrow of the Taliban in 2001. . . . Moreover, many well known cases of actual forcible regime change are missing." Downes, "Causes of Foreign-Imposed Regime Change in Interstate Wars," 20.

44. Willard-Foster, "A Peace Too Costly to Keep."

45. Noam Chomsky, *Hegemony or Survival?* (London: Hamish Hamilton, 2003); Stephen Kinzer, *Overthrow: America's Century of Regime Change from Hawaii to Iraq* (Basingstoke, UK: Macmillan, 2007); S. C. Schlesinger and Stephen Kinzer, *Bitter Fruit: The Story of the American Coup in Guatemala* (New York: David Rockefeller Center for Latin American Studies, 2005); Greg Grandin, *Empire's Workshop: Latin America, the United States, and the Rise of the New Imperialism* (Basingstoke, UK: Macmillan, 2006)

46. Daniel Yergin, *The Prize: The Epic Quest for Oil, Money & Power* (New York: Free Press, 2008), 476–78; Michael J. Sullivan, *American Adventurism Abroad: Invasions, Interventions, and Regime Changes since World War II* (Hoboken, NJ: Wiley-Blackwell, 2008), 53.

47. Kinzer, *Overthrown*, 3.

48. Arindrajit Dube, Ethan Kaplan, and Suresh Naidu. "Coups, Corporations, and Classified Information," *Quarterly Journal of Economics* 126, no. 3 (2011): 1375–1409.

49. Dube, Kaplan, and Naidu, "Coups, Corporations, and Classified Information," 1376. The authors, however, do not claim to prove that these economic incentives were the decisive factor driving U.S. policymakers to intervene.

50. Michael Grow, *U.S. Presidents and Latin American Interventions: Pursuing Regime Change in the Cold War* (Lawrence: University Press of Kansas, 2008), 185.

51. Jorge I. Domínguez, *Economic Issues and Political Conflict: US—Latin American Relations* (Amsterdam: Elsevier, 2013), 33.

52. Francis J. Gavin, "Politics, Power, and U.S. Policy in Iran, 1950–1953," *Journal of Cold War Studies* 1, no. 1 (January 1, 1999): 56–89.

53. Bissell quoted in Grow, *U.S. Presidents and Latin American Interventions*, 186.

54. Fortuny quoted in Grow, 186.

55. Henry Kissinger and Richard Nixon, "Telcon (San Clemente)," July 4, 1973, National Security Archive (hereafter cited as NSA), https://nsarchive2.gwu.edu/NSAEBB/NSAEBB313/Doc05.pdf.

56. Noam Chomsky writes, "For the USSR the Cold War has been primarily a war against its satellites, and for the U.S. a war against the Third World. For each it has served to entrench a particular system of domestic privilege and coercion." Noam Chomsky, *Deterring Democracy* (Basingstoke, UK: Macmillan, 1992), 28.

57. Maud Bracke, *Which Socialism, Whose Détente? West European Communism and the Czechoslovak Crisis of 1968* (Budapest: Central European University Press, 2007), 56.

58. Immanuel Wallerstein, *The Politics of the World-Economy: The States, the Movements and the Civilizations* (Cambridge: Cambridge University Press, 1984); Chomsky, *Deterring Democracy*, 28; Sullivan, *American Adventurism Abroad*; Daniel Berger et al., "Commercial Imperialism? Political Influence and Trade during the Cold War," *American Economic Review* 103, no. 2 (2013): 863–96.

59. Sullivan, *American Adventurism Abroad*, 5–6.

60. Berger et al., "Commercial Imperialism," 863–96.

61. G. John Ikenberry, *After Victory: Institutions, Strategic Restraint, and the Rebuilding of Order after Major Wars* (Princeton, NJ: Princeton University Press, 2009).

62. John J. Mearsheimer, *Tragedy of Great Power Politics* (New York: Norton, 2001), chap. 3; Robert Gilpin, *War and Change in World Politics* (Cambridge: Cambridge University Press, 1983).

63. Paul Zachary, Kathleen Deloughery, and Alexander B. Downes, "No Business Like FIRC Business: Foreign-Imposed Regime Change and Bilateral Trade," *British Journal of Political Science* 47, no. 4 (August 2015): 1–34.

64. Church Committee, *Final Report of the Senate Select Committee to Study Governmental Operations with Respect to Intelligence Activities* (Washington, DC: US GPO, 1976); Rhodri Jeffreys-Jones, *The CIA and American Democracy* (New Haven, CT: Yale University Press, 1991); Chalmers Johnson, *Blowback: The Costs and Consequences of American Empire* (Basingstoke, UK: Macmillan, 2000); William Blum, *Killing Hope: US Military and CIA Interventions since World War II* (London: Zed Books, 2003); Tim Weiner, *Legacy of Ashes: The History of the CIA* (New York: Anchor, 2008).

65. Church Committee, *Alleged Assassination Plots Involving Foreign Leaders* (Washington, DC: US GPO, 1975).

66. Church Committee, *Final Report of the Senate Select Committee*, 56–57.

67. On Church renouncing the "rogue elephant" characterization, see Samuel Walker, *Presidents and Civil Liberties from Wilson to Obama: A Story of Poor Custodians* (Cambridge: Cambridge University Press, 2012), 335.

68. Tim Weiner, *Legacy of Ashes*, xix.

69. Loch K. Johnson, *America's Secret Power: The CIA in a Democratic Society* (Oxford: Oxford University Press, 1991).

70. Church Committee, *Final Report of the Senate Select Committee*, 50.

71. Charles G. Cogan, "Covert Action and Congressional Oversight: A Deontology," *Studies in Conflict & Terrorism* 16, no. 2 (1993): 87–97.

72. Robert M. Gates, *From the Shadows: The Ultimate Insider's Story of Five Presidents and How They Won the Cold War* (New York: Simon and Schuster, 2007), 567.

73. Officials within and outside the CIA concur with this assessment. Gerald K. Haines, "Looking for a Rogue Elephant: The Pike Committee Investigations and the CIA," in *Inside CIA: Lessons in Intelligence*, ed. Sharad S. Chauhan (New Delhi: APH Publishing, 2004), chap. 30; Stephen Knott, "The CIA's Greatest Fear: Being Thrown under the Bus by Congress . . . Again," *National Interest*, August 8, 2014.

74. Historical accounts focusing on geostrategic considerations include Johnson, *America's Secret Power*; Thomas Bodenheimer and Robert Gould, *Rollback! Right-Wing Power in US Foreign Policy* (New York: South End Press, 1989); Roy Godson, *Dirty Tricks or Trump Cards: U.S. Covert Action and Counterintelligence* (Piscataway, NJ: Transaction, 1995); John Prados, *Presidents' Secret Wars: CIA and Pentagon Covert Operations from World War II through the Persian Gulf* (Chicago: Ivan R Dee, 1996); James M. Scott, *Deciding to Intervene: The Reagan Doctrine and American Foreign Policy* (Durham, NC: Duke University Press, 1996); Gavin, "Politics, Power, and U.S. Policy in Iran, 1950–1953," 56–89; Gregory Mitrovich, *Undermining the Kremlin: America's Strategy to Subvert the Soviet Bloc, 1947–1956* (Ithaca, NY: Cornell University Press, 2000); Peter Grose, *Operation Rollback: America's Secret War Behind the Iron Curtain* (Boston: Houghton Mifflin Harcourt, 2001); William Blum, *Killing Hope: US Military and CIA Interventions since World War II* (Monroe, ME: Common Courage Press, 2004); William Daugherty, *Executive Secrets: Covert*

Action and the Presidency (Lexington: University Press of Kentucky, 2006); Odd Arne Westad, *The Global Cold War: Third World Interventions and the Making of Our Times* (Cambridge: Cambridge University Press, 2005); John Prados, *Safe for Democracy: The Secret Wars of the CIA* (Lanham, MD: Rowman & Littlefield, 2006); James Callanan, *Covert Action in the Cold War: US Policy, Intelligence and CIA Operations* (New York: IB Tauris, 2009).

75. Scott Wolford, Dan Reiter, and Clifford J. Carrubba, "Information, Commitment, and War," *Journal of Conflict Resolution* 55, no. 4 (2011): 17. See also Suzanne Werner, "The Precarious Nature of Peace: Resolving the Issues, Enforcing the Settlement, and Renegotiating the Terms," *American Journal of Political Science* 43, no. 3 (1999): 912–34; Suzanne Werner and Amy Yuen, "Making and Keeping Peace" *International Organization* 59, no. 2 (April 2005): 261–92; Nigel Lo, Barry Hashimoto, and Dan Reiter, "Ensuring Peace: Foreign-Imposed Regime Change and Postwar Peace Duration, 1914–2001," *International Organization* 62, no. 4 (2008): 717–36.

76. Fazal, *State Death*, 173–75. Downes found that buffer states fighting against a great power engaged in an enduring rivalry are overthrown five times more often than nonbuffer states. Downes, "Causes of Foreign Imposed Regime Change in Interstate Wars," 39–40.

77. Mearsheimer, *Tragedy of Great Power Politics*, 17–18.

78. See Alexander B. Downes and Lindsey A. O'Rourke, "You Can't Always Get What You Want: Why Foreign-Imposed Regime Change Seldom Improves Interstate Relations," *International Security* 41, no. 2 (2016): 43–89, for a version of this argument.

79. Because this project focuses on a single country's interventions, it remains an open empirical question the extent to which these security-oriented motives can be generalized to explain the overt and covert regime changes of other states. For covert interventions, a lack of data on the covert regime changes of other states hinders that analysis. For overt interventions, however, there is already a large Realist literature on the causes of war. The arguments presented here would apply to the subset of wars that pursue regime change.

80. Patrick James, "Structural Realism and the Causes of War," *Mershon International Studies Review* 39, no. 2 (1995): 181–208; Mearsheimer, *Tragedy of Great Power Politics*, chap. 9.

81. Stephen M. Walt, *The Origins of Alliances* (Ithaca, NY: Cornell University Press, 1990).

82. D. Scott Bennett, "Democracy, Regime Change, and Rivalry Termination," *International Interactions* 22, no. 4 (April 1, 1997): 376.

83. Owen, *Clash of Ideas in World Politics*, 144.

84. US objectives in the Korean War did not originally include overthrowing the North Korean regime. However, they expanded to include regime change during the war.

85. National Security Council, "NSC-58 on Policy toward Eastern Europe," October 5, 1949, NSA, "Soviet Flashpoints" Collection, http://www.fransamaltingvongeusau.com/documents/dll/h5/1.5.13.pdf.

86. Joint Chiefs of Staff, January 15, 1951, quoted in Gregory Mitrovich, *Undermining the Kremlin: America's Strategy to Subvert the Soviet Bloc, 1947–1956* (Ithaca, NY: Cornell University Press, 2000), 67.

87. For more on rollback, see Bodenheimer and Gould, *Rollback!*; Scott, *Deciding to Intervene*; Mitrovich, *Undermining the Kremlin*; Grose, *Operation Rollback*.

88. Jack S. Levy, "Declining Power and the Preventive Motivation for War," *World Politics* 40, no. 1 (1987): 87.

89. This distinction comes from Silverstone, *Preventive War and American Democracy*.

90. Silverstone, *Preventive War and American Democracy*, 10.

91. Scott D. Sagan, "The Origins of the Pacific War," *Journal of Interdisciplinary History* 18, no. 4 (1988): 893–922.

92. George W. Bush, *The National Security Strategy of the United States of America* (Washington, DC: Executive Office of the President, September 2002). For a skeptical take on the preventive war argument, see Ahsan I. Butt, "Why Did the United States Invade Iraq in 2003?," *Security Studies*, forthcoming.

93. Dale C. Copeland, *The Origins of Major War* (Ithaca, NY: Cornell University Press, 2000), 4.

94. Copeland, *Origins of Major War*, 4.

95. Timothy W. Crawford, "Preventing Enemy Coalitions: How Wedge Strategies Shape Power Politics," *International Security* 35, no. 4 (March 18, 2011): 155–89.

96. For an analogous argument about proxy warfare in bipolarity, see Mark O. Yeisley, "Bipolarity, Proxy Wars, and the Rise of China," *Strategic Studies Quarterly* (January 2011): 75–91; Andrew Mumford, "Proxy Warfare and the Future of Conflict," *The RUSI Journal* 158, no. 2 (April 1, 2013): 40–46.

97. Westad, *The Global Cold War*; Berger et al., "Commercial Imperialism," 863–96.

98. Marc Trachtenberg, "Preventive War and U.S. Foreign Policy," *Security Studies* 16, no. 1 (April 16, 2007): 1–31.

99. John Lewis Gaddis, *Strategies of Containment: A Critical Appraisal of Postwar American National Security Policy* (New York: Oxford University Press, 1982); Marc Trachtenberg, "Making Grand Strategy: The Early Cold War Experience in Retrospect," *SAIS Review* 19, no. 1 (1999): 33–40; Callanan, *Covert Action in the Cold War*.

100. National Security Council, March 15, 1954, "Directive 5412: Note from Executive Secretary of the National Security Council (Lay) to the National Security Council," *Foreign Relations of the United States (FRUS), 1950–1955, Vol. IV, The Intelligence Community, 1950–1955*, ed. Douglas Keane and Michael Warner (Washington, DC: US GPO, 2007), Doc. 171.

101. National Security Council, "NSC 162/2: Basic National Security Policy," October 30, 1953, https://fas.org/irp/offdocs/nsc-hst/nsc-162-2.pdf.

102. Mearsheimer, *Tragedy of Great Power Politics*, 40.

103. "Hierarchy exists when one actor, the dominant state, possesses authority over another actor, the subordinate state." David A. Lake, "Escape from the State of Nature: Authority and Hierarchy in World Politics," *International Security* 32, no. 1 (June 26, 2007): 56.

104. Mearsheimer, *Tragedy of Great Power Politics*, 34.

105. Mearsheimer, 41.

106. Mearsheimer, *Tragedy of Great Power Politics* (2014 ed.), 365.

107. Gilpin, *War and Change in World Politics*, 1–34.

108. Gilpin, 1–34; Robert Gilpin and Jean M. Gilpin, *The Political Economy of International Relations* (Princeton, NJ: Princeton University Press, 1987); Mearsheimer, *Tragedy of Great Power Politics*, chap. 2; Fazal, *State Death*; David A. Lake, *Hierarchy in International Relations* (Ithaca, NY: Cornell University Press, 2009), chap. 4; David A. Lake, "Regional Hierarchy: Authority and Local International Order," *Review of International Studies* 35, no. Supplement S1 (February 2009): 35–58.

109. Lake, "Escape from the State of Nature: Authority and Hierarchy in World Politics," 56.

110. National Security Council 144/1, March 18, 1953, "United States Objectives and Courses of Action with Respect to Latin America, General Considerations," *FRUS, 1952–1954, Vol. IV, The American Republics*, ed. N. Stephen Kane and William F. Sanford Jr. (Washington, DC: US GPO, 1983), Doc. 3.

111. Ahsan I. Butt, "Anarchy and Hierarchy in International Relations: Examining South America's War-Prone Decade, 1932–41," *International Organization* 67, no. 3 (July 2013): 575–607.

112. Owen, *Clash of Ideas in World Politics*, 15–16.

113. Data from Alexander B. Downes and Jonathan Monten, "Appendices for 'Force to Be Free: Why Foreign-Imposed Regime Change Rarely Leads to Democratization,'" 3–4, https://alexanderdownes.weebly.com/uploads/9/2/6/8/92684520/forced_to_be_free_replication_and_appendices.zip.

114. Downes and Monten, 3–4

115. National Security Council, March 18, 1953, "NSC 144/1: United States Objectives and Courses of Action with Respect to Latin America, General Considerations," *FRUS, 1952–1954, Vol. IV, The American Republics*, Doc. 3.

116. Quoted in Weiner, *Legacy of Ashes: The History of the CIA*, 691.

117. For more on the Monroe Doctrine and regional hegemony, see Lars Schoultz, *Beneath the United States: A History of US Policy toward Latin America* (Cambridge, MA: Harvard University Press, 1998); Mearsheimer, *Tragedy of Great Power Politics*; Martin Sicker, *The Geopolitics of Security in the Americas: Hemispheric Denial from Monroe to Clinton* (Westport, CT: Greenwood, 2002); Mark T. Gilderhus, "The Monroe Doctrine: Meanings and Implications," *Presidential Studies Quarterly* 36, no. 1 (2006): 5–16; Lester D. Langley, *America and the Americas: The United States in the Western Hemisphere* (Athens: University of Georgia Press, 2010).

118. Bueno de Mesquita and Downs, "Intervention and Democracy," 627–49; Lo, Hashimoto, and Reiter, "Ensuring Peace," 717–36; Dan Reiter, *How Wars End* (Princeton, NJ: Prince-

ton University Press, 2009); Downes and O'Rourke, "You Can't Always Get What You Want."

119. Robert Axelrod, "Conflict of Interest: An Axiomatic Approach," *Journal of Conflict Resolution* 11, no. 1 (1967): 87–99. See also Robert Jervis, "Cooperation under the Security Dilemma," *World Politics* 30, no. 2 (1978): 167–214; Robert Axelrod and Robert O. Keohane, "Achieving Cooperation under Anarchy: Strategies and Institutions," *World Politics* 38, no. 1 (1985): 226–54.

120. Axelrod, "Conflict of Interest: An Axiomatic Approach," 98.

121. Jervis, "Cooperation under the Security Dilemma," 1978; Kenneth Waltz, *Theory of International Politics* (Boston: Addison-Wesley, 1979); Robert Keohane, *After Hegemony: Cooperation and Discord in the World Political Economy* (Princeton, NJ: Princeton University Press, 1984); Axelrod and Keohane, "Achieving Cooperation under Anarchy: Strategies and Institutions," 226–54; Bruce Bueno De Mesquita and David Lalman, *War and Reason: Domestic and International Imperatives* (New Haven, CT: Yale University Press, 1992); James D. Fearon, "Domestic Political Audiences and the Escalation of International Disputes," *American Political Science Review* 88, no. 3 (1994): 577–92; Mearsheimer, *Tragedy of Great Power Politics*.

122. Brian C. Rathbun, "Uncertain about Uncertainty: Understanding the Multiple Meanings of a Crucial Concept in International Relations Theory," *International Studies Quarterly* 51, no. 3 (September 1, 2007): 533.

123. Arthur A. Stein, "Coordination and Collaboration: Regimes in an Anarchic World," *International Organization* 36, no. 2 (March 1982): 299–324; Axelrod and Keohane, "Achieving Cooperation under Anarchy: Strategies and Institutions," 226–54; Joseph M. Grieco, "Understanding the Problem of International Cooperation: The Limits of Neoliberal Institutionalism and the Future of Realist Theory," in *Neorealism and Neoliberalism: The Contemporary Debate*, David A. Baldwin, ed. (New York: Columbia University Press, 1993); John J. Mearsheimer, "The False Promise of International Institutions," *International Security* 19, no. 3 (1994): 5–49.

124. Keohane, *After Hegemony*, 1984; Axelrod and Keohane, "Achieving Cooperation under Anarchy: Strategies and Institutions," 226–54; Robert O. Keohane, "Institutionalist Theory and the Realist Challenge After the Cold War," in *Neorealism and Neoliberalism* (New York: Columbia University Press, 1993), 276; Katja Weber, "Hierarchy Amidst Anarchy: A Transaction Costs Approach to International Security Cooperation," *International Studies Quarterly* 2 (1997): 321–40; Ikenberry, *After Victory*.

125. Bueno de Mesquita and Lalman, *War and Reason*, 38.

126. Charles Lipson, "International Cooperation in Economic and Security Affairs," *World Politics* 37, no. 1 (October 1984): 1–23; Axelrod and Keohane, "Achieving Cooperation under Anarchy: Strategies and Institutions," 226–54.

127. See Rathbun, "Uncertain about Uncertainty," 533, for a discussion of uncertainty's role in Realism.

128. Copeland, *Origins of Major War*, 4; Mearsheimer, *Tragedy of Great Power Politics*.

129. Classic articulation of the security dilemma from Jervis, "Cooperation under the Security Dilemma," 169. For Defensive Realist understandings of uncertainty, see Waltz, *Theory of International Politics*, 105; Charles L. Glaser, "Realists as Optimists: Cooperation as Self-Help," *International Security* 19, no. 3 (1994): 56; Joseph M. Grieco, "Understanding the Problem of International Cooperation: The Limits of Neoliberal Institutionalism and the Future of Realist Theory," in *Neorealism and Neoliberalism: The Contemporary Debate*, ed. David A. Baldwin (New York: Columbia University Press, 1993), 314; Daryl Press, *Calculating Credibility: How Leaders Assess Military Threats* (Ithaca, NY: Cornell University Press, 2005), 22.

130. Alexander Wendt, "Anarchy Is What States Make of It: The Social Construction of Power Politics," *International Organization* 46, no. 2 (March 1992): 391–425; Alexander Wendt, "Collective Identity Formation and the International State," *American Political Science Review* 88, no. 2 (June 1994): 384–96; Margaret E. Keck and Kathryn Sikkink, *Activists Beyond Borders: Advocacy Networks in International Politics* (Ithaca, NY: Cornell University Press, 1998); Finnemore and Sikkink, "International Norm Dynamics and Political Change," 887–917; Wendt, *Social Theory of International Politics*.

131. Alexander Wendt and Daniel Friedheim, "Hierarchy Under Anarchy: Informal Empire and the East German State," *Cambridge Studies in International Relations* 46, no. 1 (1996): 248–52; Krasner, *Sovereignty*, 50.

132. G. John Ikenberry and Charles A. Kupchan, "Socialization and Hegemonic Power," *International Organization* 44, no. 3 (June 1990): 285.

133. Ikenberry and Kupchan, "Socialization and Hegemonic Power," 315.
134. Alexander L. George and William E. Simons, *The Limits of Coercive Diplomacy* (Boulder, CO: Westview Press, 1994), chap. 1; Bruce Jentleson, "Coercive Diplomacy: Scope and Limits in the Contemporary World," *Stanley Foundation Policy Brief Analysis* (2006), 1–12.
135. Jentleson, "Coercive Diplomacy," 7.
136. Downes, "Causes of Foreign Imposed Regime Change in Interstate Wars."
137. For more on these dynamics, see Downes and O'Rourke, "You Can't Always Get What You Want: Why Foreign-Imposed Regime Change Seldom Improves Interstate Relations," 43–89.
138. Analogous to James D. Fearon, "Domestic Political Audiences and the Escalation of International Disputes," *American Political Science Review* 88, no. 3 (1994); Melissa Willard-Foster, "A Peace Too Costly to Keep: Why Major Powers Overthrow Foreign Governments" (paper prepared for the American Political Science Association 2012 Annual Meeting, New Orleans, LA, September 2012) makes this argument most explicitly.
139. Mearsheimer, *Tragedy of Great Power Politics*.
140. Carrubba, Reiter, and Wolford, "Information, Commitment, and War," 556–79.
141. Downes, "Causes of Foreign Imposed Regime Change in Interstate Wars"; Owen, *Clash of Ideas in World Politics*; Willard-Foster, "A Peace Too Costly to Keep"; Downes and Monten, "Forced to be Free?"
142. Bruce Bueno De Mesquita, James D. Morrow, Randolph M. Siverson, and Alastair Smith, "An Institutional Explanation of the Democratic Peace," *American Political Science Review* 93, no. 4 (1999): 791–807, make this point about democratic regimes.
143. Robert Powell, "War as a Commitment Problem," *International Organization* 60, no. 1 (2006): 189.
144. Minxin Pei and Sara Kasper, *Lessons from the Past: The American Record on Nation Building*, vol. 24. (Washington, DC: Carnegie Endowment for International Peace, 2003); Eva Bellin, "The Iraqi Intervention and Democracy in Comparative Historical Perspective," *Political Science Quarterly* 119, no. 4 (2004): 595–608; Andrew J. Enterline and J. Michael Greig, "Perfect Storms? Political Instability in Imposed Polities and the Futures of Iraq and Afghanistan," *Journal of Conflict Resolution* 52, no. 6 (2008): 880–915; Downes, "Causes of Foreign Imposed Regime Change in Interstate Wars."
145. Reisman, "Why Regime Change Is (Almost Always) a Bad Idea," 524. Similarly, Andrew Enterline and Michael Greig looked at ninety-four cases of "foreign-imposed polities" between 1816 and 1994. They found that the "key to the long-term stability . . . is the neutralization of domestic political challenges early in an imposed polity's existence." Enterline and Greig, "Perfect Storms?," 33. Likewise, Downes found that regime changes that restored a recently deposed leader were less likely to spark a civil war for precisely these reasons. Alexander Downes, "Catastrophic Success: Foreign-imposed Regime Change and Civil War" (paper prepared for delivery at the 2010 Annual Meeting of the American Political Science Association, Washington, DC, September 2–5, 2010), 10.
146. Grow, *U.S. Presidents and Latin American Interventions*, 193.
147. James F. Dobbins, "America's Role in Nation-Building: From Germany to Iraq," *Survival* 45, no. 4 (December 1, 2003): 104.
148. Pei and Kasper, *Lessons from the Past*; David M. Edelstein, *Occupational Hazards: Success and Failure in Military Occupation* (Ithaca, NY: Cornell University Press, 2011); Enterline and Greig, "Perfect Storms?"

3. Conduct

1. James Callanan, *Covert Action in the Cold War: US Policy, Intelligence and CIA Operations* (New York: IB Tauris, 2009); Austin Carson, "Secrecy, Acknowledgement and War Escalation" (PhD diss., Ohio State University, 2013); Andrew Bowen, "Two Step Intervention: Covert Action and Audience Costs during the Soviet Invasion of Afghanistan" (unpublished manuscript, Boston College, 2016).

2. "US Policy Toward the Soviet Satellite States in Eastern Europe," Policy Planning Staff Paper 59, August 25, 1949, *Foreign Relations of the United States (FRUS), 1949, Vol. V, Eastern Europe; The Soviet Union*, ed. William Z. Slany and Rogers P. Churchill (Washington, DC: US Government Printing Office [GPO], 1975), Doc. 10.

3. National Security Council Directive 174, December 11, 1953, "Statement of Policy Proposed by the National Security Council on United States Policy toward the Soviet Satellites in Eastern Europe," *FRUS, 1949, Vol. V, Eastern Europe; The Soviet Union*, Doc. 51.

4. National Security Council Directive 174, "Statement of Policy."

5. Stephen Kinzer, *All the Shah's Men: An American Coup and the Roots of Middle East Terror* (Hoboken, NJ: John Wiley and Sons, 2008), 210. In 1953 dollars, the costs were between $100,000 and $20 million.

6. Immerman estimates these costs at $5–7 million. Richard H. Immerman, *The CIA in Guatemala: The Policy of Foreign Intervention* (Austin, TX: University of Texas Press, 1982), 138. The Central Intelligence Agency puts these costs at $3 million. Central Intelligence Agency, May 12, 1975, "CIA's Role in the Overthrow of Arbenz," *FRUS, 1952–1954, Guatemala*, ed. Susan Holly and David S. Patterson (Washington, DC: GPO, 2003), Doc. 287. The $25–56 million figure is for $3–7 million in 1954 dollars.

7. That included $48.3 million to create propaganda, $18.25 million to disseminate that propaganda, $4.8 million to support private sector groups, and $1 million for the coup. Church Committee, *Covert Action in Chile, 1963–1973* (Washington, DC: US GPO, 1975), 95. In 1973 dollars, the costs were $13.4 million for the entire operation: $9 million on propaganda, $3.4 million to dissemination that propaganda, $900,000 to support private sector groups, and $200,000 for the military coup.

8. Department of State, June 29, 1971, "Memorandum for the 40 Committee, Subject: Bolivia," *FRUS, 1969–1976, Vol. E-10, Documents on American Republics, 1969–1972*, ed. Douglas Kraft and James Siekmeier (Washington, DC: US GPO, 2009), Doc. 104; Department of State, July 9, 1971, "Backchannel Message From the Ambassador in Bolivia (Siracusa) to the Assistant Secretary of State for Intern-American Affairs (Meyer), La Paz," *FRUS, 1969–1976, Vol. E-10, Documents on American Republics, 1969–1972*, Doc. 106; National Security Council, August 19, 1971, "Memorandum for Dr. Kissinger from Arnold Nachmanoff, Subject: Bolivia," *FRUS, 1961–1963, Vol. XII, American Republics*, ed. Edward C. Keefer, Harriet Dashiell Schwar, W. Taylor Fain III (Washington, DC: US GPO, 1996), Doc. 107. This is $410,000 in 1971 dollars.

9. Quoted in William Daugherty, *Executive Secrets: Covert Action and the Presidency* (Lexington: University Press of Kentucky, 2006), 175. This is $16 million in 1975 dollars.

10. For Grenada, see "Operation Urgent Fury: The 1983 U.S. Intervention in Grenada—Joseph Washecheck," Project on National Security, accessed September 25, 2017, http://www.pnsr.org/?p=842. This is $134.4 million in 1983 dollars. For Panama, see Joseph E. Kelley, *Panama: Costs of the US Invasion of Panama* (Washington, DC: US General Accounting Office, September 1990), 3. This is $163.6 million in 1989 dollars.

11. Jim Rasenberger, *The Brilliant Disaster: JFK, Castro, and America's Doomed Invasion of Cuba's Bay of Pigs* (New York: Simon and Schuster, 2011), xv. This is $46 million in 1960 dollars.

12. Assistant Secretary of Defense, October 24, 1962, "Subject: Financing and Reporting Increased Costs Associated with Current Activities Incident to Cuba," National Security Archive, Washington, DC (hereafter cited as NSA), https://nsarchive2.gwu.edu//NSAEBB/NSAEBB397/docs/Doc%2042a%20CMC%20costs%20doc%20rg%20330%20Sec%20Def%20CMC%20bx%205%20cuba%20381%20(case%20date%202%20Jan%2063)%20January%201963%20(2).pdf; Assistant Secretary of Defense, January 24, 1963, "Memorandum for the Secretary of Defense, Subject: Increased Costs Associated with Activities Incident to Cuba," NSA, https://nsarchive2.gwu.edu/NSAEBB/NSAEBB397/. The $1.3 billion figure is $165,678,738 in 1962 dollars.

13. Joint Chiefs of Staff, "Memorandum for the President, Subject: Evaluation of the Effects on US Operations Plans of Soviet Army Equipment Introduced into Cuba," November 2, 1962, NSA, https://nsarchive2.gwu.edu/NSAEBB/NSAEBB397/docs/doc%2022%2011-2-62%20memo%20to%20JFK%20re%20invasion%20plans.pdf.

14. Peter L. Bergen, *Holy War, Inc.: Inside the Secret World of Osama Bin Laden* (London: Weidenfeld & Nicolson, 2001), 68. This is $3 billion in 1985 dollars.

15. "Cost of National Security Counters," National Priorities Project, Institute for Policy Studies, accessed September 25, 2017, https://www.nationalpriorities.org/cost-of/resources /notes-and-sources/. This is $20.8 billion in 2001 dollars. Richard B. Andres, Craig Wills, and Thomas E. Griffith. "Winning with Allies: The Strategic Value of the Afghan Model," *International Security* 30, no. 3 (January 1, 2006): 124–60.

16. Powell quoted in Bob Woodward, *Plan of Attack: The Definitive Account of the Decision to Invade Iraq* (New York: Simon & Schuster, 2004), 150. On the ethical obligations of occupying states, see Noah Feldman, *What We Owe Iraq: War and the Ethics of Nation Building* (Princeton, NJ: Princeton University Press, 2009).

17. George Crile, *Charlie Wilson's War* (New York: Grove, 2003), 519.

18. National Priorities Project. The $763 billion number reflects the total cost of the war through September 25, 2017, minus the total cost of the war in the year 2001.

19. Bilmes estimated the total costs of the wars in Afghanistan and Iraq to reach between $4 and $6 trillion dollars. Linda J. Bilmes, "The Financial Legacy of Iraq and Afghanistan: How Wartime Spending Decisions Will Constrain Future National Security Budgets," Harvard Kennedy School of Government Faculty Research Working Paper Series RWP13-006, March 2013.

20. One could object that the United States faces higher reputational costs as a democracy than other regime types. However, there are reasons to doubt that assumption. Every regime has an incentive not to undermine the legitimacy of its political institutions and ideology. In the context of the Cold War, the Soviet Union frequently used covert conduct when targeting fellow communist states and when trying to support communist regimes in the third world. On this point, see Tanisha M. Fazal, *State Death: The Politics and Geography of Conquest, Occupation, and Annexation* (Princeton, NJ: Princeton University Press, 2007), 52.

21. Bruce Russett, *Grasping the Democratic Peace: Principles for a Post–Cold War World* (Princeton, NJ: Princeton University Press, 1994), 123.

22. Jaechun Kim, "Democratic Peace and Covert War: A Case Study of the US Covert War in Chile," *Journal of International and Area Studies* (2005): 25–47; Alexander B. Downes and Mary Lauren Lilley, "Overt Peace, Covert War? Covert Intervention and the Democratic Peace," *Security Studies* 19, no. 2 (2010): 266–306.

23. William P. Rogers and Henry Kissinger, "Telecon Secretary Rogers," September 14, 1970, NSA, 2, https://nsarchive2.gwu.edu/NSAEBB/NSAEBB255/19700912-1215-Rogers3.pdf.

24. Kennan quoted in Tarak Barkawi and Mark Laffey, *Democracy, Liberalism, and War: Rethinking the Democratic Peace Debate* (Boulder, CO: Lynne Rienner, 2001), 115.

25. John J. Mearsheimer, *Why Leaders Lie: The Truth About Lying in International Politics* (New York: Oxford University Press, 2011), 6.

26. Mearsheimer, *Why Leaders Lie*, 69.

27. David N. Gibbs "Secrecy and International Relations," *Journal of Peace Research* 32, no. 2 (1995): 222.

28. Dulles as quoted by Stephen Ambrose, *Ike's Spies: Eisenhower and the Espionage Establishment* (New York: Anchor Books, 1981), 244.

29. Dulles as quoted by John Prados, *The President's Secret Wars: CIA and Pentagon Secret Operations since World War II* (New York: William Morrow, 1986), 139.

30. Central Intelligence Agency, December 1979, "Official History of the Bay of Pigs Operation: Volume III, Evolution of CIA's Anti-Castro Policies, 1959-January 1961," National Archives and Records Administration, College Park, MD (hereafter cited as NARA), iii–iv, https://www.archives.gov/files/research/jfk/releases/104-10301-10004.pdf.

31. Richard Bissell quoted in Charles Lathrop, *The Literary Spy* (New Haven, CT: Yale University Press, 2008), 33.

32. Church Committee, *Alleged Assassination Plots Involving Foreign Leaders* (Washington, DC: US GPO, 1975), 277.

33. Church Committee, *Final Report of the Senate Select Committee to Study Governmental Operations with Respect to Intelligence Activities* (Washington, DC: US GPO, 1976).

34. On the marketplace of ideas, see Jack Snyder, *Myths of Empire: Domestic Politics and International Ambition* (Ithaca, NY: Cornell University Press, 2013), 31–55; Stephen Van Evera, *Causes of War: Power and the Roots of Conflict* (Ithaca, NY: Cornell University Press, 2013); Chaim

Kaufmann, "Threat Inflation and the Failure of the Marketplace of Ideas: The Selling of the Iraq War," *International Security* 29, no. 1 (2004): 5–48; Dan Reiter, "Democracy, Deception, and Entry into War," *Security Studies* 21, no. 4 (October 1, 2012): 594–623.

35. Stephen Van Evera, "Why States Believe Foolish Ideas," September 6, 2004, http://dspace.mit.edu/handle/1721.1/5533.

36. Joshua Rovner, *Fixing the Facts: National Security and the Politics of Intelligence* (Ithaca, NY: Cornell University Press, 2011), 29.

37. Church Committee, *Alleged Assassination Plots*, 77.

38. Commission on Organization of the Executive Branch of Government (1949) quoted in Anthony Stuart Farson and Mark Phythian, *Commissions of Inquiry and National Security: Comparative Approaches* (Santa Barbara, CA: ABC-CLIO, 2011), 150.

39. See appendix 4 online for a description of these committees.

40. Tim Weiner, *Legacy of Ashes: The History of the CIA* (New York: Anchor, 2008), 341. See also Brendan O'Malley and Ian Craig, *The Cyprus Conspiracy: America, Espionage and the Turkish Invasion* (New York: IB Tauris, 2001), 164.

41. Allen E. Goodman, Bruce D. Berkowitz, and the Twentieth Century Fund, *The Need to Know: The Report of the Twentieth Century Fund Task Force on Covert Action and American Democracy* (New York: Century Foundation Press, 1992), 10.

42. Helms quoted in Rhodri Jeffreys-Jones, *The CIA and American Democracy* (New Haven, CT: Yale University Press, 1991), 93.

43. Cline quoted in Ambrose, *Ike's Spies*, 251.

44. Jeffreys-Jones, *The CIA and American Democracy*, 82.

45. Edward N. Luttwak, *Coup d'état: A Practical Handbook* (Cambridge, MA: Harvard University Press, 1979); James T. Quinlivan, "Coup-Proofing: Its Practice and Consequences in the Middle East," *International Security* 24, no. 2 (October 1, 1999): 131–65; Stephen T. Hosmer, *Operations Against Enemy Leaders* (Santa Monica, CA: RAND Corp., 2001); Samuel E. Finer and Jay Stanley, *The Man on Horseback: The Role of the Military in Politics* (New Brunswick, NJ: Transaction, 2002); Ken Connor and David Hebditch, *How to Stage a Military Coup: From Planning to Execution* (New York: Skyhorse, 2009).

46. Quinlivan, "Coup-Proofing," 131–65.

47. Caitlin Talmadge, *The Dictator's Army: Battlefield Effectiveness in Authoritarian Regimes* (Ithaca, NY: Cornell University Press, 2015), 2.

48. Covert Operations Study Group quoted in Weiner, *Legacy of Ashes*, 340.

49. Roosevelt quoted in Kinzer, *All the Shah's Men*, 172.

50. First quotation from Weiner, *Legacy of Ashes*, 116. Second quotation from Martha L. Cottam, *Images and Intervention: U.S. Policies in Latin America* (Pittsburgh, PA: University of Pittsburgh Press, 1994), 43.

51. Eisenhower quoted in Evans Thomas, *The Very Best Men: Four Men Who Dared; The Early Years of the CIA* (New York: Touchstone, 1995), 120.

52. McNamara quoted Howard Jones, *The Bay of Pigs* (New York: Oxford University Press, 2010), 83.

53. Central Intelligence Agency, September 15, 1970, Richard Helms's Notes on Meeting with the President of Chile, NSA, https://nsarchive2.gwu.edu/NSAEBB/NSAEBB437/docs/Doc%203%20-%20Handwritten%20instructions%20from%20Nixon%20Sep%2015%201970.pdf.

54. For more on what types of states constitute a military threat, see Stephen M. Walt, *The Origins of Alliance* (Ithaca, NY: Cornell University Press, 1990).

55. Robert J. Art, *A Grand Strategy for America* (Ithaca, NY: Cornell University Press, 2004), chap. 2.

56. Austin Carson and Keren Yarhi-Milo discuss how states can use covert interventions to signal their intentions to adversaries and allies. Austin Carson and Keren Yarhi-Milo, "Covert Communication: The Intelligibility and Credibility of Signaling in Secret," *Security Studies* 26, no. 1 (2017): 124–56. I agree with their basic assessment about the potential for covert signaling. However, I believe that overt interventions send a stronger signal of resolve than covert interventions. On that point, see Lindsey A. O'Rourke, "H-Diplo/ISSF Article Review of Austin Carson and Keren Yarhi-Milo," *H-Diplo, International Security Studies Forum 76*, 2017.

57. Willard-Foster, "A Peace Too Costly to Keep," 4. Great powers identified by the Correlates of War data set.

58. Kenneth Waltz, *Theory of International Politics* (Boston: Addison-Wesley, 1979); Stephen M. Walt, "Alliance Formation and the Balance of World Power," *International Security* 9, no. 4 (1985): 3–43; Walt, *Origins of Alliance*; Randall L. Schweller, "Neorealism's Status-quo Bias: What Security Dilemma?," *Security Studies* 5, no. 3 (March 1, 1996): 90–121; Robert A. Pape, "Soft Balancing Against the United States," *International Security* 30, no. 1 (July 1, 2005): 7–45.

59. Robert Jervis, "Deterrence Theory Revisited," *World Politics* 31, no. 2 (1979): 289–324; Robert Powell, "Nuclear Deterrence Theory, Nuclear Deterrence, and National Missile Defense," *International Security* 27, no. 4 (2003): 86–118.

60. Jonathan Mercer, *Reputation and International Politics* (Ithaca, NY: Cornell University Press, 1996), 1–2.

61. Thomas C. Schelling, *Arms and Influence: With a New Preface and Afterword* (New Haven, CT: Yale University Press, 2008), 55–56. See also Press's (2005) discussion of past-action theory: Daryl Grayson Press, *Calculating Credibility: How Leaders Assess Military Threats* (Ithaca, NY: Cornell University Press, 2005).

62. John D. Orme, "Credibility and Deterrence," in *Deterrence, Reputation and Cold-War Cycles* (Basingstoke, UK: Palgrave Macmillan, 1992), 1–11; Paul Huth, Christopher Gelpi, and D. Scott Bennett, "The Escalation of Great Power Militarized Disputes: Testing Rational Deterrence Theory and Structural Realism," *American Political Science Review* 87, no. 3 (September 1993): 609–23.

63. Jerome Slater, "Dominos in Central America: Will They Fall? Does It Matter?," *International Security* 12, no. 2 (1987): 105–34.

64. Nixon quoted by Mercer, *Reputation and International Politics*, 2.

65. Kissinger quoted by Howard Zinn, *A People's History of the United States: 1492–Present* (New York: Routledge, 2015), 551.

66. Reagan quoted by Mercer, *Reputation and International Politics*, 2.

67. Richard Haass, *Intervention: The Use of American Military Force in the Post–Cold War World* (Washington, DC: Carnegie Endowment for International Peace, 1999), 70.

68. Richard Nixon, *1999: Victory without War* (New York: Simon and Schuster, 2013), 109.

69. John J. Mearsheimer, *Conventional Deterrence* (Ithaca, NY: Cornell University Press, 1985), 63–66. This argument builds on his theory that deterrence is more likely to hold when a potential attacker has an attrition strategy and is less likely to hold when they have a blitzkrieg strategy. (A "limited aims strategy" is not possible given the objective of regime change.)

70. Brett Ashley Leeds, "Do Alliances Deter Aggression? The Influence of Military Alliances on the Initiation of Militarized Interstate Disputes," *American Journal of Political Science* 47, no. 3 (July 1, 2003): 427–39.

71. Mearsheimer, *Conventional Deterrence*, 35–43. Other basic military principles for a clever strategy include having a clear and obtainable objective, seizing the initiative, exploiting maneuver to mass combat power at decisive points, unifying command, and simplifying plans. On this, see US Army Field Manual 100–5 (Washington, DC: Department of the Army, 1993), chap. 2.

72. Peter Paret, Gordon A. Craig, and Felix Gilbert, *Makers of Modern Strategy from Machiavelli to the Nuclear Age* (Princeton, NJ: Princeton University Press, 1986), chap. 5.

73. Mearsheimer, *Conventional Deterrence*.

74. On Iraq, see Bruce Nussbaum, "It's Time to Shelve the Rumsfeld Doctrine," *BusinessWeek*, April 26, 2004. On the RMA's potential overuse see *Strategy and the Revolution in Military Affairs: From Theory to Policy* (Collingdale, PA: Diane, 1995), 29.

75. During the Cold War, American policymakers split on the question of whether public support was necessary. Some officials, like Secretary of Defense Caspar Weinberger, explicitly cited it as a prerequisite for intervention. Others, like Colin Powell, George Shultz, and George H. W. Bush, did not include it among their prerequisites. For the purposes here, however, the important point is that both sides would agree that public support decreases the costs of intervention, which makes overt intervention more likely.

76. Benjamin I. Page and Robert Y. Shapiro, *The Rational Public: Fifty Years of Trends in Americans' Policy Preferences* (Chicago: University of Chicago Press, 2010); H. W. Brands, "Decisions on American Armed Intervention: Lebanon, Dominican Republic, and Grenada," *Political Science Quarterly* 102, no. 4 (1987): 607–24; Kaufmann, "Threat Inflation."

77. Brands, "American Armed Intervention." This coincides with Downes's observation that operations to reinstall recently deposed leaders were three times less likely to lead to civil war than missions installing a new leader. Alexander Downes, "Catastrophic Success: Foreign-imposed Regime Change and Civil War" (paper prepared for delivery at the 2010 Annual Meeting of the American Political Science Association, Washington, DC, September 2–5, 2010).

78. Department of State, July 14, 1958, Memorandum from the Record of a Meeting of the Department of State, *FRUS, 1958–1960, Vol. XI, Lebanon and Jordan*, ed. Louis J. Smith (Washington, DC: US GPO, 1992), Doc. 123.

79. Central Intelligence Agency, "A Study of Assassination," NSA, https://nsarchive2.gwu.edu/NSAEBB/NSAEBB4/ciaguat2.html.

80. Central Intelligence Agency, "A Study of Assassination."

81. Central Intelligence Agency, "A Study of Assassination."

82. For instance, one section of the working group report on the intervention, titled "Elimination of Key Figures," made the following recommendation: "In order to facilitate the action of liberative forces, reduce the capabilities of the Syrian regime to organize and direct its military actions, to hold losses and destruction to a minimum, and to bring about the desired results in the shortest possible time, a special effort should be made to eliminate certain key individuals. Their removal should be accomplished early in the course of the uprising and intervention and in the light of circumstances existing at the time. Those who should be eliminated are Sarraj, Bizri, and Khalid Bakdash." Quoted in Matthew Jones, "The 'Preferred Plan': The Anglo-American Working Group Report on Covert Action in Syria, 1957," *Intelligence and National Security* 19, no. 3 (September 1, 2004): 408.

83. Church Committee, *Alleged Assassination Plots*, "Part III. Assassination Planning and the Plots, A. Congo," 3–70.

84. Church Committee, *Alleged Assassination Plots*, "Part III. Assassination Planning and the Plots, B. Cuba," 71–180.

85. See, for example, Church Committee, *Alleged Assassination Plots*, "Introduction and Summary," footnote on page 4; Church Committee, *Alleged Assassination Plots*, "Institutionalizing Assassination: The 'Executive Action' Capability," footnote on page 181.

86. "Chile Court Confirms Salvador Allende Committed Suicide," *BBC News*, September 12, 2012, http://www.bbc.com/news/world-latin-america-19567445.

87. Church Committee, *Covert Action in Chile, 1963–1973, Staff Report on the Select Committee to Study Governmental Operations with Respect to Intelligence Activities, United States Senate* (Washington, DC: US GOP, 1975).

88. Peter Kornbluh, *The Pinochet File: A Declassified Dossier on Atrocity and Accountability* (New York: New Press, 2013). For a more skeptical view, see Kristian Gustafson, *Hostile Intent: US Covert Operations in Chile, 1964–1974* (Washington, DC: Potomac Books, 2007).

89. Henry Kissinger and Richard Nixon, "TelCon: September 16, 1973 (Home) 11:50, Mr. Kissinger/The President," NSA, https://nsarchive2.gwu.edu/NSAEBB/NSAEBB123/Box%2022,%20File%203,%20Telcon,%209-16-73%2011,50%20Mr.%20Kissinger-The%20Pres%202.pdf.

90. Gerald R. Ford, "Exec. Order 11905," 41 Fed. Reg. 7703, February 18, 1976, http://www.presidency.ucsb.edu/ws/?pid=59348.

91. Jimmy Carter, January 24, 1978, "Executive Order 12063—United States Court of Military Appeals Nominating Commission," The American Presidency Project, http://www.presidency.ucsb.edu/ws/?pid=30904; "Executive Order 12333," December 4, 1981, Federal Register, National Archives, https://www.archives.gov/federal-register/codification/executive-order/12333.html.

92. Luttwak, *Coup d'état*, 12.

93. See "Definitions and Data" section in chapter 1 for more on how I code these operations.

94. For an overview of these policies, see Joshua Muravchik, *Exporting Democracy: Fulfilling America's Destiny* (Washington, DC: American Enterprise Institute, 1992), chap. 13.

95. Ronald Reagan, June 8, 1982, "Address to the British Parliament," The History Place: Great Speeches Collection, http://www.historyplace.com/speeches/reagan-parliament.htm.

96. National Security Decision Directive 77, January 14, 1983, "Management of Public Diplomacy Relative to National Security," Ronald Reagan Library, Simi Valley, CA (hereafter cited as RRL).

97. Kate Geoghegan, "The Specter of Anarchy, the Hope of Transformation: The Role of Non-State Actors in the US Response to Soviet Reform and Disunion, 1981–1996" (PhD diss. for the University of Virginia, Department of History, December 2015).

98. Bernard Gwertzman, "Skeptics Pelt Shultz with Queries on Reagan's 'Project Democracy,'" *New York Times*, February 24, 1983; National Endowment for Democracy, "Statement of Principles and Objectives," accessed September 25, 2017, http://www.ned.org/about/statement-of-principles-and-objectives/.

99. National Endowment for Democracy, "Statement of Principles and Objectives."

100. National Endowment for Democracy, "Statement of Principles and Objectives."

101. National Endowment for Democracy, "Statement of Principles and Objectives"; Barbara Conry, "Loose Cannon: The National Endowment for Democracy," *CATO Foreign Policy Briefing* no. 27 (November 8, 1993); William Robinson, *Promoting Polyarchy: Globalization, US Intervention, and Hegemony* (Cambridge: Cambridge University Press, 1996); William Blum, *Rogue State: A Guide to the World's Only Superpower* (London: Zed Books, 2006). Two caveats are in order regarding the National Endowment for Democracy. First, I am only talking about the NED in the context of its relationship with the Reagan administration at the height of the Cold War. I am not claiming that the NED continues these same strategies today. To the contrary, as Sarah Bush's dissertation on the US democracy establishment finds, "Today's template of democracy assistance activities emphasizes technical programs that do not threaten the non-democratic regimes of the countries where the programs take place. That template contrasts with the more confrontational aid projects to dissidents, political parties, and trade unions that dominated the early era of democracy assistance in the 1980s." To show this, Bush categorized over 10,000 NED programs from its first report in 1985 to March 2013. She found that over 80 percent of the NED's programs in the 1980s were "confrontational," which she defined as "threatening the imminent survival of the incumbent regime in the host state." However, by 2013, the number of confrontational programs had dropped to less than 20 percent. Second, I do not argue that the NED's activities are illegal. Instead, I suggest that because of the NED's close relationship to the US government— particularly the NSC—it worked with the government several times during the 1980s to promote foreign democratic regime changes in a way that hid the government's role in these efforts. At the same time, however, the NED launched hundreds of programs throughout the world during this period, and I do not suggest that they were all US-backed regime changes. For this study, I only include cases where I found primary source US government data that the United States provided aid and assistance to the NED with the stated objective of bringing about regime change in that country. This conservative standard for inclusion likely underestimates the total number of cases. Sarah Bush, *The Taming of Democracy Assistance* (Philadelphia, PA: Temple University, 2011).

102. Memorandum from Alexander Haig to Reagan, "Strategy for Building Democracy in Communist and Non-Communist Countries," March 8, 1982, RRL.

103. Gershwin quoted in Blum, *Rogue State*, 239.

104. Quoted in Blum, 239.

105. Robinson, *Promoting Polyarchy*; Daugherty, *Executive Secrets*, 201–3; John Prados, *Safe for Democracy: The Secret Wars of the CIA* (Lanham, MD: Rowman & Littlefield, 2006), 505; Blum, *Rogue State*; Gregory F. Domber, *Empowering Revolution: America, Poland, and the End of the Cold War* (Chapel Hill: University of North Carolina Press, 2014). During the latter half of the 1980s, the NED was also extensively involved in the Soviet Union. However, I have decided not to code these programs as an instance of covert regime change because US behavior within the USSR appears to be geared toward maintaining pressure on Gorbachev to continue his liberal-

izing policies, rather than attempt to remove Gorbachev from power. For an overview of these programs, see Geoghegan, *Specter of Anarchy*.

106. Robinson, *Promoting Polyarchy*.

107. Robinson, 107.

108. National Security Decision Directive 101, "United States Strategy toward Liberia," September 2, 1983, RRL.

109. Robinson, *Promoting Polyarchy*, 222.

110. Robinson places this figure in the tens of millions of dollars. Robinson, *Promoting Polyarchy*, 319–26. Domber places it at $9,081,084. Domber, *Empowering Revolution*, 288.

111. Robinson, *Promoting Polyarchy*, 124–38.

112. Robinson, 111.

113. Philip Taubman, "Latin Vote: Symbol of Assertiveness, News Analysis," *New York Times*, May 5, 1983.

114. This holds true even in cases where the intervener spends a comparatively large amount on the operation—such as the $6 billion that the United States spent supporting the Mujahedeen during the 1980s. Although the costs of intervention were far higher in this case than average, they still were far lower than they would have been had the United States overtly intervened.

115. John J. Mearsheimer, *Why Leaders Lie: The Truth About Lying in International Politics* (New York: Oxford University Press, 2010), chap. 5; David N, Gibbs, "Secrecy and International Relations," *Journal of Peace Research* 32, no. 2 (May 1995): 213–28.

116. Richard Sobel, "A Report: Public Opinion About United States Intervention in El Salvador and Nicaragua," *Public Opinion Quarterly* 53, no. 1 (1989): 114–28.

117. Sobel, "A Report."

118. Gibbs "Secrecy and International Relations," 213–28.

119. Public Law 98–148, November 7, 1973, "Joint Resolution Concerning the War Powers of Congress and the President," US Government Publishing Office, Washington, DC, https://www.gpo.gov/fdsys/pkg/STATUTE-87/pdf/STATUTE-87-Pg555.pdf.

120. Christopher Felix, *A Short Course in the Secret War* (Lanham, MD: Rowman & Littlefield, 2001), 28.

121. Carson, *Secrecy, Acknowledgement and War Escalation*.

122. M. Petersen, M., "Maybe You Had to Be There: The SIGINT on Thirteen Soviet Shootdowns of US Reconnaissance Aircraft," undated, accessed September 25, 2017, Federation of American Scientists, https://fas.org/irp/nsa/maybe_you.pdf.

123. Carson, *Secrecy, Acknowledgement and War Escalation*.

124. Bruce D. Berkowitz and Allan E. Goodman. "The Logic of Covert Action," *National Interest*, no. 51 (1998): 38–46.

125. Austin Carson, "Russians over the Yalu: Deception and Escalation in the Korean War" (paper presented at the Research in Project Workshop, George Washington University, Washington, DC, 2013).

4. Consequences

1. Kenneth Andrade and Dale Conboy, *Spies and Commandos: How America Lost the Secret War in North Vietnam* (Lawrence: University Press of Kansas, 2000).

2. Church Committee, "Final Report of the Senate Select Committee to Study Governmental Operations with Respect to Intelligence Activities" (Washington, DC: US Government Printing Office [GPO], 1976), 256–57.

3. Church Committee, "Final Report of the Senate Select Committee," 281.

4. Peter L. Bergen, *Holy War, Inc. Inside the Secret World of Osama Bin Laden* (London: Weidenfeld & Nicolson, 2001), 68. This is $3 billion in 1985 dollars.

5. Reed Brody, "Inside a Dictator's Secret Police," *Foreign Policy*, March 9, 2010, http://www.foreignpolicy.com/articles/2010/03/08/inside_a_dictators_secret_police.

6. This excludes an aborted coup attempt against the democratic government in Syria in 1955 and the coup plotting against Sukarno's semi-democratic regime.

7. Caitlin Talmadge, *The Dictator's Army: Battlefield Effectiveness in Authoritarian Regimes* (Ithaca, NY: Cornell University Press, 2015), 21.

8. Samuel P. Huntington, *Political Order in Changing Societies* (New Haven, CT: Yale University Press, 1968); Jennifer Gandhi and Adam Przeworski, "Authoritarian Institutions and the Survival of Autocrats," *Comparative Political Studies*, 50, no. 11 (November 2007): 1279–301; Jason Brownlee, *Authoritarianism in an Age of Democratization* (Cambridge: Cambridge University Press, 2007); Talmadge, *The Dictator's Army*.

9. William Robinson, *Promoting Polyarchy: Globalization, US Intervention, and Hegemony* (Cambridge: Cambridge University Press, 1996), 157.

10. For size of Solidarity membership in 1981, see Tom Buchanan, *Europe's Troubled Peace: 1945 to the Present* (West Sussex, UK: John Wiley & Sons, 2012), 210.

11. Samuel P. Huntington, *The Third Wave: Democratization in the Late Twentieth Century* (Norman: University of Oklahoma Press, 1993).

12. Robinson, *Promoting Polyarchy*; James M. Scott and Carie A. Steele. "Assisting Democrats or Resisting Dictators? The Nature and Impact of Democracy Support by the United States National Endowment for Democracy, 1990–99," *Democratization* 12, no. 4 (2005): 439–60; William Blum, *Rogue State: A Guide to the World's Only Superpower* (London: Zed Books, 2006).

13. Scott and Steele, "Assisting Democrats or Resisting Dictators," 452.

14. It is coded simply as 1 = yes and 0 = no.

15. For the analysis, data on each country during the year before the covert intervention were used in order to control for the fact that the mission itself may have had an independent effect on the target state. In the ten cases where the United States supported a secessionist movement in its bid for independence or backed indigenous anti-colonial forces that were seeking to oust their colonizer, the variables reflect the capabilities of the central government or colonial power that the subnational group was trying to overthrow. Data on the subnational groups either come from Wimmer and Min (2009) or were calculated for this study. See the online appendix for more information. Andreas Wimmer and Brian Min, "The Location and Purpose of Wars around the World: A New Global Dataset, 1816–2001," *International Interactions* 35, no. 4 (2009): 390–417.

16. Regime type is measured using the Polity IV dataset. The Polity2 variable ranks states on a 21-point scale based on the competitiveness of each country's political system, its methods of executive recruitment, and constraints on executive power. Each polity2 score is calculated by subtracting a state's autocracy score from its democratic score. The resulting scale ranks states from –10 (highly autocratic) to +10 (highly democratic). To transform the polity2 scores to purely positive values, 11 was added to each state's score, thus shifting the scale from 1 (highly autocratic) to 21 (highly democratic). Monty G. Marshall and Keith Jaggers, *Polity IV Project: Political Regime Characteristics and Transitions, 1800–2010*, accessed September 25, 2017, http://www.systemicpeace.org/polity/polity4.htm.

17. Material Capabilities is measured using the Composite Index of National Capability (CINC) score from the Correlates of War (v. 4.0) dataset. Each country's CINC score is a composite average of six different factors and reflects its share of the world's total: total population, urban population, iron and steel production, primary energy consumption, military expenditures, and military personnel. J. David Singer, Stuart Bremer, and John Stuckey, "Capability Distribution, Uncertainty, and Major Power War, 1820–1965," in *Peace, War, and Numbers*, ed. Bruce Russett (Beverly Hills, CA: Sage, 1972), 19–48.

18. Instability is also measured using the Polity IV dataset. It is a dichotomous variable coded as 1 if the country experienced more than a three-point change in its polity score within the preceding three years or if the country experienced a political transition or political anarchy during the year listed.

19. Economic Development is measured using gross domestic product (GDP) per capita from the Penn World Table 8.1. Robert C. Feenstra, Robert Inklaar, and Marcel P. Timmer, "The Next Generation of the Penn World Table," *American Economic Review* 105, no. 10 (2015): 3150–82.

20. Ongoing Civil War is a dichotomous variable from the Correlates of War (v. 4.0) dataset. It is coded as 1 if the target state was experiencing a civil war in the year listed. Meredith Reid Sarkees and Frank Wayman, *Resort to War: 1816–2007* (Washington, DC: CQ Press, 2010).

21. Ethno-linguistic fractionalization measures the level of ethnic, linguistic, and religious heterogeneity of the target state or the subnational group supported by the United States. Data come from Roeder (2001) or were calculated using the CIA World Factbook. Philip G. Roeder, "Ethnolinguistic Fractionalization Indices, 1961 and 1985," February 16, 2001, http://pages .ucsd.edu/~proeder/elf.htm. Variable imported from Alexander B. Downes and Jonathan Monten, "Forced to Be Free? Why Foreign-Imposed Regime Change Rarely Leads to Democratization," *International Security* 37, no. 4 (2013): 90–131, online replication data. Central Intelligence Agency, The World Factbook, accessed August 2015, https://www.cia.gov/library /publications/the-world-factbook/.

22. Alliance reflects whether the target state was an American or Soviet ally. Data comes from the Correlates of War Formal Alliance dataset (v. 4.0). Douglas M. Gibler, *International Military Alliances, 1648–2008* (Washington, DC: CQ Press, 2009).

23. Dummy variables have been included for each of the five types of covert tactics used by the United States during the Cold War: assassination, coups, supporting dissidents, trying to influence elections, and trying to promote a democratic revolution in an authoritarian state.

24. The two most common ways to model a binary outcome are probit and logit analyses. Probit regression assumes a normal distribution of errors, whereas logit assumes a standard distribution of errors. Probit results are reported here; however, I also ran identical analyses of all the models in this book, using a logit regression, with similar results. See online appendix for more details.

25. Alliance membership was calculated using data from the Correlates of War Formal Alliance dataset and Stephen Walt's *Origins of Alliances*; all the countries in the dataset were coded as a Soviet ally, nonaligned state, or American ally at the time of the US intervention. I used both sources to assemble my alliance data because the correlates of war (COW) dataset only includes major formal alliances. Walt's data, by contrast, more accurately captures Cold War dynamics by including informal alliances. Stephen M. Walt, *The Origins of Alliances* (Ithaca, NY: Cornell University Press, 1990).

26. One potential drawback to the Pearson's chi-square test is that it assumes asymptotic approximation (i.e., that the approximation will become exact as the sample size approaches infinity). Because my sample size is small, however, it is difficult to say whether this assumption holds. As such, I also conducted a Fisher's Exact Test on the contingency table, which yields a probability of 0.00003. This strongly confirms the Chi Square test on the success of covert regime changes by Cold War alliance.

27. Memorandum from Robert P. Joyce of the Policy Planning Staff to the Deputy Under Secretary (Matthews), December 31, 1952, "Subject: [Redacted] Activities Directed against Poland," *Foreign Relations of the United States (FRUS), 1950–1955, Vol. IV, The Intelligence Community, 1950–1955*, ed. Douglas Keane and Michael Warner (Washington, DC: US GPO, 2007), Doc. 142.

28. Calculated using COW data. See replication materials for a full discussion.

29. However, they note that there was an additional spike in the success rate starting in 2003, which is beyond the time scope of my study. See Jonathan M. Powell and Clayton L. Thyne, "Global Instances of Coups from 1950 to 2010: A New Dataset," *Journal of Peace Research* 48, no. 2 (2011): 256.

30. The argument put forth in this section mirror arguments that I make with Alexander Downes in Alexander B. Downes and Lindsey A. O'Rourke, "You Can't Always Get What You Want: Why Foreign-Imposed Regime Change Seldom Improves Interstate Relations," *International Security* 41, no. 2 (2016): 43–89.

31. Glenn Palmer et al., "The MID4 Dataset, 2002–2010: Procedures, Coding Rules and Description," *Conflict Management and Peace Science* 32, no. 2 (2015): 222–42.

32. Daniel M. Jones, Stuart A. Bremer, and J. David Singer. "Militarized Interstate Disputes, 1816–1992: Rationale, Coding Rules, and Empirical Patterns," *Conflict Management and Peace Science* 15, no. 2 (1996): 163.

33. Michael Poznansky, Alexander Downes, and Lindsey O'Rourke, "Correspondence: Friends, Foes, and Foreign-Imposed Regime Change," *International Security* 42, no. 2 (Fall 2017): 191–95.

34. For examples of similar studies using matching, see Jason Lyall, "Does Indiscriminate Violence Incite Insurgent Attacks? Evidence from Chechnya," *Journal of Conflict Resolution* 53, no. 3 (2009): 331–62; Michael J. Gilligan, and Ernest J. Sergenti, "Do UN Interventions Cause Peace? Using Matching to Improve Causal Inference," *Quarterly Journal of Political Science* 3, no. 2 (2008): 89–122; Downes and Monten, "Forced to Be Free."

35. Daniel E. Ho, Kosuke Imai, Gary King, and Elizabeth A. Stuart, "Matching as Nonparametric Preprocessing for Reducing Model Dependence in Parametric Causal Inference," *Political Analysis* 15, no. 3 (2007): 216.

36. Daniel Ho, Kosuke Imai, Gary King, and Elizabeth Stuart, "MatchIt: Nonparametric Preprocessing for Parametric Casual Inference," *Journal of Statistical Software*, 48, no 2 (2011): 1–28, for a description of this program.

37. Downes and O'Rourke, "You Can't Always Get What You Want."

38. Each of these models employed the same matching techniques and control variables as the models investigating Militarized Interstate Disputes. United Nations voting behavior variable is from Anton Strezhnev, Erik Voeten, and Michael Bailey, "Estimating Dynamic State Preferences from United Nations Voting Data," IQSS Dataverse Network, 2013, https://papers .ssrn.com/sol3/papers.cfm?abstract_id=2330913. Foreign Policy Portfolio Similarity is from Frank M. Häge, "Choice or Circumstance? Adjusting Measures of Foreign Policy Similarity for Chance Agreement, *Political Analysis* 19, no. 3 (2011): 287–305.

39. Joshua Muravchik, *Exporting Democracy: Fulfilling America's Destiny* (Washington, DC: American Enterprise Institute, 1992); Charles Krauthammer, "Democratic Realism. An American Foreign Policy for a Unipolar World" (lecture delivered at AEI, Washington, DC, February 10, 2004); Condoleezza Rice, "The Promise of Democratic Peace," *Washington Post*, December 11, 2005; Susan B. Epstein, Nina M. Serafino, and Francis T. Miko, "Democracy Promotion: Cornerstone of U.S. Foreign Policy," Report for Congress, Order Code RL34296 (Washington, DC: Congressional Research Service, December 26, 2007); Tony Smith, *America's Mission: The United States and the Worldwide Struggle for Democracy* (Princeton, NJ: Princeton University Press, 2012).

40. Eva Bellin, "The Iraqi Intervention and Democracy in Comparative Historical Perspective," *Political Science Quarterly* 119, no. 4 (2004): 595–608; Nils Petter Gleditsch, Lene Siljeholm Christiansen, and Håvard Hegre, "Democratic Jihad? Military Intervention and Democracy" (paper prepared for the Workshop on "Resources, Governance Structures, and Civil War," European Consortium for Political Research [ECPR] Joint Sessions of Workshops, Uppsala, Sweden. April 13–18, 2004); Arthur A. Goldsmith, "Making the World Is Safe for Partial Democracy? Questioning the Premises of Democracy Promotion," *International Security* 33, no. 2 (2008): 120–47.

41. James Meernik, "United States Military Intervention and the Promotion of Democracy," *Journal of Peace Research* 33, no. 4 (November 1996): 391–402; Margaret G. Hermann and Charles W. Kegley Jr., "The U.S. Use of Military Intervention to Promote Democracy: Evaluating the Record," *International Interactions* 24, no. 2 (June 1, 1998): 91–114; Mark Peceny, "Forcing Them to Be Free," *Political Research Quarterly* 52, no. 3 (September 1999): 549–82; Bruce Bueno de Mesquita and George W. Downs, "Intervention and Democracy," *International Organization* 60, no. 3 (2006): 627–49; Scott Walker and Frederic S. Pearson, "Should We Really 'Force Them to Be Free?' An Empirical Examination of Peceny's Liberalizing Intervention Thesis," *Conflict Management and Peace Science* 24, no. 1 (April 1, 2007): 37–53; Downes and Monten, "Forced to Be Free."

42. Daniel Berger et al., "Do Superpower Interventions Have Short and Long Term Consequences for Democracy?," *Journal of Comparative Economics* 41, no. 1 (2013): 22–34.

43. Downes and Monten, "Forced to Be Free."

44. New variables not previously discussed in the text include *maximum level of democratization, interstate war,* and *British colony. Maximum level of democratization* was measured by a state's highest polity score in the preceding fifty years. *Interstate war,* a dichotomous variable

from the COW Interstate War (v. 4.0) dataset. *British colony* is a dichotomous variable from the COW Colonial/Dependency Contiguity (v. 3.0) dataset.

45. Goran Peic and Dan Reiter, "Foreign-imposed Regime Change, State Power and Civil War Onset, 1920–2004," *British Journal of Political Science* 41, no. 3 (2011): 474.

46. Alexander Downes, "Catastrophic Success: Foreign-Imposed Regime Change and Civil War" (paper prepared for delivery at the 2010 Annual Meeting of the American Political Science Association, Washington, DC, September 2–5, 2010).

47. Downes, "Catastrophic Success," 40.

48. For an expanded discussion of covert regime change and civil war, see Lindsey A. O'Rourke, "Covert Calamities: American-backed Covert Regime Changes and Civil War," *Canadian Foreign Policy Journal* 23, no. 3 (2017): 232–45.

49. New variables not previously discussed in the text include *percentage mountainous terrain* and *defeat in an interstate war*. *Percentage mountainous terrain* is a continuous variable from James D. Fearon and David D. Laitin, "Ethnicity, Insurgency, and Civil War," *American Political Science Review* 97, no. 1 (2003): 75–90. *Defeat in an interstate war* is a dichotomous variable created from the COW Interstate War (v. 4.0) dataset.

50. The fact that only failed covert attempts had a statistically significant effect in the linear regression model, however, likely results from the fact that all US-backed covert missions to support a foreign secessionist movement or intervene in a civil war failed to replace their target. Had some of these operations succeeded in that short-term goal, successful covert regime change may have had a positive and statistically significant effect as well.

51. Alexander B. Downes and Lindsey A. O'Rourke, "Foreign-Imposed Regime Change and Mass Killing" (paper prepared for the 2017 International Studies Association Annual Conference, Baltimore, MD, February 22–25, 2017).

52. Jay Ulfelder and Benjamin Valentino, "Assessing Risks of State-Sponsored Mass Killing," February 1, 2008, Social Science Research Network (SSRN), http://ssrn.com/abstract =1703426.

53. David A. Baldwin, "Success and Failure in Foreign Policy," *American Review of Political Science* 3, no. 1 (2000): 167–82.

5. Overview of US-Backed Regime Changes during the Cold War

1. National Security Council 58/2, December 8, 1949, "A Report to the President by the National Security Council on United States Policy Toward the Soviet Satellite States in Eastern Europe," *Foreign Relations of the United States (FRUS), 1949, Vol. V, Eastern Europe; The Soviet Union*, ed. William Z. Slany and Rogers P. Churchill (Washington, DC: US Government Printing Office [GPO], 1975), Doc. 17.

2. Melvyn P. Leffler, *For the Soul of Mankind: The United States, the Soviet Union, and the Cold War* (New York: Hill and Wang, 2008), chap. 1.

3. Holloway quoted in Leffler, *For the Soul of Mankind*, 51.

4. Melvyn P. Leffler, *The Specter of Communism: The United States and the Origins of the Cold War, 1917–1953* (New York: Hill and Wang, 1994), 24.

5. John J. Mearsheimer, *The Tragedy of Great Power Politics* (New York: Norton, 2001), 328.

6. Mearsheimer, *Tragedy of Great Power Politics*.

7. Stalin quoted in Leffler, *For the Soul of Mankind*, 49.

8. C. Clifford and G. Elsey, July 1946, "The Clifford-Elsey Report," Harry S. Truman Library, Independence, MO.

9. Clifford and Elsey, "The Clifford-Elsey Report," 71.

10. "U.S. Policy toward the Soviet Satellite States in Eastern Europe," August 25, 1949, Policy Planning Staff Paper 59, *FRUS, 1949, Vol. V, Eastern Europe; The Soviet Union*, Doc. 10.

11. George Kennan, February 22, 1946, 9 p.m., "The Charge in the Soviet Union (Kennan) to the Secretary of State," National Security Archive, Washington, DC (hereafter cited as NSA), https://nsarchive2.gwu.edu//coldwar/documents/episode-1/kennan.htm.

12. George F. Kennan, "The Sources of Soviet Conduct," *Foreign Affairs* 25 (1947): 566–82.

13. National Security Council Memorandum 4, December 17, 1947, "Coordination of Foreign Information Measures," *FRUS, 1945–1950, Emergence of the Intelligence Establishment*, ed. C. Thomas Thorne Jr. and David S. Patterson (Washington, DC: US GPO, 1996), Doc. 252; László Borhi, "Rollback, Liberation, Containment, or Inaction? U.S. Policy and Eastern Europe in the 1950s," *Journal of Cold War Studies* 1, no. 3 (September 1, 1999): 67–110.

14. National Security Directive 5412/2, December 28, 1955, "Covert Operations," *FRUS, 1950–1955, Vol. IV, The Intelligence Community*, ed. Douglas Keane and Michael Warner (Washington, DC: US GPO, 2007), Doc. 250.

15. On North Korea, see Frank Holober, *Raiders of the China Coast: CIA Covert Operations during the Korean War* (Annapolis, MD: US Naval Institute Press, 1999); Michael E. Haas, *In the Devil's Shadow: UN Special Operations during the Korean War* (Annapolis, MD: Naval Institute Press, 2000); Ben S. Malcom, *White Tigers: My Secret War in North Korea* (Washington, DC: Potomac Books, 2003); William M. Leary, *Perilous Missions: Civil Air Transport and CIA Covert Operations in Asia* (Tuscaloosa: University Alabama Press, 2006); Curtis Peebles, *Twilight Warriors: Covert Air Operations Against the USSR* (Annapolis, MD: Naval Institute Press, 2013), chap. 3; Central Intelligence Agency, Clandestine Services History, March 1964, "The Secret War in Korea: June 1950 to June 1952," https://fas.org/irp/cia/product/korea.pdf; Memorandum to the National Security Council by the Executive Secretary (Lay), July 22, 1953, "Subject: Project Solarium," *FRUS, 1952–1945, Vol. II, Part 1, National Security Affairs*, ed. Lisle A. Rose and Neal H. Petersen (Washington, DC: US GPO, 1984), Doc. 79.

16. On China, see Department of State, February 27, 1950, "A Report to the National Security Council: The Position of the United States with Respect to Indochina," https://www.mtholyoke.edu/acad/intrel/pentagon/doc1.htm; "Military Support to Anti-Communist Groups in China," JSPC 985/15, Declassified Documents Reference Service, Library of Congress, Washington, DC (hereafter cited as DDRS); Central Intelligence Agency, June 18, 1952, "Special Estimate: Present and Potential Offensive Capabilities of the Chinese Nationalists and Probable Reactions to an Identifiable US Program of Preparing the Nationalists for Offensive Operations Against the Chinese Communists," CIA Freedom of Information Act (FOIA) Electronic Reading Room, https://www.cia.gov/library/readingroom/ (hereafter cited as CIA-FOIA), Doc. CIA-RDP79R00904A000100030050-5; Central Intelligence Agency [N. Dumovic], 2006, "Two CIA Prisoners in China, 1952–73, Extraordinary Fidelity," in *Studies in Intelligence* 50, no. 4, https://www.cia.gov/library/center-for-the-study-of-intelligence/csi-publications/csi-studies/studies/vol50no4/two-cia-prisoners-in-china-1952201373.html; 303 Committee, September 8, 1969, "Subject: CIA Covert Action Program against Communist China," *FRUS, 1969–1976, Vol. XVII, China, 1969–1972*, ed. Steven E. Phillips (Washington, DC: US GPO), Doc. 30. Holober, *Raiders of the China Coast*; Kenneth Conboy and James Morrison, *The CIA's Secret War in Tibet* (Lawrence: University Press of Kansas, 2002); Peebles, *Twilight Warriors*, chaps. 4 and 7; John W. Garver, *The Sino-American Alliance: Nationalist China and American Cold War Strategy in Asia* (Abingdon, UK: Routledge, 2015).

17. National Security Council Directive 5608, July 3, 1956, "U.S. Policy Toward the Soviet Satellites in Eastern Europe," Wilson Center Digital Archive, http://digitalarchive.wilsoncenter.org/document/114689.

18. Kenneth Osgood, *Total Cold War: Eisenhower's Secret Propaganda Battle at Home and Abroad* (Lawrence: University Press of Kansas, 2006); A. Ross Johnson, *Radio Free Europe and Radio Liberty: The CIA Years and Beyond* (Palo Alto, CA: Stanford University Press, 2010).

19. On Afghanistan, see White House, July 3, 1979, "Findings Pursuant to Section 662 of the Foreign Assistance Act of 1961, as Amended, Concerning Operations in Foreign Countries Other Than Those Intended Solely for the Purpose of Intelligence Collection," NSA ; United States Army, May 1989, "Lessons from the War in Afghanistan," NSA, https://nsarchive2.gwu.edu//NSAEBB/NSAEBB57/us11.pdf; Director of Central Intelligence, November 1989, "Afghanistan: The War in Perspective," NSA, https://nsarchive2.gwu.edu//NSAEBB/NSAEBB57/us12.pdf; Steve Coll, *Ghost Wars: The Secret History of the CIA, Afghanistan, and Bin Laden, from the Soviet Invasion to September 10, 2001* (London: Penguin, 2004). On Cambodia, see White House, January 9, 1985, "National Security Decision Directive 158 on United States Policy in Southeast Asia, the Kampuchea Problem," Ronald Reagan Library, Simi Valley, CA (hereafter

cited as RRL); White House, November 14, 1988, "National Security Decision Directive 319: United States Policy towards Indochina," Federation of American Scientists (hereafter cited as FSA), https://fas.org/irp/offdocs/nsdd/nsdd-319.htm. On Nicaragua, see White House, September 19, 1983, "Findings Pursuant to Section 662 of the Foreign Assistance Act of 1961," NSA, https://nsarchive2.gwu.edu/NSAEBB/NSAEBB210/1-Reagan%20Finding%209-19-83%20(IC%2000203).pdf; National Security Council Meeting, June 25, 1984, "Meeting Minutes, Subject: Central America," NSA, https://nsarchive2.gwu.edu/NSAEBB/NSAEBB210/2-NSPG%20minutes%206-25-84%20(IC%2000463).pdf; Central Intelligence Agency, December 14, 1984, "Subject: Nicaragua," NSA, https://nsarchive2.gwu.edu/NSAEBB/NSAEBB210/3-Gates%20Memo%2012-14-84.pdf; Peter Kornbluh and Malcolm Byrne, ed., *The Iran-Contra Scandal* (New York: New Press, 1993); Lisa Klobuchar, *The Iran-Contra Affair: Political Scandal Uncovered* (Mankato, MN: Capstone, 2008); Malcolm Byrne, *Iran-Contra: Reagan's Scandal and the Unchecked Abuse of Presidential Power* (Lawrence: University Press of Kansas, 2014).

20. National Security Decision Directive 75, January 17, 1983, "U.S. Relations with the U.S.S.R.," RRL; Thomas Bodenheimer and Robert Gould, *Rollback!: Right-Wing Power in US Foreign Policy* (New York: South End Press, 1989); James M. Scott, *Deciding to Intervene: The Reagan Doctrine and American Foreign Policy* (Durham, NC: Duke University Press, 1996); Chester Pach, "The Reagan Doctrine: Principle, Pragmatism, and Policy," *Presidential Studies Quarterly* 36, no. 1 (March 1, 2006): 75–88. On Poland, see Central Intelligence Agency, December 4, 1981, Memorandum from Gates to Casey, "Subject: Assistance to Poland, Tuesday's NSC Meeting," CIA-FOI, Doc. CIA-RDP89G00720R000100050008-7; National Security Council, September 9, 1982, "NSDD 54 on Eastern Europe," CIA-FOIA Doc. CIA-RDP10M00666R000301000001-7; Department of State, December 6, 1982, Memorandum from Bremer to Clark, "NSDD 11-82—Draft NSDD and IG Study," CIA-FOIA, Doc. CIA-RDP90B01013R000300490002-0; National Endowment for Democracy Annual Reports (1984–89), http://www.ned.org/publications/annual-reports-1984–2004/.

21. There is good reason to doubt that America's covert support played a decisive role in the Polish or Nicaraguan regime changes. For instance, the anti-Soviet Solidarity movement already claimed 9 million members by the time it received American support. Second, the Polish regime change occurred amid the wave of regime changes brought about by the collapse of the Soviet Union. Because most of these regime changes occurred without American support, it is reasonable to assume that a movement as powerful as Solidarity would also have succeeded without US backing.

22. "Decisive and crushing blow," quoted by James I. Matray, "Truman's Plan for Victory: National Self-Determination and the Thirty-Eighth Parallel Decision in Korea," *Journal of American History* 66, no. 2 (1979): 325. "A return to the status quo . . ." is from Department of Defense, July 31, 1950, "U.S. Courses of Action in Korea," *FRUS, 1950, Vol. VII, Korea*, ed. John P. Glennon et al. (Washington, DC: US GPO), Doc. 379.

23. See, for instance, Central Intelligence Agency, July 17, 1968, "The Secret War in Korea, June 1950 to June 1952," CIA-FOIA, Doc. 0001459071; United State Army, Far East Air Forces, February 11, 1953, "Covert & Clandestine Activities in Korea (JLS 53)," Digital National Security Archive (hereafter cited as DNSA), Doc. no. JLS 53; 960454.

24. Tim Weiner, *Legacy of Ashes: The History of the CIA* (New York: Anchor, 2008), chap. 6.

25. See United Nations Security Council Resolutions 82, June 25, 1950, http://www.un.org/en/ga/search/view_doc.asp?symbol=S/RES/82(1950), and 83, June 27, 1950, http://www.un.org/en/ga/search/view_doc.asp?symbol=S/RES/83(1950).

26. Policy Planning Staff Draft Memo, July 22, 1950, "Problem: To Decide Upon policy regarding the advance beyond the 38th parallel of U.S. forces now engaged in Korea as part of the U.N. forces," *FRUS, 1950, Vol. VII, Korea*, Doc. 344.

27. National Security Council Directive 81/1, September 1, 1950, "Note by the Executive Secretary to the National Security Council on United States Courses of Action with Respect to Korea," *FRUS, 1950, Vol. VII, Korea*, Doc. 486.

28. Central Intelligence Agency, October 12, 1950A, "Threat of Soviet Intervention in Korea," *FRUS, 1950, Vol. VII, Korea*, Doc. 666.

29. Central Intelligence Agency, October 12, 1950B, "Threat of Full Chinese Communist Intervention in Korea," *FRUS, 1950, Vol. VII, Korea,* Doc. 665.

30. Quoted in Bruce A. Lesh, "Limited War or a Rollback of Communism? Truman, MacArthur, and the Korean Conflict," *OAH Magazine of History* 22, no. 4 (October 2008): 4.

31. Quoted in Weiner, *Legacy of Ashes,* 61.

32. Seymour Hersh, "Target Gaddafi," *New York Times Magazine* 17 (1987): 74.

33. Memorandum from Graham E. Fuller to Director of Central Intelligence, April 15, 1986, DNSA Accession no. CO01856; National Security Council, April 8, 1986, "Subject: Next Steps: Libya," Reagan Files, http://www.thereaganfiles.com/19860408-next-steps-re.pdf.

34. Quoted in Nicholas Laham, *The American Bombing of Libya: A Study of the Force of Miscalculation in Reagan Foreign Policy* (Jefferson, NC: McFarland, 2007), 115.

35. Laham, *American Bombing of Libya,* 117.

36. Central Intelligence Agency, April 21, 1986, "Talking Points for the DDI, 21 April 1986, Libyan Leader Qadafi's Residences," DNSA, Accession no. CO01862.

37. Quoted in Laham, *American Bombing of Libya,* 133.

38. Quoted in Joseph T. Stanik, *El Dorado Canyon: Reagan's Undeclared War with Qaddafi* (Annapolis, MD: Naval Institute Press, 2003), 39.

39. Quoted in Thomas Ward, "Norms and Security: The Case of International Assassination," *International Security* 25, no. 1 (2000): 125.

40. Quoted in Laham, *American Bombing of Libya,* 157.

41. "Text of the State Department Report in Libya Under Qaddafi," *New York Times,* January 9, 1986. See also Bob Woodward, *Veil: The Secret Wars of the CIA, 1981–1987* (New York: Simon & Schuster, 2007).

42. On the emergence of containment as US policy, see Marc Trachtenberg, "Making Grand Strategy: The Early Cold War Experience in Retrospect," *SAIS Review* 19, no. 1 (1999): 41; Mearsheimer, *Tragedy of Great Power Politics,* 322–27; John Lewis Gaddis, *Strategies of Containment: A Critical Appraisal of American National Security Policy during the Cold War.* (Oxford: Oxford University Press, 2005); James Callanan, *Covert Action in the Cold War: US Policy, Intelligence and CIA Operations* (New York: IB Tauris, 2009), chap. 1.

43. Kennan, July 1947.

44. George Kennan, February 22, 1946, 9 p.m., "The Charge in the Soviet Union (Kennan) to the Secretary of State," NSA, https://nsarchive2.gwu.edu/coldwar/documents/episode-1/kennan.htm

45. Gaddis, *Strategies of Containment,* chaps. 1–2.

46. Callanan, *Covert Action in the Cold War,* 86.

47. Gaddis, *Strategies of Containment,* 57–59.

48. National Security Council, October 30, 1953, NSC 162/2 "Basic National Security Policy," FSA, https://fas.org/irp/offdocs/nsc-hst/nsc-162-2.pdf.

49. Clifford and Elsey, "The Clifford-Elsey Report," 9.

50. Jerome Slater, "Dominos in Central America: Will They Fall? Does It Matter?," *International Security* 12, no. 2 (1987): 105–34.

51. Dwight Eisenhower, "President Eisenhower's News Conference, April 7, 1954," Mount Holyoke, International Relations, http://www.mtholyoke.edu/acad/intrel/pentagon/ps11.htm.

52. National Security Council 124, February 13, 1952, "United States Objectives and Courses of Action with Respect to Communist Aggression in Southeast Asia," *FRUS, 1952–1954, Vol. XII, Part 1, East Asia and the Pacific,* ed. David W. Mabon (Washington, DC: US GPO, 1984), Doc. 9.

53. Leffler, *For the Soul of Mankind.*

54. Mearsheimer, *Tragedy of Great Power Politics,* 156.

55. Odd Arne Westad, *The Global Cold War: Third World Interventions and the Making of Our Times* (Cambridge: Cambridge University Press, 2005); For the American position, see Department of State, January 19, 1955, Minutes of Meeting, Secretary Dulles' Office, "Subject: Afro-Asian Conference, Secretary's Office, 2:30 p.m., January 18, 1955," *FRUS, East Asian Security, 1955–57, Vol. XXI, Cambodia; Laos,* ed. Edward C. Keefer and David W. Mabon (Washington,

DC: US GPO, 1990), Doc. 6; For the Soviet position, see Roy Allison, *The Soviet Union and the Strategy of Non-Alignment in the Third World* (Cambridge, UK: Cambridge University Press, 2009).

56. Quoted in Jonathan Nashel, *Edward Lansdale's Cold War* (Amherst, MA: University of Massachusetts Press, 2005), 96.

57. National Security Council Directive 10/2, May 12, 1948, "Draft Report by the National Security Council," *FRUS 1945–1950: Emergence of the Intelligence Establishment*, ed. C. Thomas Thorne Jr. and David S. Patterson (Washington, DC: US GPO, 1996), Doc. 274.

58. Central Intelligence Agency, December 31, 1947, "The Current Situation in France," CIA-FOIA, Doc. CIA-RDP78-01617A003000240001-1; Central Intelligence Agency, February 1948, "The Current Situation in Italy," CIA-FOIA, Doc. 0000008669; National Security Council, March 8, 1948, "National Security Council Report: Position of the United States with Respect to Italy in Light of the Possible Communist Participation in Government by Legal Means," CIA-FOIA, Doc. CIA-RDP78-01617A003100010001-5.

59. Leffler, *For the Soul of Mankind*, 59.

60. Deputy Director of Central Intelligence, September 15, 1951, "Analysis of the Power of the Communist Parties of France and Italy and of Measures to Counter Them," CIA-FOIA, Doc. CIA-RDP80R01731R003200020013-5.

61. Deputy Director of Central Intelligence, "Analysis of the Power."

62. Deputy Director of Central Intelligence, "Analysis of the Power."

63. Summary for Secretary Marshall, May 26, 1947, "Italian and French Struggle Against Communism," NSA, https://nsarchive2.gwu.edu/NSAEBB/ciacase/EXK.pdf; Summary for Secretary Marshall, September 15, 1947, "Communist Threat in Italy," NSA, https://nsarchive2.gwu.edu/NSAEBB/ciacase/EXK.pdf; Department of State, October 24, 1947, Memorandum from the Executive Secretary of the National Security Council (Souers) to Secretary of Defense (Forrestal), *FRUS, 1945–1950, Emergence of the Intelligence Establishment*, Doc. 245; Central Intelligence Agency, November 16, 1948, "Memorandum for the File, Subject: Relationship and Proposed Course of Dealing with OPA and ECA," *FRUS, 1945–1950, Emergence of the Intelligence Establishment*, Doc. 307; Summary for Secretary Marshall, November 24, 1947, "Communist Violence in Italy and France," NSA, https://nsarchive2.gwu.edu/NSAEBB/ciacase/EXK.pdf; Summary for Secretary Marshall, January 19, 1948, "Position of Italian Communists," NSA, https://nsarchive2.gwu.edu/NSAEBB/ciacase/; Department of State, February 12, 1948, Letter from Bonner to Undersecretary of State Lovett, NARA, RG 59, Dec. File, 1945–1959, Box 6915A; National Security Council, "National Security Council Report: Position of the United States with Respect to Italy in Light of the Possible Communist Participation in Government by Legal Means," CIA-FOIA, Doc. CIA-RDP78-01617A003100010001-5. A second wave of US covert missions to influence Italian elections reemerged in 1972–73. See Department of State, September 12, 1966, "Subject: 303 Committee Consideration of the Italian Covert Action Program," *FRUS, 1964–1968, Vol. XII, Western Europe*, ed. James E. Miller (Washington, DC: US GPO, 2001), Doc. 125; Department of State, June 28, 1965, "Subject: Minutes of the Meeting of the 303 Committee, Covert Action Program in Italy for FY1966," *FRUS, Vol. 1964–1968, Vol. XII, Western Europe*, Doc., 113; Memorandum from Bundy to Johnson, August 4, 1965, "Subject: Italian Covert Political Assistance," *FRUS, 1964–1968, Vol. XII, Western Europe*, Doc. 116.

64. See *FRUS, 1968–1968, Vol. XXIX, Part 2, Japan*, ed. Karen L. Gatz (Washington, DC: US GPO, 2006), Doc. 1, Editorial Note; Psychological Strategy Board, December 22, 1952), "Psychological Strategy Program for Japan," NSA; Robert O. Blake, James D. Mason, and Horace G. Torbert, December 29, 1990, "Interview with Robert O. Blake," Manuscript/mixed material, *Library of Congress*, https://www.loc.gov/item/mfdipbib000096/.

65. George Kennan, August 20, 1948, "Comments on the General Trend of U.S. Foreign Policy," in Kennan Papers, Seeley Mudd Library, Princeton University.

66. Central Intelligence Agency, March 1954, "Clandestine Service History, Overthrow of Premier Mossadeq of Iran, November 1952–August 1953," NSA, https://nsarchive2.gwu.edu/NSAEBB/NSAEBB28/; Central Intelligence Agency, March 1954, "Appendix A: Initial Operational Plan as Cabled from Nicosia to Headquarters on 1 June 1953," NSA, http://cryptome.org/iran-cia/a.pdf; Central Intelligence Agency, March 1954, "Appendix D: Report on Military

Planning Aspect of TPAjax," NSA, https://nsarchive2.gwu.edu//NSAEBB/NSAEBB28/D-New
.pdf; Kermit Roosevelt, *Countercoup, the Struggle for the Control of Iran* (New York: McGraw-Hill,
1979); Mark J. Gasiorowski, "The 1953 Coup d'État in Iran," *International Journal of Middle East
Studies* 19, no. 3 (August 1987): 261–86; Ervand Abrahamian, "The 1953 Coup in Iran," *Science
& Society* 65, no. 2 (2001): 182–215; Stephen Kinzer, *All the Shah's Men: An American Coup and the
Roots of Middle East Terror* (Hoboken, NJ: John Wiley & Sons, 2003); Mark J. Gasiorowski and
Malcolm Byrne, *Mohammad Mosaddeq and the 1953 Coup in Iran* (Syracuse, NY: Syracuse University Press, 2004).

67. Gaddis, *Strategies of Containment*, 155–56. For an overview of Eisenhower's numerous
covert interventions, see Central Intelligence Agency, undated, "SOL-1F/C-1, Sec. IX," DDRS,
Doc. CK3100529913.

68. On Syria, see National Security Council, March 3, 1955, "Memorandum of Discussion," *FRUS, 1955–1957, Vol. XII, Near East Region; Iran; Iraq*, Doc. 18; US–UK Working Group
on Syria, September 18, 1957, "Final Report of the Joint U.S.–U.K. Working Group on Syria,"
Duncan Sandys papers 6/35, Churchill College Archives, Cambridge (hereafter cited as
DSND); US–UK Working Group on Syria, September 18, 1957, "VII: Covert Actions in Support
of the Operation," DSND; Douglas Little, "Cold War and Covert Action: The United States and
Syria, 1945–1958," *Middle East Journal* 44, no. 1 (1990): 51–75; Matthew Jones, "The 'Preferred
Plan': The Anglo-American Working Group Report on Covert Action in Syria, 1957," *Intelligence and National Security* 19, no. 3 (September 1, 2004): 408. On Lebanon, see Department of
State, July 31, 1957, "Ratio Plan for the Lebanon," *FRUS, 1955–57, Vol. XIII, Near East: Jordan-Yemen, Vol. XIII*, ed. Will Klingman, Aaron D. Miller, and Nina J. Noring (Washington, DC: US
GPO, 1988), Doc. 140; Department of State, June 9, 1958, Memorandum of Conversation, White
House, "Subject: Situation in Lebanon," *FRUS, 1958–1960, Vol. XI, Lebanon and Jordan*, ed. Louis
J. Smith (Washington, DC: US GPO, 1992), Doc. 65; Charles Stuart Kennedy and Richard B.
Parker, April 21, 1989, "Interview with Richard B. Parker," Manuscript/Mixed Materials, Library of Congress, https://www.loc.gov/item/mfdipbib000898/.

69. On Iraq (1972–75), see Department of State, May 31, 1972, "The Kurds of Iraq: Renewed
Insurgency," *FRUS, 1969–1976, Vol. E-4, Documents on Iran and Iraq, 1969–1972*, ed. Monica
Belamonte (Washington, DC: US GPO, 2006), Doc. 310; Department of State, July 18, 1972,
"Subject: Assistance to Iraqi Kurdish Leader Mulla Mustafa Barzani," *FRUS, 1969–1976, Vol.
E-4*, attachment contained in Doc. 321; Memorandum from Haig to Kissinger, July 28, 1972,
"Subject: Kurdish Problem," *FRUS, 1969–1976, Vol. E-4*, Doc. 321; Memorandum from Kissinger to Nixon, October 5, 1972, "Subject: Progress Report on the Kurdish Support Operations,"
FRUS, Vol. E-4, Doc. 325. On South Yemen, see Memorandum from Brzezinski to Carter,
February 7, 1980, "Subject: Covert Action Program for the Yemens," *FRUS, 1977–1980, Middle
East Region, Arabian Peninsula*, ed. Kelly M. McFarland (Washington, DC: US GPO, 2015), Doc.
296; Memorandum from Hoskinson to Brzezinski, August 16, 1978, "Subject: the Yemens,"
FRUS, 1977–1980, Vol. XXIII, Middle East Region; Arabian Peninsula, Doc. 252; Central Intelligence
Agency, 1979, "Proposed Covert Action Program in the Arabian Peninsula," *FRUS, 1977–1980,
Vol. XXIII, Middle East Region; Arabian Peninsula*, Doc. 272; Memorandum from Odom to Brzezinski, November 28, 1979, "Subject: Strategy for the Persian Gulf in 1980," *FRUS, 1977–1980,
Vol. XXIII, Middle East Region, Arabian Peninsula*, Doc. 34; Memorandum from William E.
Griffith to Zbigniew Brzezinski, January 31, 1979, "The Arc of Instability: What Is to Be Done,"
DNSA, Accession no. CO00460.

70. Department of State Memorandum, January 2, 1958, "United States Policy toward Indonesia," *FRUS, 1958–1960, Vol. XVII, Indonesia*, ed. Robert J. McMahon (Washington, DC: US
GPO, 1994), Doc. 1. See also National Security Council Memorandum 5518, February 10, 1958,
"Subject: U.S. Policy on Indonesia," *FRUS, 1958–1960, Vol. XVII, Indonesia*, Doc. 10; Department
of State Memorandum of Conversation, April 13, 1958, "Subject: Indonesia," *FRUS, 1958–1960,
Vol. XVII, Indonesia*, Doc. 57; Memorandum of Conversation with President Eisenhower,
April 15, 1958, *FRUS, 1958–1960, Vol. XVII, Indonesia*, Doc. 62.

71. For North and South Vietnam, see chap. 7. On Laos, see National Security Council,
September 30, 1961, "Concept for Military Intervention in Laos," DNSA, Accession no. VI00534;
National Security Council, April 22, 1963, "United States Operations in Laos and the Geneva

Accords," DNSA, Accession no. VI00759; Central Intelligence Agency, 2006, "Undercover Armies: CIA and Surrogate Warfare in Laos 1961–73," CIA-FOIA, Doc. 5076e89c993247d4d-82b62ef. On Thailand, see Department of State, September 10, 1965, "Subject: Mr. Bundy's Meeting with Mr. Colby," *FRUS, 1964–1968, Vol. XXVI, Indonesia; Malaysia-Singapore; Philippines*, ed. Edward C. Keefer (Washington, DC: US GPO, 2000), Doc. 304; 303 Committee, September 28, 1965, "Covert U.S. Government Financial Report to Thai Elections," *FRUS, 1964–1968, Vol. XXVI, Indonesia; Malaysia-Singapore; Philippines*, Doc. 305; 303 Committee, October 8, 1965, "Minutes of the Meeting of the 303 Committee, 7 October 1965, Topic: Thailand—Covert U.S. Government Financial Support to Thai Elections," *FRUS, 1964–1968, Vol. XXVI, Indonesia; Malaysia-Singapore; Philippines*, Doc. 306.

72. Central Intelligence Agency, May 16, 1973; Central Intelligence Agency Cable, August 26, 1960, "Dulles to Station Officer," *FRUS, 1958–1960, Vol. XIV, Africa*, ed. Harriet Dashiell Schwar and Stanley Shaloff (Washington, DC: US GPO, 1992), Editorial Note 189; Church Committee, *Alleged Assassination Plots Involving Foreign Leaders*, "Chapter III: Assassination Planning and the Plots, A. Congo."

73. On Mozambique, see Department of State, April 29, 1964, Memorandum from Assistant Secretary of State for African Affairs (Williams) to Secretary of State Rusk, "Subject: Portuguese African Colonies," *FRUS, 1964–1968, Vol. XXIV, Africa*, ed. Nina Davis Howland (Washington, DC: US GPO, 1999), Doc. 418; Department of State, October 27, 1967, "Minutes of the Meeting of the 303 Committee," *FRUS, 1964–1968, Vol. XXIV, Africa*, Doc. 449; Department of State, October 28, 1964, "Subject: Mozambique," *FRUS, 1964–1968, Vol. XXIV, Africa*, Doc. 426. On Angola, see Department of State, April 29, 1964; Central Intelligence Agency, May 4, 1964, "Meeting May 4, 1964, re U.S. Policy Towards the Portuguese Possessions in Africa," *FRUS, 1964–1968, Vol. XXIV, Africa*, Doc. 419; Department of State, May 21, 1964, Memorandum for the Record, "Subject: Minutes of the Meeting of the Special Group, 21 May 1964," *FRUS, 1964–1968, Vol. XXIV, Africa*, Doc. 421. On Somalia, "Editorial Note," *FRUS, 1964–1968, Vol. XXIV, Africa*, Doc. 283.

74. National Security Council, June 27, 1975, "Minutes. Subject: Angola," Ford Library, https://www.fordlibrarymuseum.gov/library/document/0312/1552391.pdf; National Security Council Intergovernmental Group for Africa, June 13, 1975, "Response to NSSM 224: United States Policy toward Angola," CIA-FOIA, Doc. LOC-HAK-104-6-3-6; Department of State, 1975, "Discussion of U.S. Policy and Soviet Involvement in Angola," DNSA, Accession no. SA00483.

75. On Chad, see National Security Council, September 17, 1984, "Subject: An Assessment of Administration Strategies in Africa, 1981–84," DNSA, Accession no. CO01556; Kennedy, Charles Stuart, and Donald R. Norland, December 15, 1992, "Interview with Donald R. Norland," Manuscript/Mixed Materials, Library of Congress, Washington, DC, https://www.loc.gov/item/mfdipbib000873/; Charles Stuart Kennedy and David Blakemore, November 7, 1997, "Interview with David Blakemore," Manuscript/Mixed Materials, Library of Congress, https://www.loc.gov/item/mfdipbib000098/; Bishop, James k, and Charles Stuart Kennedy, November 15, 1995, "Interview with James K. Bishop Jr." Manuscript/Mixed Materials, Library of Congress, https://www.loc.gov/item/mfdipbib000091/; National Security Decision Directive 322, December 14, 1988, "U.S. Interests and Policy in Chad," FAS, https://fas.org/irp/offdocs/nsdd/nsdd-322.pdf. On Ethiopia, see National Security Council, April 4, 1980, "Subject: Ethiopia—A Brief Political Assessment," DNSA, Accession no. CO00808; National Security Decision Directive 57, September 17, 1982, "United States Policy Towards the Horn of Africa," DNSA Accession no. PD01670; Thomas J. Dunnigan and Joseph P. O'Neill, May 19, 1998, "Interview with Joseph P. O'Neill," Manuscript/Mixed Materials, Library of Congress, https://www.loc.gov/item/mfdipbib000885/. Charles Stuart Kennedy and David A. Korn, December 11, 1990, "Interview with David A. Korn," Manuscript/Mixed Materials, Library of Congress, https://www.loc.gov/item/mfdipbib000635/. Charles Stuart Kennedy and William Hubert Lewis, October 24, 1996, "Interview with William H. Lewis," Manuscript/Mixed Materials, Library of Congress, https://www.loc.gov/item/mfdipbib001586/. On Liberia, see National Security Study Directive 4–38, April 5, 1983, "U.S. Strategy Towards Liberia," DNSA, Accession no. PR01676; National Security Decision Directive 101, September 2, 1983, "United

States Strategy toward Liberia," FAS, https://fas.org/irp/offdocs/nsdd/nsdd-101.htm; National Endowment for Democracy, 1988, Annual Report, http://www.ned.org/docs/annual/1988%20NED%20Annual%20Report.pdf. On Libya, see National Security Council, January 21, 1982, "Subject: Libya," NARA; Central Intelligence Agency, January 28, 1986, "Qadhafi's Vulnerabilities," CIA-FOIA, Doc. 0000389216; White House, August 14, 1986, "Subject: NSPg on Libya, August 14, 1986," DNSA Accession no. CO01903; National Security Decision Directive 234, August 16, 1986, "Libya Policy," https://www.fas.org/irp/offdocs/nsdd/nsdd-234.pdf; Memorandum from Graham E. Fuller to Director of Central Intelligence, April 15, 1986, "Subject: A Successor to Qadhafi," DNSA Accession no. CO01856; Directorate of Intelligence, April 30, 1986, "Libya: What If Qadhafi Is Ousted?," CIA-FOIA, Doc. CIA-RDP88G01117R000100130003-3. On Angola, see State Department, January 1986, "U.S. Africa Policy: The Opportunity and Need for a Pro-American Strategy," DNSA Accession no. SA01983; White House, February 10, 1986, "National Security Decision Directive 212: United States Policy toward Angola," DNSA, Accession no. SA02008; White House, May 7, 1987, "National Security Decision Directive, NSDD 274, United States Policy toward Angola," FAS, https://fas.org/irp/offdocs/nsdd/nsdd-274.htm.

76. Salim Yaqub, *Containing Arab Nationalism: The Eisenhower Doctrine and the Middle East* (Chapel Hill, NC: University of North Carolina Press, 2004).

77. Public Law 85–7, March 9, 1957, "Joint Resolution to Promote Peace and Stability in the Middle East," http://en.wikisource.org/wiki/Page:United_States_Statutes_at_Large_Vol. _71. djvu/41; see also National Security Council 5428, July 23, 1954, "United States Objectives and Policies with Respect to the Near East," *FRUS, 1952–1954, Vol. IX, Part 1, The Near and Middle East*, ed. Paul Claussen, Joan M. Lee, and Carl N. Raether (Washington, DC: US GPO, 1986), Doc. 219.

78. Little, "Cold War and Covert Action," 32.

79. Little, 35; for accounts by CIA operatives, see Miles Copeland, *The Game of Nations: The Amorality of Power Politics* (New York: Simon and Schuster, 1970); David Atlee Phillips, *The Night Watch: 25 Years of Peculiar Service* (New York: Athenaeum, 1977); Wilbur Crane Eveland, *Ropes of Sand: America's Failure in the Middle East* (London: Norton, 1980).

80. Little, "Cold War and Covert Action," 36.

81. Kennedy and Parker, "Interview with Richard B. Parker."

82. Department of State, May 11, 1958, "Telegram from the Embassy in Lebanon to the Department of State," *FRUS, 1958–1960, Vol. XI, Lebanon and Jordan*, Doc. 25.

83. White House, May 13, 1958, "Subject: Lebanese Crisis," *FRUS, 1958–1960, Vol. XI, Lebanon and Jordan*, Doc. 30.

84. Department of State, June 9, 1958.

85. Department of State, July 14, 1958, Memorandum from the Record of a Meeting of the Department of State, "Subject: Meeting re Iraq," *FRUS, 1958–1960, Vol. XI, Lebanon and Jordan*, Doc. 123.

86. Little, "Cold War and Covert Action."

87. Quoted in John M. Benson, "The Polls: U.S. Military Intervention," *Public Opinion Quarterly* 46, no. 4 (1982): 594.

88. Because the United States intervened in Lebanon to maintain a pro-American regime, this operation could reasonably be described as regime maintenance. However, I have decided to include it as an example of regime change because of the role that the United States played in convincing both sides to reach a compromise and elect Chehab as president. Because I argue that states will generally not launch overt regime changes, this is the harder assumption for my theory. If I were to drop the overt Lebanese intervention from my data set, my argument that states prefer covert conduct would be stronger.

89. Lars Schoultz, *Beneath the United States: A History of US Policy toward Latin America* (Cambridge, MA: Harvard University Press, 1998); Martin Sicker, *The Geopolitics of Security in the Americas: Hemispheric Denial from Monroe to Clinton* (Westport, CT: Greenwood, 2002); Mark T. Gilderhus, "The Monroe Doctrine: Meanings and Implications," *Presidential Studies Quarterly* 36, no. 1 (2006): 5–16; Lester D. Langley, *America and the Americas: The United States in the Western Hemisphere* (Athens: University of Georgia Press, 2010).

90. Mearsheimer, *Tragedy of Great Power Politics*, 236.

91. James Monroe, December 2, 1823, "Seventh Annual Message to Congress," commonly referred to as the Monroe Doctrine, The Avalon Project, Yale Law School, http://avalon.law.yale .edu/19th_century/monroe.asp.

92. Theodore Roosevelt, December 6, 1904, "Fourth Annual Message to Congress," Teaching American History, http://teachingamericanhistory.org/library/document/roosevelt-corollary -to-monroe-doctrine/.

93. Greg Grandin, *Empire's Workshop: Latin America, the United States, and the Rise of the New Imperialism* (Basingstoke, UK: Macmillan, 2006), 3.

94. Franklin D. Roosevelt, March 4, 1933, "Inaugural Speech," Wyzant, http://www.hpol .org/fdr/inaug/.

95. Cited in Stephen D. Krasner, *Sovereignty: Organized Hypocrisy* (Princeton, NJ: Princeton University Press, 1999), 21–22.

96. Krasner, *Sovereignty.*

97. Leffler, *Specter of Communism*, 22.

98. Dulles quoted in Richard H. Immerman, *The CIA in Guatemala: The Foreign Policy of Intervention* (Austin: University of Texas Press, 2010), 10.

99. National Security Council 141, January 19, 1953, quoted in Michael D. Gambone, *Eisenhower, Somoza, and the Cold War in Nicaragua, 1953–1961* (Westport, CT: Greenwood, 1997), 85.

100. Eisenhower, Dwight, August 24, 1960, "President's News Conference," The American Presidency Project, http://www.presidency.ucsb.edu/ws/?pid=11915.

101. Quoted in Rodney P. Carlisle, *Manifest Destiny and the Expansion of America* (Santa Barbara, CA: ABC-CLIO, 2007), 55.

102. Ronald Reagan, January 27, 1987, "Address Before a Joint Session of Congress on the State of the Union," The American Presidency Project, http://www.presidency.ucsb.edu/ws/?pid=34430.

103. Lars Schoultz, *Beneath the United States: A History of US Policy toward Latin America* (Cambridge, MA: Harvard University Press, 1998), chap. 6; Michael C. Desch, "The Keys That Lock Up the World: Identifying American Interests in the Periphery," *International Security* 14, no. 1 (1989): 86–121; Michael C. Desch, *When the Third World Matters: Latin America and the United States Grand Strategy* (Baltimore, MD: Johns Hopkins University Press, 1993).

104. Michael Grow, *U.S. Presidents and Latin American Interventions: Pursuing Regime Change in the Cold War* (Lawrence: University Press of Kansas, 2008), x.

105. Once an alliance with the Soviet Union was formalized, I reclassified these operations as offensive.

106. Schoultz, *Beneath the United States*, 38.

107. Grow, *U.S. Presidents and Latin American Interventions*, xii.

108. On this logic, see Robert Powell, "War as a Commitment Problem," *International Organization* 60, no. 1 (2006): 189.

109. Grow, *U.S. Presidents and Latin American Interventions*, xii.

110. See "Normative Explanations" section in chap. 2.

111. David A. Lake, *Hierarchy in International Relations* (Ithaca, NY: Cornell University Press, 2009), 14.

112. The White House, November 5, 1970, "Memorandum for the President, Subject: NSC Meeting November 6—Chile," NSA, https://nsarchive2.gwu.edu/NSAEBB/NSAEBB437 /docs/Doc%204%20-%20Kissinger%20to%20Nixon%20re%20Nov%206%20NSC%20meeting .pdf.

113. National Security Council, August 20, 1956, "Draft Statement of Policy on U.S. Policy toward Latin America," *FRUS, 1955–1957, Vol. VI, American Republics: Multilateral; Mexico, Caribbean*, ed. N. Steven Kane et al. (Washington, DC: US GPO, 1957), Doc. 12.

114. Quoted by Grow, *U.S. Presidents and Latin American Interventions*, 9. See also Susanne Jonas, "Guatemala: Land of Eternal Struggle," in *Latin America: The Struggle with Dependency and Beyond*, ed. Ronald H. Chilcote and Joel C. Edelstein (New York: John Wiley, 1974): 89–215; José M. Aybar De Soto, *Dependency and Intervention: The Case of Guatemala in 1954* (Boulder, CO:

Westview Press, 1978); Stephen Schlesinger and Stephen Kinzer, *Bitter Fruit: The Story of the American Coup in Guatemala* (Cambridge, MA: Harvard University Press, 1999).

115. Grow, *U.S. Presidents and Latin American Interventions*, 9.

116. Grow, 9.

117. Most notably, Eisenhower's secretary of state, John Foster Dulles, and his brother, CIA Director Allen Dulles, who had spent years working closely with UFCO through their law firm Sullivan and Cromwell.

118. Quoted in Richard H. Immerman, *The CIA in Guatemala: The Policy of Foreign Intervention* (Austin: University of Texas Press, 1982), 181.

119. Scholars who argue that America's intervention was motivated by the desire to protect UFCO's interests include Jonas, "Guatemala"; de Soto, *Dependency and Intervention*; and Schlesinger and Kinzer, *Bitter Fruit*. Arguments against this interpretation come from Immerman, *The CIA in Guatemala* (2010); Piero Gleijeses, *Shattered Hope: The Guatemalan Revolution and the United States, 1944–1954* (Princeton, NJ: Princeton University Press, 1992); Schoultz, *Beneath the United States*; and Grow, *U.S. Presidents and Latin American Interventions*.

120. Department of State, May 29, 1964, "The Acting Secretary of State to Certain Diplomatic Offices in the American Republics," *FRUS, 1952–1954, Vol. VI, American Republics*, ed. N. Steven Kane and William F. Sanford Jr. (Washington, DC: GPO, 1983), Doc. 458.

121. Even after Arbenz was overthrown, Eisenhower did not pressure the new regime to help the UFCO. To the contrary, his administration proceeded with antitrust litigation against UFCO, which ultimately forced them to divest from Guatemala.

122. Dulles quoted in Schlesinger and Kinzer, *Bitter Fruit*, 136; Schoultz, *Beneath the United States*, 342.

123. National Security Council, August 19, 1953, "NSC Guatemala," *FRUS, 1952–1954, Vol. IV, American Republics*, Doc. 424.

124. Policy Planning Staff, May 28, 1954, "Our Guatemala Policy," *FRUS, 1952–1954, Vol. IV, American Republics*, Doc. 457.

125. National Security Council, August 19, 1953.

126. National Security Council, August 19, 1953.

127. Central Intelligence Agency, ca. 1953, "A Suggested Plan for Psychological Warfare Operations in Connection with Over-all Guatemalan Operations," CIA-FOIA, Doc. 0000914764.

128. Central Intelligence Agency, November 12, 1953, "Subject: Program for BCSUCCESS," *FRUS, 1952–1954, Guatemala*, ed. Susan Holly (Washington, DC: US GPO, 2003), Doc. 65.

129. Central Intelligence Agency, May 12, 1975, "CIA's Role in the Overthrow of Arbenz," *FRUS, 1952–1954, Guatemala*, Doc. 287.

130. At this point, there were actually three coups in short succession. Arbenz turned power over to Chief of the Armed Forces Carlos Enrique Diaz. However, the United States considered Diaz unacceptable and pressed him to appoint Colonel Elfego Monzon. Diaz then double-crossed the United States and appointed Monzon Minister of Government, thus maintaining power for himself. However, Diaz reversed his position after serious coercive diplomacy by US officials. In early July, Monzon relinquished control to Armas in exchange for a position of authority within the junta.

131. For three primary source documents on each intervention, see as following. On Brazil, see White House Audio Tape, March 31, 1964, "President Lyndon B. Johnson discussing the impending coup in Brazil with Undersecretary of State George Ball," https://nsarchive2.gwu .edu/NSAEBB/NSAEBB118/index.htm#docs; Department of State, March 27, 1964, "Top Secret Cable from Rio de Janeiro," NSA, https://nsarchive2.gwu.edu/NSAEBB/NSAEBB118 /bz02.pdf; Department of State, March 28, 1964, "Telegram from the Ambassador to Brazil (Gordon) to the Department of State," *FRUS, 1964–1968, Vol. XXXI, South and Central America; Mexico*, ed. David C. Geyer and David H. Herschler (Washington, DC: US GPO, 2004), Doc. 127; Department of State, March 29, 1964, "Top Secret Cable from Ambassador Lincoln Gordon," NSA, https://nsarchive2.gwu.edu/NSAEBB/NSAEBB118/bz03.pdf. On Bolivia (1963–66), see 303 Committee, January 29, 1965, "Provide Support to [less than 1 line of source text not declassified] and the Popular Christian Movement in Bolivia," *FRUS, 1964–1968, Vol. XXXI, South and Central America; Mexico*, Doc. 153; 303 Committee, July 13, 1965, "Expansion of

Political Action Program in Bolivia," *FRUS, 1964–1968, Vol. XXXI, South and Central America; Mexico*, Doc. 158; 303 Committee, July 15, 1966, "Results of the Political Action Program for Bolivia," *FRUS, 1964–1968, Vol. XXXI, South and Central America; Mexico*, Doc. 161. On Bolivia (1971), see Department of State, June 29, 1971, "Memorandum for: the 40 Committee, Subject: Bolivia," *FRUS, 1969–1972, Documents on the American Republics*, Doc. 104; Department of State, July 9, 1971, Backchannel Message From the Ambassador in Bolivia (Siracusa) to the Assistant Secretary of State for Inter-American Affairs (Meyer), La Paz, *FRUS, 1969–1976, Vol. E-10, Documents on the American Republics, 1969–1972*, ed. Douglas Kraft and James Siekmeier (Washington, DC: US GPO, 2009), Doc. 106; National Security Council, August 19, 1971, Memorandum for Dr. Kissinger from Arnold Nachmanoff "Subject: Bolivia," *FRUS, 1969–1976, Vol. E-10, Documents on the American Republics, 1969–1972*, Doc. 107. On British Guiana/Guyana, see Memorandum from Schlesinger to Kennedy, August 30, 1961, "Subject: British Guiana," *FRUS, 1961–1963, Volume XII, American Republics*, ed. Edward C. Keefer, Harriet Dashiell Schwar, and W. Taylor Fain III (Washington, DC: US GPO, 1996), Doc. 249; Department of State, March 15, 1962, "Possible Courses of Action in British Guiana," *FRUS, 1961–1963, Volume XII, American Republics*, Doc. 272; Memorandum from Schlesinger to Kennedy, September 5, 1962, "Subject: British Guiana," *FRUS, 1961–1963, Volume XII, American Republics*, Doc. 288. On Chile, see Senate Select Committee on Intelligence Activities Staff Report, "Covert Action in Chile, 1963–1973," https://www.archives.gov/files/declassification/iscap/pdf/2010-009-doc17.pdf; Central Intelligence Agency, November 18, 1970, "Report of CIA Chilean Task Force Activities, 15 September to 3 November 1970," NSA, https://nsarchive2.gwu.edu//NSAEBB/NSAEBB8/docs/doc01.pdf; Department of State, September 18, 2000, "Hinchey Report: CIA Activities in Chile," Homeland Security Digital Library, https://www.hsdl.org/?abstract&did=438476. On Cuba, see Memorandum from Lansdale to the Special Group, July 25, 1962, "Subject: Review of Operation Mongoose," NSA; Central Intelligence Agency, October 1961, "Inspector General's Survey of the Cuba Operation," NSAhttps://nsarchive2.gwu.edu//NSAEBB/NSAEBB341/IGrpt1.pdf; Central Intelligence Agency, January 18, 1962, "An Analysis of the Cuban Operation," NSA, https://nsarchive2.gwu.edu/NSAEBB/ciacase/EXF.pdf. On the Dominican Republic, see chap. 8. On Haiti, see Department of State, April 15, 1969, "Minutes of the Meeting of the 303 Committee," Nixon Library, https://www.nixonlibrary.gov/virtuallibrary/releases/dec10/14.pdf; 303 Committee, May 27, 1969, "Subject: Termination of U.S. Government Support to the Haitian Coalition for Radio Broadcasts to Haiti," *FRUS, 1969–1976, Vol. E-10, Documents on the American Republics, 1969–1972*, Doc. 383; 303 Committee, June 6, 1968, Memorandum from Jessup to Rostow, "Subject: Notes on 303 for PFIAB," *FRUS, 1964–1968, Vol. XXXII, Dominican Republic; Cuba; Haiti; Guyana*, ed. Daniel Lawler and Carolyn Lee (Washington, DC: US GPO, 2005), Doc. 279. On Panama, see Department of Defense, October 5, 1989, "Panama Crisis Chronology," DDRS; Joint Chiefs of Staff, *Operation Just Cause: Panama*, (Washington, DC: Joint History Office, Office of the Joint Chiefs of Staff, 1995). L. A. Yates, *The U.S. Military Intervention in Panama: Origins, Planning, and Crisis Management, June 1987–December 1989* (Washington, DC: Center of Military History, United States Army, 2008).

132. National Security Council Meeting, March 13, 1987, "Subject: South American Democracy," DNSA, Accession no. CO01941.

133. For three primary source documents on each intervention, see as following. On Chile, see National Security Council, November 13, 1986, "Subject: Meeting with the NSC," DNSA, Accession no. CL02473; National Security Council, November 17, 1986, "Subject: NSC Meeting on Chile," DNSA, Accession no. CL02474; National Security Council, November 18, 1986, "Subject: Chile," DNSA, Accession no. CL02477. On Haiti, see White House, April 22, 1986, "National Security Decision Directive Number 220: Haiti," FAS, https://fas.org/irp/offdocs/nsdd/nsdd-220.pdf; State Department cable from American embassy to Secretary of State, August 12, 1987, "Subject: Forces at Play in Haitian Crisis," Department of State (DOS) FOIA Electronic Reading Room, https://www.foia.state.gov/searchapp/DOCUMENTS/FOIADocs/00005557.pdf; National Endowment for Democracy, 1988, Annual Report, http://www.ned.org/docs/annual/1988%20NED%20Annual%20Report.pdf; Charles Stuart Kennedy and Clayton E. McManaway, June 29, 1993, "Interview with Clayton E. McManaway Jr.," Manuscript/Mixed Materials, Library of Congress, https://www.loc.gov/item/mfdipbib000799/.

On Nicaragua, see National Security Decision Directive 248, October 22, 1986, "Central America," FAS, https://fas.org/irp/offdocs/nsdd/nsdd-248.htm; National Security Council, March 12, 1987, "Subject: PRG Meeting on Nicaragua, February 27, 1987," CIA-FOIA, Doc. CIA-RDP89B00224R000802750002-3; Central Intelligence Agency, February 6, 1987, "Subject: CIA Response to National Security Study Directive on Central America," CIA-FOIA, Doc. 0001265255; National Security Decision Directive 264, February 27, 1987, "Central America," FAS, https://fas.org/irp/offdocs/nsdd/nsdd-264.htm. On Suriname, see White House, June 28, 1984, "Issues in Latin America," DNSA, Accession no. CO01502; National Endowment for Democracy, 1985, Annual Report, http://www.ned.org/wp-content/uploads/annualreports/1985-ned-annual-report.pdf; National Security Council, March 13, 1987, "Subject: South American Democracy," DNSA, Accession no. CO01941; Charles Stuart Kennedy and John J. Crowley Jr., June 27, 1989, "Interview with John J. Crowley Jr.," Manuscript/Mixed Materials, Library of Congress, https://www.loc.gov/item/mfdipbib000252/.

134. Quoted in D. J. Lecce, "International Law Regarding Prodemocratic Intervention: A Study of the Dominican Republic and Haiti," *Naval Law Review* 45 (1998): 258.

135. Quoted in H. W. Brands, "Decisions on American Armed Intervention: Lebanon, Dominican Republic, and Grenada," *Political Science Quarterly* 102, no. 4 (1987): 614.

136. Quoted in Benson, "The Polls," 594.

137. This is not to say that the invasion of Grenada was motivated in response to the Beirut attack. By the time of the attack in the barracks bombing, the invasion plans for Grenada were well underway, and Reagan had all but approved of the operation. Denise M. Bostdorff, "The Presidency and Promoted Crisis: Reagan, Grenada, and Issue Management," *Presidential Studies Quarterly* 21, no. 4 (1991): 737–50; Alan J. Rosenblatt, "Aggressive Foreign Policy Marketing: Public Response to Reagan's 1983 Address on Lebanon and Grenada," *Political Behavior* 20, no. 3 (September 1998): 225–40.

138. Quoted in Gary Williams, *US-Grenada Relations: Revolution and Intervention in the Backyard* (Basingstoke, UK: Macmillan, 2007), 170.

139. Ronald Reagan, October 25, 1983, "Remarks of the President and Prime Minister Eugenia Charles of Dominica Announcing the Deployment of United States Forces in Grenada," The American Presidency Project, http://www.presidency.ucsb.edu/ws/index.php?pid=40681#axzz1vAGJUucU.

140. Brands, "Decisions on American Armed Intervention," 614.

141. Quoted in "Invading Grenada," *FAIR*, January 1, 2007, http://fair.org/extra/book-excerpt-invading-grenada/.

142. Seymour M. Hersh, "Panama Strongman Said to Trade in Drugs, Arms and Illicit Money," *New York Times*, June 12, 1986, sec. World; Tom H. Carothers, *In the Name of Democracy: U.S. Policy toward Latin America in the Reagan Years* (Berkeley: University of California Press, 1991).

143. Carothers, *In the Name of Democracy*; Margaret E. Scranton, *The Noriega Years: US–Panamanian Relations, 1981–1990* (Boulder, CO: Lynne Rienner, 1991); Ronald Ratcliff, "Panama—The Enduring Crisis 1985–1989," in *Case Studies in Policy Making and Implementation* (Newport, RI: Naval War College, 2002).

144. Ratcliff, *Panama—The Enduring Crisis.*

145. Quoted in Yates, *U.S. Military Intervention in Panama*, 252.

146. Quoted in Yates, 294–63.

147. "Fighting in Panama: The President; A Transcript of Bush's Address on the Decision to Use Force in Panama," *New York Times*, December 21, 1989, sec. World.

148. Quoted in Russell Crandall, *Gunboat Democracy: U.S. Interventions in the Dominican Republic, Grenada, and Panama* (Lanham, MD: Rowman & Littlefield, 2006), 208–9.

6. Rolling Back the Iron Curtain

1. This is what Slater and Ziblatt refer to as "typological representativeness." Dan Slater and Daniel Ziblatt, "The Enduring Indispensability of the Controlled Comparison," *SAGE Publications Comparative Political Studies* 46, no. 10 (2013): 1301–27, DOI: 10.1177/0010414012472469.

2. Slater and Ziblatt, "Enduring Indispensability," 1301–27.

3. National Security Council 58/2, December 8, 1949, "A Report to the President by the National Security Council on United States Policy toward the Soviet Satellite States in Eastern Europe," *Foreign Relations of the United States (FRUS), 1949, Eastern Europe, The Soviet Union, Volume V*, ed. William Z. Slany and Rogers P. Churchill (Washington, DC: US Government Printing Office [GPO], 1975) Doc. 17.

4. Gregory Mitrovich, *Undermining the Kremlin: America's Strategy to Subvert the Soviet Bloc, 1947–1956* (Ithaca, NY: Cornell University Press, 2000), 20.

5. Clark Clifford and George Elsey, July 1946, "The Clifford-Elsey Report," 77, Harry S. Truman Library, Independence, MO, https://trumanlibrary.org/whistlestop/study_collections/coldwar/documents/pdf/4-1.pdf.

6. Tanisha M. Fazal, *State Death: The Politics and Geography of Conquest, Occupation, and Annexation* (Princeton, NJ: Princeton University Press, 2007); and Alexander B. Downes, "The Causes of Foreign Imposed Regime Change in Interstate Wars" (paper prepared for delivery at the 2008 Annual Meeting of the American Political Science Association, Boston MA, August 28–31, 2008).

7. Timothy *Bloodlands: Europe Between Hitler and Stalin* (New York: Basic Books, 2012).

8. Soviet losses cited Richard Overy, *Russia's War: A History of the Soviet Effort: 1941–1945.* (New York: Penguin Books, 1998), 445–46.

9. On the Soviet's desire for a sphere of influence, see Arthur Schlesinger, "Origins of the Cold War," *Foreign Affairs* 46, no. 1 (1967): 22–52; Albert Resis, "Spheres of Influence in Soviet Wartime Diplomacy," *Journal of Modern History* 53, no. 3 (1981): 417–39; Friedrich Kratochwil, "Of Systems, Boundaries, and Territoriality: An Inquiry into the Formation of the State System," *World Politics* 39, no. 1 (October 1986): 27–52; Martha Finnemore, *The Purpose of Intervention: Changing Beliefs About the Use of Force* (Ithaca, NY: Cornell University Press, 2004), 124–29.

10. Stalin quoted in Melvyn P. Leffler, For *the Soul of Mankind: The United States, The Soviet Union, and the Cold War* (New York: Hill and Wang, 2008), 51.

11. Christopher Lawrence Zugger, *The Forgotten: Catholics of the Soviet Empire from Lenin Through Stalin* (Syracuse, NY: Syracuse University Press, 2001), 380.

12. Peter Grose, *Operation Rollback: America's Secret War Behind the Iron Curtain* (Boston: Houghton Mifflin Harcourt, 2001), 19–20.

13. Dmitriĭ Antonovich Volkogonov, *Stalin: Triumph and Tragedy* (Phoenix, AZ: Prima Lifestyles, 1991), 531.

14. Tom Bower, *The Red Web: MI6 and the KGB Master Coup* (London: Arrow Books, 1989); J. B. Sedaitis and V. S. Vardys, *Lithuania: The Rebel Nation* (Boulder, CO: Westview Press, 1997): chap. 4.

15. Peter Grose, *Operation Rollback*, 35.

16. Central Intelligence Agency, 1998, "Cold War Allies: The Origins of CIA's Relationships with Ukrainian Nationalists," 19, CIA Freedom of Information Act (FOIA) Electronic Reading Room, https://www.cia.gov/library/readingroom/, (hereafter cited as CIA-FOIA), Doc. 519697e8993294098d50c281.

17. In English, they are called the National Union of Labor Solidarists. Christopher Simpson, *Blowback: America's Recruitment of Nazis and Its Effects on the Cold War* (New York: Weidenfeld and Nicolson, 1988); Grose, *Operation Rollback*; John Prados, *Safe for Democracy: The Secret Wars of the CIA* (Lanham, MD: Rowman & Littlefield, 2006); Tim Weiner, *Legacy of Ashes: The History of the CIA* (New York: Anchor, 2008); James Callanan, *Covert Action in the Cold War: US Policy, Intelligence and CIA Operations* (New York: IB Tauris, 2009).

18. Quoted in Grose, *Operation Rollback*, 40.

19. Prados, *Safe for Democracy*.

20. Quoted in Grose, *Operation Rollback*, 4.

21. George Kennan, February 22, 1946, 9 p.m., "The Charge in the Soviet Union (Kennan) to the Secretary of State," National Security Archive, George Washington University, Washington, DC (hereafter cited as NSA), https://nsarchive2.gwu.edu//coldwar/documents/episode-1/kennan.htm.

22. Kennan, "The Charge of the Soviet Union."

23. Kennan.

24. Clifford and Elsey, "The Clifford-Elsey Report."

25. Clifford and Elsey.

26. Patrick K. O'Donnell, *Operatives, Spies, and Saboteurs: The Unknown Story of the Men and Women of World War II's OSS*. (New York: Free Press, 2004); Richard Harris Smith, *OSS: The Secret History of America's First Central Intelligence Agency* (Guildford, CT: Lyons Press, 2005); Douglas Waller, *Wild Bill Donovan: The Spymaster Who Created the OSS and Modern American Espionage* (New York: Free Press, 2011).

27. Richard A. Best, *Proposals for Intelligence Reorganization, 1949–2004* (Library of Congress, Congressional Research Service, July 29, 2004).

28. US Congress, "The National Security Act of 1947" in *Decisions of the Highest Order: Perspectives on the National Security Council* (Pacific Grove, CA: Brooks, 1988): 37–39.

29. Central Intelligence Agency "Office of Policy Coordination: 1948–52," CIA-FOIA, Doc. 5166d49299326091c6a60241.

30. Bower, *Red Web*, 55; Richard Breitman, Norman J. W. Goda, Timothy Naftali, and Robert Wolfe, *U.S. Intelligence and the Nazis* (Cambridge: Cambridge University Press, 2005).

31. US Army Intelligence, May 1, 1952, "Report of Initial Contact with General Gehlen's Organization," 23–24.

32. Simpson, *Blowback*; Breitman, Goda, Naftali, and Wolfe, *U.S. Intelligence and the Nazis.*

33. Hilberg quoted in Simpson, *Blowback*, 24.

34. Mary Ellen, *General Reinhard Gehlen: The CIA Connection* (Fairfax, VA: George Mason University Press, 1990)

35. Simpson, *Blowback*; Breitman, Goda, Naftali, and Wolfe, *U.S. Intelligence and the Nazis.*

36. Simpson, *Blowback*, 53.

37. Weiner, *Legacy of Ashes*, 32, places this figure at 5 percent of the Marshall Plan budget; Callanan, *Covert Action in the Cold War*, 53, questions that figure.

38. Grose, *Operation Rollback*, 114.

39. National Security Council Directive 10/2, May 12, 1948, "Draft Report by the National Security Council," *FRUS, 1945–1950, Emergence of the Intelligence Establishment*, ed. C. Thomas Thorne Jr. and David S. Patterson (Washington, DC: US GPO, 1996), Doc. 274.

40. National Security Council 20/1, "U.S. Objectives with Respect to Russia," in *Containment: Documents on American Policy and Strategy, 1945–1950* (New York: Columbia University Press, 1978): 173–203.

41. National Security Council 20/4, November 23, 1948, "Note By the Executive Secretary on U.S. Objectives With Respect to the USSR to Counter Soviet Threats to U.S. Security," *FRUS, 1948, Vol. I, Part 2, General; The United Nations*, ed. Neal H. Petersen et al. (Washington, DC: US GPO, 1976), Doc. 61.

42. National Security Council 174, "Statement of Policy Proposed by the National Security Council on United States Policy toward the Soviet Satellites in Eastern Europe," December 11, 1953, *FRUS, 1952–1954, Vol. VIII, Eastern Europe; Soviet Union; Eastern Mediterranean*, ed. David M. Baehler et al. (Washington, DC: US GPO, 1988), Doc. 51.

43. Policy Planning Staff Paper 59, "U.S. Policy toward the Soviet Satellite States in Eastern Europe," August 25, 1949, *FRUS, 1949, Vol. V, Eastern Europe, The Soviet Union*, ed. William Z. Slany and Rogers P. Churchill (Washington, DC: US GPO, 1975), Doc. 10.

44. Quoted by Jeffrey Burds, *The Early Cold War in Soviet West Ukraine, 1944–1948* (Pittsburgh, PA: University of Pittsburgh, 2001).

45. For an excellent internal history, see Psychological Strategy Board, December 1951, "The Development of American Psychological Operations, 1945–41," NARA, https://archive.org/details/TheDevelopmentofAmericanPsychologicalOperations-1945-51devpsychops.

46. National Security Council 20/1, "U.S. Objectives with Respect to Russia."

47. National Security Council 20/1.

48. Harry S. Truman, "Truman Doctrine, March 12, 1947," UVA Miller Center, https://millercenter.org/the-presidency/presidential-speeches/march-12-1947-truman-doctrine.

49. National Security Council 58/2, "A Report to the President by the National Security Council," 5.

50. Quoted in Mitrovich, *Undermining the Kremlin*, 10.

51. Melvyn P. Leffler, *The Specter of Communism: The United States and the Origins of the Cold War, 1917–1953* (New York: Hill and Wang, 1994).

52. Policy Planning Staff 13, November 6, 1947, "Resume of World Situation," *FRUS, 1947, General; The United Nations, Vol. 1*, ed. Ralph E. Goodwin, Neal H. Petersen, Marvin W. Kranz, and Willian Slany (Washington, DC: US GPO, 1973), Doc. 393.

53. Matthew A. Evangelista, "Stalin's Post War Army Reappraised," *International Security* 7, no. 3 (Winter 1982–83): 110. These figures were grossly inflated, in part due to erroneous intelligence provided by the Gehlen Organization.

54. Evangelista, "Stalin's Post War Army."

55. National Security Council 68, April 14, 1950, "United States Objectives and Programs for National Security," *FRUS, 1950, Vol. I, National Security Affairs; Foreign Economic Policy*, ed. Neal H. Peterson et al. (Washington, DC: US GPO, 1950), Doc. 85.

56. Grose, *Operation Rollback*.

57. Beatrice Heuser, "Covert Action within British and American Concepts of Containment, 1948–51," in *British Intelligence, Strategy and the Cold War, 1945–51*, ed. Richard J. Aldrich (London: Routledge, 1993), 76.

58. Lindsay quoted in Grose, *Operation Rollback*, 188.

59. National Security Council 174, "Statement of Policy Proposed by the National Security Council on United States Policy toward the Soviet Satellites in Eastern Europe."

60. National Security Council 174.

61. National Security Council 5606, July 18, 1956, "Note by the Executive Secretary to the National Security Council on U.S. Policy toward the Soviet Satellites in Eastern Europe," *FRUS, 1955–1957, Vol. XXV, Eastern Europe*, ed. Edward C. Keefer, Ronald D. Landa, and Stanley Shaloff (Washington, DC: US GPO, 1990), Doc. 73.

62. Quoted in Prados, *Safe for Democracy*, 59.

63. King Zog is sometimes also known as King Zogu.

64. Sometimes translated as the National Liberation Army (NLA) or National Liberation Front (NLF).

65. I introduced them here for the sake of simplicity, but the Legaliteti were not formally organized until December 1943. Prior to that point, Royalist forces were disunified across several organizations.

66. Peter Lucas, *The OSS in World War II Albania: Covert Operations and Collaboration with Communist Partisans* (Jefferson, NC: McFarland, 2007): 28.

67. Dusan Batakovic, "Kosovo and Metohija: Serbia's Troublesome Province," *Balcanica* 39 (2008): 243–76.

68. Nigel Thomas and Peter Abbott, *Partisan Warfare 1941–45* (Oxford: Osprey, 2010), 25–27.

69. Albert Lulushi, *Operation Valuable Fiend: The CIA's First Paramilitary Strike against the Iron Curtain* (New York: Arcade, 2014), 24.

70. Carl Savich, "Macedonia in World War II: Debar and the Skanderbeg Division," Balkanalysis, October 4, 2005, http://www.balkanalysis.com/blog/2005/10/04/macedonia-in-world-war-ii-debar-and-the-skanderbeg-division/.

71. Simpson, *Blowback*, 123.

72. R. J. Crampton, *The Balkans Since the Second World War* (London; New York: Routledge, 2002), 38–43.

73. Miranda Vickers, *The Albanians: A Modern History* (London: IB Tauris, 2011), 169–70.

74. Mitrovich, *Undermining the Kremlin*, 44.

75. Mitrovich, 44.

76. Stephen Dorril, *MI6: Inside the Covert World of Her Majesty's Secret Intelligence Service* (New York: Simon and Schuster, 2002), 369–70.

77. Burton Hersh, *The Old Boys: The American Elite and the Origins of the CIA* (St. Petersburg, FL: Scribner's, 1992), 262.

78. Office of Policy Coordination, "Outline Plan for Project No. EE-10," NARA, RG 263, Entry ZZ-19, Vol. 02, Box. 46.

79. Office of Policy Coordination, "Outline Plan for Project No. EE-10"; Lulushi, *Operation Valuable Fiend*, 52.

80. Central Intelligence Agency, October 7, 1949, "Central BGFIEND Sub-Project Outline" CIA-FOIA, Doc. 519a2b76993294098d50f3d8.

81. Callanan, *Covert Action in the Cold War*, 74.

82. Central Intelligence Agency, "Central BGFIEND Sub-Project Outline."

83. Quoted in Owen Pearson, *Albania as Dictatorship and Democracy: From Isolation to the Kosovo War, 1946–1998* (London: IB Taurus, 2006), 348.

84. Central Intelligence Agency, July 1951, "Albania—Jugoslavia," NARA.

85. Quoted in Callanan, *Covert Action in the Cold* War, 71.

86. Central Intelligence Agency, undated, "Advantages and Disadvantages of an Attempted Coup in Albania," NARA, RG 263, Entry ZZ-19, Vol. 1, Box 45. See also Central Intelligence Agency, "Pros and Cons of Proposal to Detach Albania from the Soviet Orbit," NARA, RG. 263, Entry ZZ-19, Vol. 01, Box 45.

87. Memorandum from Kermit Roosevelt to the Assistant Director for Policy Coordination, November 29, 1949, CIA-FOIA, Doc. 519a2b76993294098d50f3d1.

88. O'Donnell, *Operatives, Spies, and Saboteurs*, 37.

89. O'Donnell, 37.

90. Central Intelligence Agency, July 1951, "Albania—Jugoslavia," NARA.

91. Quoted in Lulushi, *Operation Valuable Fiend*, 42.

92. Memorandum from Wisner to the Assistant Director for Policy Coordination, June 4, 1952, CIA-FOIA, Doc. No. 519a2b76993294098d50f3b5.

93. Memorandum from Wisner to Assistant Director for Policy Coordination, June 4, 1952.

94. Memorandum from Kermit Roosevelt to the Assistant Director for Policy Coordination, November 29, 1949.

95. Central Intelligence Agency, undated, ca. 1949, "Country Plan: Albania," CIA-FOIA, Doc. 519a2b76993294098d50f3c0.

96. Simpson, *Blowback*; Breitman, Goda, Naftali, and Wolfe, *U.S. Intelligence and the Nazis*; Richard Breitman and Norman J. W. Goda. *Hitler's Shadow: Nazi War Criminals, U.S. Intelligence, and the Cold War* (Washington, DC: National Archives, 2010).

97. Central Intelligence Agency, January 8, 1954, "Decadal Views on NCFA Reorganization," CIA-FOIA, Doc. 519a2b76993294098d50f39d.

98. CIA, "Decadal Views."

99. CIA, "Decadal Views."

100. Prados, *Safe for Democracy*, 63.

101. Quoted in Lulushi, *Operation Valuable Fiend*, 63–64.

102. Quoted in Lulushi, 63–64.

103. Hersh, *The Old Boys*, 262.

104. The visa issue was resolved relatively quickly after some bureaucratic maneuvering, and NCFA leaders visited New York and Washington in September 1949.

105. Central Intelligence Agency, May 1, 1952, "Report of Initial Contact with General Gehlen's Organization," NSA, https://nsarchive2.gwu.edu/NSAEBB/NSAEBB146/doc06.pdf. Lulushi, *Operation Valuable Fiend*, 71, argues that Dosti's ties to the Italian and German occupying powers have been exaggerated and that he has served as cabinet minister as part of a Balli Kombëtar plan to infiltrate the government. He notes that Dosti suffered greatly at the hands of the Germans, who murdered his brother and wife.

106. Central Intelligence Agency, July 12, 1949, "Subject; Deva, Djafer (also Shaver, Diafar and Khafer)," CIA-FOIA, Doc. 519a6b27993294098d51121b.

107. Central Intelligence Agency, "Country Plan: Albania," 83.

108. Central Intelligence Agency, October 7, 1949, "Sub-Project: PW Annex to Project BG-FIEND," CIA-FOIA, Doc. 519a2b76993294098d50f3d8. For an example of the type of propaganda distributed by the NCFA, see H. Dosti (undated), "The Position of Albania and the Establishment of the Communist Regime," CIA-FOIA, Doc. 519a6b23993294098d510a77.

109. Central Intelligence Agency, August 3, 1950, "Proposed Joint PW Policy Guidance for BGFIEND," CIA-FOIA, Doc. 519a2b76993294098d50f3c7.

110. Andrew V. Noble, *Bullets and Broadcasting: Methods of Subversion and Subterfuge in the CIA War against the Iron Curtain* (Reno: University of Nevada, 2008), 73.
111. Burke Quoted in Grose. *Operation Rollback*, 157.
112. Wisner quoted in Prados, *Safe for Democracy*, 59.
113. This refers to the ten agents dropped in early September and the eleven agents dropped on October 6, 1949. Lulushi, *Operation Valuable Fiend*.
114. Lulushi, *Operation Valuable Fiend*, 81.
115. Simpson, *Blowback*; Grose, *Operation Rollback*; Mitrovich, *Undermining the Kremlin*; Prados, *Safe for Democracy*; Sarah-Jane Corke, *US Covert Operations and Cold War Strategy: Truman, Secret Warfare and the CIA, 1945–53* (London: Routledge, 2007); Weiner, *Legacy of Ashes*; Callanan, *Covert Action in the Cold War*.
116. Quoted in Noble, *Bullets and Broadcasting*, 77.
117. For a typical summary, see Central Intelligence Agency, January 4, 1951, "Memo from Policy Coordination to OPC," CIA-FOIA, Doc. CIA-RDP83-00036R001100010019-8.
118. Central Intelligence Agency "Country Plan: Albania."
119. Central Intelligence Agency, November 14, 1950, "Subject: First Team Drop into HBPixie, 11–12, November 1950," NARA, RG 263, Vol. 5, Box. 46.
120. Lulushi, *Operation Valuable Fiend*, 115.
121. Curtis Peebles, *Twilight Warriors: Covert Air Operations against the USSR* (Annapolis, MD: Naval Institute Press, 2013).
122. Michael Clodfelter, *Warfare and Armed Conflicts*, Jefferson, NC: McFarland, 539. For a case-by-case account of these operations, see Peebles, *Twilight Warriors*, chap. 1.
123. Noble, *Bullets and Broadcasting*, 80.
124. Prados, *Safe for Democracy*, 63.
125. Lulushi, *Operation Valuable Fiend*, 159.
126. Lulushi, 159.
127. Lulushi, 161.
128. Lulushi, 161.
129. S. J. Hamrick, *Deceiving the Deceivers: Kim Philby, Donald Maclean and Guy Burgess* (New Haven, CT: Yale University Press, 2004).
130. Weiner, *Legacy of Ashes*, 52.
131. Hamrick, *Deceiving the Deceivers*, 138.
132. Central Intelligence Agency, April 4, 1951, "Intelligence Summary No. 10: Increasing Unrest in Albania," CIA-FOIA, Doc. 519a2b7a993294098d50fe80.
133. Noble, *Bullets and Broadcasting*, 80.
134. Central Intelligence Agency, December 18, 1951, "CIA/opc 1952 Albanian Operations," CIA-FOIA, Doc. 519a2b76993294098d50f3ca.
135. Central Intelligence Agency, May 3, 1954, "Memorandum for Chief SE Division, Two Year Plan of Operations for Albania," CIA-FOIA, Doc. 519a2b76993294098d50f3a8.
136. Hoxha quote in Noble, *Bullets and Broadcasting*, 81.
137. Central Intelligence Agency, "Text of Albanian Spy Trial Verdict," April 21, 1954, CIA-FOIA, Doc. 519a2b7e993294098d5106e4; Albanian Home Services, April 5, 1954, "Trial of U.S. Diversionists to Begin," CIA-FOIA, Doc. 519a2b7a993294098d50fdd1.
138. Central Intelligence Agency, April 16, 1956, "Subject; National Committee for a Free Albania (NCFA)," CIA-FOIA, Doc. 519a2b76993294098d50f39b; See also, Central Intelligence Agency, June 14, 1956, "Subject: Termination of OBLIVIOUS Project," CIA-FOIA, Doc. 519a2b76993294098d50f3a0.
139. Central Intelligence Agency, November 25, 1949 "Dosti, Hasan," NARA, https://archive.org/details/DOSTIHASAN-0026.
140. Central Intelligence Agency, "Country Plan: Albania," 81; Central Intelligence Agency, "Central BGFIEND Sub-Project Outline."
141. CIA, "Country Plan."
142. Callanan, *Covert Action in the Cold War*, 76.
143. Corke, *US Covert Operations and Cold War Strategy*, 98.
144. Callanan, *Covert Action in the Cold War*, 78.

145. Callanan, 78.

146. Peebles, *Twilight Warriors*, 34.

147. Lulushi, *Operation Valuable Fiend*, 66.

148. Wisner quoted in Lulushi, 66.

149. Office of Policy Coordination, September 7, 1949, "Memorandum for: CCP, Subject: Revaluation of Project BGFIEND," NARA, RG. 263, Entry ZZ-19 Vol. 02. Box 46.

150. Hamrick, *Deceiving the Deceivers*, 200.

151. Smith quoted in Mitrovich, *Undermining the Kremlin*, 45.

152. Burke quoted in Prados, *Safe for Democracy*, 64.

153. Lindsay quoted in Callanan, *Covert Action in the Cold* War, 84.

154. Snyder, *Bloodlands*, 27.

155. Snyder, 27.

156. Central Intelligence Agency, undated, "Stepan Bandera," Complete file at: https://iwpchi.files.wordpress.com/2014/03/cia_nazi_war_criminals_files_bandera.pdf; Breitman, Goda, Naftali, and Wolfe, *U.S. Intelligence and the Nazis*, 249–55.

157. The other faction was OUN-M, led by Andrei Melynik. Like Bandera's group, OUN-M collaborated with the Nazis and later worked with Anglo-American intelligence agencies. However, I have omitted them from this account for the sake of simplicity.

158. Viktor Polishchuk, *Bitter Truth: The Criminality of the Organization of Ukrainian Nationalists (OUN) and the Ukrainian Insurgent Army (UPA): The Testimony of a Ukrainian* (W. Poliszczuk, 1999), 146.

159. Quoted in Breitman and Goda, *Hitler's Shadow*, 74.

160. Quoted in Breitman and Goda, 74.

161. Simpson, *Blowback*, 163; Breitman and Goda, *Hitler's Shadow*, 75.

162. Simpson, 163; Breitman and Goda, 75.

163. Central Intelligence Agency, undated, "Stepan Bandera."

164. Quoted by Breitman, Goda, Naftali, and Wolfe, *U.S. Intelligence and the Nazis*, 250.

165. Lebed quoted in Breitman and Goda, *Hitler's Shadow*, 75.

166. Lebed quoted in Breitman and Goda, 75.

167. Benjamin Lieberman, *Terrible Fate: Ethnic Cleansing and the Making of Modern Europe* (Lanham, MD: Rowman & Littlefield), 210.

168. Simpson, *Blowback*, 162.

169. Maltz quoted in Breitman and Goda, *Hitler's Shadow*, 76.

170. Quoted in Breitman and Goda, 77.

171. Burds, "The Early Cold War in Soviet West Ukraine, 1944–1948," 8.

172. Simpson, *Blowback*, 162.

173. Central Intelligence Agency, 1998, "Cold War Allies," 20.

174. The SSU was the postwar successor of the OSS and a precursor to the CIA.

175. Quoted in Burds, "The Early Cold War in Soviet West Ukraine, 1944–1948, 13.

176. Central Intelligence Agency, 1998, "Cold War Allies," 29.

177. Central Intelligence Agency, December 27, 1946, "Country: Ukraine, Subject: Operation Belladonna," CIA-FOIA, Doc. 519a2b75993294098d50f11d.

178. Quoted in Breitman and Goda, *Hitler's Shadow*, 86.

179. Quoted in Burds, "The Early Cold War in Soviet West Ukraine, 1944–1948," 16.

180. Prados, *Safe for Democracy*, 28.

181. Quoted in Grose, *Operation Rollback*, 45.

182. Grose, 45; Prados, *Safe for Democracy*, 29.

183. Quoted in Burds, "The Early Cold War in Soviet West Ukraine, 1944–1948," 15.

184. Central Intelligence Agency, December 12, 1950, "Joint OSO-OSP Report on the Ukrainian National Resistance Movement," NARA.

185. Central Intelligence Agency, 1998, "Cold War Allies," 21–22.

186. Central Intelligence Agency, "Joint OSO-OSP Report on the Ukrainian National Resistance Movement."

187. Central Intelligence Agency, November 28, 1950, "Operations in Ukraine," NARA.

188. Central Intelligence Agency, "Operations in Ukraine."

189. Central Intelligence Agency, January 4, 1951, "Memorandum from Wisner to Director of Central Intelligence, Joint OSO/OPC Report on the Ukrainian Resistance Movement," NARA, RG. 263, Entry ZZ-19 Subject Files (2nd Release), Box 9, Aerodynamic Vol. 9.

190. Central Intelligence Agency, December 22, 1950, "Subject: Project PBCRUET-Aero-Dynamic," CIA-FOIA, Doc. 519a2b75993294098d50f142.

191. Central Intelligence Agency, April 23, 1951, "Subject: Ukrainian Position Paper," NARA, https://archive.org/details/AERODYNAMICVOL9DEVELOPMENTANDPLANS-0039; Central Intelligence Agency, March 1951, "Specific arrangements suggested for inclusion in operational framework for coordinated U.S.-British operations with Russian émigré groups," NARA, RG. 263, Entry ZZ-19, Box 9, Vol. 9.

192. Central Intelligence Agency, February 28, 1956, "Aerodynamics—English Language Publication," CIA-FOIA, Doc. 519a2b7d993294098d510670. See Jeffrey Burds, "Borderland Wars: The Soviet War to Crush Ukrainian Nationalism, 1944–1948" (unpublished manuscript).

193. Central Intelligence Agency, "Aerodynamics"; Burds, "Borderland Wars."

194. Grose, Operation Rollback, 172; Prados, Safe for Democracy, 73.

195. Central Intelligence Agency, July 29, 1954, "Subject: Letter from RECAVATINA/6 Operational Leader from Drohobycz Okrug," CIA-FOIA Doc. 519a2b74993294098d50f0a9.

196. Prados, Safe for Democracy, 51; Breitman and Goda, Hitler's Shadow, 88.

197. Central Intelligence Agency "Cold War Allies."

198. Burds, "The Early Cold War in Soviet West Ukraine, 1944–1948," 33–35.

199. Sudoplatov quoted in Burds, "Early Cold War," 44.

200. Sudoplatov quoted in Grose, Operation Rollback, 180.

201. Velimir Vuksic, Tito's Partisans 1941–45 (New York: Bloomsbury, USA: Osprey, 2003).

202. Sabrina P. Ramet, The Three Yugoslavias: State-Building and Legitimation, 1918–2005 (Bloomington: Indiana University Press, 2006), 146.

203. Kennan, "The Charge of the Soviet Union."

204. Truman, "Truman Doctrine, March 12, 1947."

205. Simpson, Blowback; Breitman, Goda, Naftali, and Wolfe, U.S. Intelligence and the Nazis.

206. Ivo Banac, With Stalin against Tito: Cominformist Splits in Yugoslav Communism (Ithaca, NY: Cornell University Press, 1988).

207. Policy Planning Staff Directive 35, June 30, 1948, "The Attitude of This Government toward Events in Yugoslavia," FRUS, 1948, Vol. V, Eastern Europe; The Soviet Union, ed. William Z. Slany and Rogers P. Churchill (Washington, DC: US GPO, 1975), Doc. 702.

208. Policy Planning Staff Directive 35, "Attitude of This Government."

209. Policy Planning Staff Directive 49, February 10, 1949, "Economic Relations between the United States and Yugoslavia," DNSA, Accession no. PD00053.

210. Mitrovich, Undermining the Kremlin, 38.

211. National Security Council 58/2, "A Report to the President by the National Security Council."

212. National Security Council 58/2.

213. National Security Council 58/2.

214. Kennan quoted in Mitrovich, Undermining the Kremlin, 38.

215. National Security Council 174, "Statement of Policy Proposed by the National Security Council on United States Policy toward the Soviet Satellites in Eastern Europe."

216. National Security Council 174.

217. Rositzke quoted in Burds, "The Early Cold War in Soviet West Ukraine, 1944–1948," 18.

218. Bedell Smith quoted in Mitrovich, Undermining the Kremlin, 39.

219. Quoted in Grose, Operation Rollback, 110.

220. Bower, Red Web; Vardys and Sedaitis, Lithuania, chap. 4; Grose, Operation Rollback.

221. Quoted in Kevin Ruffner, April 2003, "Eagle and Swastika: CIA and Nazi War Criminals and Collaborators, Draft Working Paper," 237, CIA-FOIA, Doc. 519697e8993294098 d50c2a4.

222. Harry Rositzke, "America's Secret Operations: A Perspective," Foreign Affairs 53, no. 2 (1975): 334–51.

7. Containment, Coup d'Etat, and the Covert War in Vietnam

Epigraph: Lyndon B. Johnson, "Conversation with Eugene McCarthy," https://millercenter .org/the-presidency/secret-white-house-tapes/conversation-eugene-mccarthy-february-1 -1966-0.

1. Vietnamese casualty estimates from Rudolph J. Rummel, *Statistics of Democide: Genocide and Mass Murder Since 1900* (Münster, Germany: LIT Verlag, 1997), chap. 6. US casualty estimate from National Archives, "Vietnam War U.S. Military Fatal Casualty Statistics," April 29, 2008, http://www.archives.gov/research/military/vietnam-war/casualty-statistics .html.

2. Based on this project's coding rules, I do not consider America's overt actions against North Vietnam during the Vietnam War to be a regime change operation because Washington's objectives stopped short of overthrowing Ho Chi Minh's regime. Instead, US policymakers sought to coerce Hanoi into stopping its aggressive policies toward the south and accepting an independent, non-communist government in Saigon.

3. Gary King and Langche Zeng, "Explaining Rare Events in International Relations," *International Organization* 55, no. 3 (June 2001): 693–715.

4. State-Saigon Cable 243, August 23, 1963, "Action: AmEmbassy Saigon," National Security Archive, Washington, DC (hereafter cited as NSA), https://nsarchive2.gwu.edu/NSAEBB /NSAEBB101/vn02.pdf.

5. John F. Kennedy, October 29, 1963, 4:20 p.m., "President Kennedy Meets with His National Security Council on the Question of Supporting a Coup in South Vietnam," in *The White House Tapes: Eavesdropping on the President*, ed. John Prados (New York: New Press, 2003).

6. Robert S. McNamara and Brian Van De Mark, *In Retrospect: The Tragedy and Lessons of Vietnam* (New York: Vintage Books, 1996), 129–39.

7. John Lewis Gaddis, *Strategies of Containment: A Critical Appraisal of Postwar American National Security Policy* (New York: Oxford University Press, 2005), 29.

8. Dixee Bartholomew-Feis, *The OSS and Ho Chi Minh: Unexpected Allies in the War against Japan* (Lawrence: University Press of Kansas, 2006).

9. William Duiker, *U.S. Containment Policy and the Conflict in Indochina* (Palo Alto, CA: Stanford University Press, 1994), chap. 1.

10. Pentagon Papers, 1969, *Part I, Vietnam and the United States, 1940–1950*, Pentagon Papers collection at National Archives and Records Administration, https://www.archives.gov /research/pentagon-papers (hereafter cited as NARA-PP), C-38.

11. Pentagon Papers, 1969, *Part I*, B-4.

12. Pentagon Papers, 1969, *Part I*, A-3.

13. Pentagon Papers, 1969, *Part I*, C-4.

14. Duiker, *U.S. Containment Policy*, chap. 3.

15. Pentagon Papers, 1969, *Part I*, A-42.

16. Pentagon Papers, 1969, *Part I*, A-49.

17. Pentagon Papers, 1969, *Part I*, A-49.

18. Pentagon Papers, 1969, *Part II, U.S. Involvement in the Franco-Viet Minh War, 1950–1954*, (NARA-PP), A-2.

19. Pentagon Papers, 1969, *Part I*, A-61.

20. Duiker, *U.S. Containment Policy*, 93.

21. John Prados, *Vietnam: The History of an Unwinnable War, 1945–1975* (Lawrence: University Press of Kansas, 2009), 23.

22. Thomas L. Ahern, *CIA and the House of Ngo: Covert Action in South Vietnam 1954–1961* (Washington, DC: Central Intelligence Agency, Center for the Study of Intelligence, 2000), 3, CIA-FOIA, no. 5076e89c993247d4d82b62eb.

23. Ted Morgan, *Valley of Death: The Tragedy at Dien Bien Phu That Led America into the Vietnam War* (New York: Random House, 2010).

24. Eisenhower quoted in George C. Herring and Richard H. Immerman, "Eisenhower, Dulles, and Dienbienphu: 'The Day We Didn't Go to War' Revisited," *Journal of American History* 71, no. 2 (1984): 349.

25. Herring and Immerman, "Eisenhower, Dulles, and Dienbienphu," 362.

26. Herring and Immerman, 362.

27. Herring and Immerman, 362.

28. Herring and Immerman, 362; Prados, *Vietnam*, 29.

29. Elizabeth Nathan Saunders, *Leaders at War: How Presidents Shape Military Interventions* (Ithaca, NY: Cornell University Press, 2011), 73.

30. Eisenhower quoted in Saunders, *Leaders at War*, 74.

31. Pentagon Papers, 1969, *Part IV, A-3, Evolution of the War: U.S. and France's Withdrawal from Vietnam, 1954–56*, NARA-PP, 3.

32. Ahern, *CIA and the House of Ngo*, 14.

33. National Security Council Memorandum, January 21, 1954, quoted in Kenneth Andrade and Dale Conboy, *Spies and Commandos: How America Lost the Secret War in North Vietnam* (Lawrence: University Press of Kansas, 2000), 2.

34. Conboy and Andrade, *Spies and Commandos*, 3.

35. NSC 5429/2, August 20, 1954, "Current U.S. Policy toward the Far East," in Pentagon Papers, 1969, *Part V, Justification for the War, The Internal Documents*, NARA-PP, 731.

36. NSC 5429/3, November 19, 1954, "Current U.S. Policy toward the Far East," in *Foreign Relations of the United States (FRUS), 1952–1954, Vol. XII, Part 1, East Asia and the Pacific*, ed. David W. Mabon (Washington, DC: US Government Printing Office [GPO], 1984), Doc. 394. Whether Eisenhower hoped these operations could overthrow the Vietminh regime is unclear. For the purposes here, I have decided not to code them as a regime change. Given their small scale and stated objectives, I believe that US policymakers employed these covert missions for objectives short of regime change—that is, supporting the South Vietnamese regime, harassing Ho Chi Minh's government, and creating an underground infrastructure to wage a guerilla war in the event of a Soviet or Chinese invasion. Having just observed the French collapse, Eisenhower does not seem to believe that the United States would be able covertly to overthrow the Vietminh regime. Nevertheless, these early actions are important because they help pave the way for America's subsequent covert regime changes in the country.

37. Conboy and Andrade, *Spies and Commandos*, 4.

38. Richard H. Shultz, Jr., *The Secret War against Hanoi: The Untold Story of Spies, Saboteurs, and Covert Warriors in North Vietnam* (New York: Harper Perennial, 1999), 14.

39. Conboy and Andrade, *Spies and Commandos*, 6.

40. Sedgwick D. Tourison, *Secret Army, Secret War: Washington's Tragic Spy Operation in North Vietnam* (Annapolis, MD: US Naval Institute Press, 1995), 9.

41. Conein quoted in Tourison, *Secret Army, Secret War*, 9.

42. Ho quoted in Shultz, *Secret War against Hanoi*, 14.

43. Ahern, *CIA and the House of Ngo*, 5–6.

44. Some historians have argued that the CIA played an active role in convincing Bao Dai to appoint Diem. I have found no evidence of this and thus do not code it as a regime change. As evidence to the contrary, an internal CIA history notes in response to this question that "Agency records do not entirely resolve the question, but suggest, at most, a peripheral CIA role." Ahern, *CIA and the House of Ngo*, 24.

45. Pentagon Papers, 1969, *Part IV, A-3*, 5.

46. Pentagon Papers, 1969, *Part IV, A-3*, 3.

47. Pentagon Papers, 1969, *Part IV, A-4, Evolution of the War: U.S. Training of Vietnamese National Army, 1954–59*, NARA-PP, 1.1.

48. Pentagon Papers, 1969, *Part IV*, 13.

49. State Department Telegram, November 7, 1954, "The Ambassador in Vietnam (Heath) to the Department of State," *FRUS, 1952–1954, Vol. XIII, Part 2, Indochina*, ed. Neal H. Peterson; (Washington, DC: US GPO, 1982), Doc. 1308.

50. Pentagon Papers, 1969, *Part IV, A-3*, 18.

51. Pentagon Papers, 1969, *Part IV, A-3*, 21.

52. Pentagon Papers, 1969, *Part IV, A-3*, 21.

53. Pentagon Papers, 1969, *Part IV, A-3*, 22.

54. Pentagon Papers, 1969, *Part IV, A-3*, 23.

55. Pentagon Papers, 1969, *Part IV, A-3*, 25.

56. Ahern, *CIA and the House of Ngo*, 77.

57. Pentagon Papers, 1969, *Part IV, A-3*, 31.

58. Pentagon Papers, 1969, *Part IV, A-3*, 32.

59. State Department Telegram, May 1, 1955, "Telegram from the Secretary of State to the Embassy in Vietnam," *FRUS, 1955–1957, Vol. I, Vietnam*, ed. Edward C. Keefer and David W. Mabon (Washington, DC: US GPO, 1985), Doc. 164.

60. Pentagon Papers, 1969, *Part IV, A-3*, 34.

61. Pentagon Papers, 1969, *Part IV, A-5, Evolution of the War: Origins of the Insurgency*, NARA-PP, 5.

62. First quote from Director of the Office of Philippines and Southeast Asian Affairs "U.S. Policy on All Vietnam Elections," March 28, 1955. Second quote from NSC report, "U.S. Policy on All-Vietnam Elections," March 28, 1955. Both quotes in Kathryn C. Statler, *Replacing France: The Origins of American Intervention in Vietnam* (Lawrence: University Press of Kentucky, 2007), 158 and 160, respectively.

63. Statler, *Replacing France*, 161.

64. Ahern, *CIA and the House of Ngo*, 13.

65. State Department Telegram, April 7, 1955, "Telegram from the Special Representative in Vietnam (Collins) to the Department of State," *FRUS, 1955–1957, Vol. I, Vietnam*, Doc. 106.

66. Pentagon Papers, 1969, *Part IV, A-4*, 1.

67. Pentagon Papers, 1969, *Part IV, A-4*, 2.1-5.1.

68. Quoted in David Elliott, *The Vietnamese War: Revolution and Social Change in the Mekong Delta, 1930–1975* (Abingdon, UK: Routledge, 2003), 228.

69. Quoted in Shultz, *Secret War against Hanoi*, 14.

70. Howard Jones, *Death of a Generation: How the Assassinations of Diem and JFK Prolonged the Vietnam War* (New York: Oxford University Press, 2003), 18.

71. Edward Lansdale, January 17, 1961, "Memorandum for the Secretary of Defense, Deputy Secretary of Defense, From: BrigGen Lansdale, OSO/OSD, Subj: Vietnam," in Pentagon Papers, 1969, *Part V, Justification for the War, The Internal Documents, The Kennedy Administration, Book II*, NARA-PP, 1–12.

72. Quoted in Jones, *Death of a Generation*, 13.

73. Country Team Staff Committee, January 4, 1961, "Basic Counterinsurgency Plan for Viet-Nam," *FRUS, 1964–1968, Vol. I, Vietnam, 1964*, ed. Edward C. Keefer and Charles S. Sampson (Washington, DC: US GPO, 1992), Doc. 1.

74. Quoted in Tourison, *Secret Army, Secret War*, 37.

75. Shultz, *Secret War against Hanoi*, 3.

76. Thomas L. Ahern, *The Way We Do Things: Black Entry Operations into North Vietnam, 1961–1964* (Central Intelligence Agency: Center for the Study of Intelligence, 2005), 10, CIA-FOIA no. 5076e89c993247d4d82b62ec.

77. National Security Action Memorandum 28, March 9, 1961, "Subject: Guerilla Operations in Viet-Minh Territory," John F. Kennedy Library, Boston, MA (hereafter cited as JFKL).

78. Ahern, *The Way We Do Things*, 1; Conboy and Andrade, *Spies and Commandos*, 34.

79. Colby quoted in Jones, *Death of a Generation*, 74–75.

80. See Curtis Peebles, *Twilight Warriors: Covert Air Operations Against the USSR* (Annapolis, MD: Naval Institute Press, 2013), chap. 10, for more on the CIA's covert air operations in North Vietnam.

81. Panagiotis Dimitrakis, *Secrets and Lies in Vietnam: Spies, Intelligence and Covert Operations in the Vietnam Wars* (New York: IB Tauris, 2016), 137.

82. Ahern, *The Way We Do Things*, 10.

83. Ahern, 12.

84. Ahern, 13.

85. Robert Gillespie, *Black Ops, Vietnam: An Operational History of MACVSOG* (Annapolis, MD: Naval Institute Press, 2011), 137.

86. Gillespie, *Black Ops, Vietnam*.

87. Shultz, *Secret War Against Hanoi*, 82.

88. See online appendix for a breakdown of these operations.

89. Shultz, *Secret War Against Hanoi*, 58.

90. Memorandum from Lansdale to Taylor, October 23, 1961, "Subject: Unconventional Warfare," *FRUS, Vietnam, 1961–1963, Vol. I, Vietnam, 1961*, ed. Ronald D. Landa and Charles S. Sampson (Washington, DC: US GPO, 1988), Doc. 186.

91. Ahern, *The Way We Do Things*, 21.

92. NSAM 57 stated that any paramilitary mission "wholly covert or disavowable, may be assigned to the CIA" except those that "require significant numbers of militarily trained personnel [and] amounts of military equipment," which were to be taken over by the Department of Defense. See National Security Action Memorandum 57, June 28, 1961, "Responsibility for Paramilitary Operations," JFKL.

93. Shultz, *Secret War against Hanoi*, 31.

94. See Tourison, *Secret Army, Secret War*, 216–17; Shultz, *Secret War against Hanoi*, chap. 4; Conboy and Andrade, *Spies and Commandos*, 74–80; Gillespie, *Black Ops, Vietnam*, 28–29, for more on the SSPL.

95. Shultz, *Secret War against Hanoi*, 31; Conboy and Andrade, *Spies and Commandos*, 77.

96. MACSOG Documentation Study, July 10, 1970, "Appendix A to Appendix C: Psychological Operations," https://drive.google.com/file/d/1K77NtENcaoHR4TQ-qLjYGLxRB XRr0Xcd/view?usp=sharing, c-a-16.

97. Conboy and Andrade, *Spies and Commandos*, 79; Gillespie, *Black Ops, Vietnam*, 27–29.

98. Ahern, *The Way We Do Things*, 47.

99. Conboy and Andrade, *Spies and Commandos*, 80.

100. Ahern, *The Way We Do Things*, 57.

101. Shultz, *Secret War against Hanoi*, 29.

102. Quoted in Shultz, 30.

103. Shultz, 31.

104. Quoted in Shultz, 29, 36–37.

105. Country Team Staff Committee, January 4, 1961, "Basic Counterinsurgency Plan for Viet-Nam," *FRUS, 1961–1963, Vol. I, Vietnam, 1961*, Doc. 1.

106. National Security Action Memorandum 52, May 11, 1961, "U.S. Approval, in 1961, of Steps to Strengthen South Vietnam," Mount Holyoke Academics, https://www.mtholyoke.edu /acad/intrel/pentagon2/doc99.htm.

107. Jones, *Death of a Generation*, 201.

108. Jones, 53.

109. Thomas L. Ahern, *CIA and the Generals: Covert Support to Military Government in South Vietnam* (Central Intelligence Agency: Center for the Study of Intelligence, 1998), 1, CIA-FOIA, no. 5076e89c993247d4d82b62ed.

110. Caitlin Talmadge, *The Dictator's Army: Battlefield Effectiveness in Authoritarian Regimes* (Ithaca, NY: Cornell University Press, 2015), chap. 4.

111. Ahern, *The Way We Do Things*, 7.

112. Quoted in Jones, *Death of a Generation*, 132.

113. Walt Rostow, December 22, 1961, "Subject: Diem's Fear of a Coup and Command Arrangements," *FRUS, 1961–1963, Vol. I, Vietnam, 1961*, Doc. 335.

114. Department of State, October 20, 1961, "Suggested Contingency Plan," *FRUS, 1961–1963, Vol. I, Vietnam, 1961*, Doc. 181.

115. Taylor Report, November 3, 1961, "Paper Prepared by the President's Military Representative (Taylor), General Conclusions," *FRUS, 1961–1963, Vol. I, Vietnam, 1961*, Doc. 210.

116. Taylor Report.

117. Taylor Report.

118. National Security Action Memorandum 111, November 22, 1961, "Subject: First Phase of Vietnam Program," JFKL.

119. Central Intelligence Agency, January 11, 1963, "Subject: Current Status of the War in South Vietnam," *FRUS, 1961–1963, Vol. III, Vietnam, January–August 1963*, ed. Edward C. Keefer, Louis J. Smith (Washington, DC: US GPO, 1991), Doc. 11.

120. Jones, *Death of a Generation*, 235.

121. Memorandum for the Record of the Secretary of Defense Conference, May 6, 1963, "Subject: Notes and Necessary Actions Resulting from SecDef Honolulu Conference on Vietnam, 6 May 1963," *FRUS, 1961–1963, Vol. III, Vietnam, January–August 1963*, Doc. 107.

122. Pentagon Papers, 1969, *Part IV, B-5, Evolution of the War, Counterinsurgency: The Overthrow of Ngo Dinh Diem, May-November 1963*, NARA-PP, ix.

123. Pentagon Papers, 1969, *Part IV, B-5*, ii.

124. Pentagon Papers, 1969, *Part IV, B-5*, ii.

125. Central Intelligence Agency, July 10, 1963, "The Situation in South Vietnam," Mount Holyoke Academics, https://www.mtholyoke.edu/acad/intrel/pentagon2/doc125.htm.

126. Ahern, *CIA and the House of Ngo*, 166.

127. Robert Templer, "Madame Nhu Obituary," April 26, 2011, *Guardian*, https://www.theguardian.com/world/2011/apr/26/madame-nhu-obituary.

128. Pentagon Papers, 1969, *Part IV, B-5*, iii.

129. Pentagon Papers, 1969, *Part IV, B-5*, iii.

130. Director of Central Intelligence, July 9, 1963, "DCI Briefing: South Vietnam," NSA, https://nsarchive2.gwu.edu/NSAEBB/NSAEBB101/vn01.pdf.

131. Pentagon Papers, 1969, *Part, IV, B-5*, 17–18.

132. Lodge to the Department of State, August 24, 1963, "Telegram from the Embassy in Vietnam to the Department of State," *FRUS, 1961–1963, Vol. III, Vietnam, January–August 1963*, Doc. 276.

133. Lodge to the Department of State, August 24, 1963.

134. Conversation recounted in numerous places, including Jones, *Death of a Generation*, 314–15.

135. Jones, *Death of a Generation*, 316.

136. Ball to embassy in Saigon, August 24, 1963, "Cable 243: Telegram from the Department of State to the embassy in Vietnam," *FRUS, 1961–1963, Vol. III, Vietnam, January–August 1963*, Doc. 281.

137. Victor Krulak, August 26, 1963, 12 p.m., "Memorandum for the record, Subject: Vietnam," *FRUS, 1961–1963, Vol. III, Vietnam, January–August 1963*, Doc. 289.

138. Bromley Smith, August 28, 1963, Memorandum of Conference with the President, "Subject: Vietnam," *FRUS, 1961–1963, Vol. IV, Vietnam, August–December 1963*, ed. Edward C. Keefer (Washington, DC: US GPO, 1991), Doc. 1.

139. Lodge to Department of State, August 29, 1963, 4 p.m., "Telegram from the Embassy in Vietnam to the Department of State," *FRUS, 1961–1963, Vol. IV, Vietnam, August–December 1963*, Doc. 11.

140. Lodge to Department of State, August 29, 1963, 6 p.m., "Telegram from the Embassy in Vietnam to the Department of State," *FRUS, 1961–1963, Vol. IV, Vietnam, August–December 1963*, Doc. 12.

141. Harkins to Taylor, August 29, 1963 5:30 p.m., "Telegram from the Commander, Military Assistance Command, Vietnam (Harkins) to Chairman of the Joint Chiefs of Staff (Taylor)," *FRUS, 1961–1963, Vol. IV, Vietnam, August–December 1963*, Doc. 13.

142. Rusk to Lodge and Harkins, August 29, 1963, 5:03 p.m., "Telegram from the Department of State to the Embassy in Vietnam," *FRUS, 1961–1963, Vol. IV, Vietnam, August–December 1963*, Doc. 16.

143. Central Intelligence Agency, August 28, 1963, "Current Intelligence Memorandum, Subject: Cast of Characters in South Vietnam," NSA, https://nsarchive2.gwu.edu/NSAEBB/NSAEBB101/vn08.pdf; Taylor to President, August 30, 1963, "Probable Loyalties of Vietnamese Units and Commanders," *FRUS, 1961–1963, Vol. IV, Vietnam, August–December 1963*, Doc. 24.

144. Kennedy to Lodge, August 29, 1963, "Message from the President to the Ambassador in Vietnam," *FRUS, 1961–1963, Vol. IV, Vietnam, August–December 1963*, Doc. 18.

145. Kennedy to Lodge, August 29, 1963.

146. White House, August 30, 1963, 2:30 p.m., "Memorandum of Conversation, Subject: Vietnam," *FRUS, 1961–1963, Vol. IV, Vietnam, August–December 1963*, Doc. 26.

147. Central Intelligence Agency, August 25, 1963, "Telegram from the Central Intelligence Agency Station in Saigon to Headquarters," *FRUS, 1961–1963, Vol. IV, Vietnam, August–December 1963*, Doc. 284.

148. Michael Forrestal, August 26, 1963, "Memorandum from Michael V. Forrestal of the National Security Council Staff to the President, Subject: Vietnam, Lodge-Diem Discussion," *FRUS, 1961–1963, Vol. IV, Vietnam, August–December 1963*, Doc. 296.

149. Bromley Smith, August 29, 1963, 12 p.m., "Memorandum of Conference with the President, Subject: Vietnam," *FRUS, 1961–1963, Vol. IV, Vietnam, August–December 1963*, Doc. 15.

150. Central Intelligence Agency, August 30, 1963, "Telegram from the Central Intelligence Agency Station in Saigon to the Agency," *FRUS, 1961–1963, Vol. IV, Vietnam, August–December 1963*, Docs. 21–23.

151. Memorandum from Rusk to Lodge, August 30, 1963, 8:30 p.m., "Telegram from the Department of State to the Embassy in Vietnam," *FRUS, 1961–1963, Vol. IV, Vietnam, August–December 1963*, Doc. 31.

152. Central Intelligence Agency, August 31, 1963, 2:39 a.m., "Telegram from the Central Intelligence Agency Station in Saigon to the Agency," *FRUS, 1961–1963, Vol. IV, Vietnam, August–December 1963*, Doc. 32.

153. Pentagon Papers, 1969, *Part IV, B-5*, iv.

154. White House, September 10, 1963, "Memorandum of Conversation, Subject: Vietnam," *FRUS, 1961–1963, Vol. IV, Vietnam, August–December 1963*, Doc. 83.

155. McNamara-Taylor Report, October 2, 1963, "Subject: Report of McNamara-Taylor Mission to South Vietnam," *FRUS, 1961–1963, Vol. IV, Vietnam, August–December 1963*, Doc. 167.

156. McNamara-Taylor Report, October 2, 1963.

157. McNamara-Taylor Report.

158. National Security Council, October 2, 1963, "McNamara-Taylor Report on Vietnam," *FRUS, 1961–1963, Vol. IV, Vietnam, August–December 1963*, Doc. 170.

159. Central Intelligence Agency, October 3, 1963, "Telegram from the Central Intelligence Agency Station in Saigon to Headquarters," *FRUS, 1961–1963, Vol. IV, Vietnam, August–December 1963*, Doc. 171.

160. White House, October 5, 1963, "Memorandum for the files of the President, Subject: Presidential Conference on South Vietnam," *FRUS, 1961–1963, Vol. IV, Vietnam, August–December 1963*, Doc. 179.

161. Pentagon Papers, 1969, *Part IV, B-5*, xxii.

162. Central Intelligence Agency, October 5, 1963, "Telegram from the Central Intelligence Agency Station in Saigon to Headquarters," *FRUS, 1961–1963, Vol. IV, Vietnam, August–December 1963*, Doc. 177.

163. Pentagon Papers, 1969, *Part IV, B-5*, xxiii.

164. Memorandum from Lodge to Bundy, October 25, 1963, "Telegram from the Ambassador in Vietnam (Lodge) to the President's Special Assistant for National Security (Bundy)," *FRUS, 1961–1963, Vol. IV, Vietnam, August–December 1963*, Doc. 216.

165. Memorandum from Lodge to Bundy, October 25, 1963.

166. Memorandum from Bundy to Lodge, October 25, 1963, "Telegram from the President's Special Assistant for National Security (Bundy) to the Ambassador in Vietnam (Lodge)," *FRUS, 1961–1963, Vol. IV, Vietnam, August–December 1963*, Doc. 217.

167. Memorandum from Lodge to Secretary of State, October 28, 1963, 6 p.m., "Telegram from the Embassy in Vietnam to the Department of State," *FRUS, 1961–1963, Vol. IV, Vietnam, August–December 1963*, Doc. 306.

168. Colby, William, October 29, 1963, 4:20 p.m., "President Kennedy Meets with His National Security Council on the Question of Support a Coup in South Vietnam," WHT.

169. Smith, Bromley, October 29, 1963, 6 p.m., "Memorandum of a Conference with the President, Subject: Vietnam," *FRUS, 1961–1963, Vol. IV, Vietnam, August–December 1963*, Doc. 235.

170. Memorandum from Bundy to Lodge, October 30, 1963, "Telegram from the President's Special Assistant for National Security (Bundy) to the Ambassador in Vietnam (Lodge)," *FRUS, 1961–1963, Vol. IV, Vietnam, August–December 1963*, Doc. 249.

171. Memorandum from Kennedy to Lodge, November 6, 1963, 7:50 p.m., "Eyes Only from the President to Ambassador Lodge," *FRUS, 1961–1963, Vol. IV, Vietnam, August–December 1963,* Doc. 304.

172. Church Committee, *Alleged Assassination Plots Involving Foreign Leaders* (Washington, DC: US GPO, 1975), 256.

173. Pentagon Papers, 1969, *Part IV, B-5,* viii.

174. Conein testimony to the Church Committee, *Alleged Assassination Plots Involving Foreign Leaders,* 222.

175. Central Intelligence Agency, October 25, 1963, "Check-list of Possible U.S. Actions in Case of Coup," DNSA, Accession no. VI01033.

176. Pentagon Papers, 1969, *Part IV, B-5,* 57–58.

177. Quoted in Jones, *Death of a Generation,* 429.

178. Central Intelligence Agency, November 2, 1963, Telegram from Saigon, to Department of State, No. 888, NSA, https://nsarchive2.gwu.edu/NSAEBB/NSAEBB101/vn26.pdf.

179. Taylor quoted in an Editorial Note, *FRUS, 1961–1963, Vol. IV, Vietnam, August–December 1963,* Doc. 274.

180. Memorandum from Bundy to Lodge, November 2, 1963, 6:31 p.m., "Telegram from the President's Special Assistant for National Security (Bundy) to the Ambassador in Vietnam (Lodge)," *FRUS, 1961–1963, Vol. IV, Vietnam, August–December 1963,* Doc. 235.

181. White House, November 4, 1963, "Memorandum for the Record at Discussion at Daily White House Staff Meeting," *FRUS, 1961–1963, Vol. IV, Vietnam, August–December 1963,* Doc. 288.

182. White House, November 4, 1963.

183. Memorandum from Harkins to Joint Chiefs of Staff, November 4, 1963, 1:05 a.m., "MAC J-3 8587. Summary Evaluation South Vietnam," *FRUS, 1961–1963, Vol. IV, Vietnam, August–December 1963,* Doc. 287.

184. State Department quoted in Jones, *Death of a Generation,* 443.

185. Memorandum from Lodge to State Department, November 4, 1963, 8 p.m., "Report of Conversation with General Minh and General Don, Lt. Colonel Conein was with me," *FRUS, 1961–1963, Vol. IV, Vietnam, August–December 1963,* Doc. 291.

186. Memorandum from Kennedy to Lodge, November 6, 1963, 7:50 p.m., "Eyes Only from the President to Ambassador Lodge," *FRUS, 1961–1963, Vol. IV, Vietnam, August–December 1963,* Doc. 304.

187. Pentagon Papers, 1969, *Part IV, B-5,* 62–63.

188. Pentagon Papers, 1969, *Part IV, B-5,* i.

189. Ahern, *CIA and the Generals,* 2.

190. Pentagon Papers, 1969, *Part IV, C-1, Evolution of the War, U.S. Programs in South Vietnam, November 1963–April 1965: NASM 273–NSAM 288–Honolulu,* NARA-PP, i.

191. Department of Defense, March 16, 1964, "Memorandum from the Secretary of Defense (McNamara) to the President," *FRUS, 1961–1963, Vol. IV, Vietnam, August–December 1963* Doc. 84.

192. NLF quoted in Jones, *Death of a Generation,* 420.

193. Pentagon Papers, 1969, *Part IV, A-5,* 68.

194. CIA quoted in Tourison, *Secret Army, Secret War,* 102.

195. Conboy and Andrade, *Spies and Commandos,* 83.

196. Gillespie, *Black Ops, Vietnam,* 15.

197. Memorandum for the Record of Meeting, November 24, 1963, 3 p.m., "Subject: South Vietnam Situation," *FRUS, 1961–1963, Vol. IV, Vietnam, August–December 1963,* Doc. 330.

198. Pentagon Papers, 1969, *Part IV, C-2-a, Evolution of the War, Military Pressures against NVN, February–June, 1964,* NARA-PP, 1.

199. Operation Plan 34A outlined in MACSOG Documentation Study, July 16, 1970, https://web.archive.org/web/20110205144335/http://www.dod.mil/pubs/foi/reading_room/520-22.pdf.

200. Quoted in Shultz, *Secret war against Hanoi,* 38.

201. Robert S. McNamara, *In Retrospect: The Tragedy and Lessons of Vietnam* (New York: Vintage Books, 1996), 103.

202. McNamara quoted in Conboy and Andrade, *Spies and Commandos*, 89.

203. National Security Action Memorandum 273, November 26, 1963, "South Vietnam," Lyndon B. Johnson Library (LBJL), Austin, TX.

204. MACSOG Documentation Study, July 16, 1970, B-159.

205. Quoted in Shultz, *Secret War against Hanoi*, 39.

206. Quoted in Shultz, 40.

207. Gillespie, *Black Ops, Vietnam*, 10.

208. Joint Chiefs of Staff, July 16, 1970, B-1.

209. MACSOG Documentation Study, July 10, 1970, "Appendix A to Appendix C," https://web.archive.org/web/20110205144015/http://www.dod.mil/pubs/foi/reading_room/520-1.pdf, C-a-2.

210. Memorandum for the Record of Meeting, November 24, 1963.

211. MACSOG Documentation Study, July 10, 1970, "Appendix A to Appendix C," C-a-7.

212. MACSOG Documentation Study, C-a-8.

213. MACSOG Documentation Study, C-a-9.

214. MACSOG Documentation Study, C-a-12.

215. MACSOG Documentation Study, C-a-16.

216. MACSOG Documentation Study, C-a-20.

217. Central Intelligence Agency, January 20, 1964, "CAS Saigon 3902. Following are Ambassador Lodge's Comments on Ref.," *FRUS, 1964–1968, Vol. I, Vietnam, 1964*, Doc. 13.

218. Johnson quoted in Arthur Schlesinger, *Robert Kennedy and His Times* (Boston: Houghton Mifflin Harcourt, 2012), 726.

219. Lyndon B. Johnson, *Public Papers of the Presidents of the United States: Lyndon B. Johnson, 1963–1964*, 607.

220. Johnson, *Public Papers*, 1126.

221. Pentagon Papers, 1969, *Part IV, C-1*, iv.

222. McNamara quoted in Jones, *Death of a Generation*, 454.

223. John Prados, August 4, 2004, "The Gulf of Tonkin Incident, 40 Years Later," *National Security Archive Electronic Briefing Book, No. 132*, NSA, http://nsarchive.gwu.edu/NSAEBB/NSAEBB132/.

224. Gulf of Tonkin Resolution, August 10, 1964, "Joint Resolution to Promote the Maintenance of International Peace and Security in Southeast Asia," ourdocuments.gov, https://www.ourdocuments.gov/doc.php?doc=98&page=transcript.

225. Colby quoted in James Callanan, *Covert Action in the Cold War: US Policy, Intelligence and CIA Operations* (New York: IB Tauris, 2009), 86.

226. Central Intelligence Agency, October 10, 1961, "SNIE 10-3-61, Probable Communist Reactions to Certain SEATO Undertakings in South Vietnam," CIA-FOIA, no. 0001166423.

227. Joint Chiefs of Staff Memorandum to McNamara, August 24, 1961, "JSCM 583–61, Subject: North Vietnam," *FRUS, 1961–1963, Vol. I, Vietnam, 1961*, Doc. 123.

228. See Gaddis, *Strategies of Containment*, chap. 7; Gary A. Donaldson, *The Making of Modern America: The Nation from 1945 to the Present* (Lanham, MD: Rowman & Littlefield, 2012), chap. 5.

229. Country Team Staff Committee, January 4, 1961.

230. Jones, *Death of a Generation*, 27.

231. Testimony of Lucien Conein to the Church Committee, June 20, 1975, Mary Farrell Foundation, Church Committee Boxed Files, https://www.maryferrell.org/php/showlist.php?docset=1015, 68–73.

232. Quoted in Jones, *Death of a Generation*, 143.

233. Central Intelligence Agency, October 10, 1961, "SNIE 10-3-61."

234. Smith, Bromley, November 1, 1963, 10 a.m., "Memorandum of Conversation with the President, Subject: Vietnam," NSA, https://nsarchive2.gwu.edu/NSAEBB/NSAEBB101/vn22.pdf.

235. Conboy and Andrade, *Spies and Commandos*, 82.

236. Quoted in Jones, *Death of a Generation*, 428.

237. William Egan Colby and Peter Forbath, *Honorable Men: My Life in the CIA* (New York: Simon & Schuster, 1978), 203.

8. Dictators and Democrats in the Dominican Republic

Epigraph: John F. Kennedy, "Address before the American Society of Newspaper Editors," April 20, 1961, John F. Kennedy Library, Boston MA (hereafter cited as JFKL), https://www.jfklibrary.org/Asset-Viewer/Archives/JFKWHA-024-001.aspx.

1. Bruce J. Calder, *The Impact of Intervention: The Dominican Republic during the U.S. Occupation of 1916–1924* (Princeton, NJ: Wiener, 1984); Lars Schoultz, *Beneath the United States: A History of US Policy toward Latin America* (Cambridge, MA: Harvard University Press, 1998), chap. 11; Eric Paul Roorda, *The Dictator Next Door: The Good Neighbor Policy and the Trujillo Regime in the Dominican Republic, 1930–1945* (Durham, NC: Duke University Press, 1998), chap. 1; Russell Crandall, *Gunboat Democracy: U.S. Interventions in the Dominican Republic, Grenada, and Panama* (Lanham, MD: Rowman & Littlefield, 2006), chap. 1; Greg Grandin, *Empire's Workshop: Latin America, the United States, and the Rise of the New Imperialism* (Basingstoke, UK: Macmillan, 2006), chap. 1. Noel Maurer, *The Empire Trap: The Rise and Fall of U.S. Intervention to Protect American Property Overseas, 1893–2013* (Princeton, NJ: Princeton University Press, 2013); Ellen D. Tillman, *Dollar Diplomacy by Force: Nation-Building and Resistance in the Dominican Republic* (Chapel Hill: University of North Carolina Press, 2016).

2. Memorandum from Goodwin to Bundy, June 8, 1961, "June 7 Meeting at the White House Mansion," *Foreign Relations of the United States (FRUS), 1961–1963, Vol. XII, American Republics,* ed. Edward C. Keefer, Harriet Dashiell Schwar, W. Taylor Fain III, and Glenn W. LaFantasie (Washington, DC: US Government Printing Office [GOP], 1996), Doc. 312.

3. Thomas Ward "Norms and Security: The Case of International Assassination," *International Security* 25, no. 1 (2000): 105–33.

4. Department of State, March 22, 1961, Airgram from the Consulate General in the Dominican Republic to the Department of State, *FRUS, 1961–1963, Vol. XII, American Republics,* Doc. 304.

5. This was also Dearborn's interpretation of events. Tim Weiner, *Legacy of Ashes: The History of the CIA* (New York: Anchor, 2008), 198.

6. Church Committee, *Alleged Assassination Plots Involving Foreign Leaders* (Washington, DC: US Government Printing Office, 1975), 202.

7. Church Committee, *Alleged Assassination Plots,* 204.

8. Church Committee, 191.

9. Piero Gleijeses, *The Dominican Crisis: The 1965 Constitutional Revolt and American Intervention* (Baltimore, MD: Johns Hopkins University Press, 1978); G. Pope Atkins and Larman Curtis Wilson, *The Dominican Republic and the United States: From Imperialism to Transnationalism* (Athens: University of Georgia Press, 1998); Michael R. Hall, *Sugar and Power in the Dominican Republic: Eisenhower, Kennedy, and the Trujillos* (Westport, CT: Greenwood, 2000); Eric Thomas Chester, *Rag-Tags, Scum, Riff-Raff and Commies: The U.S. Intervention in the Dominican Republic, 1965–1966* (New York: Monthly Review Press, 2001); Maurer, *The Empire Trap.*

10. Chester, *Rag Tags, Scum, Riff-Raff and Commies,* 31.

11. Gleijeses, *The Dominican Crisis,* 239–40.

12. Chester, *Rag Tags, Scum, Riff-Raff and Commies,* 31.

13. C. Lloyd Brown-John, "Economic Sanctions: The Case of the O.A.S. and the Dominican Republic, 1960–1962," *Caribbean Studies* 15, no. 2 (1975): 73–105; Hall, *Sugar and Power in the Dominican Republic.*

14. Jonathan Kirshner, "The Microfoundations of Economic Sanctions," *Security Studies* 6, no. 3 (1997): 32–64.

15. Chester, *Rag Tags, Scum, Riff-Raff and Commies,* 31–35; See also John Bartlow Martin, *Overtaken by Events: The Dominican Crisis from the Fall of Trujillo to the Civil War* (New York: Doubleday, 1966).

16. Crandall, *Gunboat Democracy,* 39.

17. James Monroe, "Seventh Annual Message to Congress," December 2, 1823, Yale Law School, The Avalon Project, http://avalon.law.yale.edu/19th_century/monroe.asp; commonly referred to as the Monroe Doctrine.

18. Theodore Roosevelt, "Roosevelt Corollary to the Monroe Doctrine," December 6, 1904, Teaching American History, http://teachingamericanhistory.org/library/document/roosevelt -corollary-to-monroe-doctrine/.

19. Maurer, *The Empire Trap*, 60–75.

20. Maurer, 164–66.

21. Maurer, 102; Roorda, *The Dictator Next Door*, 21–22.

22. Crandall, *Gunboat Democracy*, 45.

23. Crandall, 45.

24. Maurer, *The Empire Trap*, 166; Crandall, *Gunboat Democracy*, 46.

25. Roorda, *The Dictator Next Door*.

26. Giancarlo Soler Torrijos, *In the Shadow of the United States: Democracy and Regional Order in the Latin Caribbean* (Boca Raton, FL: Brown Walker Press, 2008), 35.

27. Torrijos, *In the Shadow of the United States*, 37. A January 1958 survey by the director of the Office of Middle American Affairs identified America's primary interests in the Dominican Republic during this period as "its strategic position in relation to the Panama Canal, a U.S. guided missile tracking station on the northeast coast, and general Dominican support for U.S. policies." *FRUS, American Republics, 1958–1960, Vol. V*, Preface by William Z. Slany (Washington, DC: US GPO, 1991), Editorial Note, Doc. 305.

28. Dearborn quoted in Weiner, *Legacy of Ashes*, 198.

29. Dearborn quoted in Weiner, 198.

30. Bernard Diederich, *Trujillo: The Death of the Dictator* (Princeton, NJ: Markus Wiener, 2017), chap. 1.

31. Diederich, *Trujillo*.

32. Department of State, January 15, 1957, "Subject: Disappearance of Gerald Lester Murphy and Death of Octavio de la Maza," *FRUS, 1955–1957, Vol. VI, American Republics: Multilateral; Mexico; Caribbean*, ed. N. Stephen Kane et al. (Washington, DC: US GPO, 1987), Doc. 314.

33. Department of State, "Disappearance of Gerald Lester Murphy."

34. Department of State, February 15, 1957, "Subject: Re-Evaluation of Overall U.S. Strategy in Relation to the Dominican Republic in Light of the Murphy Case Developments," *FRUS, 1955–1957, Vol. VI, American Republics: Multilateral; Mexico; Caribbean*, Doc. 318.

35. Torrijos, *In the Shadow of the United States*, 37.

36. Special National Intelligence Estimate 80–59, June 30, 1959, "The Situation in the Caribbean through 1959," *FRUS, 1958–1960, Vol. V, American Republics*, Preface by William Z. Slany, Doc. 122.

37. Department of State, March 15, 1959, Letter from Joseph S. Farland, National Archives and Records Administration, College Park, MD (hereafter cited as NARA), RG. 59, Decimal Files 739.00/8-1457.

38. Johnson quoted in Chester, *Rag Tags, Scum, Riff-Raff and Commies*, 15.

39. MFM B-2/52, August 7, 1959, "Situation in the Caribbean," *FRUS, 1958–1960, Vol. V, American Republics*, Doc. 90.

40. Special National Intelligence Estimate 80/1-59, December 29, 1959, "The Situation in the Caribbean through 1960," *FRUS, 1958–1960, Vol. V, American Republics*, Doc. 126.

41. Farland quoted in Torrijos, *In the Shadow of the United States*, 42.

42. Department of State, June 30, 1960, "Views on the political problems in the Dominican Republic and suggestions for possible courses of action by our Government in its future negotiations with the Government of Dominican Republic," NARA, RG 59, Decimal Files 739.00/6-3060.

43. Memorandum from Rubottom to the Secretary of State, June 25, 1959, "Subject: Possible Action by the Organization of American States regarding the Caribbean Situation," *FRUS, 1958–1960, Vol. V, American Republics*, Doc. 80.

44. Herter quoted in Torrijos, *In the Shadow of the United States*, 40.

45. Rubottom quoted in Torrijos, *In the Shadow of the United States*, 41.

46. *FRUS, Vol. V, American Republics, 1958–1960*, Editorial Note, Doc. 305.

47. Special Group Minutes, February 10, 1960, referenced in Church Committee, *Alleged Assassination Plots Involving Foreign Leaders*, 192.

48. Church Committee, *Alleged Assassination Plots*, 192.

49. Stephen G. Rabe, "The Caribbean Triangle: Betancourt, Castro and Trujillo and U.S. Foreign Policy, 1958–1963," in *Empire and Revolution: The United States and the Third World since 1945*, ed. Peter L. Hahn and Mary Ann Heiss (Columbus: Ohio State University Press, 2001), 48–70.

50. Rabe, "The Caribbean Triangle," 55.

51. Bernard Diederich, *Trujillo: The Death of a Dictator* (Princeton, NJ: Markus Wiener, 2000), 42.

52. Church Committee, *Alleged Assassination Plots Involving Foreign Leaders*, 193.

53. CIA quoted in Church Committee, *Alleged Assassination Plots Involving Foreign Leaders*, 192.

54. Quoted in Church Committee, *Alleged Assassination Plots*, 192–93.

55. Quoted in Church Committee, 192–93.

56. Quoted in Church Committee, 193.

57. Quoted in Church Committee, 193.

58. Quoted in Church Committee, 195.

59. Rabe, "The Caribbean Triangle," 57.

60. Hall, *Sugar and Power in the Dominican Republic*, 97–99.

61. Dearborn quoted in Rabe, "The Caribbean Triangle," 58.

62. Church Committee, *Alleged Assassination Plots Involving Foreign Leaders*, 196.

63. Dearborn quoted in Church Committee, *Alleged Assassination Plots*, 195.

64. Quoted by Joel Westra, *International Law and the Use of Armed Force: The UN Charter and the Major Powers* (Abingdon, UK: Routledge, 2007), 79.

65. Church Committee, *Alleged Assassination Plots Involving Foreign Leaders*, 196.

66. Church Committee, 197.

67. Quoted in Chester, *Rag Tags, Scum, Riff-Raff and Commies*, 16.

68. Memorandum from Rusk to Kennedy, February 15, 1961, "Subject: The Dominican Republic," *FRUS, 1961–1963, Vol. XII, American Republics*, Doc. 302.

69. Airgram from the Consulate General in the Dominican Republic to the Department of State, March 22, 1961.

70. Chester, *Rag Tags, Scum, Riff-Raff and Commies*, 16.

71. Michael E. Latham, "Ideology, Social Science, and Destiny: Modernization and the Kennedy-Era Alliance for Progress," *Diplomatic History* 22, no. 2 (1998): 199–229.

72. Rabe, "The Caribbean Triangle," 59.

73. Church Committee, *Alleged Assassination Plots Involving Foreign Leaders*, 199.

74. Memorandum from Rusk to Kennedy, February 15, 1961.

75. Church Committee, *Alleged Assassination Plots Involving Foreign Leaders*, 203.

76. Church Committee, 198.

77. Dearborn quoted by the Church Committee, *Alleged Assassination Plots Involving Foreign Leaders*, 199.

78. Airgram from the Consulate General in the Dominican Republic to the Department of State, March 22, 1961.

79. Church Committee, *Alleged Assassination Plots Involving Foreign Leaders*, 201.

80. Church Committee, *Alleged Assassination Plots*, 200.

81. Church Committee, 200.

82. Church Committee, 205.

83. Department of State, April 28, 1961, 9:05 p.m., Telegram from the Department of State to the Consulate General in the Dominican Republic, *FRUS, 1961–1963, Vol. XII, American Republics*, Doc. 305.

84. See Diederich, *Trujillo*, for a detailed account of the assassination plot.

85. Díaz quoted in Diederich, *Trujillo*, 170.

86. Church Committee, *Alleged Assassination Plots Involving Foreign Leaders*, 205–7.

87. Church Committee, 206.

88. Church Committee, 206.

89. Cable quoted in Chester, *Rag Tags, Scum, Riff-Raff and Commies*, 17.

90. Diederich, *Trujillo*, 96.

91. David Belin, May 30, 1975, "Summary of Facts—Investigation of CIA Involvement in Plans to Assassinate Foreign Leaders," NARA, https://www.archives.gov/files/research/jfk/releases/docid-32112745.pdf.

92. Church Committee, *Alleged Assassination Plots Involving Foreign Leaders*, 213.

93. Church Committee, 214.

94. State Department Telegram, May 31, 1961, From: Smith and Clifton, To: Bundy for the President, JFKL, Digital Identifier: JFKPOF-115-019-p0006.

95. Memorandum from the Under Secretary of State Bowles, June 3, 1961, "Notes on Crisis involving the Dominican Republic," *FRUS, 1961–1963, Vol. XII, American Republics*, Doc. 310.

96. See Diederich, *Trujillo*, for a detailed account of this assassination.

97. Garcia quoted in Diederich, *Trujillo*, 137–38.

98. Huascar quoted in *Trujillo*, 176.

99. Kirk Semple, "Antonio Imbert Barrera, Who Helped Assassinate Dominican Dictator Trujillo, Dies at 95," *New York Times*, June 7, 2016.

100. The Associated Press, "Son of Trujillo Takes Command of Armed Forces," *New York Times*, June 2, 1961.

101. Memorandum from the Under Secretary of State Bowles, June 3, 1961.

102. Church Committee, *Alleged Assassination Plots Involving Foreign Leaders*, 215.

103. Department of State, June 1, 1961, 11:54 a.m., Telegram from the Department of State to the Consulate General in the Dominican Republic), *FRUS, 1961–1963, Vol. XII, American Republics*, Doc. 309.

104. Department of State, June 5, 1961, 6:29 a.m., Telegram from the Department of State to Secretary of State Rusk, at Paris, *FRUS, 1961–1963, Vol. XII, American Republics*, Doc. 311.

105. State Department, June 12, 1961.

106. Telegram from Dearborn to Department of State, February 24, 1961, 9:56 p.m., *FRUS, 1961–1963, Vol. XII, American Republics*, Doc. 303.

107. White House, July 10, 1961, "Memorandum from President Kennedy to the Assistant Secretary of State for Inter-American Affairs (Woodward)," *FRUS, 1961–1963, Vol. XII, American Republics*, Doc. 314.

108. Department of State, July 17, 1961, "Courses of Action in the Dominican Republic," *FRUS, 1961–1963, Vol. XII, American Republics*, Doc. 315.

109. State Department quoted in Torrijos, *In the Shadow of the United States*, 47.

110. State Department Memo quoted in Torrijos, *In the Shadow of the United States*, 48.

111. Memorandum from Goodwin to Kennedy, October 3, 1961, "Memorandum for the President," JFKL, Digital identifier: JFKPOF-115-019-p0056.

112. Department of State, November 16, 1961, 11:00 a.m., "Telegram from the Consulate General in the Dominican Republic to the Department of State," *FRUS, 1961–1963, Vol. XII, American Republics*, Doc. 325.

113. *FRUS, 1961–1963, Vol. XII, American Republics*, Editorial Note, Doc. 330.

114. White House, December 16, 1961, "PRWHO5. From Naval Aide to the President. To Mr. Bundy, WASHDC, Sec Rusk, State Department," *FRUS, 1961–1963, Vol. XII, American Republics*, Doc. 332.

115. White House, December 16, 1961.

116. Department of State, December 17, 1961, "Developments in the Dominican Republic," *FRUS, 1961–1963, Vol. XII, American Republics*, Doc. 335.

117. *FRUS, 1961–1963, Vol. XII, American Republics*, Doc. 336, Editorial Note.

118. Department of State, January 17, 1962, "Telegram from the Department of State to the Embassy in the Dominican Republic," *FRUS, 1961–1963, Vol. XII, American Republics*, Doc. 338.

119. Department of State, March 4, 1962, "Telegram from the Embassy in the Dominican Republic to the Department of State," *FRUS, 1961–1963, Vol. XII, American Republics*, Doc. 339.

120. Department of State, July 17, 1961.

121. CIA quoted in Chester, *Rag Tags, Scum, Riff-Raff and Commies*, 18.

122. Special National Intelligence Estimate 86.2-61, July 25, 1961, "The Dominican Situation," *FRUS, 1961–1963, Vol. XII, American Republics*, Doc. 317.

123. Central Intelligence Agency (ca. 1962) "Clandestine Activities and Plans in the Dominican Republic," JFKL, Digital Identifier: JFKPOF-115-019-p0088.

124. Central Intelligence Agency, (ca. 1962).

125. Central Intelligence Agency, (ca. 1962).

126. Central Intelligence Agency, (ca. 1962).

127. Quoted in Chester, *Rag Tags, Scum, Riff-Raff and Commies*, 21.

128. Jonathan Hartlyn, *The Struggle for Democratic Politics in the Dominican Republic* (Chapel Hill: The University of North Carolina Press, 1998), 76.

129. Crandall, *Gunboat Democracy*, 50.

130. Crandall, 50.

131. Chester, *Rag Tags, Scum, Riff-Raff and Commies*, 30.

132. Chester, 30–34.

133. Johnson quoted in Crandall, *Gunboat Democracy*, 51.

134. Ball quoted in Crandall, *Gunboat Democracy*, 51.

135. Chester, *Rag Tags, Scum, Riff-Raff and Commies*, 33.

136. Johnson quoted in Chester, *Rag Tags, Scum, Riff-Raff and Commies*, 35.

137. State Department quoted in Torrijos, *In the Shadow of the United States*, 60,

138. Airgram from the embassy in the Dominican Republic to the Department of State, September 22, 1963, "Subject: Six Months in a Quandary," *FRUS, 1961–1963, Vol. XII, American Republics*, Doc. 357.

139. Martin quoted in Chester, *Rag Tags, Scum, Riff-Raff and Commies*, 38.

140. Martin quoted in Crandall, *Gunboat Democracy*, 52.

141. Ball quoted in Chester, *Rag Tags, Scum, Riff-Raff and Commies*, 39.

142. Special National Intelligence Estimate 86.2-64, January 17, 1964, "Instability and Insurgency Threat in the Dominican Republic," *FRUS, 1964–1968, Vol. XXXII, Dominican Republic; Cuba; Haiti; Guyana*, ed. Daniel Lawler and Carolyn Lee (Washington, DC: US GPO, 2005), Doc. 1.

143. Special NIE, "Instability and Insurgency Threat."

144. Department of State, October 17, 1963, 6:33 p.m., "Telegram from the Department of State to the Embassy in the Dominican Republic," *FRUS, 1961–1963, Vol. XII, American Republics*, Doc. 361.

145. Department of State, "Telegram to DR Embassy."

146. Department of State, "Telegram to DR Embassy."

147. Crandall, *Gunboat Democracy*, 53.

148. State Department quoted in Chester, *Rag Tags, Scum, Riff-Raff and Commies*, 42.

149. Airgram from the embassy in the Dominican Republic to the Department of State, December 5, 1964, "Subject: The Reid Government, January–November 1964: A Review," *FRUS, 1964–1968, Vol. XXXII, Dominican Republic; Cuba; Haiti; Guyana*, Doc. 17.

150. Quoted in Chester, *Rag Tags, Scum, Riff-Raff and Commies*, 44.

151. Telegram from the embassy in the Dominican Republic to the Department of State, May 21, 1964, 2 p.m., "1053. For ARA, Subject: Prospects for the Dominican Republic," *FRUS, 1964–1968, Vol. XXXII, Dominican Republic; Cuba; Haiti; Guyana*, Doc. 5.

152. Airgram from the embassy in the Dominican Republic to the Department of State, February 19, 1964, "Subject: Conversation with Donald Reid," *FRUS, 1964–1968, Vol. XXXII, Dominican Republic; Cuba; Haiti; Guyana*, Doc. 4.

153. Telegram from the embassy in the Dominican Republic to the Department of State, May 21, 1964, 2 p.m.

154. State Department quoted in Chester, *Rag Tags, Scum, Riff-Raff and Commies*, 43.

155. CIA quoted in Crandall, *Gunboat Democracy*, 54.

156. White House, April 26, 1965, 9:35 a.m., "Telephone Conversation Between the Under Secretary of State for Economic Affairs (Mann) and President Johnson," *FRUS, 1964–1968, Vol. XXXII, Dominican Republic; Cuba; Haiti; Guyana,* Doc. 22.

157. Torrijos, *In the Shadow of the United States,* 67.

158. Quoted in Michael Grow, *U.S. Presidents and Latin American Interventions: Pursuing Regime Change in the Cold War* (Lawrence: University Press of Kansas, 2008), 83.

159. US Service Attaches quoted in Torrijos, *In the Shadow of the United States,* 67.

160. Crandall, *Gunboat Democracy,* 63.

161. Central Intelligence Agency, April 27, 1965, "CIA Report on Whether the Dominican Republic Will Turn into Another Cuba," Declassified Documents Reference Service (DDRS), Library of Congress, Washington, DC (hereafter cited as DDRS). See also Crandall, *Gunboat Democracy,* 64.

162. Telegram from the Department of State to the embassy in the Dominican Republic, April 27, 1965, "644. Establishment of the Provisional Government," *FRUS, 1964–1968, Vol. XXXII, Dominican Republic; Cuba; Haiti; Guyana,* Doc. 24.

163. Torrijos, *In the Shadow of the United States,* 67.

164. Chester, *Rag Tags, Scum, Riff-Raff and Commies,* 66.

165. White House, April 27, 1965, quoted in Crandall, *Gunboat Democracy,* 65.

166. Department of State, April 28, 1965, 1718Z, "Telegram from the Embassy in the Dominican Republic to the Department of State," *FRUS, 1964–1968, Vol. XXXII, Dominican Republic; Cuba; Haiti; Guyana,* Doc. 27.

167. Department of State, April 28, 1965, 1900Z, "Telegram from the Embassy in the Dominican Republic to the Department of State," *FRUS, 1964–1968, Vol. XXXII, Dominican Republic; Cuba; Haiti; Guyana,* Doc. 28.

168. Transcript of Teleconference between the Department of State and the Embassy in the Dominican Republic, April 28, 1965, 2230Z, "Subject; Dominican Situation," *FRUS, 1964–1968, Vol. XXXII, Dominican Republic; Cuba; Haiti; Guyana,* Doc. 33.

169. Joint Chiefs of Staff, May 1, 1965, quoted in *FRUS, 1964–1968, Vol. XXXII, Dominican Republic; Cuba; Haiti; Guyana,* Editorial Note, Doc. 43.

170. Johnson, May 2, 1965, "Radio and Television Report to the American People on the Situation in the Dominican Republic," The American Presidency Project, http://www.presidency.ucsb.edu/ws/?pid=26932.

171. Congressional Resolution 124, quoted in Myres S. McDougal and Florentino P. Feliciano, *The International Law of War: Transnational Coercion and the World Public Order* (Leiden, NL: Martinus Nijhoff, 1994), xlix.

172. Gallup poll quoted in Grow, *U.S. Presidents and Latin American Interventions,* 91.

173. Chester, *Rag Tags, Scum, Riff-Raff and Commies,* 7.

174. *FRUS, 1964–1968, Vol. XXXII, Dominican Republic; Cuba; Haiti; Guyana,* Doc. 30, Editorial Note.

175. Johnson quoted in Lawrence A. Yates, *Power Pack: U.S. Intervention in the Dominican Republic, 196501966* (Fort Leavenworth, KS: Combat Studies Institute, 1988), 171.

176. Special National Intelligence Estimate 86.2-64, January 17, 1964.

177. Cable from the British embassy quoted in Torrijos, *In the Shadow of the United States,* 68.

178. Rusk quoted in Crandall, *Gunboat Democracy,* 71.

179. Johnson quoted in Grow, *U.S. Presidents and Latin American Interventions,* 85.

180. Johnson quoted in Crandall, *Gunboat Democracy,* 75.

181. Johnson quoted in Crandall, 76.

182. Johnson, April 30, 1965, quoted in *FRUS, Vol. XXXII, Dominican Republic; Cuba; Haiti; Guyana,* Editorial Note, Doc 48.

183. Bruce Palmer, *Intervention in the Caribbean: The Dominican Crisis of 1965* (Lexington, KY: University Press of Kentucky, 1989), 5.

184. Palmer, *Intervention in the Caribbean,* 8.

185. State Department quoted in Torrijos, *In the Shadow of the United States,* 68.

186. Chester, *Rag Tags, Scum, Riff-Raff and Commies;* Torrijos, *In the Shadow of the United States;* Grow, *U.S. Presidents and Latin American Interventions.*

187. White House, November 10, 1965, "Memorandum from Administrator of the Agency for International Development Bell to President Johnson," *FRUS, Vol. XXXII, Dominican Republic; Cuba; Haiti; Guyana*, Doc. 143.

188. Torrijos, *In the Shadow of the United States*, 75.

189. Central Intelligence Agency Special Memorandum No. 24–65, October 27, 1965, "Subject: Some Perspectives on the Dominican Problem," *FRUS, Vol. XXXII, Dominican Republic; Cuba; Haiti; Guyana*, Doc. 139.

190. Department of State, December 8, 1965, "Subject: ARA-Agency Meeting December 8, 1965," *FRUS, Vol. XXXII, Dominican Republic; Cuba; Haiti; Guyana*, Doc. 147.

191. 303 Committee, December 30, 1965, "Subject: Presidential Election in the Dominican Republic," *FRUS, Vol. XXXII, Dominican Republic; Cuba; Haiti; Guyana*, Doc. 152.

192. 303 Committee, January 6, 1966, "Subject: Minutes of the 303 Committee, January 6, 1966," *FRUS, Vol. XXXII, Dominican Republic; Cuba; Haiti; Guyana*, Doc. 155.

193. National Security Council, January 11, 1966, "Subject: Contingency Plan for Dominican Elections," *FRUS, Vol. XXXII, Dominican Republic; Cuba; Haiti; Guyana*, Doc. 157.

194. NSC, "Contingency Plan."

195. Department of State, March 17, 1966, "Subject; Visit to Bosch of Ambassadors Bunker and Bennett," *FRUS, Vol. XXXII, Dominican Republic; Cuba; Haiti; Guyana*, Doc. 164.

196. Central Intelligence Agency, March 12, 1966, "Subject: At 1100, 12 March, Meeting was held in The Office of Deputy Under Secretary U. Alexis Johnson to Discuss the Election Situation in the Dominican Republic," *FRUS, Vol. XXXII, Dominican Republic; Cuba; Haiti; Guyana*, Doc. 163.

197. Memorandum from the President's Special Assistant (Rostow) to President Johnson (ca. April 12, 1965) "Subject: Recent Dominican Developments," *FRUS, Vol. XXXII, Dominican Republic; Cuba; Haiti; Guyana*, Doc. 169.

198. National Intelligence Estimate 86.2-66, April 28, 1966, "Prospects for Stability in the Dominican Republic," *FRUS, Vol. XXXII, Dominican Republic; Cuba; Haiti; Guyana*, Doc. 171.

199. NIE 86.2-66, "Prospects for Stability."

200. NIE 86.2-66.

201. 303 Committee, April 30, 1965, "Subject: Dominican Election Operation," *FRUS, Vol. XXXII, Dominican Republic; Cuba; Haiti; Guyana*, Doc. 172.

202. White House, May 10, 1966, 7:45 p.m., "Memorandum from the President's Special Assistant (Rostow) to President Johnson," *FRUS, Vol. XXXII, Dominican Republic; Cuba; Haiti; Guyana*, Doc. 175.

203. State Department quoted in Chester, *Rag Tags, Scum, Riff-Raff and Commies*, 245.

204. *FRUS, 1964–1968, Vol. XXXII, Dominican Republic; Cuba; Haiti; Guyana*, Doc. 178, Editorial Note.

205. Crandall, *Gunboat Democracy*, 90.

206. Torrijos, *In the Shadow of the United States*, 74.

207. Torrijos, 74.

208. Special National Intelligence Estimate 86.2-2-66, September 19, 1966, "Prospects for Stability in the Dominican Republic," *FRUS, Vol. XXXII, Dominican Republic; Cuba; Haiti; Guyana*, Doc. 184.

209. Memorandum from the President's Special Assistant (Rostow) to President Johnson, November 18, 1966, "Subject: Dominican Situation," *FRUS, Vol. XXXII, Dominican Republic; Cuba; Haiti; Guyana*, Doc. 186.

210. Memorandum from William G. Bowdler of the National Security Council Staff to the President's Special Assistant (Rostow), November 29, 1966, 2:30 p.m., "Subject: Our Meeting on the Dominican Republic," *FRUS, Vol. XXXII, Dominican Republic; Cuba; Haiti; Guyana*, Doc. 187.

211. National Intelligence Estimate 86.2-67, April 20, 1967, "Prospects for Stability in the Dominican Republic Over the Next Year or So," *FRUS, Vol. XXXII, Dominican Republic; Cuba; Haiti; Guyana*, Doc. 197.

212. National Intelligence Estimate 86.2-67, April 20, 1967.

213. Information Memorandum from the President's Special Assistant (Rostow) to President Johnson, January 16, 1968, "Subject: Dominican Situation," *FRUS, Vol. XXXII, Dominican Republic; Cuba; Haiti; Guyana*, Doc. 210.

214. 303 Committee, January 29, 1968, "Subject: Covert Financial Contribution to the Revolutionary Social Christian Party for the May 1968 Municipal Elections in the Dominican Republic," *FRUS, Vol. XXXII, Dominican Republic; Cuba; Haiti; Guyana*, Doc. 211.

215. 303 Committee Memorandum, June 28, 1968, "Subject: Results of Covert Financial Contributions to the Revolutionary Social Christian Party for the May 1968 Municipal Elections in the Dominican Republic," *FRUS, Vol. XXXII, Dominican Republic; Cuba; Haiti; Guyana*, Doc. 215.

216. *FRUS, Vol. XXXII, Dominican Republic; Cuba; Haiti; Guyana*, Doc.213, Editorial Note.

217. 303 Committee Memorandum, June 28, 1968.

218. Central Intelligence Agency Intelligence Memorandum No. 0606/68, July 15, 1968, "Dominican President Balaguer at Mid-Term," *FRUS, Vol. XXXII, Dominican Republic; Cuba; Haiti; Guyana*, Doc. 216.

219. Central Intelligence Agency Intelligence Memorandum No. 0606/68, July 15, 1968, "Dominican President Balaguer at Mid-Term,"

220. David A. Lake, *Hierarchy in International Relations* (Ithaca, NY: Cornell University Press, 2009), 14.

221. National Security Council, August 19, 1952, "Subject: Status of United States Programs for National Security as of June 30, 1952," *FRUS, 1950–1955, Vol. IV, The Intelligence Community*, ed. Douglas Keane and Michael Warner (Washington, DC: Government Printing Office, 2007), Doc. 127.

222. Department of State, May 15, 1961, "Memorandum from the Cuban Task Force of the National Security Council to the President's Special Assistant for National Security Affairs (Bundy)," *FRUS, 1961–1963, Vol. XII, American Republics*, Doc. 307.

223. Grow, *U.S. Presidents and Latin American Interventions*, 92.

224. National Security Council, January 11, 1966.

225. CIA quoted in Crandall, *Gunboat Democracy*, 64.

226. CIA quoted in Crandall, 65.

9. Covert Regime Change after the Cold War

1. G. John Ikenberry, *After Victory: Institutions, Strategic Restraint, and the Rebuilding of Order after Major Wars* (Princeton, NJ: Princeton University Press, 2009).

2. Woolsey quoted in Charles Lathrop, *The Literary Spy* (New Haven, CT: Yale University Press, 2008), 79.

3. Ahmed Rashid, *Taliban: Islam, Oil and the New Great Game in Central Asia* (New York: IB Tauris, 2002), 18; Milton Bearden, "Afghanistan, Graveyard of Empires," *Foreign Affairs* (November–December 2001): 17–30.

4. Peter L. Bergen, *Holy War, Inc.: Inside the Secret World of Osama bin Laden* (New York: Simon and Schuster, 2002), chaps. 2–3.

5. "Bergen: Bin Laden, CIA Links Hogwash," CNN, September 6, 2006, http://www.cnn.com/2006/WORLD/asiapcf/08/15/bergen.answers/index.html.

6. For Peikney's statement, see Richard Miniter, "Dispelling the CIA-Bin Laden Myth," *Fox News*, September 24, 2003; for Bearden, see Milton Bearden and James Risen, *The Main Enemy: The Inside Story of the CIA's Final Showdown with the KGB* (New York: Random House Digital, 2004), 237; For Cannistraro, see Peter Beinart, "TRB: Back to Front," *New Republic*, September 26, 2001; Sageman, *Understanding Terror Networks*, 57–58.

7. Michael Rubin, "Who Is Responsible for the Taliban?," *Middle East Review of International Affairs* 6, no. 1 (2002): 1–16.

8. Rubin, "Who Is Responsible for the Taliban?"

9. David Robarge, "DCI John McCone and the Assassination of President John F. Kennedy," *Studies in Intelligence* 57, no. 3 (2013), National Security Archive, Washington, DC (hereafter cited as NSA), https://nsarchive2.gwu.edu/NSAEBB/NSAEBB493/docs/intell_ebb_026.PDF.

10. Lisa Hoffman, "Screwy Theories about JFK Jr's Crash Fill Internet," *Scripps Howard News Service*, July 22, 1999.

11. Rory McKeown, "Shock Claim: John Lennon 'Murdered by the CIA,'" *Daily Star*, October 9, 2017.

12. "CIA Denies Plotting to Kill Diana," *Irish Times*, April 30, 1998.

13. *Russian Times*, "CIA Linked to Benazir Bhutto's Assassination?," July 14, 2009.

14. Darryl Fears, "Study: Many Blacks Cite AIDS Conspiracy," *Washington Post*, January 25, 2005.

15. Tom Jensen, "Democrats and Republicans Differ on Conspiracy Theory Beliefs," Public Policy Polling, April 2, 2013, https://www.publicpolicypolling.com/polls/democrats-and-republicans-differ-on-conspiracy-theory-beliefs/.

16. Jensen, "Democrats and Republicans Differ."

17. "International Poll: No Consensus on Who Was Behind 9/11," World Public Opinion, September 10, 2008, https://majorityrights.com/uploads/who-did-911-poll.pdf.

18. "22% Believe Bush Knew about 9/11 in Advance," Rasmussen Reports, May 4, 2007, http://www.rasmussenreports.com/public_content/politics/current_events/bush_administration/22_believe_bush_knew_about_9_11_attacks_in_advance.

19. William Webster, "Remarks by William H. Webster, Director of Central Intelligence Before the Phoenix Rotary Club, Phoenix, Arizona, January 15, 1988," CIA, FOIA Electronic Reading Room, Doc. no. CIA-RDP99-00777R000301900001-1.

20. Charles Krauthammer, "The Unipolar Moment," *Foreign Affairs* 70, no. 1 (1990): 23.

21. William C. Wohlforth, "The Stability of a Unipolar World," *International Security* 24, no. 1 (1999): 5–41.

22. Wohlforth, "The Stability of a Unipolar World"; Stockholm International Peace Research Institute, *SIPRI Yearbook 2015: Armaments, Disarmament, and International Security* (New York: Oxford University Press, 2015).

23. Barry R. Posen, "Command of the Commons: The Military Foundation of US Hegemony," *International Security* 28, no. 1 (2003): 5–46; Wohlforth, "The Stability of a Unipolar World," 17–18.

24. On unipolarity's positive influence on military intervention, see Nuno P. Monteiro, *Theory of Unipolar Politics* (Cambridge: Cambridge University Press, 2014).

25. Krauthammer, "The Unipolar Moment," 33.

26. Jonathan Monten, "The Roots of the Bush Doctrine: Power, Nationalism, and Democracy Promotion in US Strategy," *International Security* 29, no. 4 (2005): 112–56.

27. Francis Fukuyama, "The End of History?," *National Interest* 16 (1989): 4.

28. National Endowment for Democracy, *1984–85 Annual Report* and *2015 Annual Report*, http://www.ned.org/publications/.

29. National Endowment for Democracy (2016), "About the National Endowment for Democracy," accessed September 25, 2017, http://www.ned.org/about/.

30. Sarah Sunn Bush, *The Taming of Democracy Assistance* (Cambridge: Cambridge University Press, 2015), 5.

31. Bush, *The Taming of Democracy Assistance*, 219.

32. Nuland's estimation has been taken out of context by some critics of US policy in Ukraine. For a discussion of its context see: Katie Sanders, "The United States Spent $5 billion on Ukraine anti-government riots," *Politifact*, March 19, 2014, http://www.politifact.com/punditfact/statements/2014/mar/19/facebook-posts/united-states-spent-5-billion-ukraine-anti-governm/.

33. National Endowment for Democracy (NED) (2016) "Ukraine 2016," accessed September 25, 2017, https://web.archive.org/web/20170301131752/http://www.ned.org/region/central-and-eastern-europe/ukraine-2016/.

34. Max Fisher, "In D.N.C. Hack, Echoes of Russia's New Approach to Power," *New York Times*, July 25, 2016.

35. Darya Korsunskaya, "Putin Says Russia Must Prevent 'Color Revolution,'" Reuters, November 20, 2014, https://www.reuters.com/article/us-russia-putin-security/putin-says-russia-must-prevent-color-revolution-idUSKCN0J41J620141120.

36. Alec Luhn, "National Endowment for Democracy Is First 'Undesirable' NGO Banned in Russia," *Guardian*, July 28, 2015; NED (2015) "Russia 2015," accessed September 25, 2017, https://web.archive.org/web/20170608155633/http://www.ned.org:80/region/eurasia /russia-2015/.

37. Philip Taubman, "Editorial Observer: The Battle Baghdad That Might Have Been," *New York Times*, February 8, 1998.

38. Bill Clinton, *National Security Strategy of Engagement and Enlargement* (Washington, DC: The White House, 1994), 22.

39. Thomas Carothers, *The Clinton Record on Democracy Promotion* (Washington, DC: Carnegie Endowment for International Peace, 2000).

40. Carothers, *The Clinton Record*, 3.

41. Anthony Lake, "Confronting Backlash States," *Foreign Affairs* (1994): 45–46.

42. Lake, "Confronting Backlash States."

43. Lake, 55.

44. Walter Edward Kretchik, Robert F. Baumann, and John T. Fishel, *Invasion, Intervention, Intervasion": A Concise History of the US Army in Operation Uphold Democracy* (Collingdale, PA: Diane, 1998).

45. William J. Clinton, "Statement on Signing the Iraq Liberation Act of 1998," The White House, Washington, DC (1998).

46. Gregory L. Schulte, "Regime Change Without Military Force: Lessons from Overthrowing Milosevic," *Prism: A Journal of the Center for Complex Operations* 4, no. 2 (2013): 45–55.

47. Joe Klein, "It's Time For Extreme Peacekeeping," *Time*, 11, 2003.

48. He continued, "Afghanistan was the ultimate nation building mission." George W. Bush, *Decision Points* (New York: Crown Publishing, 2010), 205.

49. Brian C. Schmidt and Michael C. Williams, "The Bush Doctrine and the Iraq War: Neoconservatives versus Realists," *Security Studies* 17, no. 2 (2008): 191–220.

50. Charles Krauthammer, "Its [*sic*] Time to Change Regimes," *Townhall*, September 28, 2001, https://townhall.com/columnists/charleskrauthammer/2001/09/28/its-time-to-change -regimes-n1003596.

51. National Commission on Terrorist Attacks upon the United States, "Diplomacy, Staff Statement No. 5" (2004), accessed September 25, 2017, http://govinfo.library.unt.edu/911/staff _statements/staff_statement_5.pdf.

52. Stephen Biddle, "Allies, Airpower, and Modern Warfare: The Afghan Model in Afghanistan and Iraq," *International Security* (2005–6): 161–76.

53. iCauslaties.org. *Operation Enduring Freedom.* http://icasualties.org/oef/

54. Carlotta Gall, "Election of Karzai Is Declared Official," *New York Times*, November 4, 2004.

55. Lindsey A. O'Rourke and Alexander B. Downes, "Picking Your Friends: Foreign-Imposed Regime Change and Foreign Policy Portfolio Similarity" (unpublished manuscript, Boston College and George Washington University, 2017).

56. Seth G. Jones, "The Rise of Afghanistan's Insurgency: State Failure and Jihad," *International Security* 32, no. 4 (2008): 7–40; Alissa Rubin, "Karzai Bets on Vilifying U.S. to Shed His Image as a Lackey," *New York Times*, March 12, 2013; Dexter Filkins, "Charm and the West Keep Afghan in Power, for Now," *New York Times*, March 25, 2002.

57. Matthew Rosenberg, "Karzai Says He Was Assured CIA Would Continue Delivering Bags of Cash," *New York Times*, May 4, 2013; Joby Warrick, "Little Blue Pills among the Ways CIA Wins Friends in Afghanistan," *Washington Post*, December 26, 2008.

58. Rod Nordland, Alissa J. Rubin, and Matthew Rosenberg, "Gulf Widens Between U.S. and a More Volatile Karzai," *New York Times*, March 17, 2012.

59. Kevin Sieff, "Interview: Karzai Says 12-year Afghanistan War Has Left Him Angry at U.S. Government," *Washington Post*, March 2, 2014.

60. Emily Ekins, "Poll Reveals Americans Supported Iraq War in 2003 Far More Than They Admit Today," Reason.com, October 16, 2014.

61. Frank Newport, "Seventy-Two Percent of Americans Support War Against Iraq," Gallup, March 24, 2003, http://news.gallup.com/poll/8038/seventytwo-percent-americans-support -war-against-iraq.aspx.

62. Michael MacDonald, *Overreach: Delusions of Regime Change in Iraq* (Cambridge, MA: Harvard University Press, 2014), 4.

63. Obama quoted by Jeffrey Goldberg, "The Obama Doctrine," *Atlantic*, April 2016.

64. Jo Becker and Scott Shane, "Hillary Clinton, 'Smart Power' and a Dictator's Fall," *New York Times*, February 27, 2016; Scott Shane and Jo Becker, "A New Libya, with 'Very Little Time Left,'" *New York Times*, February 27, 2016.

65. E. Londono and G. Miller, "CIA Begins Weapons Delivery to Syrian Rebels," *Washington Post*, September 11, 2013; M. Mazzetti and M, Apuzzo, "U.S. Relies Heavily on Saudi Money to Support Syrian Rebels," *New York Times*, January 23, 2013.

66. Office of the Director of National Intelligence, "Background to 'Assessing Russian Activities and Intentions in Recent US Elections': The Analytic Process and Incident Attribution," January 6, 2017, https://www.dni.gov/files/documents/ICA_2017_01.pdf.

67. Louis Nelson, "Trump Tweets Praise of Putin: 'I Always Knew He Was Very Smart!'" *Politico*, December 30, 2016.

68. Max Fisher, "Uncertainty Over Donald Trump's Foreign Policy Risks Global Instability," *New York Times*, November 9, 2016; Krishnadev Calamur, "NATO Shmato?," *Atlantic*, July 21, 2016; redstatemedia, *Trump Loves Putin*, YouTube, published September 7, 2016, https://www.youtube.com/watch?v=5pHgcOz2SVQ; Emily Schultheis, "Trump Says He May Let Russia Keep Crimea," CBS News, July 31, 2016.

69. Mazzetti and Lichtblau, "C.I.A. Judgment on Russia Built on Swell of Evidence," *New York Times*, December 11, 2016.

70. CNN, Dan Merica, and Jeff Zeleny, "Clinton Says Putin Grudge Led Russia to Hack, Podesta Says Something 'Deeply Broken' at FBI," CNN, December 16, 2016.

71. Ray Cline quoted in William Daugherty, *Executive Secrets: Covert Action and the Presidency* (Lawrence: University Press of Kentucky, 2006), 131.

72. Lindsey A. O'Rourke, "Analysis | The U.S. Tried to Change Other Countries' Governments 72 Times during the Cold War," *Washington Post*, December 23, 2016.

73. Office of the Director of National Intelligence, "Background to 'Assessing Russian Activities and Intentions," 5.

74. Jim Zarroli, "Want to Set Up a Shell Corporation To Hide Your Millions? No Problem," NPR, April 13, 2016.

75. Jim Rutenberg, "RT, Sputnik and Russia's New Theory of War," *New York Times*, September 13, 2017.

76. Mike Isaac and Daisuke Wakabayashi, "Russian Influence Reached 126 Million Through Facebook Alone," *New York Times*, October 30, 2017;

77. Nicholas Fandos and Scott Shane, "Senator Berates Twitter Over 'Inadequate' Inquiry into Russian Meddling, *New York Times*, September 28, 2017.

78. Siva Vaidhyanathan, "Facebook Wins, Democracy Loses," *New York Times*, September 8, 2017.

79. Scott Shane, "The Fake Americans Russia Created to Influence the Election," *New York Times*, September 7, 2017.

80. Nicole Perlroth, Michael Wines, and Matthew Rosenberg, "Russian Election Hacking Efforts, Wider Than Previously Now, Draw Little Scrutiny," *New York Times*, September 1, 2017.

81. James Vincent, "Artificial Intelligence Is Going to Make It Easier Than Ever to Fake Images and Video," *Verge*, December 20, 2016.

82. Julie Hirschfeld Davis, "Trump Says Putin 'Means It' About Not Meddling," *New York Times*, November 11, 2017.

83. Gerald F. Seib, "Listen Closely: Donald Trump Proposes Big Mideast Strategy Shift," *Wall Street Journal*, December 12, 2016.

84. On Iraq see: "Trump Repeats Wrong Claim That He Opposed Iraq War," *Politifact*, September 7, 2016, http://www.politifact.com/truth-o-meter/statements/2016/sep/07/donald -trump/trump-repeats-wrong-claim-he-opposed-iraq-war/; on Libya, see "Fact Check: Clinton's Claim That Trump Supported an Intervention in Libya," *Washington Post*, September 26, 2016.

85. Michael Crowley, "Trump Allies Push White House to Consider Regime Change in Iran," *Politico*, June 25, 2017.

86. President's Board of Consultants on Foreign Intelligence Activities, 1961 Report to President Eisenhower, quoted in Allan Goodman, "Reforming U.S. Intelligence," *Foreign Policy* (Summer 1987).

87. Gregory F. Treverton, *Covert Action: The Limits of Intervention in the Postwar World* (New York: Basic Books, 1989), 85.

88. Richard Helms and William Hood, *A Look Over My Shoulder: A Life in the Central Intelligence Agency* (New York: Random House Publishing Group, 2004), 184.

Index

Page numbers in italics refer to illustrations.

Vlasov Army, 132, 133
Voice of America, 134
Volhynia, 146
Volkogonov, Dmitri, 129
voting systems, hacking and, 235

Walker, William, 17
war: causes of, 36; preventive, 38; Realist
    theories on, 13; risk of, 9, 81, 139 (*see also*
    security costs). *See also* civil wars
war crimes, 155. *See also* mass killings
War Powers Act, 70
weak states: anti-Americanism in, 16; as
    buffer states, 35–36; covert regime change
    in, 9–10, 73; defensive measures, 56;
    resistance by, 45–46; as targets, 74, 82–83
Webster, William, 228
Weinberger, Caspar, 254n75
Weinstein, Allen, 67
Weisshart, Herbert, 76, 173–74
Wessin y Wessin, Elías, 210, 213, 215–17
Western Europe: economy, 107, 128; elections,
    98; preventive operations, 108–10; Soviet
    threat to, 100; US interventions in, 39

Western Hemisphere, 82, 97; economic
    interests in, 32–34; hemispheric solidar-
    ity, 40–41, 118 (*see also* regional hege-
    mony)
West Germany, 89. *See also* Germany
Westphalian state sovereignty, 17, 24
WikiLeaks, 234
William of Orange, 12
Wilson, Woodrow, 12, 198
Wisner, Frank, 131, 137, 140, 142, 145, 150
Woolsey, R. James, 226
World War I, 38
World War II, 37, 38, 41, 108, 128–29, 131,
    133; French Indochina and, 162–63;
    Yugoslavia and, 152. *See also* Nazi
    Germany

Yemen, 39
Yugoslavia, 20, 127, 137, 139, 152–57
Yugoslav Partisans, 152–53

Zawahiri, Ayman al-, 226
Zhou Enlai, 17, 104
Zog I, 137–38, 140

Lightning Source UK Ltd.
Milton Keynes UK
UKHW012000250319
339739UK00006B/232/P